T0323677

REVOLUTIONARY THOUGHT AFTER THE PARIS COMMUNE, 1871–1885

This first comprehensive account of French revolutionary thought in the years between the crushing of France's last nineteenth-century revolution and the re-emergence of socialism as a meaningful electoral force offers new interpretations of the French revolutionary tradition. Drawing together material from Europe, North America, and the South Pacific, Julia Nicholls pieces together the nature and content of French revolutionary thought in this often-overlooked era. She shows that this was an important and creative period, in which activists drew upon fresh ideas they encountered in exile across the world to rebuild a revolutionary movement that was both united and politically viable in the changed circumstances of France's new Third Republic. The relative success of these efforts, moreover, has significant implications for the ways in which we understand the founding years of the Third Republic, the nature of the modern revolutionary tradition, and the origins of European Marxism.

JULIA NICHOLLS is Lecturer in French and European Studies at King's College, London. An intellectual historian of modern France, her research focuses on ideas of freedom and revolution, subjection, and social exclusion. She is particularly interested in how these ideas travelled across European borders and beyond.

IDEAS IN CONTEXT

Edited by David Armitage, Richard Bourke, Jennifer Pitts,
and John Robertson

The books in this series will discuss the emergence of intellectual traditions and of related new disciplines. The procedures, aims and vocabularies that were generated will be set in the context of the alternatives available within the contemporary frameworks of ideas and institutions. Through detailed studies of the evolution of such traditions, and their modification by different audiences, it is hoped that a new picture will form of the development of ideas in their concrete contexts. By this means, artificial distinctions between the history of philosophy, of the various sciences, of society and politics, and of literature may be seen to dissolve.

The series is published with the support of the Exxon Foundation.

A list of books in the series can be found at the end of the volume.

REVOLUTIONARY THOUGHT AFTER THE PARIS COMMUNE, 1871–1885

JULIA NICHOLLS

King's College London

CAMBRIDGE
UNIVERSITY PRESS

CAMBRIDGE
UNIVERSITY PRESS

University Printing House, Cambridge CB2 8BS, United Kingdom

One Liberty Plaza, 20th Floor, New York, NY 10006, USA

477 Williamstown Road, Port Melbourne, VIC 3207, Australia

314–321, 3rd Floor, Plot 3, Splendor Forum, Jasola District Centre, New Delhi – 110025, India

79 Anson Road, #06–04/06, Singapore 079906

Cambridge University Press is part of the University of Cambridge.

It furthers the University's mission by disseminating knowledge in the pursuit of
education, learning, and research at the highest international levels of excellence.

www.cambridge.org
Information on this title: www.cambridge.org/9781108499262
DOI: 10.1017/9781108634199

First published 2019

Printed and bound in Great Britan by Clays Ltd, Elcograf S.p.A.

A catalogue record for this publication is available from the British Library.

Library of Congress Cataloging-in-Publication Data
NAMES: Nicholls, Julia, 1987- author.
TITLE: Revolutionary thought after the Paris Commune, 1871-1885 / Julia Nicholls.
DESCRIPTION: Cambridge, United Kingdom ; New York, NY : Cambridge University Press, 2019. |
SERIES: Ideas in context | Includes bibliographical references and index.
IDENTIFIERS: LCCN 2019008057 | ISBN 9781108499262 (hardback : alk. paper)
| ISBN 9781108713344 (pbk. : alk. paper)
SUBJECTS: LCSH: France–Politics and government–1870-1940. | France–History–Third Republic,
1870-1940. | Paris (France)–History–Commune, 1871. | Socialism–France–History–19th century.
| Revolutionaries–France–History–19th century.
CLASSIFICATION: LCC DC340 . N53 2019 | DDC 944.081/2–dc23
LC record available at https://lccn.loc.gov/2019008057

ISBN 978-1-108-49926-2 Hardback

Contents

Acknowledgements   *page* vi

Introduction   1

PART I THE PARIS COMMUNE AND ACCOUNTING FOR FAILURE   19
1   The Commune as Quotidian Event   21
2   The Commune as Violent Trauma   49

PART II REVOLUTION AND THE REPUBLIC   79
3   The French Revolutionary Tradition   81
4   Rehabilitating Revolution   112

PART III MARX, MARXISM, AND INTERNATIONAL SOCIALISM   147
5   Texts in Translation   149
6   The Origins of Marxism in Modern France   179

PART IV EMPIRE AND INTERNATIONALISM   207
7   Deportation, Imperialism, and the Republican State   209
8   Exile and Universal Solidarity   239
Conclusion   269

Bibliography   278
Index   300

v

Acknowledgements

This book is the product of many years of work, and as a result I have many people to thank.

Tracing a group of exiles across the world has involved visits to numerous libraries and archives. Chief among these are the British Library and its former newspaper archive in Colindale, where I spent many hours squinting at old documents and microfilm. I am grateful to everyone there who provided me with assistance. Staff at the Bibliothèque nationale de France, the Archives de la Préfecture de Police in Paris, the Bibliothèque universitaire de Genève, and especially at the International Institute of Social History in Amsterdam also provided me with invaluable assistance during my visits.

This project began life as a PhD in the School of History at Queen Mary University of London. While there, Miri Rubin and Georgios Varouxakis provided me with encouragement and a wealth of opportunities. Richard Bourke did all of this and more, regularly giving me invaluable guidance and insightful comments on pieces of work. Most of all, I am grateful to Gareth Stedman Jones, whose help, support, and advice have been unparalleled. I cannot now imagine a better supervisor.

At King's College London, colleagues in the French and European Studies departments provided a stimulating environment in which to bring the project to a close. Stathis Kouvelakis and Alex Callinicos in particular gave stimulating feedback and alerted me to interesting new ways of framing my conclusions.

Many others have helped along the way. I am particularly thankful to Robert Tombs, who has read many iterations of this work. My PhD examiners, Sudhir Hazareesingh and David Todd, provided invaluable comments and encouragement, while Jeremy Jennings and Quentin Deluermoz pointed me towards relevant and unpublished work. I have benefitted immensely from discussions at the Modern French History and Political Ideas seminars at the Institute of Historical Research, particularly with Joanne Paul, Signy Gutnick Allen, Caroline Ashcroft, and Emily Jones. Mary-Rose Cheadle has been constantly supportive. I am also extremely grateful to Liz Friend-Smith at Cambridge University Press for all of her help.

Finally, special thanks are due to Arthur Asseraf, Callum Barrell, Joshua Chauvin, and my parents, who are there through everything.

Introduction

Following the defeat of the Paris Commune in late May 1871, its participants and supporters were frequently moved to declare that while 'le
cadavre est à terre ... l'idée est debout': 'the body may have fallen, but
the idea still stands'.[1] Historians, political commentators, and world
leaders alike have advanced their own interpretations of the events of
spring 1871 since the last shots were fired. What precisely ex-
Communards believed this idea to be, however, has never been clear. This
book addresses itself to this question. Through an exploration of the nature
and content of French revolutionary thought from the years immediately
following the Commune's fall, it demonstrates that this idea was not a
specific policy or doctrine. Rather, by extensively redefining familiar
concepts and using their circumstances creatively, it was the idea of a
distinct, united, and politically viable French revolutionary movement that
activists sought to preserve. The relative success of these efforts, furthermore, has significant implications for the ways in which scholars understand both the founding years of the French Third Republic and the
nature of the modern revolutionary tradition.

In the small hours of 18 March 1871, troops from the French Army
marched into Paris. Their objective was the removal of a number of
cannons that had formed part of the capital's defence during the four-
month-long Siege of Paris that brought to an end the Franco-Prussian
War. News of the soldiers' early morning arrival spread quickly through
the working-class districts of Belleville, Buttes-Chaumont, and
Montmartre where the artillery was being stored. Still aggrieved by the

---

[1] See for example the cover of P.-O. Lissagaray, *Les huit journées de mai derrière les barricades* (Brussels:
Au bureau du *Petit journal*, 1871); Pilotell, 'La Commune de Paris: le cadavre est à terre et l'idée est
debout (Victor Hugo)' (1871. Musée Carnavalet, Paris); *La Bataille* (Paris), 19 March 1885. This is
also the motto of the *Association des Amies et Amis de la Commune de Paris 1871*. The phrase was
originally Victor Hugo's. See V. Hugo, *La voix de Guernesey* (Guernsey: Imprimerie T.-M. Bichard,
1867), p.14.

city's treatment at the hands of the Prussians and the French government during the war and subsequent peace negotiations, angry residents and *fédérés* from the National Guard poured out into the streets. Pleas for calm fell on deaf ears, and before long the military operation had precipitated an armed revolt. By the end of the day, two generals lay dead, rebels had assumed control of key strategic buildings in the city, and what remained of the army had beaten a hasty retreat to Versailles with the government hot on its heels.

For the next two months, Paris ruled itself as a revolutionary commune. It swiftly held municipal elections, passed legislation, and waged war against the national government. This situation came to an end on 21 May 1871 when the French Army re-entered Paris, commencing a week of street battles that quickly came to be known as the Semaine Sanglante.[2] As the army overcame the Communards one street and one barricade at a time, the capital went up in flames around them; the City of Light was now a city on fire. Fleeing revolutionaries killed a number of hostages including the Archbishop of Paris, while the advancing troops were liable to shoot anyone they suspected of participation in the Commune. By the time the final Communards were defeated on 28 May amidst the graves of Père-Lachaise cemetery, thousands had been killed – the vast majority revolutionaries – in what Robert Tombs has termed 'the worst violence committed against civilians in Europe between the French and Russian Revolutions'.[3]

In the weeks, months, and years that followed, the war against the Commune did not dissipate, but merely changed form. In the immediate aftermath, 40,000 people were arrested and marched to holding camps in and around Versailles, where hundreds died as a result of the poor conditions. Over the next five years, thousands of prisoners were tried for crimes of varying gravity by a series of specially created *conseils de guerre*. Ninety-five were sentenced to death (although only twenty-three were executed[4]) and a further 4,500 were deported to New Caledonia, a French penal colony in the South Pacific.

While the courts martial dispensed death and justice to the Communards, the rattled Assemblée Nationale set about ensuring that the events

---

[2] For more on the genesis of this narrative see Chapter 1, as well as A. Dowdall, 'Narrating *la Semaine Sanglante*, 1871–1880' (unpublished MPhil thesis, University of Cambridge, 2010).

[3] '[L]a pire violence contre des civils en Europe entre la Révolution française et la révolution russe'. R.P. Tombs, *Paris, bivouac des révolutions: La Commune de 1871* (trans.) J. Chatroussat (Paris: Éditions Libertalia, 2014. First published in English, 1999), p.360.

[4] Ibid., p.363.

of spring 1871 would not and could not be repeated. It swiftly introduced legal restrictions upon revolutionaries' principal means of communication – the press and association – and left the state of siege in place in Paris and other parts of France until 1876.[5] The defeat of the Commune, they hoped and claimed, was more than simply the defeat of *a* revolution: it brought to a definitive close the era of modern European revolutions begun in 1789.

Revolutionaries escaping immediate death or arrest in May 1871 fled France in a mass exodus. Where previously the majority of revolutionaries had been concentrated in Paris, they now found themselves defeated, depleted, and scattered across the globe. Approximately 1500 headed for Belgium, while the same number followed in the footsteps of their *quarante-huitard* predecessors and made for Britain and Jersey. A further 750 settled in Switzerland, predominantly in and around French-speaking Geneva.[6] Smaller numbers headed west to the United States, while several individuals travelled as far afield as China and Sudan. It was not until the Opportunist Republican government reluctantly granted a full amnesty in July 1880 that the surviving exiles and deportees were able to return freely to France.

The Paris Commune has captured imaginations for almost 150 years. Mindful of Karl Marx's claim that 1871 represented 'the glorious harbinger of a new society',[7] communist world leaders and activists during the late nineteenth and twentieth centuries rushed to associate themselves with the Commune. Lenin's body was famously shrouded in a Communard flag. Chinese theorists including Mao Zedong, meanwhile, claimed the events of 1871 were their social inspiration during the Cultural Revolution; the 1967 Shanghai People's Commune was explicitly modelled on the Paris Commune.[8] Commentators on the right, meanwhile, have been

---

[5] C. Bellanger, *Histoire générale de la presse française*, 5 vols. (Paris: Presses universitaires de France, 1969–1976), vol.3 (1972), p.152.

[6] Dowdall, 'Narrating *la Semaine Sanglante*', p.12. For contemporary estimates of numbers in Geneva, see Intelligence report to the Préfecture de Police, 30 November 1873. Archives de la Préfecture de Police (APP) Ba431/891. For contemporary estimates of refugees in Britain and Jersey, see 'Les réfugiés à Londres' (1876). APP Ba429/1346.

[7] K. Marx, *The Civil War in France* (London: Martin Lawrence Ltd, 1933. First published, 1871), p.34.

[8] For more on the Paris Commune in Chinese thought, see J.B. Starr, *Continuing the Revolution: The Political Thought of Mao* (Princeton, NJ: Princeton University Press, 2015. First published, 1979), pp.188–201; Y. Wu, *The Cultural Revolution at the Margins: Chinese Socialism in Crisis* (Cambridge, MA: Harvard University Press, 2014), p.192. See also V.I. Lenin, *The Paris Commune* (London: Martin Lawrence, 1931); G. Kozintsez and L. Trauberg (dirs.), *Новый Вавилон* (The New Babylon) (1929).

equally eager to engage with the Commune in an effort to disinvest such a celebrated socialist symbol of its power and heuristic value.[9]

After a brief lull in popularity following the end of the Cold War, the Commune has recently been experiencing something of a cultural renaissance. In 2009, it was reborn as an altogether different kind of symbol in the form of the French clothing and lifestyle brand Commune de Paris 1871, which draws inspiration from the imagery of 1871 and names its products after famous streets, events, and revolutionaries.[10] This development has in turn sparked an aggrieved call to arms demanding that the Commune not be left to 'rich *bobo* hipsters' pricing 'the revolutionary experience' at €150.[11] In November 2016, renewed interest in 1871 culminated in socialist deputies in the Assemblée National voting – to the chagrin of the right – to posthumously exonerate the Communard victims of official repression.[12] Whether as a major turning point in modern revolutionary history or the aesthetic inspiration for moderately priced shirts and watches, the Paris Commune has always possessed the power to spark admiration and debate. Indeed, it is one of the most abiding symbols of modern global social and political history.

The Commune has also proved perennially academically popular. 1871 has attracted the passing interest of numerous distinguished scholars eager to interpret its social significance, from C.L.R. James to Henri Lefebvre, while others such as Jacques Rougerie have devoted their careers to chronicling its events and aftermath.[13] Much of this attention undoubtedly resulted from the Commune's political significance during the

---

[9] See for example E.S. Mason, *The Paris Commune: An Episode in the History of the Socialist Movement* (New York: The Macmillan Company, 1930).

[10] Www.communedeparis1871.fr/fr [last accessed 25 May 2015].

[11] '[B]obos-hipsters fortunés'. 'Ne laissons pas la Commune de Paris aux hipsters!' www.poisson-rouge.info/2015/06/02/ne-laissons-pas-la-commune-de-paris-aux-hipsters/ [last accessed 7 September 2015].

[12] 'L'Assemblée réhabilite les communards victimes de la répression', *Le Monde* (Paris), 30 November 2016, www.lemonde.fr/societe/article/2016/11/30/l-assemblee-rehabilite-les-communards-victimes-de-la-repression_5040565_3224.html [last accessed 3 April 2018].

[13] See for example C.L.R. James, 'They showed the way to labor emancipation: on Karl Marx and the 75th anniversary of the Paris Commune', *Labor Action* 10 (18 March 1946); H. Lefebvre, *La proclamation de la Commune, 26 Mars 1871* (Paris: Gallimard, 1965); E. Schulkind, *The Paris Commune of 1871* (London: The Historical Association, 1971); E. Kamenka, *Paradigm for Revolution? The Paris Commune 1871–1971* (Canberra: Australian National University Press, 1972); *Colloque universitaire pour la commémoration du centenaire de la Commune de 1871: Le mouvement social* 79 (April–June 1972). For Rougerie, see J. Rougerie, *Procès des Communards* (Paris: Julliard, 1964); J. Rougerie, *Paris libre 1871* (Paris: Éditions du Seuil, 1971); J. Rougerie, *1871: jalons pour une histoire de la Commune de 1871* (Paris: Presses universitaires de France, 1973); J. Rougerie, *La Commune 1871* (Paris: Presses universitaires de France, 1988); J. Rougerie, *Paris insurgé: la Commune de 1871* (Paris: Gallimard, 1995).

twentieth century, yet such academic interest cannot simply be diagnosed as the result of Cold War mentalities. Unlike the political attention it once received, academic interest in the Commune has not waned since the 1980s.[14] The 2014 publication of John Merriman's *Massacre: The Life and Death of the Paris Commune* and the recent success of Tombs's *Paris, bivouac des révolutions: la Commune de 1871* is testament to the attention that it continues to command in both Anglophone and Francophone circles.[15] While its political power may have waned since 1989, the academic allure of the Commune remains as strong as ever.

In the long historiographical shadows cast by the Commune, however, its participants and supporters have been somewhat lost. Much of 1871's posthumous political utility derived from its violent end, and particularity the staggering estimates of 20,000 or more dead that quickly emerged and gained traction after the Commune's fall.[16] For its critics, as for the French government in 1871, death on such a scale signified the finality of the revolution's defeat. For the likes of Marx, Lenin, and Mao, meanwhile, it was amidst the flames and sacrifice of the Semaine Sanglante that a new era of revolution was born. In these interpretations, the Communards have accordingly been characterised primarily as dead bodies and mortality statistics rather than historical actors with agency and ideas.

Historians of the Commune have paid more attention to revolutionaries' fates in the wake of its fall. In *Procès des Communards*, Rougerie extensively detailed the trials that followed the Commune,[17] while many

---

[14] For work from the late twentieth century, see for example R. Bellet and P. Régnier (eds.), *Écrire la Commune: témoignages, récits et romans (1871–1931)* (Tusson: Du Lérot, 1994); A. Boime, *Art and the French Commune: Imagining Paris after War and Revolution* (Princeton, NJ: Princeton University Press, 1995); M.P. Johnson, *The Paradise of Association: Political Culture and Popular Organisations in the Paris Commune of 1871* (Ann Arbor: University of Michigan Press, 1996); M.P. Johnson, 'Memory and the cult of revolution in the 1871 Paris Commune', *Journal of Women's History* 9 (1997), 39–57; R.P. Tombs, *The Paris Commune, 1871* (London: Longman, 1999).

[15] J. Merriman, *Massacre: The Life and Death of the Paris Commune of 1871* (New Haven, CT: Yale University Press, 2014); Tombs, *Paris, bivouac des révolutions*. For other recent work, see G. Larguier and J. Quaretti (eds.), *La Commune de 1871: utopie ou modernité?* (Perpignan: Presses universitaires de Perpignan, 2000); C. Latta (ed.), *La Commune de 1871: l'événement, les hommes et la mémoire* (Saint-Étienne: Publications de l'Université de Saint-Étienne, 2004); D. Shafer, *The Paris Commune: French Politics, Culture, and Society at the Crossroads of the Revolutionary Tradition and Revolutionary Socialism* (Basingstoke: Palgrave Macmillan, 2005); P. Starr, *Commemorating Trauma: The Paris Commune and Its Cultural Aftermath* (New York: Fordham University Press, 2006); J.-C. Caron, *Paris, l'insurrection capitale* (Seyssel: Champ Vallon, 2015).

[16] See for example P.-O. Lissagaray, *Histoire de la Commune de 1871* (Paris: E. Dentu, 1896. First published, 1876), p.27. For an analysis of this phenomenon, see R.P. Tombs, 'How bloody was *la semaine sanglante* of 1871? A revision', *The Historical Journal* 55 (September 2012), 679–704.

[17] J. Rougerie, *Procès des Communards* (Paris: Julliard, 1964).

others have traced its participants into exile and deportee life in New Caledonia.[18] Colette Wilson, Albert Boime, and J.M. Przyblyski, meanwhile, have examined the fate of revolutionary Paris in the 1870s and the concerted attempts to erase the Commune from contemporary French memory.[19] Whether in the form of the scale and creativity of the State's repression, the penury and dislocation of life outside of France, or the unlikely employment exiles found in order to survive, the conclusions reached about life after 1871 have remained essentially the same.[20] In all interpretations, the Commune has been characterised as a watershed defeat that severely damaged, if not put a decisive end, to revolutionaries' political ideas and careers. Their political careers and ideas, in other words, have been folded into the history of the event itself.

The broader literature on France in the years after 1871 has further reinforced the perception of the Commune as the end of revolutionary relevance. French historians such as Claude Nicolet, François Furet, and Mona Ozouf traditionally characterised 1870–1885 as a period in which revolution, Bonapartism, and monarchism were successfully relegated to the margins of French political life as a result of the Opportunist Republicans' rise to power and the legislative reforms they enacted between 1880 and 1885.[21] More recently scholars have sought to complicate these classic accounts of Republican *enracinement*, yet revolutionaries have nonetheless remained largely absent from their work.[22]

[18] For New Caledonia, see J. Baronnet and J. Chalou, *Communards en Nouvelle-Calédonie: Histoire de la déportation* (Paris: Mercure de France, 1987); G. Mailhé, *Déportations en Nouvelle-Calédonie des communards et des révoltés de la grande Kabylie (1872–1876)* (Paris: L'Harmattan, 1994); A. Bullard, *Exile to Paradise: Savagery and Civilization in Paris and the South Pacific, 1790–1900* (Stanford, CA: Stanford University Press, 2000). For exile, see P.K. Martinez, 'Paris Communard refugees in Britain, 1871–1880' (unpublished PhD thesis, University of Sussex, 1981); Tombs, *Paris, bivouac des révolutions*, pp.365–366.

[19] C.E. Wilson, *Paris and the Commune 1871–78: The Politics of Forgetting* (Manchester: Manchester University Press, 2007); J.M. Przyblyski, 'Revolution at a standstill: photography and the Paris Commune of 1871', *Yale French Studies* 101 (2001), 54–78; A. Boime, *Art and the French Commune: Imagining Paris after War and Revolution* (Princeton: Princeton University Press, 1995). See also J.T. Joughin, *The Paris Commune in French Politics, 1871–1880*, 2 vols. (Baltimore, MD: Johns Hopkins University Press, 1955).

[20] This narrative was also popular in certain radical circles at the time. See Jenny Longuet, quoted in G. Stedman Jones, *Karl Marx: Greatness and Illusion* (London: Allen Lane, 2016), p.511.

[21] C. Nicolet, *L'Idée républicaine en France (1789–1924)* 2nd edn (Paris: Éditions Gallimard, 1994. First published, 1982), p.472; F. Furet, *La Révolution de Turgot à Jules Ferry* (Paris: Hachette, 1988); F. Furet and M. Ozouf (eds.), *Le siècle de l'avènement républicain* (Paris: Gallimard, 1993).

[22] See for example P. Nord, *The Republican Moment: Struggles for Democracy in Nineteenth-Century France* (Cambridge, MA: Harvard University Press, 1995); S. Hazareesingh, *Intellectual Founders of the Republic: Five Studies in Nineteenth-Century French Republican Political Thought* 2nd edn (Oxford: Oxford University Press, 2005. First published, 2001); P. Rosanvallon, *The Demands of Liberty: Civil Society in France since the Revolution* (trans.) A. Goldhammer (Cambridge, MA:

The objective of these accounts was of course not to write the history of socialist or revolutionary thought, but the absence of revolutionaries from them has nonetheless contributed to the perception that they played little part in the political or social life of the early Third Republic. Whether a victory for a new brand of Republicans or a more lengthy and complex process, work on French politics has overwhelmingly characterised the early Third Republic as a period in which moderate politics and ideas broadly defined became increasingly entrenched, confident, and popular. While revolutionaries may have continued to exist after the Commune, they were of little significance to France or French politics. This consensus has in turn indirectly reinforced the perception that revolution and revolutionaries simply disappeared after 1871.

These revolutionaries have not, however, been entirely written out of history. Since the 1970s, historians have produced a string of biographies and intellectual biographies of notable figures such as Paul Lafargue, Paul Brousse, and Louis Auguste Blanqui, which provide valuable, if partial, insights into the state of revolutionary activism after the Commune.[23] Ex-Communards have also featured prominently in work on broader movements and intellectual trends. Michel Cordillot, for example, has recently detailed Communard exiles' involvement in the International Workingmen's Association, while Zeev Sternhell and Emmanuel Jousse have located the origins of French fascism and reformist socialism respectively in the 1870s and 1880s.[24] Unlike other bodies of literature, these studies have focused not on the devastation caused by the Commune, but on revolutionaries' attempts to bounce back from it through the adoption of new ideas and ideologies such as Marxism and public service socialism.

Harvard University Press, 2007. First published in French, 2004); C. Gaboriaux, *La République en quête des citoyens: les républicains français face au bonapartisme rural (1848–1880)* (Paris: Presses de la Fondation Nationale des Sciences Politiques, 2010).

[23] S. Bernstein, *Auguste Blanqui and the Art of Insurrection* (London: Lawrence and Wishart, 1971); M. Dommanget, *Auguste Blanqui au début du IIIe République (1871–1880): dernière prison et ultimes combats* (Paris: Mouton, 1971); D. Stafford, *From Anarchism to Reformism: A Study of the Political Activities of Paul Brousse within the First International and the French Socialist Movement 1870–90* (London: Cox & Wyman, 1971); L. Derfler, *Paul Lafargue and the Founding of French Marxism 1842–1882* (Cambridge, MA: Harvard University Press, 1991); C. Willard, *Jules Guesde, l'apôtre et la loi* (Paris: Éditions ouvrières, 1991); K.S. Vincent, *Between Marxism and Anarchism: Benoît Malon and French Reformist Socialism* (Berkeley: University of California Press, 1992); L. Derfler, *Paul Lafargue and the Flowering of French Socialism, 1882–1911* (Cambridge, MA: Harvard University Press, 1998);

[24] M. Cordillot, *Aux origines du socialisme moderne: La Première Internationale, la Commune de Paris, l'exil* (Paris: Éditions de l'Atelier, 2010); Z. Sternhell, *La droite révolutionnaire 1885–1914: les origines françaises du fascisme* (Paris: Éditions du Seuil, 1978); E. Jousse, *Les hommes révoltés: les origines intellectuelles du réformisme en France (1871–1917)* (Paris: Fayard, 2017).

This attention is undoubtedly welcome, yet the complexities of the 1870s and 1880s have often been lost in the long chronological reach of such studies. While they ostensibly deal with this period, much of this work has focused primarily upon explaining the genesis either of individuals' more 'mature' thought or later events and organisations, from the Boulanger and Dreyfus Affairs to the Second International, and even the First World War. Indeed, this inclination can be glimpsed in historians' tendency project the (as yet unheard of) appellations and groupings of later years – 'reformist socialism', 'the revolutionary right' – back onto this period. While the 1870s and 1880s are often fulsomely discussed, then, these years have been treated primarily as a stepping-stone, and insights into them are few. Where elsewhere this period and these revolutionaries have been overshadowed by 1871, in this literature they have often been eclipsed by the more attention-grabbing and immediately relevant events and ideas of the late 1880s and beyond.

From these diverse bodies of literature, a clear portrait of the immediate post-Commune period and revolutionaries' place in it emerges. The Commune marked a definitive break, after which old revolutionary ideas and associations lost their potency. While French politics, society, and government were remade without revolution, the vanquished of 1871 were relegated – both physically and intellectually – to the sidelines. Revolutionaries with any hope of remaining politically relevant were forced to change considerably, abandoning their previous ideas and drifting towards a series of prefabricated intellectual orthodoxies such as Marxian socialism or more moderate republicanism. Certainly, they had few distinct ideas of their own. Intellectually and politically, it is suggested, the 1870s and 1880s was a fallow holding period suspended between momentous events, characterised primarily by intellectual stagnation and injurious factional infighting.

The French government's initial characterisation of the Commune as the end of revolution, in other words, has been surprisingly durable. Recently, however, historians have begun to chip away at this portrayal. Revising his earlier work in 2012, Tombs offered a reinterpretation of the Semaine Sanglante in which substantially fewer revolutionaries were killed and forty-eight of the Commune's fifty-three-strong government escaped unharmed.[25] A new generation of French historians has also played a leading role in these efforts. Laure Godineau, for example, has assessed the impact of the return of Communard exiles to France at the beginning

---

[25] Tombs, 'How bloody was *la semaine Sanglante* of 1871?', at p.702.

of the 1880s,[26] while in *La Commune n'est pas morte* Éric Fournier cast a critical gaze over the subsequent political uses of 1871, transforming the Commune from a vehicle for predicting future events into a prism through which to study modern history.[27] In these interpretations the Commune was not a fork in the road, but rather 'a roundabout, where different temporalities crossed and overlapped'.[28]

It is this body of historiography that this study seeks to place itself within and build upon. While Godineau, Tombs, and others have dealt extensively with revolutionaries' physical and practical circumstances, their ideas are still relatively unexamined. Perhaps the closest work is Charles Rihs's *La Commune de Paris: sa structure et ses doctrines*, but this deals with the revolution itself rather than its aftermath, and has never been translated into English.[29] In fact, there remains more on the right's ideas on revolution than those of revolutionary activists themselves.[30] This book addresses this historiographical gap. It asks not just where revolutionaries went in 1871 or what they did, but also what they thought.

The revolutionary movement during this period is difficult to define, and groups, allegiances, and appellations were often diffuse and shifting. Revolutionaries are here defined as activists who either took part in the Commune or expressed strong affinities with it after its fall. This encompasses the groups of activists often described as French Marxists,[31] Possibilists or federalist socialists,[32] and Blanquists.[33] It also includes a variety of more independent theorists such as Élisée Reclus and Gustave Lefrançais, as well as others who occupied the boundaries between revolutionary and radical thought such as Arthur Arnould and Charles Longuet, and numerous anonymous journalists and pamphleteers.

---

[26] L. Godineau, 'Retour d'exil: les anciens Communards au début de la Troisième République' (unpublished PhD thesis, Université de Paris I Panthéon-Sorbonne, 2000). See also P.K. Martinez, 'Paris Communard refugees in Britain, 1871–1880'.

[27] É. Fournier, *La Commune n'est pas morte: les usages politiques du passé de 1871 à nos jours* (Paris: Éditions Libertalia, 2013).

[28] '[U]n carrefour où s'entrecroisent et se chevauchent différentes temporalités'. Tombs, *Paris, bivouac des révolutions*, p.417.

[29] C. Rihs, *La Commune de Paris (1871): sa structure et ses doctrines* (Paris: Éditions du Seuil, 1973). First published, 1955).

[30] P. Lidsky, *Les écrivains contre la Commune* (Paris: Maspero, 1970); J.M. Roberts, 'The Paris Commune from the Right', *English Historical Review*, supplement 6 (1973); A. Dowdall, 'Narrating la Semaine Sanglante' (unpublished MPhil thesis, University of Cambridge, 2010).

[31] For example Jules Guesde, Paul Lafargue, and Gabriel Deville.

[32] Including Paul Brousse, Benoît Malon, and Jean Allemane.

[33] Such as Henri Rochefort, Louise Michel, and of course Louis Auguste Blanqui himself.

Intellectually, revolutionaries in this period were connected to rich and diverse traditions of French radicalism. This was especially true of its more extreme strands. All revolutionaries during our period, for example, shared the concern for economic equality that had motivated François Noël 'Gracchus' Babeuf in the 1790s. Louis Auguste Blanqui was likewise consistently venerated, variously as a source of ideas and as a figurehead. By the 1860s, though, many revolutionaries were edging away from active engagement in the kind of conspiratorial violence practised by Babeuf and Blanqui. Younger revolutionaries increasingly came to radicalism through the nascent trade union movement, which presented a more organised, international, and accessible alternative to traditional action. Under the Second Empire, meanwhile, revolutionaries and student radicals had often joined forces with more moderate republicans in an effort to oust Napoleon III.

Indeed, the question of what precisely separated revolutionaries and so-called 'advanced radicals' was much discussed from the 1860s until well into the twentieth century. As we shall see, there existed many similarities between the two groups during the 1870s and early 1880s, but several important differences set revolutionaries apart. These differences lay in both the extent of the social changes that they supported and the means they advocated for bringing them about. Specifically, the majority of revolutionaries continued to be open to the possibility of violent action, even if after 1871 this commitment was largely theoretical. By contrast, although radical republicans such as Georges Clemenceau, Camille Pelletan, and Victor Hugo frequently attempted to intercede on revolutionaries' behalf during the 1870s, they also systematically distanced themselves from such ideas and acts. Thus, while this study deals with them insofar as they influence or interacted with revolutionaries, it does not consider them as principal actors.

Through a comprehensive examination of these figures and their work, it shall become clear that that the 1870s and 1880s were far from a barren intellectual wasteland, marooned between the more dramatic events of 1871 and the late 1880s. Although cut off from France and their previous lives, revolutionaries were neither intellectually defeated by their physical loss, nor overwhelmed by the situations they found themselves in. Rather, they accepted their circumstances and even attempted to turn them to their advantage. Whether in New Caledonia, America, or Europe, revolutionaries attempted to use the 1870s productively, interacting with various international radical and revolutionary figures from Marx and Mikhail Bakunin to Algerians involved in the 1871 Kabyle Rebellion, and forging new alliances that they would carry back with them to France in the early 1880s. While the Commune may have prompted a distinct drop in revolutionary activity in France in other words, the ideas kept coming.

It was not only individual revolutionaries that survived the fall of the Commune, however, but also the idea of the revolutionary movement. While French activists voraciously sought out new ideas and alliances during this period, they did not do so in search of access to prefabricated orthodoxies like 'Marxism' or 'anarchism'. Neither were they willing to subjugate themselves to intellectual frameworks of other people's making. Rather, their primary objective remained the preservation of a French revolutionary movement that was at once unified, autonomous, and politically viable. The Commune was thus more than simply an historical roundabout at which different ideas and temporalities overlapped, crossed, and moved on: the brief unity that it engendered continued to provide inspiration for revolutionary actors and theorists well into the Third Republic. Although activists frequently differed, clashed, and changed their minds as to what precisely a unified and viable revolutionary movement constituted and how to achieve it, they nonetheless remained steadfast and united in their desire to do so.

Revolutionaries pursued this aim primarily through the redefinition of words and concepts with which French audiences were already conversant. Activists drew extensively upon new work including Marx's thought on factory labour and Élisée Reclus's new universal geography, as well as experiences such as deportee life in New Caledonia to invest familiar terms such as 'universal equality', 'the right to work', and most importantly 'revolution' itself with new meanings that were more attuned to the circumstances that they found themselves in after 1871. In doing so, revolutionaries in the post-Commune period hoped to demonstrate their intellectual flexibility and thus continued political viability, whilst simultaneously maintaining their connections to and reconstituting their historical identity. It is for these reasons that a serious history of their ideas matters. While social, political, and cultural histories have demonstrated that these revolutionaries remained active in French and international politics following the fall of the Commune, it is only with an intellectual history that we can understand why they remained so committed to their historical identity, what precisely it constituted, and how they managed to preserve its relevance.

As a result of its closer examination of the period after the Commune, this book also suggests that it is necessary to re-evaluate the ways in which we think about the revolutionary movement and French politics more generally in the second half of the nineteenth century. Not only did revolutionaries remain close to other parts of the republican community after the Commune, but perhaps more significantly, the ways in which they operated bore far more similarities to the pre-1871 period than has previously been thought. The Commune, in other words, was quite literally an extraordinary episode. Rather than a great watershed, it represented an interruption in a longer intellectual trajectory. While the circumstances and the content of their ideas may have changed, their connections and the ways in which they thought did not. Rather than an entirely separate period, this book thus suggests that these years marked the tail end of a longer phase in French politics, which began in the 1840s and ended not in 1871, but in the 1880s.

The end date of December 1885 reflects this revised interpretation. It is a central claim of this book that in order to properly understand and appreciate the revolutionary thought of the immediate post-Commune period, we must dispense with the formulations of later years. Revolutionary thought in the years following the Commune bore little to no resemblance to the more clearly defined socialisms and nationalisms of the Second International, the Boulanger Affair, and beyond. The year 1885 has been selected to coincide with the French presidential and legislative elections of that year, in which the Opportunists lost their parliamentary majority, bringing to an end an important wave of republican legislation. Several important events also occurred in Asia and Africa around 1885, such as the Tonkin Affair and the suspicious death of the French revolutionary Olivier Pain, as did various incremental leadership changes within international socialism. Although none of these individual events should be considered synonymous with radical intellectual change, collectively they mark an apposite end point.

The sources required for such a study are nominally abundant, but often surprisingly difficult to come by. Much revolutionary correspondence during this period was destroyed immediately after reading, but even surviving material is often difficult to locate. Barring the Lucien Descaves collection held in Amsterdam's International Institute of Social History few exhaustive or even substantial archives exist. More abundant printed sources, which were often produced cheaply on poor quality paper, have deteriorated substantially over time. As a result, many valuable titles have been lost, while others such as the important Blanquist exile newspaper *La Fédération*, held at the British Library, have deteriorated to such an extent that they can no longer be viewed. Even as scholarly interest in the subject matter rises, the sources render sustained study increasingly challenging.

In an effort to counteract such difficulties, this book has cast an extremely wide net. It draws upon printed and manuscript sources – many rare, and some previously unstudied – authored by diverse French revolutionaries and their allies primarily from the 1870s to the late 1880s. These include the archives of international organisations to which many French activists belonged, including the International Workingmen's Association and the Jura Federation; the political programmes of parties such as the *Fédération des travailleurs socialistes de France* and the *Parti ouvrier français*; and a diverse array of books, pamphlets, and almanachs. Originally produced in Europe, North America, and Oceania, these sources are now housed in various libraries and archives across Europe. Although this book focuses upon the years 1871–1885, in an effort to satisfactorily contextualise revolutionaries' thoughts and actions during this period, where relevant it draws upon sources produced anywhere between the 1840s and 1890s.

Two specific bodies of sources play particularly important roles in this study. The archives of the Parisian *préfecture de police* have proved extremely useful. Despite the scale of the Communards' defeat, French officials (particularly under the Moral Order governments of the 1870s) continued to fear their influence and frequently tasked police spies with infiltrating revolutionary circles. These informants produced a wealth of material including detailed reports on political meetings and commemorations.[34] Wary of precisely such surveillance, activists themselves rarely kept records of these meetings. The official reports are thus the only window onto the quotidian lives of activists during this period and the ways in which ideas were privately discussed and formed. While of course these sources reflect official paranoia and preoccupations as much as they do revolutionaries' ideas, they nonetheless provide invaluable insights into otherwise inaccessible areas of revolutionary life.

Newspapers formed the crux of French revolutionary intellectual life during this period. Revolutionary titles were printed in huge numbers during the Commune (one had a print run of around 100,000[35]), and they continued to do so even under the tight restrictions imposed after its fall. Activists from all six corners of France and across the ideological spectrum poured their attention and their funds into producing papers, while editors constantly sang their praises.[36] Dailies and weeklies were widely

---

[34] See for example 'Les réfugiés à Londres' (1876). APP Ba429/1346; APP Ba429/2313.
[35] C. Bellanger, *Histoire générale de la presse française*, 5 vols. (Paris: Presses universitaires de France, 1969–1976), vol.2 (1969), p.371.
[36] See for example 'Les journaux ouvriers', *Le Prolétaire*, 27 December 1879.

acknowledged to be revolutionaries' principal means of communication. In 1882, for example, Friedrich Engels observed to Eduard Bernstein that '[i]n Paris . . . if one wants to influence the masses one must have a daily'.[37]

Yet it was also in the pages of newspapers that ideas (many of which would later be published as books or pamphlets) were first articulated, debated, and formulated. The correspondence sections of larger titles, meanwhile, offered even obscure activists the opportunity to air their opinions. Newspapers were not simply a vehicle for dissemination, but rather a public service circulating ideas and connecting activists: the physical manifestation revolutionaries' intellectual aims. As such, newspapers afford access to the ideas of a wide variety of revolutionaries, rather than simply those of the movement's leaders.

Newspaper sources from this period present certain difficulties. The early Third Republic saw a meteoric rise in the number of titles published. Parisian dailies jumped from 40 titles published in 1874 to 90 in 1882, while those published in the provinces grew from 179 to 252 over the same period.[38] Yet in spite of its status as 'the golden age of the newspaper', it is virtually impossible to determine circulation figures for individual titles during the early years of the Third Republic. Although the Ministry of the Interior requested that circulation figures were recorded, archives rarely complied, and the figures in the *Annuaire de la presse* are, as Claude Bellanger noted in his seminal *Histoire de la presse française*, 'fantasies more often than not'.[39] Unofficial means of measuring circulation, such as compulsory stamp duties and postal tariffs, were also progressively eradicated during the 1870s.[40]

Where it is possible to determine circulation figures, however, they indicate that newspapers provide an unparalleled insight into French revolutionary thought and life during this period. According to Bellanger, the most popular titles during the Commune had huge outputs: over 60,000 for *Le Père Duchêne*, and a print run of over 100,000 for Jules Vallès's *Cri du Peuple*.[41] Almost a decade later, the initial issue of Henri Rochefort's *L'Intransigeant*, published just days after the general amnesty was declared, had a print run of over 70,000, although subsequent issues

---

[37] 197: F. Engels to E. Bernstein (4 November 1882, London), in K. Marx and F. Engels, *Marx/Engels Collected Works* (trans.) R. Dixon et al., 50 vols (London: Lawrence and Wishart, 1975–2004), vol.46 (1992), 359–363, at p.361. Later historians are in agreement with this sentiment. See Bellanger, *Histoire générale de la presse française*, vol.3 (1972), pp.370–371.

[38] Bellanger, *Histoire générale de la presse française*, vol.3, p.138.

[39] '[P]lus souvent fantaisistes'. Ibid., pp.147–148.   [40] Ibid., pp.147–148.

[41] Bellanger, *Histoire générale de la presse française*, vol.2, p.371.

quickly dropped by over half.[42] Numbers reduced further after the initial euphoria of the amnesty wore off and as titles multiplied, but according to estimates by their contributors, figures for important Parisian daily titles still remained well into the thousands.[43]

Close attention to both the form and the content of their newspapers is therefore vital to understanding the nature of French revolutionary thought during this period. This book draws upon a wide variety. The major Parisian daily papers of the 1880s including *L'Égalité*, *Le Prolétaire*, *Le Citoyen*, *L'Intransigeant*, and *La Bataille* plus titles published outside of Paris such as Malon's *Émancipation* and Vallès's *Cri du peuple* provide invaluable insight into some of the revolutionary movement's key ideas as well as their complicated relationships with French politics and with each other. Exile newspapers such as *La Fédération*, *Le Travailleur*, and *Qui Vive!* elaborate the nature of revolutionary thought during the 1870s as well as ex-Communards' interaction and collaboration with foreign activists such as Vera Zasulich, James Guillaume, Mikhail Bakunin, and Karl Marx. Finally, in order to gain further perspective upon these, I have also examined a number of more mainstream contemporary titles, several prominent revolutionary publications from the 1860s such as Rochefort's *La Lanterne*, and around forty ephemeral newspapers published during the Commune.

The book is divided into four parts, each of which has a triple purpose. First, the chapters all explore themes or subjects that were prominent in revolutionary thought during this period: the Commune, revolution, Marxism, and empire. These themes also represent the 'crises' that supposedly put an end to the revolutionary movement: the defeat of the Commune, the rise of the Third Republic and the consequent unfeasibility of traditional revolutionary action, the increasing prominence of Marxian international socialism, and deportation and exile. Finally, the successive parts may also be seen as a series of concentric circles, radiating progressively outwards to cover all of the contexts in which revolutionaries thought and operated. The first deals with the fallout of largely Parisian events, the second with the supposedly national character of revolution, the third with revolutionary involvement in (largely) European socialist organisations, and the fourth with the wider world.

---

[42] Bellanger, *Histoire générale de la presse française*, vol.3, p.341.
[43] See, for example, 63: P. Lafargue to F. Engels (Paris, 24 November 1882), in F. Engels and P. and L. Lafargue, *Correspondence*, 3 vols. (trans.) Y. Kapp (Moscow: Foreign Languages Publishing House, 1959), vol.1, 110–115, at p.113; 195: F. Engels to E. Bernstein, 2–3 November 1882 (London), in Marx and Engels, *Marx/Engels Collected Works*, vol.46, 353–358, at p.356.

While not an exhaustive encyclopaedia of all the subjects they covered, this approach enables us to better explore the forms, contexts, and languages that characterised revolutionary thought during this period. This in turn provides a much clearer picture of the shifting shape of revolutionaries' ideas and alliances, strengths and weaknesses, and successes and failures, as well as their complex interactions with French politicians, the French public, and the international revolutionary movement.

Part I examines the defeat of the Commune and revolutionary reactions to it. Through the examination of a wide range of revolutionary work on the Commune from the period immediately after its fall, it establishes that its surviving participants were neither crushed by the events of 1871 nor often considered it a significant defeat of their ideas. Through accounts of both its tenure of power and its violent end, revolutionaries attempted to simultaneously counteract the widespread image of the Communards as lawless barbarians and repurpose their defeat as a unifying experience.

Far from attempting to forget about the Commune, revolutionaries embraced it, creatively using its memory to navigate the new circumstances in which they found themselves and to establish a foundation upon which to rebuild the idea and image of a unified French revolutionary movement that was at once autonomous and politically viable. This work cannot be classified in terms of neat later categories such as 'left' and 'right', or even those frequently used during the period such as 'socialist', 'anarchist', or 'nationalist'. As well as the revolutionary movement's survival, accounts of the Commune are thus also indicative of its participants' intellectual heterogeneity.

The next three parts delve further into the content, character, and contexts of this thought. Part II asks what precisely it meant to be a French revolutionary during this period. With the failure and repression of the Commune, and the accession to power several years later of the actively reforming Opportunist republicans, traditional revolutionary action became increasingly unlikely and unpopular over the course of this period. It is therefore tempting to assume that activists' vaunted revolutionary unity was based upon little more than memories.

Part II demonstrates that this was not the case. Rather, using a variety of different languages and temporalities, activists from across the revolutionary movement including supposed 'traditionalists' such as Blanqui attempted to redefine revolution in broad, expansive terms more attuned to the political, social, and cultural circumstances of early Third Republic France. While these attempts met with mixed success, they nevertheless demonstrate that both activists and other sections of the French population continued to believe that revolution was an active and potentially viable concept.

Using the example of Marxism, Part III addresses the suggestion that revolutionary thought during this period was irreparably divided along factional, ideological lines. It shows that Marx and Marx's thought were both far more prevalent and used more reflexively than the acrimonious social and organisational history of French revolutionary socialism may suggest. Neither Marx nor his thought was the exclusive intellectual property of the self-proclaimed French Marxists. Rather, they were creatively and concurrently used by a wide variety of French revolutionaries to discuss pressing social problems, and to reinforce their marginal, revolutionary credentials in French politics. While bitter personal and political divisions certainly existed within the movement, at the same time revolutionaries noticeably struggled to ensure that it was not defined or consumed by them.

Revolutionaries, moreover, did not simply import a clearly defined 'Marxism' into French thought. Early French Marxism was not a distortion or a misunderstanding of an authentic original, but rather a nuanced variation upon a theme. As these chapters demonstrate, Marx himself, in the various abridgements and French translations of his work that he oversaw, went to considerable efforts to adjust his arguments to what he thought the French might like to hear. It was thus not only French thought that was flexible, creative, and collaborative during this period, but that of the international socialist movement more generally. French revolutionaries could not be divided along hard ideological lines, for no such intellectual orthodoxies existed.

Finally, Part IV places this thought within a global context. French revolutionaries had always seen their ideas as universally applicable. This took on new resonance during the 1870s and 1880s, though, as thousands of revolutionaries were deported to the South Pacific and the French state began to approach imperial ventures with increasing enthusiasm and moral certainty. A purely national or continental treatment of French revolutionary thought would therefore fail to capture the multiple spheres in which these activists saw themselves as operating.

Part IV delineates the ways in which activists both in Europe and in New Caledonia thought about and interacted with issues concerning the wider world during this period. Such issues, furthermore, were more than simply prevalent and prominent in French revolutionary thought: they occupied a position of vital importance. The diverse ways in which activists dealt with these concerns served variously to demarcate the boundaries and highlight the possibilities of supposedly universal ideas such as equality, fraternity, and revolution which, as we shall see, were central to revolutionary thought during this period.

This study has three principal aims. First, it intends to begin to piece together the nature and content of French revolutionary thought in the years that immediately followed the fall of the Commune. This shall provide us with a richer and more comprehensive account of how and why both revolutionary activists and the idea of a unified revolutionary movement continued to influence French politics for years after the prospect of traditional revolutionary action had disappeared. Second, in the process of delineating these imbrications, it hopes to revise the characterisation of the 1870s and early 1880s as a period in which both French and wider European politics became increasingly moderate and homogenous. Finally, through re-examining the thought of one of the founding moments of the modern revolutionary tradition, I aim to interrogate and provide a new perspective on a form, or forms, of politics that has played a pivotal role in Western political thought and practice for substantial periods of the nineteenth and twentieth centuries.

While the Paris Commune may have been defeated in May 1871, the French revolutionary movement did not simply collapse and disappear along with it. Neither did its erstwhile members disband and drift towards a series of prefabricated political and intellectual orthodoxies. Rather, the years that immediately followed the Commune's defeat were a far more creative moment than has previously been suggested. Activists spent the 1870s and early 1880s working hard to reconstruct the idea of a French revolutionary movement capable of being at once united, autonomous, and politically viable. This was achieved largely through the creative use of both new ideas and their new circumstances to redefine revolution and what it meant to be a revolutionary. The continued visibility and survival of French revolution, in other words, was ensured at least for a time through intellectual flexibility rather than deference to staid traditions or rigid doctrines.

PART I

The Paris Commune and Accounting for Failure

CHAPTER I

The Commune as Quotidian Event

On the edges of Père-Lachaise cemetery in Paris, the Mur des Fédérés stands as a permanent monument to the revolutionaries who lost their lives during the Paris Commune of 1871. The wall stands on the south-eastern outer limit of the famous cemetery, and marks the final resting place of the Commune's last defenders. On 28 May 1871, 147 Communards were lined up against the wall, shot by the French Army, and buried in a mass grave at its base. Facing the wall are the graves of various *fin-de-siècle* activists and politicians, their commitment to the Commune immortalised in strategically placed stone. Some, such as the anarchist Gustave Lefrançais and the socialist Benoît Malon, had taken an active part in the Commune. Many, like the French Marxists Paul and Laura Lafargue, had not.

In the years following the Commune's fall, activists and writers such as Malon, Lefrançais, and the Lafargues would come to enjoy success within both revolutionary and national political arenas. Paul Lafargue, for example, became the first socialist deputy elected to the Assemblée Nationale in 1891, while in 1880 Malon launched the *Revue socialiste* – a monthly journal on left politics that is still running today.[1] The Paris Commune, on the other hand, was defeated in little over two months, and was widely regarded as a definitive political failure. Yet clearly it remained of paramount importance for both its participants and its observers alike. It was this event – this failure – that they elected to be associated with in perpetuity.

This singular attachment to the Commune continued well into the twentieth century. In 1974, *Le Mouvement social* declared the Commune 'indecipherable', but others were far more certain of their allegiance.[2]

---

[1] For more, see M. Rebérioux, '*La revue socialiste*', *Cahiers Georges Sorel* 5 (1987), 15–38.

[2] J. Estèbe, 'Le centenaire de la Commune par le livre', in *Le Mouvement social* 86 (January–March 1974), 89–112, at p.89. See also *Paris Match* 1142 (Paris), 27 March 1971.

Marches through Paris to the Mur des Fédérés had taken place annually since the late 1800s, and they functioned as a rallying point for the French left throughout the twentieth century. In 1935, for example, thousands of marchers turned out to protest the rising wave of fascism in France and support the Popular Front coalition assembled by the Socialist, Communist, and Radical Parties. In May 1971, over 50,000 people took part in the centenary demonstrations.[3] The year was also marked by both an attempt to blow up the tomb of Adolphe Thiers (*chef du pouvoir exécutif* during the Commune and one of the architects of the harsh punishment meted out to its participants), and memorial services for Georges Darboy, Archbishop of Paris and one of the hostages executed by Communards in May 1871.[4] Even a century later, the Commune retained the power to provoke powerful reactions.

These strong opinions were doubtless heightened by the tense geopolitical climate of the Cold War. Since the 1917 Russian Revolution at least, international politics had been riven by the competition between capitalism and communism, and the two ideologies' radically different ideas of how society should be structured. The Commune played a significant part in these battles. Following in the textual footsteps of Karl Marx, who in May 1871 had declared the Commune 'the glorious harbinger of a new society', Communist leaders from Vladimir Lenin to Mao Zedong regularly invoked the memory of 1871.[5] Conservative commentators and later liberal historians, meanwhile, sought to minimise the emotional and political impact of such assertions, depicting it as the definitive end to a peculiarly French revolutionary tradition.[6] Writings on the Commune have rarely been free from this symbolism. As Martin Johnson noted in *The Paradise of Association*, 'explaining the Commune has always been more than a historical exercise'. [7]

Despite their overt political differences, these competing interpretations display a certain consensus as to what the Commune was and where its

---

[3] *Paris jour* (Paris), 24 May 1971.
[4] *France soir* (Paris), 3 November 1971; *L'Aurore* (Paris), 3 November 1971.
[5] K. Marx, *The Civil War in France: Address of the General Council of the International Working-Men's Association* (London: Edward Truelove, 1871), p.34. See also V.I. Lenin, *The Paris Commune* (London: Martin Lawrence, 1931).
[6] D. Thomson, *Democracy in France since 1870* (London: Cassell, 1989. First published, 1946), p.26.
[7] M.P. Johnson, *The Paradise of Association: Political Culture and Popular Organisations in the Paris Commune of 1871* (Ann Arbor: University of Michigan Press, 1996), p.7. For similar sentiments, see J.-C. Caron, *Frères de sang: la guerre civile en France au XIXe siècle* (Seyssel: Champ Vallon, 2009), p.229; C. Rihs, *La Commune de Paris (1871): sa structure et ses doctrines* (Paris: Éditions du Seuil, 1973. First published in Geneva, 1955), p.9.

significance lay. Intellectual and political uses of the Commune have principally derived their saliency from two factors. The first of these has been the belief that the Commune represented above all a significant historical break. For some, it was the glorious, albeit flawed, dawn of a new era, whereas for others it represented the end of a tradition. In both interpretations, however, the story of the Commune has traditionally been portrayed as one of unambiguous rupture: a watershed moment in terms of ideas, politics, and personnel.[8]

The second – and related – factor in accounting for the Commune's continued popularity has been its symbolic purchase. Whether, in the evocative words of its most distinguished chronicler Jacques Rougerie, the Commune was an 'aurore' or a 'crépuscule', its historic importance has overwhelmingly been derived from its symbolic value.[9] The Commune has been an empty vessel into which writers unconnected to it have poured their own ideas and interpretations. Certainly some, such as the renowned labour historian Jean Maitron and the film-maker Peter Watkins, have advanced more nuanced readings of the Commune's place in history.[10] Yet the 'symbolic break' interpretation first formulated by Marx in *The Civil War in France* in 1871 and taken up with such enthusiasm by many in the twentieth century has proved so powerful that it still dominates even recent historiography of the Commune and its afterlife.[11]

---

[8] S. Bernstein, *The Beginnings of Marxian Socialism in France* (New York: Russell & Russell Inc, 1965. First published, 1933), p.xxi; P. Hutton, *The Cult of the Revolutionary Tradition: The Blanquists in French Politics, 1864–1893* (Berkeley: University of California Press, 1981), p.36; C. Sowerwine, *Sisters or Citizens? Women and Socialism in France since 1876* (Cambridge: Cambridge University Press, 1982), p.4; F. Furet, *La Révolution de Turgot à Jules Ferry* (Paris: Hachette, 1988), p.489.

[9] J. Rougerie, *Procès des Communards* (Paris: Julliard, 1964), p.241. See also C.L.R. James, 'They showed the way to labor emancipation: on Karl Marx and the 75th anniversary of the Paris Commune', *Labor Action* 10 (New York, 18 March 1946); J. Chastenet, 'La Commune de Paris, aube des révolutions modernes ou flamboyant crépuscule?', in P. Dominique, *La Commune de Paris* (Paris: Hachette, 1962. First published, 1948).

[10] J. Maitron, 'Avant-propos', in P.-O. Lissagaray, *Histoire de la Commune de 1871* (Paris: Maspero, 1967. First published 1876.), 5–13, at p.12; P. Watkins (dir.), *La Commune (Paris, 1871)* (2000). See also H. Lefebvre, *La Proclamation de la Commune, 26 Mars 1871* (Paris: Gallimard, 1965), p.139; R. Dubois in 'Débat: "La Commune: utopie ou modernité?"', in G. Larguier and J. Quaretti (eds.), *La Commune de 1871: utopie ou modernité?* (Perpignan: Presses universitaires de Perpignan, 2000), 407–424, at p.412.

[11] For a critical look at this, see É. Fournier, *La Commune n'est past morte: les usages politiques du passé de 1871 à nos jours* (Paris: Éditions Libertalia, 2013). For examples, see P. Darriulat, 'Le patriotisme révolutionnaire de la déclaration de guerre à la Semaine sanglante', in C. Latta (ed.), *La Commune de 1871: L'événement, les hommes et la mémoire* (Saint-Étienne: Publications de l'Université de Saint-Étienne, 2004), 93–105, at p.105; D. Tartakowsky, 'La Commune: "Mémoires vives", résurgences et réfoulements', in Latta (ed.), *La Commune de 1871*, 319–336, at p.319.

The Commune's symbolic purchase has rendered it and its participants superficially well known, however on an intellectual level it has effectively removed them from history. For those seeking to invest the event with their own meaning, the ideas of the Communards themselves have proved an inconvenience. Historians such as Rougerie, Johnson, and Robert Tombs have undertaken valuable work on the Commune itself,[12] while Jean Joughin and more recently Laure Godineau have produced absorbing studies of the Commune's role in the French politics of the 1870s and 1880s. Yet as Joughin reminds his reader at the beginning of *The Paris Commune in French Politics*, 'the substance of this book is practical politics', and this statement could be applied equally to Godineau's work.[13]

By contrast, very little has been written on how French revolutionaries *thought* about (and therefore understood) the Commune in its immediate aftermath. While one intellectual history, Charles Rihs's 1955 *La Commune de Paris (1871): sa structure et ses doctrines*, exists, this work concentrates upon the two months of the Commune's existence, rather than the period immediately afterwards.[14] Works such as James Leith's *Images de la Commune* and Éric Fournier's recent *La Commune n'est pas morte* critically examine uses of the Commune after its fall, but cover a much broader time period.[15] These dual concentrations on either practical politics or symbolic power have, whether directly or indirectly, reinforced the idea that the Commune's primary import is its symbolic power, and that its ideas (unlike its images) have had no afterlife.[16]

Part I of this book demonstrates that this was not the case. It explores how French revolutionaries narrated, interpreted, and debated the Commune in the years immediately following its suppression during the Semaine Sanglante in May 1871. Using memoirs and articles on the Commune from the 1870s and early 1880s, it argues that for ex-Communards and revolutionaries, the Commune was of far more than

[12] See, for example, Rougerie, *Procès des Communards*; Johnson, *Paradise of Association*; R.P. Tombs, *The Paris Commune, 1871* (London: Longman, 1999).

[13] J.T. Joughin, *The Paris Commune in French Politics, 1871–1880*, 2 vols. (Baltimore, MD: Johns Hopkins University Press, 1955), vol.1, p.13. See also L. Godineau, 'Retour d'exil: les anciens Communards au début de la Troisième République' (unpublished PhD thesis, Université Paris 1 Panthéon-Sorbonne, 2000).

[14] Rihs, *La Commune de Paris (1871)*.

[15] J.A. Leith (ed.) *Images of the Commune: Images de la Commune* (Montreal: McGill-Queen's Unviersity Press, 1978); É. Fournier, *La Commune n'est pas morte: les usages politiques du passé de 1871 à nos jours* (Paris: Éditions Libertalia, 2013).

[16] See, for example, L. Assier-Andrieu, 'La Commune de 1871 et l'idéologie française', in Larguier and Quaretti (eds.), *La Commune de 1871*, 57–67, at p.66.

simply symbolic value. Rather than attempting to forget the failure of March–May 1871, the Commune loomed large in French revolutionary thought during this period. It is further possible to identify two predominant revolutionary interpretations of the events of spring 1871: the 'realist' and the 'violent'. The first of these comprised highly detailed, personal accounts of the Commune and focused on quotidian events, while the second eschewed this style in favour of commemoration and highly rhetorical uses of violence. Indeed, it could be said that with its focus on either practical politics or symbolic turning points, subsequent historiography has often mirrored these two interpretations. While the two interpretations presented very different accounts of the Commune, both, however, were indicative of the continued engagement with and attachment to the Commune in French revolutionary circles immediately after its defeat.

This attachment to the Commune, whether in the form of its ideas or commemoration, has often been construed as a sign that revolutionaries during this period were becoming increasingly anachronistic.[17] This was not the case. Rather, these uses of the Commune represented precise political interventions on several levels. For French revolutionaries at this time, discussion and commemoration of the Commune acted as a means by which they could emphasise their continued unity in a decade of division and exile. Improbably, ex-Communards were able to use the Commune to their benefit, harnessing their memories of it to create and reinforce a diverse array of politically viable revolutionary identities, whilst simultaneously projecting an image of unity. By employing precisely the failure that had threatened them with obsolescence, revolutionaries and ex-Communards aimed to reassert their relevance, and indeed their social and political necessity in a period marked by increasingly stable and republican government.

Chapter 1 examines the 'realist' interpretation of the Commune. These accounts focused on the practical dimensions of the Commune, heavily contextualising its inception and acknowledging the organisational flaws that had contributed to its defeat. In doing so, exponents of this interpretation aimed to reverse the prevailing narrative of the Commune, which cast revolutionaries as dangerous criminals and the army as agents of order. 'Realist' writers, who were primarily advocates of a federal socialism, also celebrated the Commune's concrete political achievements and drew attention to its progressive ideas, which they argued offered a genuine

---

[17] Hutton, *Cult of the Revolutionary Tradition*, p.36.

alternative to contemporary French society. In doing so, revolutionaries attempted not only to counter interpretations advanced by hostile and official actors, but also to wrest back control of the left's narrative of the Commune from Karl Marx and reconstruct themselves as both legitimate revolutionaries and responsible political actors.

In order to establish this, this chapter draws upon a number of revolutionary pamphlets and memoirs on the Commune published between 1871 and 1885. Revolutionaries penned numerous accounts of the Commune, but in the interests of ensuring a wide contemporary readership, the chapter focuses primarily upon some of the most widely known, such as Arthur Arnould's three-volume *Histoire populaire et parlementaire de la Commune de Paris*, Gustave Lefrançais's *Étude sur le mouvement communaliste à Paris en 1871*, Benoît Malon's *La troisième défaite du prolétariat français*, and Prosper-Olivier Lissagaray's *Histoire de la Commune de 1871*.[18] The chapter also draws upon shorter contemporary accounts of the Commune published in newspapers such as *L'Égalité*, *Le Prolétaire*, and the international exile journal *Qui Vive!* In order to satisfactorily contextualise revolutionary ideas on 1871, they have also been compared with other contemporary works on the Commune, including Maxime du Camp's *Les convulsions de Paris*, Camille Pelletan's *Questions d'histoire*, and Karl Marx's *The Civil War in France*, as well as earlier nineteenth-century French writings on revolution.[19]

Sanja Perovic recently noted of the historiography of the French Revolution that both 'liberal' interpretations emphasising chronology and 'socialist' readings focused on utopian futures fail to convey the complexities and possibilities that revolution signified for contemporaries.[20] Similarly, the dichotomy of the end of traditional revolutions versus the dawn of a Marxist future is an inadequate perspective from which to examine the

[18] For example, A. Arnould, *Histoire populaire et parlementaire de la Commune de Paris*, 3 vols. (Brussels: Imprimerie A. Lefevre, 1878); C. Beslay, *1830–1848–1870: Mes souvenirs* (Neuchâtel: James Attinger, 1873); G. Lefrançais, *Étude sur le mouvement communaliste à Paris en 1871* (Neuchâtel: G. Guillaume Fils, 1871); B. Malon, *La troisième défaite du prolétariat français* (Neuchâtel: G. Guillaume Fils, 1871); J. Andrieu, *Notes pour servir à l'histoire de la Commune de Paris en 1871* (Paris: Payot, 1971). Although not published until 1971, Andrieu's *Notes* was widely known within the revolutionary community during the 1870s and 1880s. For more, see M. Rubel, 'Introduction', in Andrieu, *Notes pour servir à l'histoire de la Commune*, 7–40.

[19] For example, P.-J. Proudhon, *Idée générale de la révolution au XIXe siècle: Choix d'études sur la pratique révolutionnaire et industrielle* (Paris: Garnier Frères, 1851); C. Pelletan, *Questions d'histoire: le comité central et la Commune* (Paris: Lagny, 1879); Marx, *The Civil War in France*; M. du Camp, *Les convulsions de Paris*, 4 vols., 5th edn (Paris: Hachette, 1881. First published, 1878–1880).

[20] S. Perovic, *The Calendar in Revolutionary France: Perceptions of Time in Literature, Culture, Politics* (Cambridge: Cambridge University Press, 2012), p.240.

place of the Commune in French revolutionary thought during the 1870s and early 1880s. The Commune represented both more and less than these teleological interpretations suggest. Rather than a beginning or an end, an 'aurore' or a 'crépuscule', revolutionaries during this period interpreted the Commune using something more akin what Peter Starr has termed 'a historical logic in a tripartite form, neither/nor/and yet'.[21] For contemporary revolutionaries, there were many different iterations of the Commune. It represented not a single, definitive, symbolic break, but rather an intricate patchwork of smaller tears and continuities.[22] It was a model for the future that drew its strength and legitimacy in large part from the past, and provided revolutionaries with a means by which to reassert their relevance, indeed their necessity in the present.

I

The Paris Commune, it was generally agreed at the time, had been a spectacular political failure. By March 1871, there had long been rumblings of discontentment in Paris regarding the government's handling of the Franco-Prussian War, including two attempted insurrections in October 1870 and January 1871. The uprising on 18 March in Montmartre, however, had not been planned, and erupted spontaneously in response to the army's attempt to remove several old cannons from the capital and the hands of the historically radical National Guard. The speed with which it spread was also a surprise, and within a matter of hours the rebels found themselves in control of large swathes of Paris. The extent to which certain *quartiers* rallied instinctively to the revolution was a matter of celebration, and this festival atmosphere has been much emphasised by scholars such as Henri Lefebvre, as well as French student protesters in May 1968, who sought to emulate it.[23] The rapidity and spontaneity with which it emerged, however, also left revolutionaries with little time to formulate clear or unified responses to key questions such as who the Commune should represent or how it should govern.

---

[21] For the definition of this logic, see P. Starr, *Commemorating Trauma: The Paris Commune and Its Cultural Aftermath* (New York: Fordham University Press, 2006), p.61.

[22] Robert Tombs has similarly suggested that we approach the Commune not as a stopping point, but as 'un carrefour où s'entrecroisent et se chevauchent différentes temporalités'. See R. Tombs, *Paris, bivouac des révolutions: la Commune de 1871* (trans.) J. Chatroussat (Paris: Éditions Libertalia, 2014. First published in English, 1999), p.417.

[23] Lefebvre, *La proclamation de la Commune*, pp.20–26; A.L. Conklin, S. Fishman, and R. Zaretsky, *France and Its Empire since 1870* (Oxford: Oxford University Press, 2011), p.296.

These issues became increasingly apparent as the Commune progressed. Among those charged with running the administration and effecting revolutionary wishes, many were young and had not participated in revolutionary action before. Of the 86 elected members who took up their seats on the Commune's legislative and executive body, the Conseil de la Commune, half were 35 or under. The youngest members, Raoul Rigault and Théophile Ferré, were 25 and 26 respectively. Still more were inexperienced in matters of administration and municipal government. Rather than politicians or soldiers, many members of the Commune were ordinary workers such as cobblers, carpenters, dyers, and wine merchants. The experienced revolutionaries, meanwhile, had spent their careers in small, secretive cells under hostile regimes rather than in administration. Few, in other words, possessed any of the bureaucratic experience or knowledge required for quotidian politics.[24]

So evident were these shortcomings that they were recognised even by the Communards themselves. Several months after the Commune's fall, Jules Andrieu, a member of the Conseil de la Commune and its delegate in charge of public services, penned an account of the revolution for the *Fortnightly Review*, a magazine run by the English Positivists Edward Spencer Beesley and Frederic Harrison. Andrieu was one of the only Communards with bureaucratic experience (having previously worked as chief of staff at the Hôtel de Ville[25]), and took a dim view of the Communards' expertise. He likened the Commune to the populist street melodramas common in nineteenth-century Paris, observing that it was 'staged worse than a drama on the boulevards',[26] and wrote privately that while revolutionaries may have had designs upon national government, in reality they had 'no more administrative capabilities than an office boy'.[27]

The Communards, furthermore, were not only unqualified to exercise their newfound power, but also divided about what precisely to do with it. After 18 March, the National Guard swiftly arranged municipal elections in the hopes of creating a representative and efficient government, or Conseil de la Commune. Only weeks after its election, however, the

---

[24] For more on traditional French revolutionary tactics, see, for example, S. Bernstein, *Auguste Blanqui and the Art of Insurrection* (London: Lawrence and Wishart, 1971).

[25] J. Maitron et al. (eds.), *Dictionnaire biographique du mouvement ouvrier français*, 44 vols. (Paris: Éditions ouvrières, 1964–1997), vol.4 (1967), p.121.

[26] J. Andrieu, 'The Paris Commune: A Chapter Towards Its Theory and History', in *The Fortnightly Review* vol.X (October 1871), 571–598, at pp.590–591.

[27] '[N]'avait au point de vue administratif que les facultés d'un garçon de bureau'. Andrieu, *Notes pour servir à l'histoire de la Commune*, p.98. See also G. Lefrançais, *De la dictature* (Geneva: Ziegler, 1875), p.14.

Conseil descended into factional infighting. The most significant of these political divisions was that between the majority and minority factions. The former was comprised primarily of neo-Jacobin adherents of the veteran revolutionary Louis Auguste Blanqui and some independents, all of whom supported the establishment of a dictatorial Committee of Public Safety in conscious emulation of Maximilien Robespierre's government during the first French Revolution. The minority, meanwhile, was largely made up of federalists, internationalists, and self-proclaimed socialists, who opposed the creation of a Committee of Public Safety and insisted that the Commune's government remain democratic.

Neither was the Commune welcomed by much of the capital's population. Several thousand residents left Paris with the government after 18 March, while others (including hostile sections of the National Guard) protested the new regime on 21 and 22 March. Indeed, even those initially amenable to the revolutionary administration became increasingly disillusioned with it. Abstention levels in the Commune's initial municipal elections on 26 March were roughly the same as those in the plebiscite of 3 November 1870 and the elections of 8 February 1871. In the new elections of 16 April, however, abstention rose to over 70 per cent.[28] Even by Communards' own accounts, then, the Commune had clearly been a failure. Revolutionaries had spent several decades criticising those in power, yet as soon as they were handed the reins, they had proved themselves divided and unable to rule a single city effectively, let alone an entire country.

Non-revolutionary writers and politicians seized upon the Commune's failings following its fall. Drawing upon sensationalist images such as that of the *pétroleuse* – an ugly, anarchic woman who roamed Paris, pouring petrol into buildings so that they would burn more effectively – official and reactionary accounts had from the beginning of the Commune represented its participants as thoughtlessly destructive.[29] In his popular 1871 memoir *Les 73 journées de la Commune*, the poet Catulle Mendès condemned the Communards as 'nothing but rioters', while the conservative historian Hippolyte Taine similarly likened them to 'savage wolves and brigands'.[30]

---

[28] J. Rougerie, *Paris libre 1871* (Paris: Éditions du Seuil, 1971), pp.145–146.

[29] For more on *pétroleuses*, see G.L. Gullickson, *Unruly Women of Paris: Images of the Commune* (Ithaca, NY: Cornell University Press, 1996). For more on hostile interpretations of the Commune, see J.M. Roberts, 'The Paris Commune from the Right', *English Historical Review*, supplement 6 (1973).

[30] '[V]ous n'êtes que des émeutiers'. C. Mendès, *Les 73 journées de la Commune*, 5th edn (Paris: E. Lachaud, 1871), p.153. For Taine, see J. Jennings, *Revolution and the Republic: A History of*

The Commune, hostile accounts argued, had been an event 'outside history'. Its participants' actions in spring 1871 had demonstrated that they had none of the characteristics required to be good citizens, and as a result posed a serious danger to modern European society.

The most prominent and comprehensive of these hostile accounts was Maxime du Camp's four-volume *Les convulsions de Paris*, published between 1878 and 1880. A renowned essayist and frequent contributor to the *Revue des deux mondes*, du Camp had also been involved (and injured) in the suppression of working-class protesters by the National Guard in June 1848. Du Camp condemned the Commune as an abhorrent event reminiscent of the worst excesses of the Terror, in which 'idiocy seemed to march side by side with violence'.[31] Drawing upon widespread fears about the 'contamination' of the social body by the working class,[32] he characterised the Commune's participants as 'an unmotivated population, who spent the best part of their time in wine merchants',[33] and were easily stirred to immoral and destructive acts by degenerate leaders and journalists.[34] This view of the Communards reflected that of the government and the army, who reacted to events with particular ferocity. Over 15,000 arrests were made during the final week of the Commune, of which around 4,500 were in the last two days alone.[35]

Moderate republicans also took a dim view of the Commune. During the Second Empire, revolutionary, radical, and moderate republicans had been united in their efforts to remove Napoleon III from power and restore a more democratic constitution. In March 1871, however, the groups took very different paths, and both radical and moderate republicans went to great pains to distance themselves from their former allies, often leaving Paris and offering explicit condemnations of the Commune. Unlike their conservative counterparts, many republicans were willing to show clemency to the Commune's participants after its fall. Camille Pelletan, for example, a journalist and leading member of the Radicals,

---

Political Thought in France since the Eighteenth Century (Oxford: Oxford University Press, 2011), p.288.

[31] 'Tout fut sinistre dans cette Commune où la niaiserie semblait marcher de pair avec la violence'. du Camp, *Les convulsions de Paris*, vol.2, p.60. For comparisons to Marat and the Terror, see p.1; p.40.

[32] S.A. Toth, *Beyond Papillon: The French Overseas Penal Colonies, 1854–1952* (Lincoln: University of Nebraska Press, 2006), p.3; A. Bullard, *Exile to Paradise: Savagery and Civilization in Paris and the South Pacific, 1790–1900* (Stanford, CA: Stanford University Press, 2000), p.29.

[33] '[U]ne population désoeuvrée qui passait la meilleure partie de son temps chez les marchands de vin'. du Camp, *Les convulsions de Paris*, vol.2, p.43.

[34] For immoral leadership, see ibid., vol.2, p.42. For the widespread violence of Communards, see p.100.

[35] Tombs, *Paris, bivouac des révolutions*, p.344.

was horrified by the events of the Semaine Sanglante. He opposed reactionary attempts to demonise the Communards or position them as enemies of civilisation, and campaigned vigorously for a general amnesty.

He was not, however, sympathetic to the Commune itself. In *Questions d'histoire*, his 1879 inquest into 1871, he sought to separate both the Commune and its participants from the heritage of previous French revolutions. Unlike 1789, 1830, and 1848, he argued, 1871 'was not a revolution, for it had prepared neither a programme nor a government'.[36] While reactionary and republican writers strongly disagreed on the reasons for their condemnation of the Commune and its participants, they were nevertheless in agreement on a key point. Whether they classed the Commune as maliciously criminal or a tragic mistake, both agreed that it had been undeniably wrong. Moreover, both made use of similar tactics in their efforts to discredit the Commune, seizing specifically upon its most notable and incontrovertible failings, rather than simply voicing their disapproval.

Perhaps surprisingly, prominent commentators on the left were barely more sympathetic. As the remaining revolutionaries were rounded up in the days after the Commune's final defeat, Karl Marx delivered an address on recent French events to the General Council of the International Workingmen's Association. The speech was published in pamphlet form as *The Civil War in France* several weeks later, and proved extremely successful. English readers devoured the text: within two months it had already been reissued twice, and the second edition alone sold 2,000 copies.[37] The text is now widely considered the paradigmatic defence of the Commune. Samuel Bernstein in *The Beginnings of Marxian Socialism in France*, for instance, observed that '[e]very page of it breathed a spirit of hatred for the conquerors of the Commune.'[38]

Marx was certainly blistering in his condemnation of the Commune's opponents and detractors. The Government of National Defence, for instance, was 'a cabal of place-hunting barristers'.[39] Adolphe Thiers, meanwhile, was a 'monstrous gnome',[40] who waged 'banditti-warfare against Paris', while his ministers worked towards 'the establishment, throughout France, of a reign of terror'.[41] Indeed, '[t]o find a parallel for

---

[36] '[C]e n'est pas une révolution, car il n'y a pas de programme ni de gouvernement préparé'. Pelletan, *Questions d'histoire*, pp.68–69.

[37] K. Marx and F. Engels, *Marx/Engels Collected Works* (trans.) R. Dixon et al., 50 vols. (London: Lawrence and Wishart, 1975–2004), vol.22 (1986), p.666.

[38] Bernstein, *The Beginnings of Marxian Socialism in France*, p.44.

[39] Marx, *The Civil War in France*, p.3.   [40] Ibid., p.5.   [41] Ibid., pp.26–27.

the conduct of Thiers and his bloodhounds', Marx claimed, 'we must go back to the times of Sulla and the two Triumvirates of Rome'.[42] His condemnation, moreover, was not restricted to the government. Bourgeois Parisians, he argued, had considered

> the civil war but an agreeable diversion, eyeing the battle going on through their telescopes, counting the rounds of cannon, and swearing by their own honour and that of their prostitutes, that the performance was far better got up than it used to be at Porte St-Martin. The men who fell were really dead; the cries of the wounded were in good earnest; and, besides, the whole thing was so intensely historical.[43]

Its opponents, in other words, were certainly censured.

At the same time, though, he was not concerned with resuscitating the reputations of the Communards themselves. In *The Civil War in France* he applauded the Communards' effort and accepted that they had been motivated by firm convictions, celebrating the '[w]orking, thinking, fighting, bleeding Paris' that stood 'radiant in the enthusiasm of its historic initiative'.[44] Simultaneously, however, he noted that these ideas had ultimately failed. The failure of the Commune, moreover, represented more than simply the failure of a single revolution. Rather, it indicated that the time of both Paris and its revolutionaries was over. The end of the Commune, Marx concluded, was an act of 'heroic self-holocaust'.[45]

Privately, Marx was even more dismissive of the Commune. In a letter to the Dutch socialist Ferdinand Domela Nieuwenhuis in 1881, he observed that 'the majority of the Commune was in no sense socialist, nor could it have been'.[46] Indeed, he had predicted that it would fall since 6 April 1871.[47] While, unlike du Camp and Pelletan, Marx celebrated the Commune's occurrence, neither *The Civil War in France* nor his private correspondence constituted a glowing endorsement. For Marx, the Commune's utility lay in what it could inspire later socialists to do, rather than in the event itself. While his reading and use of the Commune required him to praise the event in public, it did not necessitate a rehabilitation of either its participants or ideas.

The Civil War in France was by no means the only interpretation of the Commune on the contemporary European left. As we have seen, English Positivists such as Beesley and Harrison attempted to defend the

---

[42] Ibid., p.29.   [43] Ibid., p.23.   [44] Ibid., p.25.   [45] Ibid., p.31.
[46] 42: K. Marx to F. Domela Nieuwenhuis (22 February 1881, London), *Marx/Engels Collected Works*, vol.46 (1992), 65–67, at p.66.
[47] Tombs, *Paris, bivouac des révolutions*, p.309.

Commune more vigorously, and gave a platform to its participants at the *Fortnightly Review*.[48] Yet by the mid-1880s the domination of Marx's interpretation was clear. In an 1886 speech celebrating the anniversary of the Commune, for example, the Russian anarchist Peter Kropotkin paraphrased Marx, claiming that while '[t]he Commune *did but little* . . . the little it did sufficed to throw out to the world a grand idea'.[49] Across Europe, then, on both the right and the left, the general perception of the Commune was one of failure. This failure, moreover, was celebrated (although in different ways and for different reasons) by both friends and enemies alike.

II

Communards and French revolutionaries were well aware of the potential of these interpretations for further damaging their credibility as political actors, and alive to the subsequent need to challenge their legitimacy by formulating an alternative.[50] As Kristin Ross has recently noted,

> The necessity all these refugees apparently felt, in the midst of their struggle . . . to write their personal experiences and analyses of what had occurred in Paris, shows their acute awareness of the battle over the Commune's memory that had begun to rage even as the Bloody Week was ending.[51]

Many began this work by approaching the Commune in a soberer and less rhetorical fashion than du Camp or Marx. Charles Longuet, the radical journalist and one of Marx's two French sons-in-law, participated in the Commune in 1871 as an elected member of the governing Conseil and was also involved in its *Journal Officiel*. During a speech to Communard exiles in London in 1880, however, he warned revolutionaries against publishing emotive or sensationalist accounts of 1871, arguing that for their purposes, 'it is more useful to talk about the causes of defeat than glorification of the past'.[52]

---

[48] For other interpretations of the Commune, see G. Stedman Jones, *Karl Marx: Greatness and Illusion* (London: Allen Lane, 2016), p.509; p.555.

[49] 'The Celebration of the Commune', *Commonweal* (London, 1 April 1886), p.31. Emphasis mine.

[50] *Lettres de la Nouvelle-Calédonie*, Fonds Louise Michel, International Institute for Social History (IISH), 930.

[51] K. Ross, *Communal Luxury: The Political Imaginary of the Paris Commune* (London: Verso, 2015. First published in French, 2015), p.102.

[52] 'Le citoyen *Longuet* croit qu'il est plus utile de parler des causes de la défaite que de glorification du passé.' 'Le 18 mars à Londres', *Le Prolétaire* (Paris), 3 April 1880. See also Joseph Lane, quoted in 'Celebration of the Commune', *Commonweal* (April 1886), p.31.

Other revolutionaries exhibited a similar attitude. Throughout the 1870s, newspapers such as the international exile journal *Qui Vive!* reported on the military court hearings held at Versailles, in which thousands of ex-Communards were tried. Others, such as *L'Égalité* and *Les Droits de l'homme*, presented 'evidence' of official wrongdoing in the form of unamended government speeches and pro-government newspaper articles from during the Semaine Sanglante.[53] A number of revolutionaries, then, sought to distinguish themselves from rival accounts of 1871 by presenting their recollections as attempts to precisely recover the facts of the Commune and tell its history 'as it actually happened', rather than as judgements upon its worth. Whilst it is not surprising that an author would seek to distinguish their work by claiming that it was the authoritative truth (or at least a unique take on the truth), such a style was notably different from many other contemporary accounts of the Commune.

This style of account has received relatively little attention from historians. Scholars such as Emmanuel Jousse have noted that certain contemporary accounts of the Commune emphasised qualities including precision and truth-claims. Such observations, however, have mainly been made in passing, with scholars moving swiftly back to more familiar territory like revolutionary memories of the Commune that emphasise its quality as a 'traumatic' or 'sensory' experience.[54] As we shall see in the next chapter, these ideas certainly played a central role in some revolutionary accounts of the Commune. The historiographical concentration on them, however, has given the impression that this was the primary form in which revolutionary thought on the Commune was articulated, and thus that accounts framed as truth-claims were either uncommon or unremarkable.

This regard for precision, however, was to be found in a wide variety of revolutionary publications from this period. Newspaper columnists frequently emphasised the importance of factual accuracy, agreeing with Prudent Dervillers in the widely read Parisian daily *Le Prolétaire* that the falsification of history was a serious offence.[55] This attitude was also

---

[53] For the war council minutes, see, for example, *Qui Vive!* (London), 19 October 1871; 20 October 1871. For the Semaine Sanglante material, see, for example, *Les Droits de l'homme* (Paris), 26 May 1876; 'La décade sanglante', *L'Égalité* (Paris), 26 May 1878.

[54] E. Jousse, 'La construction intellectuelle du socialisme réformiste en France, de la Commune à la Grande Guerre' (unpublished PhD thesis, Sciences-Po, 2013), pp.121–122. See also K.S. Vincent, *Between Marxism and Anarchism: Benoît Malon and French Reformist Socialism* (Berkeley, CA: University of California Press, 1992), p.40; Starr, *Commemorating Trauma*; Godineau, 'Retour d'exil', p.466; pp.518–519.

[55] 'Les responsabilités devant l'histoire', *Le Prolétaire*, 18 March 1879. See also Lefrançais, *Étude sur le mouvement communaliste*, p.12; 'L'avènement', *Le Citoyen & La Bataille* (Paris), 19 March 1883;

manifest in works such as Prosper-Olivier Lissagaray's *Histoire de la Commune de 1871*. A republican journalist and revolutionary socialist, Lissagaray had been involved in the Commune in 1871 and spent the 1870s in exile, largely in London. In London he undertook the writing of his inquest into the Commune and became briefly engaged to Marx's youngest daughter before returning to Paris after the amnesty.

Lissagaray's *Histoire*, first published in 1876, was perhaps the period's most widely read revolutionary account of the Commune. The book was banned in France upon publication, but was successfully smuggled into the country until the relaxation of press restrictions in 1881,[56] and it eventually ran to many editions.[57] The book's success was also long-lasting. Newspapers (including but by no means limited to Lissagaray's own) repeatedly reproduced extracts of the book,[58] and in 1896 the Parisian municipal council donated 121 copies to local libraries.[59]

In the *Histoire*, Lissagaray expressly positioned himself as a truth-teller. Writers 'who amuse themselves with uplifting histories', he argued, were 'just as criminal as the geographer who draws up incorrect maps for navigators'.[60] This was especially pertinent with regards to 1871, which, as we have seen, was the subject of revolutionary glorification as well as establishment horror. According to Lissagaray, however, '[a]ll the revolutionary eulogising about 18 March 1871 is not worth one page of true history'.[61] For Lissagaray, then, as well as for many other writers, the Commune was of far more than merely symbolic importance.

Given the concern for this particular kind of truth in prominent publications such as *Le Prolétaire* and Lissagaray's *Histoire*, it seems accurate to term this both a popular and a widespread interpretation, and it is this that this chapter shall henceforth be concerned with. These accounts derived primarily from former members of the Commune's minority faction, such as Arthur Arnould, Gustave Lefrançais, and Benoît Malon. For the purposes of the chapter, these accounts shall be referred to as

---

F. Jourde quoted in A. Dowdall, 'Narrating *la Semaine Sanglante*, 1871–1880' (unpublished MPhil dissertation, University of Cambridge, 2010), p.35.

[56] For details of revolutionaries' success in smuggling literature and propaganda into France during the 1870s, see Dowdall, 'Narrating *la Semaine Sanglante*', pp.14–20.

[57] Maitron, 'Avant-propos', in Lissagaray, *Histoire de la Commune*, at p.9.

[58] *Bulletin de la Fédération jurassienne* (Geneva), 3 June 1877; 24 June 1877. *Le Citoyen & La Bataille* (Paris), 12 December 1882; 29 March 1883; 2 April 1883; 21 May 1883.

[59] Godineau, 'Retour d'exil', pp.514–515.

[60] 'Celui qui fait au peuple de fausses légendes révolutionnaires, celui qui l'amuse d'histoires chantantes, est aussi criminel que le géographe qui dresserait des cartes menteuses pour les navigateurs.' 'Preface to the first edition', in Lissagaray, *Histoire de la Commune*, p.14.

[61] *La Bataille* (Paris), 19 March 1885.

'realist' interpretations of the Commune. This appellation is intended neither as an allusion to contemporary literary currents nor as an evaluation of the factual accuracy of such accounts. Rather, it reflects the authors' professed aims and intentions in presenting the Commune in this way.

This regard for the truth was frequently accompanied by an acknowledgement that it would in fact be impossible to determine the precise truth about the Commune. When reviewing the veteran revolutionary Charles Beslay's account of the Commune in 1877, for example, the Swiss-exile periodical *Le Travailleur* criticised the title. *La vérité sur la Commune*, it wrote, was '[m]uch too weighty a title in our opinion ... he cannot presume to tell *the truth about the Commune.*'[62] Similarly, when reviewing Lissagaray's *Histoire*, the same journal judged 'the best part of the work' to be 'that which deals with the Comité Central', for '[t]his the author saw with his own eyes'.[63] Truth, in other words, derived from first-hand personal experience, and was not an objective moral standard.

Realist accounts of the Commune thus indicated a more complicated vision of truth than simply the recitation of received facts. Despite the vocal commitment to clarity in many works on the Commune, the majority of these writers made no claims to universality for their own thought. Given that knowledge was derived from personal experience, it was impossible for any one author to ever know 'the whole truth' about anything, including the Commune. In such accounts, there therefore existed a tension or duality between the author's high valuation of 'truth' and the simultaneous recognition of their own inability to provide it. They were defined by the failure to offer what they themselves had identified as most valuable.

Revolutionary writers, however, did not regard such admissions of fallibility as a failing. As we have seen, this period witnessed the publication of numerous accounts of the Commune, often with vividly competing narratives. This was equally the case internally to the revolutionary movement as it was externally. Combining claims about the importance of truth and their own authorial inadequacies enabled Communards both individually and collectively to assert control over this situation. By acknowledging, through the definition of truth as personal experience,

---

[62] 'Titre trop lourd à porter selon nous ... il ne peut prétendre à dire *la vérité sur la Commune.*' *Le Travailleur* (Geneva), October 1877, p.30. Emphasis original.

[63] 'A nos yeux, la partie la mieux traitée de l'ouvrage est celle qui a trait au Comité Central. Ici l'auteur a vu de ses yeux'. Ibid., May 1877, p.27.

that multiple histories of the event could coexist, revolutionary authors were able to rationalise the uncontrolled publication of multiple, competing accounts of the Commune.

Indeed, they were even able make a virtue of this multiplicity. The suggestion that collaboration could lead to further clarification emphasised the need for the Commune's participants to overcome their differences, unite, and discuss their experiences. By acknowledging that individually they were ignorant, but that collectively they could hold the truth (or were at least able to approach it), realist writers were able to frame their accounts as a kind of forum for consultation, or an alternative inquest into the Commune: a collective post-mortem to establish what precisely had gone wrong. The form and professed objective of these works thus also began the work of repositioning revolutionaries as rational and responsible actors, offering a direct contrast to the image popularised by other accounts of the Commune.

At the same time, this conceptualisation of truth also served to discredit non-Communard accounts of the events of spring 1871. Relatively few people, after all, had actually been inside Paris during the Commune. The government, of course, had repaired to Versailles, and many other residents had joined the exodus. Moreover, while the Commune was later blamed on foreign subversion at the hands of the socialist International Workingmen's Association, it was in fact a largely national affair.[64] Several foreign revolutionaries, such as the Poles Walery Wroblewski and Jaroslav Dombrowski (who were both in exile in France already) had joined the Commune, but activists such as Marx certainly had not.

If truth required personal experience, then only the Communards themselves were qualified to dispense it. Focusing on truth therefore united revolutionaries in a number of ways. First, and most obviously, it promoted the exchange of ideas and responsible discussion within the movement at a time when calm collaboration was sorely needed. At the same time, it also provided a negative form of unification, distinguishing personal recollections from the second-hand accounts of authors like du Camp and Marx who had not been present in Paris during the Commune. Focusing on this conception of the truth as personal experience, then, also served to reclaim the Commune and its legacy for the Communards themselves.

---

[64] For more, see Q. Deluermoz, 'The IWMA and the Commune: a reassessment', in F. Bensimon, Q. Deluermoz, and J. Moisand (eds.), *'Arise Ye Wretched of the Earth': The First International in a Global Perspective* (Leiden: Brill, 2018), 107–126.

III

Realist writers married their claims about truth based on personal experience with a programme of intensive contextualisation. In 1878, *L'Égalité* pronounced 18 March 'a complex event'.[65] Similarly, the teacher and ex-Communard Raoul Urbain criticised writers who restricted their analysis to the immediate circumstances of the 18 March uprising. 'A lot has been said about the cannons', he remarked. Yet while the army's attempt to remove the cannons from Montmartre was undoubtedly a flashpoint, '[t]he cannons were not the cause of this revolution at all. They were merely the opportunity.'[66] *Le Travailleur* likewise argued that 'the Commune is only understandable when it is explained in the context of the facts that brought it about', but placed these even further in the past, listing 'June [1848], December [1851], the awakening of the final years of the empire' as particularly pertinent.[67] In a direct challenge to assertions that the Commune had been an exceptional event outside of history, then, revolutionaries argued that only through contextualisation within the previous months, years, and even decades could the Commune be properly understood.

This recontextualisation also partially shifted the burden of responsibility for 18 March from revolutionaries to the contemporary French political class. Following the French army's defeat by the Prussians at the Battle of Sedan and the humiliating capture of both Napoleon III and most of the French army on the battlefield, the Second Empire was overthrown and the imperial family fled Paris for England. On 4 September 1870, the Third Republic was proclaimed, and direction of both the country and the war was undertaken by a Government of National Defence, headed by General Louis-Jules Trochu.

The new government initially attracted cross-party support, but republicans and revolutionaries quickly became disillusioned with its decisions. Many officials appointed under the Empire were not replaced,

---

[65] '[U]n fait complexe'. 'Le 18 mars', *L'Égalité* (Paris), 24 March 1878. See also Beslay, *Mes souvenirs*, p.461; V. Marouck, 'Le Socialisme officiel sous la Commune', in *La revue socialiste* 7 (Paris, 5 June 1880), 330–336, at p.330. For a similar sentiment from a radical republican, see Pelletan, *Questions d'histoire*, p.157.

[66] 'On a beaucoup parlé de ces canons. Les canons ne furent pas du tout la cause de cette révolution. Ils n'en étaient que l'opportunité'. R. Urbain, 'Vae Victis', Fonds Lucien Descaves (IISH), 1035, p.16.

[67] '[L]a Commune n'est compréhensible que tout autant qu'elle est éclairée, expliquée par le récit des faits qui l'ont engendrée: Juin, Décembre, le réveil des dernières années de l'empire'. *Le Travailleur*, May 1877, p.27. See also 'Origines du 18 mars', *Le Prolétaire*, 19 March 1881.

and the government ignored working-class and socialist groups such as the Parisian Comité central républicain des vingt arrondissements. The government's most widely despised decision came following the war's end in January 1871, when it ceded the eastern region of Alsace and parts of Lorraine to the newly formed Germany as part of a peace treaty. Several republicans, including Malon and Victor Hugo, immediately resigned their seats in the Assemblée Nationale in protest. Revolutionaries consistently emphasised their initial high hopes and subsequent disappointment in the Government of National Defence. Gustave Lefrançais, for example, who had been a member of both the Comité républicain des vingt arrondissements and the Commune, wrote that, as honourable men, Gustave Tridon and Malon had felt compelled to resign from government 'less than *one month* after their election … convinced of the impossibility of retaining their dignity in such a milieu'.[68]

Revolutionaries supplemented these complaints of political profligacy with descriptions of the state of the capital during the Franco-Prussian War. For four months during the war, Paris was besieged by the Prussian army. Most of the national government, however, evacuated the capital, with the Assemblée Nationale removing to Bordeaux in September 1870 and another delegation (including the minister for war Léon Gambetta, who escaped in a hot air balloon) to Tours. Describing the devastation in Paris during the siege, Andrieu, for example, wrote that 'there may have been men in military dress in Paris, but there were no longer soldiers, there was no longer an army'.[69] Paris, in other words, was a lawless landscape, and during the war most national politicians had abjured their responsibility to their capital, and thus to their state.

This sense of desertion was compounded by the legislative elections of February 1871. Revolutionaries and socialists saw some success in the elections, including the victories of Benoît Malon and Gustave Tridon in Parisian constituencies. Nationally, however, the elections returned an overwhelming majority of conservative, rural deputies, many of whom favoured a return to monarchical government. As if to reinforce these sentiments, rather than returning to the newly liberated capital to take up

---

[68] '[L]es sincères, les honnêtes, qui donneront alors leur démission … moins *d'un mois* après leur élection … convaincus de l'impossibilité de rester dignes dans un pareil milieu.' G. Lefrançais, *Un Communard aux électeurs français* (Geneva: Publications de la Revue Socialiste, 1875), p.14. Emphasis original. See also *Le Travailleur*, May 1877, p.3. For an example of such disappointment, see 'La patrie en danger', *La Patrie en danger* (Paris), 7 September 1870.

[69] Andrieu, 'The Paris Commune', at p.585. See also P.-O. Lissagaray, 'Lions et ânes', *La Bataille*, 11 August 1883.

their seats, the new Assemblée chose to establish their seat of government at the palace of Versailles.

In such conditions, revolutionaries implied, Paris had been obliged to rebel in order to reassert a semblance of civilisation, and most importantly to save the Republic. As Malon argued in *La revue socialiste*, '[a]fter the ruin of the *patrie*, the Parisian proletariat ... had to take up arms'.[70] Indeed, this desire to reassert the rule of law and representative democracy was reflected in some of the Commune's immediate actions, including the organisation of municipal elections several days after the uprising. It is certainly true that such measures ultimately achieved only limited success. Only the Comité des vingt arrondissements presented lists in every arrondissement, several candidates elected to the Conseil refused to take up their seats, and some (such as Blanqui, who was in prison) were unable to do so.[71] Others quickly vacated theirs – either in protest at certain decisions, or because they were killed – leaving the Commune's legal frameworks more unsteady than had been intended. Nonetheless, however, legal frameworks had been put in place, and drawing attention to the Commune's broader context enabled revolutionaries to contrast their own regard for due process with what they regarded as others' neglect.

By throwing light upon the wider context of the Commune, realist writers thus attempted to shift some of the blame for 18 March (which, in most other accounts, fell squarely upon the Communards) away from themselves. As one Citizen Combault was at pains to stress at a banquet in London, while the removal of the cannons may have been unexpected, '[i]t is not right to say that the Revolution of 18 March was a surprise'.[72] Some form of civil unrest, in other words, was bound to happen in such a situation. Indeed, several uprisings had already occurred in Paris prior to the Commune. Adequately contextualised within the wider circumstances of 1870–1871, they argued, 18 March was simply the inevitable result of broader and deeper injustices. Simultaneously, by abnegating its obligations to the capital, the state and the political class themselves became equal players in the outbreak of revolution. In this interpretation, the Communards were far from disruptive; rather, they had been pushed into action by the inaction of others.

---

[70] 'Après la ruine de la patrie, les prolétaires parisiens ... durent prendre les armes.' B. Malon, 'Les Partis ouvriers en France', in *La revue socialiste* 5 (5 May 1880), 257–269, at p.262.

[71] For the Comité des vingt arrondissements, see Rougerie, *Paris libre*, p.136.

[72] 'Il n'est pas vrai de dire que la Révolution du 18 mars a été une surprise.' 'Le 18 Mars à Londres: le banquet des réfugiés', *Le Prolétaire*, 3 April 1880.

This context not only reflected badly upon the Commune's opponents but, equally importantly, reflected well upon the Communards themselves. Writers such as the novelist and journalist Arthur Arnould stressed that rather than a radical attempt to tear down the French polity, the Commune had been 'essentially *conservative*' in nature 'against the official government', who had cravenly abandoned France's capital and its citizens to the Prussian onslaught.[73] The London exiles agreed, asserting that

> without them [the Communards] there would be no Republic. They fought for it under the Empire and when a monarchy was being prepared on 17 March. Remember that without the dogged resistance of Paris, today you would be ruled by a Bonaparte, a Chambord, or an Orléans.[74]

The national government, revolutionaries reminded their readers, had retreated first to Bordeaux in 1870, and then to Versailles on 18 March. Rather than engaging with their constituents' concerns, politicians had systematically abandoned the national capital, 'carrying off ledgers and coffers, taking employees, and leaving Paris in complete disorganisation'.[75] In contrast, *Le Prolétaire* argued, the people (or, the Communards) 'did not recoil in the face of responsibilities abandoned by others'.[76]

By emphasising so forcefully the context in which the Commune came about, revolutionaries aimed to justify an event that, in its immediate aftermath, was widely considered unjustifiable. Thus viewed, the Commune ceased to be an inexplicable event or an act of barbarity. Rather, it was a legitimate, even necessary reaction to official neglect and injustice. Likewise, the Communards themselves became responsible actors rather than the 'savage wolves and brigands' that Taine had complained about to his wife.[77] Contextualising the Commune in this way, then, enabled revolutionary writers to adjust the balance of responsibility for the events of spring 1871. This interpretation implicated the Government of

---

[73] '[E]ssentiellement *conservateur* contre le gouvernement officiel'. Arnould, *Histoire populaire et parlementaire*, vol.2, p.34. Emphasis original.

[74] '[S]ouvenez-vous qu'il n'y aurait pas sans eux de République, qu'ils lutteraient pour elle sous l'Empire, que la monarchie était préparée le 17 mars, que, sans la résistance acharnée de Paris, vous seriez aujourd'hui sous un Bonaparte, un Chambord ou un d'Orléans'. J. Joffrin, C. Langevin, L. Landrin, P. Vichard, and E. Maujean, address to London exiles. London (undated, May–June 1877). Archives de la Préfecture de Police, Paris (APP), Ba429/2254. See also 'L'anniversaire du 18 mars 1871', *Le Prolétaire*, 18 March 1879; P.-O. Lissagaray, 'La loi du drapeau', *La Bataille*, 4 June 1885.

[75] '[L]e gouvernement fuyait à Versailles, important livres et caisse, emmenant les employés et laissant Paris dans la plus complète désorganisation.' Malon, *La troisième défaite*, p.70. See also Lissagaray, *Histoire de la Commune*, p.131.

[76] 'L'anniversaire du 18 mars 1871', *Le Prolétaire*, 18 March 1879.

[77] Jennings, *Revolution and the Republic*, p.288.

National Defence as well as the Communards in the 18 March uprising, and established the Paris Commune as a foundation upon which to begin to recast themselves as responsible political actors.

This perspective tapped into well-established prejudices against the government that had arisen in the wake of Napoleon III's fall. Many relatively radical republicans also blamed the Government of National Defence for the conflict that occurred in spring 1871, as did numerous writers and politicians on the right. The *Enquête*, for example, was full of denunciations of folly on the part of Government of National Defence. 'Realist' revolutionary writers, then, were not the only ones to blame the Government of National Defence for the Commune. Rather, their accounts both drew upon and formed a part of a broader narrative regarding the Government of National Defence's inefficacy, and this similarity between their own criticisms and those of others enhanced their claims to truth.

Contextualising the Commune enabled its participants to acknowledge its failings without discrediting themselves, however they often simultaneously used it to absolve themselves of precisely these failings. As we have seen, many revolutionaries including Andrieu and Arnould freely accepted blame for the Commune's administrative and political deficiencies.[78] Ultimately, though, while it was generally agreed that the Communards had failed in many ways, revolutionary writers ascribed the Commune's more serious shortcomings largely to circumstance. The circumstances that the Communards found themselves in were indeed disruptive. During the two months of its existence, the Commune was engaged near constantly with the national government at Versailles – in attempts to negotiate during the first few days and, from April, in military offensives and counter-offensives.[79] These not only claimed the lives of two prominent revolutionaries, Gustave Flourens and Émile Duval, but also saw the Commune gradually lose most of its strategic outposts.[80]

Realist interpretations frequently drew attention to this environment. Malon, for instance, concluded that while the Communards may have been 'beneath their task', regardless 'they could not do in those tempestuous days what they would have done in calmer times. Neither theories nor

---

[78] Andrieu, 'The Paris Commune', at p.597. See also Arnould, *Histoire populaire et parlementaire*, vol.1, p.85; Malon, *La troisième défaite*, p.221.
[79] Tombs, *Paris, bivouac des révolutions*, pp.307–308.   [80] Ibid., p.310.

men can be fairly judged'.[81] Arnould pushed this line of reasoning further, arguing:

> these failings are nothing to be ashamed of . . . They were the result of such overwhelming circumstances that even a union of geniuses would not have been able to navigate the reefs and make it into port without mistakes, no longer the ship of State, but a wave-beaten bark bearing the people and their fortune.[82]

In the same way that contextualising the Commune rendered its occurrence less shocking, it also enabled revolutionaries to offer alternative reasons for the vices and failings that had manifested themselves during its brief existence. In this interpretation, the Commune's most grievous shortcoming (if it could even be called that) had been its circumstances rather than its ideas. If its actors had been foiled by events beyond their control and almost certain defeat, it became harder to blame the Communards for its failure and its excesses. Importantly, the focus on context thus also enabled revolutionaries to partially relieve themselves of culpability whilst simultaneously accepting the events and failings of the Commune.

Contextualising the Commune therefore not only helped to shed light on the 'truth' of its circumstances, but also played an important role in combating the widespread hostile perceptions of it and its participants. The depiction of the Commune, in Arnould's words, as an embattled ship trying to steer itself and the nation to safety was designed to take the heat out of the hostile images created of it in the years immediately following its fall. In this reading the Communards were not enraged or wantonly destructive, but desperate patriots attempting (although often failing) to make responsible decisions – decisions that nobody else had been willing to make. Elaborating the difficult conditions in which the Commune found itself, it was hoped, would render the decisions made by revolutionaries during spring 1871 more understandable to the general public, and their failings more excusable.

This seemingly responsible take on the Commune was not simply exculpatory, though, and it also enabled its participants to recast

---

[81] 'Les hommes de la révolution communale furent au-dessous de leur tâche . . . mais ils ne purent pas donner dans ces jours de tempête ce qu'ils auraient pu donner dans des temps plus calmes. Ni les théories, ni les hommes ne peuvent être équitablement jugés'. Malon, *La troisième défaite*, p.177.

[82] '[C]es fautes n'ont rien de honteux . . . Elles ont été le résultat de circonstances tellement écrasantes que l'on peut se demander si même une réunion d'hommes de génie aurait pu éviter tous les écueils et conduire au port, sans fausse manoeuvre, non plus le vaisseau de l'Etat, mais la barque battue des flots qui portrait le peuple et sa fortune.' Arnould, *Histoire populaire et parlementaire*, vol.2, p.104. See also *Le Travailleur*, October 1877, p.32.

themselves as responsible political actors in the present. If the course of the Commune had been dictated by fate and circumstance, then neither the surviving Communards nor their ideas could be blamed for its worst excesses or its failure. Indeed, despite their apparent willingness to accept responsibility for their actions, the primary aim of these realist interpretations was arguably to remove the Commune from revolutionary control. The preoccupation with identifying unfavourable circumstances, mistakes, and scapegoats permitted these writers to not only show that the Commune could have succeeded, but also simultaneously absolve themselves of responsibility for the fact that it had not.

IV

Thus absolved of responsibility for the Commune's more egregious acts, realist writers returned to its ideas. As we have seen, both hostile and Marxist accounts of the Commune centred upon the idea that its participants had been either intellectually barren or severely misguided. This was not an entirely fair accusation. Upon taking power in late March 1871, the Conseil de la Commune addressed itself immediately to some of the most pressing problems that residents had experienced since the beginning of the war, including high rents. It also established ten 'commissions' to administer different areas of municipal life, including education, justice, and public services, as well as passing more ideologically motivated legislation that had long been central to radical manifestos. It established maximum salaries for civil servants, for example, and legislated for the separation of church and state.[83]

Realists emphasised these qualities. Contradicting assertions that the Commune had lacked a proper programme, Lefrançais argued in his *Étude sur le mouvement communaliste* that in fact its actions had been motivated by ideas of a better society. The 'part that we played in the movement that began on 18 March', he affirmed, 'was the result of firm convictions rather than thoughtless, reckless momentum'.[84] Arnould similarly emphasised the Communards' intellectual engagement, contrasting them favourably (unlike Pelletan) with previous revolutionaries. Whereas 'in 1830, in Lyons, on 24 February 1848 the people had nothing but vague aspirations',

---

[83] Tombs, *Paris, bivouac des révolutions*, p.160.

[84] 'La part que nous avons prise au mouvement commencé le 18 mars, étant le résultat de convictions arrêtés et non d'un entraînement irréfléchi et inconscient'. Lefrançais, *Étude sur le mouvement communaliste*, pp.11–12. See also 'Souvenons-nous!', *Le Prolétaire*, 18 March 1880.

he argued, '[i]n 1871, this was not the case.'[85] Indeed, he characterised the Communards as 'not merely soldiers, but *living ideas*', performing their thought through their revolutionary actions.[86] In addition to their emphasis on the importance of context, realist interpretations were simultaneously eager to emphasise that the Commune had been more than simply a tragic event. While its possibilities may have been foreclosed by the circumstances it found itself in and the Communards may have been below their task, the Commune itself had nonetheless been intellectually motivated.

More importantly, they claimed, the Commune's ideas remained relevant even after its fall. Many writers proudly drew attention to its reforms on matters such as divorce, education, and night work, as well as its declaration of the separation of church and state.[87] Significantly, as well as its specific legislation, writers also defended the Commune's broader ideology and sense of purpose. In 1878, the French- and Swiss-edited anarchist journal *Bulletin de la Fédération jurassienne* observed that currently '[i]deas that were still confused in 1870 and 1871 are being clarified daily through discussion.'[88] While the article acknowledged that the ideas of the Commune and the early 1870s had lacked definition, nonetheless, its reference to their ongoing discussion suggested that the content of the Commune's ideas was essentially the same as that of those held by socialist revolutionaries in the late 1870s. Likewise, writing of the imperative need for workers to establish 'a new plan of action', Lefrançais affirmed, '[w]e believe that the revolutionary movement of 18 March 1871 provided the necessary principles, and that will be its honour in the history of humanity.'[89]

Realist interpretations, then, were not merely interested in a symbolic rehabilitation or celebration of the Commune. For these writers, the afterlife of the Commune lay not in symbolism, but in its ideas. Few commentators disputed that the Commune had been of historical

[85] 'Mais en 1830, mais à Lyon, mais le 24 février 1848, ce peuple n'avait que de vagues aspirations . . . En 1871, rien de semblable.' Arnould, *Histoire populaire et parlementaire*, vol.3, pp.50–51.

[86] '[N]on seulement des soldats, mais qui sont des *idées vivantes*'. Ibid., vol.2, p.150. Emphasis original.

[87] Malon, *La troisième défaite*, p.272; 'Souvenons-nous!', *Le Prolétaire*, 18 March 1880; 'La Semaine de sang', *Le Prolétaire*, 22 May 1880; *Le Prolétariat*, 14 March 1885. See also James, 'They showed the way to labor emancipation'.

[88] 'Les idées, encore confuses en 1870 et 1871, s'éclaircissent chaque jour par la discussion'. *Bulletin de la Fédération jurassienne*, 18 March 1878.

[89] 'Or, ce plan d'action, nous pensons que le mouvement révolutionnaire du 18 mars 1871 en a fourni les principales données. Ce sera son honneur dans l'histoire de l'humanité.' G. Lefrançais, *L'idée libertaire dans la Commune de 1871* (Paris: Cahiers de contre-courant, 1958. First published, 1874), p.16. See also 'Souvenons-nous!', *Le Prolétaire*, 18 March 1880.

significance, whether positive or negative. For Pelletan, it marked a parting of the ways between revolutionaries and other republicans after several decades of cooperation. For conservatives such as du Camp and Taine, it manifested the moral bankruptcy of the Parisian working class. For Marx, the Commune was an historic Rubicon on the path to genuine social revolution. By linking its ideas to those of later revolutionaries, though, realists sought in addition to go beyond mere historical significance, demonstrating its continued intellectual significance as well, and depicting it as an event that had both developed and given a platform to important new ideas.

While realist depictions of the Commune as a new socialist dawn may have been superficially similar to Marx's conceptualisation of it as 'the glorious harbinger of a new society', in qualitative terms they were extremely different. For Marx, the Commune's significance lay in its status as the symbolic beginning of a new era of social revolution. For realist writers, it meant this and more. Not only was it symbolically important, but it was the Commune's ideas, its intellectual content, that would power this new revolution.

The most significant of the Commune's intellectual contributions, they suggested, was its delineation of progressive social ideas. Arnould, for example, averred that

> The idea [of the Commune] was great and just ... *the Paris Commune was something more than and entirely different from a revolt.* It was the advent of a principle, the affirmation of a politics. In a word, it was not merely *another* revolution. It was a *new* revolution, carrying in the folds of its flag an entirely original programme.[90]

Lefrançais similarly argued in 1873 that it was 'precisely the solution to the social question, which grows more and more important each day, that particularly preoccupied the partisans of the movement of 18 March 1871'.[91] By emphasising the Commune's links to questions of social equality, revolutionaries aimed to strengthen the case for the Commune's

---

[90] 'L'idée était grande, juste ... la *Commune de Paris fut* plus *et* autre chose *qu'un soulevement.* Elle fut l'avénement d'un principe, l'affirmation d'une politique. En un mot, elle ne fut pas seulement une révolution *de plus,* elle fut une révolution *nouvelle,* portant dans le plis de son drapeau tout un programme original et caratérisique.' Arnould, *Histoire populaire et parlementaire,* vol.2, pp.80–81. Emphasis original.

[91] 'Or, c'est précisément de la solution de la question sociale, qui se pose d'elle-même chaque jour d'avantage, qu'étaient particulièrement préoccupés les partisans du mouvement du 18 mars 1871'. G. Lefrançais, *République et Révolution: de l'attitude à prendre par le prolétariat en présence des parties politiques* (Geneva: V. Blanchard, 1873), p.21.

lasting intellectual, as well as historical, significance. They thus positioned it as an early example of discussions that would come to dominate French revolutionary circles in this period.[92] At the same time, this emphasis on the Commune's social qualities also served to separate their ideas on the Commune from those of radical republicans such as Pelletan, who classified it as an 'exclusively political' event.[93]

The problem, revolutionaries argued, was not that the Commune had been intellectually bankrupt, but rather that it was too progressive. Not only had it been a rational reaction to circumstances, but it was also (and more importantly) an incubator of highly ambitious and vital new ideas. Arnould, for example, classified it as 'one of the most prodigious efforts to conquer the future';[94] a 'new step in revolutionary thought', presenting a vision of the future that circumstances were unable to accommodate.[95] The Commune not only had been a desperate response to current circumstances, but also had been a manifestation of a genuine intellectual and social alternative to contemporary French society. By classifying the Commune thus, realist writers were able to at once explain away the Commune's failure and credibly retain their faith in what they claimed had been the Commune's ideas. As an event that was simply too progressive for its own circumstances, revolutionaries implied, the Commune had been bound to fail, and there was nothing that could have been done about it. It was now their responsibility to preserve these ideas for the future.

Revolutionary accounts of the Commune that adopted a 'realist' interpretation, then, differed from their contemporary rivals in a number of ways. Where reactionary, republican, and even sympathetic socialist narratives primarily characterised the Commune as a failure and sought to exaggerate the scale of either the Commune's defeat or its symbolic importance, realist writers did not. These accounts were less pugnacious, and concentrated primarily upon placing the Commune back into context – whether the Siege of Paris, the new Republic, or the circumstances of the Commune itself. Such a focus set realist writers apart from their contemporaries and achieved a number of aims. First, it enabled French revolutionaries to discredit contemporary rival accounts on a more meaningful level. Rather than explicitly contesting rival accounts, realist writers

---

[92] For such a diagnosis, see, for example, A. Theisz, 'Le mouvement social: la grève des mineurs de Denain', *L'Intransigeant* (Paris), 1 November 1880.

[93] Pelletan, *Questions d'histoire*, p.84.

[94] '[U]n des plus prodigieux efforts pour la conquête de l'avenir'. Arnould, *Histoire populaire et parlementaire*, vol.2, p.21.

[95] '[L]'étape nouvelle de la pensée révolutionnaire'. Ibid., vol.1, p.9.

simply drew attention to events and claims that were undeniably true, thus reducing the potential for others to contest the veracity of their claims. Even du Camp, for instance, admitted that Thiers had 'temporarily sacrificed Paris in order to defend France' during the Commune.[96] Second, and more importantly, by placing the Commune back into its context, revolutionaries were able to redistribute the blame for both its occurrence and its end, enabling them to recover some of the Commune's ideas from the wreckage of its failure.

[96] '[A] sacrifié momentanément Paris pour defender la France'. Du Camp, *Les convulsions de Paris*, vol.2, p.39.

CHAPTER 2

The Commune as Violent Trauma

Realist interpretations of 1871, then, focused on context and quotidian events in an attempt to restore intellectual content to the Paris Commune. More prominent in the general historiography of the Commune, however, have been accounts centred upon violence. While Paris was besieged by the Prussians for four months during the winter of 1870–1871, defiant denizens of the capital were wont to declare that they would 'rather be buried in the ruins of Paris' than give it up to their enemies.[1] In late May 1871, these declarations seemed to come true for many members of the Commune. After just over two months of revolutionary rule, divisions of the national army entered Paris on 21 May 1871, commencing seven days of destructive fires and pitched street battles that came to be known as the Semaine Sanglante, or 'bloody week'. In this contest, the Communards were hopelessly outnumbered. The invading Versailles army totalled around 120,000 soldiers, while the Commune could boast only a fraction of this figure. In the second arrondissement, 25,000 soldiers (or *versaillais*) faced off against no more than dozens of Communards behind barricades.[2]

Both revolutionaries and the invading troops engaged in remarkable acts of brutality during the Semaine Sanglante. On 28 May, the 31-year-old internationalist and member of the Conseil de la Commune, Eugène Varlin, was recognised in central Paris and transported to Montmartre, where he was reportedly beaten by an angry crowd and by soldiers, before eventually being shot.[3] Communards, meanwhile, executed several clergymen including Georges Darboy, the Archbishop of Paris, in their prison at La Roquette on 24 May, and over fifty more hostages on rue Haxo in the north-east of Paris two days later. The narrative of unparalleled violence

---

[1] Préferer 'nous enterrer sous les ruines de Paris plutôt que de nous rendre'. R.P. Tombs, *Paris, bivouac des révolutions: la Commune de 1871* (trans.) J. Chatroussat (Paris: Éditions Libertalia, 2015), p.337.
[2] Ibid., p.335.
[3] J. Merriman, *Massacre: The Life and Death of the Paris Commune of 1871* (New Haven, CT: Yale University Press, 2014), p.221.

has captured attention since 1871. Both contemporary writers and later historians during the twentieth century have drawn fulsomely upon such imagery, depicting the Paris Commune primarily in terms of its violent end.[4] Indeed, the success of John Merriman's recent *Massacre: The Life and Death of the Paris Commune* is proof of the continued power of such a narrative.[5]

This chapter reconstructs the production and popularisation of this narrative, which I term the 'violent' interpretation of the Commune, in revolutionary circles immediately after the Commune's fall in May 1871. It demonstrates that rather than shying away from the violent end of their attempt at revolutionary government, many ex-Communards embraced it. This was particularly true of surviving Blanquists, who were more inclined to promote violent insurrection and state interventionism, and who had been in the governing majority during the Commune. By focusing upon violence rather than the Commune's ideas and its duration, Blanquists hoped to use it to simultaneously criticise Third Republic politicians, gloss over the Commune's own mistakes, and project an image of revolutionary unity based on the shared experience of violent trauma.

Yet although this interpretation ultimately proved more enduring, it was neither as widespread nor as beneficial to revolutionaries as its 'realist' counterpart during the 1870s and early 1880s. Whereas writers adopting a 'realist' approach were able to draw positive lessons from the Commune, those using the violent narrative were unable to characterise it as anything other than a tragic event. While revolutionary writings on the Commune provided a bedrock upon which revolutionaries of various stripes began to reconstruct their thought and image, there remained significant limitations to the Commune's revolutionary possibility, and its interpretation visibly benefited certain groups more than others. Ideas on the Commune thus also unintentionally served to illustrate the fragility of revolutionary solidarity, accentuating and visualising deep ideological cracks in the movement even as they were deployed as evidence of the Communards' solidarity.

---

[4] See, for example, B.H. Moss, *The Origins of the French Labor Movement 1830–1914: The Socialism of Skilled Workers* (Berkeley: University of California Press, 1976), p.62; E. Bottigelli and C. Willard (eds.), *La naissance du Parti ouvrier français: Correspondance inédite de Paul Lafargue, Jules Guesde, José Mesa, Paul Brousse, Benoît Malon, Gabriel Deville, Victor Jaclard, Léon Camescasse et Friedrich Engels* (Paris: Editions Sociales, 1981), p.12.

[5] Merriman, *Massacre: The Life and Death of the Paris Commune*. See also J. Moreau, *Les socialistes français et le mythe révolutionnaire* (Paris: Hachette, 2003), p.53.

The chapter draws upon a wide range of published and unpublished sources. These include full-length works such as Prosper-Olivier Lissagaray's *Les huit journées de mai derrière les barricades*.[6] Unlike realist accounts, however, during this period the violent interpretation of the Commune was developed primarily in newspaper articles and through commemoration. As a result, the chapter draws heavily upon exile newspapers from the 1870s such as *Qui Vive!* and *La Fédération*, as well as Parisian papers published after the amnesty, including *L'Intransigeant* and *L'Égalité*. Police intelligence reports, meanwhile, provide immediate insights into the extent and form of commemorations of the Commune, as well as the ways in which they changed from year to year.

I

The narrative of violent immolation emerged swiftly after the fall of the Paris Commune. The most recent work on the Semaine Sanglante, Robert Tombs's 2012 'revision' in *The Historical Journal*, estimates that the final death toll was far less than previously imagined. On the basis of various sources including highway department records and ledgers of daily burials, Tombs suggests that the number of revolutionaries executed in cold blood at the end of the Commune was probably around 1,400.[7] In the 1870s, however, reports quickly circulated that it had been ten times this number.[8] Estimates continued to climb over the next few years, and by 1885, the initial figure had doubled, with Prosper-Olivier Lissagaray reporting in *La Bataille* that 40,000 revolutionaries had been murdered.[9]

Unlike the realist interpretation discussed in Chapter 1, this was something of a collaborative effort. In the immediate aftermath of the Commune, a wide variety of writers contributed to the construction of this narrative of violent holocaust. Hostile accounts, such as that of Hippolyte Taine or Maxime du Camp's *Convulsions de Paris*, often focused on the lawlessness and brutality of the Communards. In particular, these writers emphasised the destruction of property, from private houses in wealthy neighbourhoods to monuments such as the Tuileries Palace and

---

[6] P.-O. Lissagaray, *Les huit journées de mai derrière les barricades* (Brussels: Bureau du *Petit journal*, 1871).

[7] R. Tombs, 'How bloody was *la semaine sanglante* of 1871? A revision', *The Historical Journal* 55 (September 2012), 679–704, at p.697.

[8] Ibid., at pp.701–702.

[9] See, for example, P.-O. Lissagaray, 'La loi du drapeau', *La Bataille* (Paris), 4 June 1885.

thoroughfares such as the rue de Rivoli.[10] Neither, though, did they shy
away from the violence meted out by the French army; indeed, the literary
critic Edmond Goncourt claimed to have been pleased that the Semaine
Sanglante was so violent.[11] As Alex Dowdall has demonstrated, early
commentators on the right often embraced the Semaine Sanglante as an
'event to be inscribed on the memory and consciousness of the nation
itself, in order to teach lessons, ensure vigilance, and guard against future
social extremism'.[12] Violence – both illegal and official – was thus central
to their interpretations of the Commune.

Radical republicans such as Camille Pelletan also promulgated the idea
of unprecedented official violence, although for different reasons. Although
they had vigorously opposed the Commune, many republicans including
moderates such as Jules Ferry were alarmed by the scale of the official
violence perpetrated during the Semaine Sanglante, and by its aftermath.[13]
While former Communards were convicted in their thousands in the years
after 1871, neither the French army nor the government at the time faced
any meaningful inquiry into or recriminations for their actions in the last
days of the Commune. In fact, conservative Moral Order politicians went
from strength to strength in the years after 1871, forming successive
governments and attempting to effect a monarchical restoration.
Republicans from Ferry to Pelletan regarded such politicians as a threat
to both the Republic and the stability of France, and sought in works such
as Pelletan's *La Semaine de mai* to highlight their extra-judicial actions and
thus discredit them.[14]

Ex-Communards were no exception to this fixation, and violence often
featured prominently in memories of 1871. This mainly took the form of
criticisms of the state's actions during spring 1871, and many Communards claimed it was this that had motivated them to write.[15] In some
exceptional cases, ex-Communards even embraced the Communards' own
violence, such as the executions of Generals Lecomte and Thomas on
18 March or the rue Haxo executions on 26 May 1871, in which

---

[10] See, for example, M. du Camp, *Les convulsions de Paris*, 4 vols., 5th edn (Paris: Hachette, 1881.
     First published, 1878–1880), vol.2, p.59; p.100. For more on the fires, see Tombs, *Paris, bivouac
     des révolutions*, p.337.
[11] Tombs, *Paris, bivouac des révolutions*, p.362.
[12] A. Dowdall, 'Narrating *la Semaine Sanglante*, 1871–1880' (Unpublished MPhil dissertation,
     University of Cambridge, 2010), p.34.
[13] Tombs, *Paris, bivouac des révolutions*, p.362.
[14] C. Pelletan, *La semaine de mai* (Paris: M. Dreyfous, 1880).
[15] J. Bergeret, *Le 18 Mars: Journal Hébdomadaire* (London and Brussels, 1871), p.1.

Communards shot fifty-one hostages, including eleven priests.[16] As Chapter 1 demonstrated, the 'realist' claim that the Commune had incarnated legitimate ideas and demands was fiercely contested by a spectrum of different commentators, from du Camp to Marx. When it came to the violence that had surrounded the Commune, and particularly its end, however, this was not the case. Rather, the construction of the Paris Commune as a uniquely violent event was something of a collaborative effort between writers of vastly different political persuasions.

Which revolutionaries in particular were involved in constructing and promulgating this interpretation of the Commune? Writers and publications occasionally employed both realist and violent interpretations. The most notable example of this was perhaps Lissagaray. As demonstrated in Chapter 1, his 1876 *Histoire de la Commune de 1871* was doubtless a 'realist' account. His initial analysis of the Commune, however, written during his time in Belgium and published in 1871, was a mainstay of the violent narrative. In *Les huit journées de mai derrière les barricades*, he described in copious detail individual violent acts committed by soldiers against the Parisian population, and pronounced the Semaine Sanglante as a whole to have been one of the worst massacres in history.[17] 'The great massacres of the Bible, the King of Dahomey's bloody ceremonies', he wrote, 'can give but an idea of this butchery of proletarians.'[18] He was also, through his newspaper *La Bataille*, responsible for progressively escalating the estimated number of Communards killed in the Semaine Sanglante.[19]

It is nonetheless possible, however, to make certain general distinctions between the two. Propagators of realist interpretations such as Arthur Arnould and Gustave Lefrançais had for the large part been members of the Commune's minority faction. These members of the Conseil had espoused more federalist and socialist ideas, and had voted against the creation of a 'Committee of Public Safety' in emulation of Robespierre in the final days of the Commune. In contrast, those advancing violent interpretations were overwhelmingly Blanquists, and members of the Commune's majority. Jules Bergeret, author of *Le 18 mars*, was one of the Communards responsible for the fire at the Tuileries Palace, while Gustave-Paul Cluseret had attempted to transform the National Guard

---

[16] See, for example, É. Vaillant, 'Aux communeux' (1874), in L. Michel, *La Commune* (Paris: P.V. Stock, 1898), 413–423, at p.422.

[17] See, for example, Lissagaray, *Les huit journées de mai derrière les barricades*, p.154.

[18] 'Les grandes tueries de la Bible, les fêtes sanglantes du roi de Dahomey, peuvent seules donner une idée de ces boucheries de prolétaires.' Ibid., p.155.

[19] See, for example, P.-O. Lissagaray, 'La loi du drapeau', *La Bataille*, 4 June 1885.

into an army.[20] At different points, both acted as the Conseil's delegate for war.

In the violent interpretations published by revolutionaries, the Semaine Sanglante played a key role. The lyricist Jean-Baptiste Clément, who wrote the French radical anthem *Le temps des cerises*, participated in the Commune and was a leading member of several commissions. After its fall, however, he concentrated primarily on its violent end, asking in an article in *Le Prolétaire* whether it was 'possible to forget the bloody saturnalia of the week of May...?'[21] Many of the revolutionary movement's most prominent and prolific journalists adopted similar tactics. By 1871, Henri Rochefort was a veteran radical journalist and former editor of renowned extremist papers such as *La Lanterne* and *La Marseillaise*. He edited *Le Mot d'ordre* during the Commune, and was later deported to New Caledonia, returning to France in 1880 as soon as the amnesty was declared.

In an editorial in *L'Intransigeant*, the newspaper he founded upon his return to France, Rochefort glossed over the duration of the Commune, and concentrated instead upon the Semaine Sanglante. After briefly mentioning the Commune as 'a battle of two and a half months' in an article on the legacy of 1871, he swiftly moved on to a discussion of the Semaine Sanglante, describing a scene in which '[c]orpses floated down the Seine, and the swollen streams bathed the pavements in blood.'[22] This article, like many others, not only provided a description of the violence of the Commune, but placed it in a position of primary symbolic and intellectual importance. Likewise, Édouard Vaillant, who was director (*gérant*) of the Commune's *Journal officiel* and masterminded its initiative for universal secular education, later suggested that in spring 1871, '[t]he fighting, the struggle for existence and power was everything, the rest only an accident.'[23] This was in marked contrast to realist interpretations. Whereas realist writers were primarily concerned with explaining the Commune's beginning and detailing its duration, violent interpretations focused

---

[20] For more, see J. Maitron (ed.), *Dictionnaire du mouvement ouvrier français, 2ème partie: 1864–1871, de la fondation de la première Internationale et la Commune*, 6 vols. (Paris: Éditions ouvrières, 1967–1971). For Bergeret, see vol.4 (1967), pp.258–259; for Cluseret, see vol.5 (1968), pp.134–136. For more on Cluseret, see F. Braka, *L'honneur perdu de Gustave Cluseret (1823–1900)* (Paris: Hemisphères, 2018).

[21] 'Est-il possible d'oublier les saturnales sanglantes de la semaine de mai'. 'Le prolétariat ne peut pas désarmer', *Le Prolétaire* (Paris), 29 May 1880. See also 'Les fusillés du Père-Lachaise', *Le Prolétaire*, 29 May 1880.

[22] 'Une lutte de deux mois et demi ... Pendant huit jours, la Seine charria des cadavres, et les ruisseaux gonflés baignèrent de sang les trottoirs.' 'De 1871 à 1885', *L'Intransigeant* (Paris), 19 March 1885.

[23] É. Vaillant, 'Vive la Commune!', *Commonweal* (London, April 1885), p.1.

overwhelmingly on its end and its failure. Indeed, they argued, these factors defined the Commune.

This is not to say that realist interpretations ignored such violence, but rather that their interpretations were distinct from their more violent counterparts. In 1871, for example, Lefrançais spoke of the Commune's end not as a failure but as a pragmatic act, arguing that the blood of labourers would 'purify the city and reaffirm *good principles*'.[24] Similarly, in his 1878 *Histoire populaire et parlementaire de la Commune de Paris*, Arnould wrote that:

> There are occasions when one must know how to die, for dying is to confess one's faith. Dying is to affirm a principle, to fly a flag, to launch a new and true idea into the world with one's blood.[25]

In both realist and violent interpretations, then, the Communards who died had made a heroic sacrifice, but the nature of the sacrifice was different in each. While realist writers such as Arnould and Lefrançais focused on the pragmatic nature of the Communards' deaths, in violent accounts the same sacrifice was transformed into a desperate one. In the former, the emphasis lay upon the creative possibility and future potential engendered by people 'know[ing] how to die'. For violent writers, on the contrary, the Semaine Sanglante's significance lay in the fact that it had been 'sanglante' – in other words in its decisive violence, and its finality.

The Commune of violent interpretations was thus notably and distinctly different from that of realist ones. Specifically, the Commune's ideas were nowhere to be seen. Henri Brissac, a writer and secretary to the well-known Blanquist journalist Félix Pyat, described the Commune's principles in an 1882 article as 'embryonic, undecided, and confused',[26] and similar sentiments can be inferred from the vague interpretations of many other publications.[27] In 1885, Malon claimed in *L'Intransigeant* that the Commune was regarded as 'the new political axis of peoples', but this did not result from respect for or even engagement with its intellectual

---

[24] '[C]ela épure la cité, en même temps que les *bons principes* s'en raffermissent.' G. Lefrançais, *Étude sur le mouvement communaliste à Paris en 1871* (Neuchâtel: Imprimerie G. Guillaume Fils, 1871), p.386. Emphasis original.

[25] 'Il y a des circonstances où il faut savoir mourir, lorsque mourir, c'est confesser sa foi, lorsque mourir, c'est affirmer un principe, arborer un drapeau, jeter dans le monde avec son sang une idée nouvelle et vraie.' A. Arnould, *Histoire populaire et parlementaire de la Commune de Paris*, 3 vols. (Brussels: Imprimerie A. Lefevre, 1878), vol.2, p.22; see also pp.116–117.

[26] 'Où nous en sommes', *Le Citoyen* (Paris), 30 April 1882.

[27] See, for example, 'Le dix-huit mars', *L'Intransigeant*, 20 March 1881; 'L'avènement', *Le Citoyen & La Bataille* (Paris), 19 March 1883.

content. Rather, he observed, people 'glorify its acts, adopt its martyrs' and invest it with 'the importance of a popular religion'.[28]

While the two interpretations may have shared their veneration of the Commune, the definition and content of 'the Commune' was strikingly different in each. Namely, in violent interpretations, the Commune's importance was no longer tied to the value of its ideas. In fact, these ideas were not simply overlooked, but were considered actively unnecessary.[29] The Commune's form became more important than its content, and violent interpretations effectively argued that the Commune had not had any thought.

This was reflected in other aspects of revolutionaries' interaction with the Commune, especially their parallel engagement with commemoration. Vaillant expounded the importance of commemoration to French activists in an article in the English socialist William Morris's journal *Commonweal*, writing that

> Every people has its days of revolution. These it justly holds as festivals, celebrating them as so many acts of vengeance wherein it has chastised its oppressors, as halting-places along the path that leads to freedom.[30]

Revolutionaries certainly put these ideas into practice. Following their return to Paris after the 1880 amnesty, they conducted a long campaign for the construction of a permanent memorial to the Commune in the capital.[31] They succeeded at the Mur des Fédérés, to which a memorial and a plaque commemorating those who had died during the Commune were eventually added.

Funerals were also focal points for revolutionary association. By 1880, funerals had been invaluable events for French revolutionaries and radicals for some time, as they enabled them to sidestep laws restricting association and gather in large numbers.[32] In 1870, for example, the funeral of Victor Noir, the radical journalist killed in a duel by Napoleon III's cousin, Prince

---

[28] '[I]ls glorifièrent ses actes, adoptèrent ses martyrs ... toute l'importance d'une religion populaire'. 'Étudiants et prolétaires', *L'Intransigeant*, 22 February 1885. For a similar comparison, see 'Le dix-huit mars', *L'Intransigeant*, 20 March 1881.

[29] 'Le banquet du *Prolétaire*', *Le Prolétaire*, 2 December 1882. See also 'Infamies politiciennes', *Le Prolétaire*, 20 January 1883; 'Souvenirs de Mars 1871', *Le Prolétariat*, 14 March 1885; 21 March 1885.

[30] É. Vaillant, 'Vive la Commune!', p.1.

[31] For the campaign, see 'Le droit au souvenir', *L'Intransigeant*, 4 December 1880; 'Souscription pour le monument des fédérés', *Le Prolétaire*, 12 January 1884; 'La tombe des fédérés', *Le Prolétaire*, 26 January 1884. See also M. Rebérioux, 'Le mur des fédérés', in P. Nora (ed.), *Les lieux de mémoire, tome 1: la République* (7 vols.) (Paris: Gallimard, 1984–1992. 1984), 619–649, at p.620.

[32] Tombs, *Paris, bivouac des révolutions*, p.392.

Pierre Bonaparte, functioned as a focal point for discontent with the imperial regime, when thousands of protesters (200,000, according to Lissagaray) joined the cortège.[33] Shortly after the renowned journalist Jules Vallès's death in 1885, Paul Lafargue remarked on this enthusiasm for commemorative events in a letter to Friedrich Engels:

> That lucky beggar Vallès had the finest funeral in Paris since Gambetta's: over a hundred thousand people followed it: it made a great many people envious, they would kill themselves to be buried so magnificently: funerals are one of the most important ceremonies in the Frenchman's life.[34]

Revolutionary enthusiasm for commemoration, though, was perhaps most visible in the ongoing reaction to Blanqui's death in January 1881.[35] *L'Intransigeant*, for example, voiced its concern that revolutionaries organise 'a funeral fitting of this great citizen',[36] and a year later suggested erecting a monument to Blanqui.[37] By 1885, Malon noted that Blanqui's grave had 'become a place of revolutionary pilgrimage'.[38] This commemoration, with its emphasis on ritual and 'revolutionary pilgrimage', was indicative of the stylistic and intellectual differences between realist and violent interpretations of the Commune. Unlike their realist counterparts, violent interpretations were more interested in symbolism than ideas, and in the transformation of violence into martyrdom.[39]

II

The violent interpretation of the Paris Commune underwent a pronounced rise in popularity in revolutionary circles over the course of the period 1871–1885.[40] An examination of several successive writings by

---

[33] P.-O. Lissagaray, *Histoire de la Commune de 1871* (Paris: E. Dentu, 1896. First published, 1876), p.27.

[34] 143: P. Lafargue to F. Engels, 27 February 1885 (Paris), in F. Engels, P. and L. Lafargue, *Correspondence*, 3 vols. (trans.) Y. Kapp (Moscow: Foreign Languages Publishing House, 1959), vol.1, 267–269, at pp.268–269.

[35] Over 100,000 people attended Blanqui's funeral, and over 60,000 that of Vallès. For figures, see D. Tartakowsky, *Nous irons chanter sur vos tombes: le Père-Lachaise, XIXe-XXe siècle* (Paris: Aubier, 1999), note 11, p.230.

[36] '[D]es funérailles dignes de ce grand citoyen'. 'Blanqui', *L'Intransigeant*, 4 January 1881.

[37] 'Un monument à Blanqui', *L'Intransigeant*, 15 February 1881; 28 February 1881.

[38] 'La tombe de Blanqui est devenue un lieu de pèlerinage révolutionnaire.' B. Malon, 'Blanqui socialiste', in *La revue socialiste* 7 (Paris, July 1885), 586–597, at p.587.

[39] Tombs has also briefly linked this rise in commemoration to interest in the end of the Commune. See Tombs, *Paris, bivouac des révolutions*, p.392.

[40] For a similar suggestion, see R. Bellet, 'Trois représentations de la Commune de Paris par Jules Vallès: *Le Cri du peuple, La Commune de Paris, L'Insurgé*', in G. Larguier and J. Quaretti (eds.), *La*

both authors and newspapers that published regularly on the Commune clearly manifests this shift. In 1879, for instance, *Le Prolétaire* urged revolutionaries not to dwell extensively on martyrs, asking '[l]et us move on: the dead are dead. We are in 1879 not 1871'.[41] A year later, however, the paper's attitude had shifted, and it now encouraged its readers to '[t]hink on your heroic defeats, on the periodic massacres whose victims were all of your class'.[42] It was also especially noticeable in discussions of the Semaine Sanglante. In his initial 1871 account of the Commune, *La troisième défaite du prolétariat français*, Benoît Malon barely addressed the Semaine Sanglante at all. Several years later in the May 1880 edition of his fledgling journal *La revue socialiste*, he made it the centrepiece of another account of the Commune, describing it as an event that had 'apotheosised' the social revolution.[43] Similar shifts can also be observed in the bodies of work of other writers, such as Gustave Lefrançais.[44]

The distinction between Blanquist violent writers and minority realists, then, did not account entirely for these two different revolutionary interpretations of the Commune. It is also possible to discern a shift in language and focus in the work of revolutionaries writing frequently on the Commune between 1871 and 1885. Whereas the period before 1880 saw the publication of many accounts that focused on the workings and ideas of the Commune, increasingly writers such as Malon and Lefrançais distanced themselves from such interpretations, and concentrated instead upon the violence and failure that had characterised its final week.

Commemoration provided the clearest example of this temporal shift. In *The Paris Commune in French Politics*, Jean Joughin suggested that by 1875 a 'cult of the Commune' was already emerging.[45] On the contrary, though, revolutionaries in the 1870s – scattered and in exile – appear to have taken a largely sober approach to remembrance. This was

Commune de 1871: utopie ou modernité? (Perpignan: Presses universitaires de Perpignan, 2000), 353–367, at p.367.

[41] 'Le socialisme et le parti radical', *Le Prolétaire*, 14 June 1879.

[42] 'Aux Travailleurs!', *Le Prolétaire*, 17 January 1880.

[43] B. Malon, 'Les Partis ouvriers en France', in *La revue socialiste* 5 (5 May 1880), 257–269, at p.262.

[44] Compare Lefrançais, *Étude sur le mouvement communaliste*, p.336; with G. Lefrançais, *Souvenirs d'un révolutionnaire*, 2nd edn, (ed.) J. Černy (Paris: Société Encyclopédique française et Éditions de la Tête de Feuilles, 1972. First published 1903), p.435.

[45] J.T. Joughin, *The Paris Commune in French Politics, 1871–1880*, 2 vols. (Baltimore, MD: Johns Hopkins University Press, 1955), vol.1, p.88; see also p.499. Dowdall has also suggested that accounts of the Commune increasingly 'crystallised' around violence in the 1870s. See Dowdall, 'Narrating *la Semaine Sanglante*', p.57. Ross suggests the Commune was widely celebrated during this period, but her examples all date from after 1885. See K. Ross, *Communal Luxury: The Political Imaginary of the Paris Commune* (London: Verso, 2015. First published in French, 2015), p.97.

undoubtedly partly a practical issue, especially in London, where public opinion was broadly hostile to the Communard exiles. Marx's daughter Eleanor, for example, recalled that a landlord had cancelled a booking for his hall on the first anniversary of the Commune upon learning that his customers were French revolutionary refugees.[46]

Even in more hospitable continental locales, though, French revolutionaries rarely commemorated the Commune during the 1870s.[47] As a police agent tailing Communard exiles noted in an 1872 report to the Paris Préfecture de Police, '[t]he majority of the exiles do not want to make common cause with the Genevans. They prefer to celebrate it [18 March] alone amongst themselves.'[48] Indeed, in Brussels in 1878 there was no commemoration at all.[49] Although, as another police report noted 1877, exiles were proud to have taken part in the Commune,[50] for the most part French revolutionary remembrance of it in exile remained tightly regulated and detached.[51] Clearly, then, the lack of commemoration was not simply the result of a lack of space. Rather than openly displaying their adherence to the Commune in public demonstrations, many exiled revolutionaries in the 1870s preferred to draw as little attention to themselves as possible, marking anniversaries *en famille*, in private or educational gatherings. Their method of commemoration was effectively a physical manifestation of the more muted, introspective realist written accounts.

By the 1880s, partly due to the Communards' shifting circumstances, this had begun to change. The majority of those exiled or deported in the 1870s returned to Paris at the turn of the decade following the declaration of a full amnesty on 11 July 1880. They returned, however, to a much-changed France. Although it was officially established in September 1870 following the fall of the Second Empire, the early years of the Third Republic had been a time of considerable political uncertainty. The first decade of its existence was marked by political turmoil. Martial law was

---

[46] G. Stedman Jones, *Karl Marx: Greatness and Illusion* (London: Allen Lane, 2016), p.510.

[47] For the contrast between British and continental attitudes to Communard exiles, see Stedman Jones, *Karl Marx: Greatness and Illusion*, p.511.

[48] 'Les proscrits en majorité ne veulent plus faire cause commune avec les Génévois [sic]; ils veulent être seuls et le célébrer entre eux.' Intelligence report to the Préfecture de Police, Geneva, 15 March 1872. Archives de la Préfecture de Police (APP), BA431/99. For a similar attitude, see *Bulletin de la Fédération jurassienne* (Sonvilier), 25 March 1877; *Le Républicain* (Geneva), 19 March 1878.

[49] Communication to the Préfecture de Police. Brussels, 21 March 1878. APP, BA427/491. This was not always for want of trying. See, for example, 'La liberté des manifestations', *Le Prolétaire*, 15 May 1880.

[50] Intelligence report to the Préfecture de Police, March 1877 (London). APP Ba429/2152.

[51] For tight regulation, see intelligence report to the Préfecture de Police, Geneva, 20 March 1875. APP, BA432/1438.

not lifted in Paris until five years after the Commune, and the legislative elections of February 1871 returned a large majority of conservative, royalist, and rural deputies, who spent the next several years attempting to bring about a monarchical restoration. As Joughin has noted, 'at the beginning of the 1870s France had a Republic in name, a strong body of convinced Monarchists, and an uneasy bloc of convinced Republicans'.[52] This changed only in 1877, with the resignation of President MacMahon and the installation of an actively republican and reforming government. In these circumstances, revolutionary action was neither possible nor popular, and publicly remembering the Commune represented an alternative way for ex-Communards to reassert their revolutionary identity.

This period also saw a widespread rise in the popularity of politicised commemorative sentiment.[53] In *Communal Luxury*, Kristin Ross noted that the 1879 'Address to the Heroes and Martyrs of the Commune' marked a key turning point in uniting the London exile community.[54] In Paris, the first of many annual marches to Père-Lachaise cemetery took place in May 1880, several months before the declaration of amnesty. Newspapers noted a sharp rise in the number of attendees over the next few years, probably as ex-Communards returned from exile and deportation, and once again raised the visibility of the revolutionary movement in the capital.[55] By 1885, *La Bataille* was listing thirty-six separate events across France (although mainly concentrated in Paris) to mark the Semaine Sanglante.[56]

Communards were also increasingly willing to view themselves as part of an international revolutionary or socialist community. After 1880, major French revolutionary newspapers such as *L'Intransigeant* and *Le Prolétaire* increasingly published salutations on 18 March from various places including Portugal, Romania, and Algeria.[57] This was in stark

---

[52] Joughin, *The Paris Commune in French Politics*, vol.1, p.62. See also M. Agulhon, *The French Republic 1879–1992* (trans.) A. Nevill (Oxford: Blackwell, 1993. First published in French, 1990), p.1.

[53] K. Varley, *Under the Shadow of Defeat: The War of 1870–1871 in French Memory* (Basingstoke: Palgrave Macmillan, 2008).

[54] Ross, *Communal Luxury*, p.95.

[55] 'Anniversaire de mai 1871', *Le Prolétaire*, 3 June 1882; 'L'anniversaire', *Le Prolétaire*, 2 June 1883; 'Anniversaire de la Semaine Sanglante', *L'Intransigeant*, 27 May 1884. Numbers attending social events also grew, see, for example, 'Le 18 mars', *L'Intransigeant*, 19 March 1884. For more on this, see Rebérioux, 'Le mur des fédérés', at p.620.

[56] *La Bataille*, 23 May 1885. See also 'Ce qu'a été l'anniversaire du 18 mars', *Le Prolétaire*, 22 May 1880; 'L'anniversaire du 18 mars', *Le Citoyen & La Bataille*, 4 March 1883; 6 March 1883.

[57] For Portugal, see 'Echos de l'anniversaire du 18 mars', *Le Prolétaire*, 1 April 1882; for Romania, *L'Intransigeant*, 19 March 1884; for Algeria, 'L'anniversaire du 71 en Algérie', *L'Intransigeant*,

contrast to the previous years. Whereas in the 1870s, French revolutionaries had worked hard to establish their exclusive ownership of the Commune and had preferred to remember it privately, they now appeared
willing to share ownership of their memories with others – whether
marchers in Paris, or socialists in other countries. Indeed, a decade later,
Friedrich Engels would claim that the 'anniversary of the Paris Commune
became the first common festive day for the entire proletariat'.[58]

Whereas commemorative events for the Commune during the 1870s
had largely been small or insular affairs, during the 1880s they both
multiplied in number and grew considerably in size.[59] The shift in written
work towards a focus on violence, then, was accompanied by the increasing visibility of a symbolic, and more evocative, Commune in general life
(at least in Paris). Moreover, while it goes without saying that commemorations in Paris prior to the amnesty would have been small, gatherings were
also small in large and active exile communities that were not subject to the
same restrictive legislation as Paris.[60] A definite chronological shift in
thought on the Commune is thus identifiable, along with the minority–
majority intellectual distinction that persisted throughout the period.

III

The focus on the Commune's violent end may seem surprising. Given the
resounding nature of their defeat, it may be assumed that revolutionaries
would be eager to forget about or distance themselves from the violence
that had brought the Commune to a close rather than increasing their
attention to it over time. The Semaine Sanglante had drained the revolutionary movement of many of its members and the death toll functioned as
a visible reminder of the drastic drop in revolutionary support. The
circulation of such high casualty numbers for the Semaine Sanglate served
to further compound this actual loss, publicising the fact that the revolutionary movement had been decimated. As we have seen, however, the

---

7 June 1884. For an example of foreign commemorations of the Commune, see 'Celebration of the
  Commune', *Commonweal* (April 1886), p.31.
[58] F. Engels, 'Preface' (1895), in K. Marx, *The Class Struggles in France, 1848–1850* (trans.) H. Kuhn
  (New York: New York Labor News Co., 1924. First published in German, 1850), 1–30, at p.15.
[59] Laure Godineau has also observed this shift. See L. Godineau, 'Retour d'exil: les anciens
  Communards au début de la Troisième République' (Unpublished PhD thesis, Université de
  Paris I Panthéon-Sorbonne, 2000), p.592.
[60] For more on remembrance in Paris prior to the amnesty, see Tartakowsky, *Nous irons chanter sur vos
  tombes*, p.61; É. Fournier, *La Commune n'est pas morte: les usages politiques du passé de 1871 à nos
  jours* (Paris: Éditions Libertalia, 2013), pp.34–36.

mythologisation of violence constituted a central and fiercely active part of many revolutionary accounts of the Commune.

The violence of the Semaine Sanglante was often more uncomfortable for others than it was for revolutionaries themselves. Whereas in 1848, republicans and revolutionaries had at least initially presented a united front during the revolution, this had not happened in 1871. Instead, many of the republican politicians of the 1870s and 1880s had openly supported the Versailles government during the Commune, or had at least openly opposed the revolutionaries. This was as true of radicals such as Pelletan and even Georges Clemenceau as it was of more moderate republicans such as Jules Ferry. Clemenceau was a fiery critic of moderate republicanism and had been the radical mayor of the 18th arrondissement when (and where) the Commune broke out. In the early days of the administration, he was involved in efforts to open negotiations between the national government and the Commune, and even stood again for his seat in the 26 March elections. After losing resoundingly, though, he had elected to play no further part in the Commune.

Revolutionary writers frequently drew attention to these facts.[61] Lefrançais advised against voting for either radical republicans or Opportunists, reminding his readers of their complicity in the reaction to the Commune: 'do not forget that ... Gambetta himself has not stopped glorifying the ex-Bonapartist army for having flooded Paris ... with the blood of the *fédérés*.'[62] Prudent Dervillers, one of the founders of the French workers' party, similarly emphasised the Communards' separation from other republicans, castigating radicals such as Louis Blanc, Victor Schoelcher, Henri Tolain, and Clemenceau for not having endorsed the Commune when their voters had clearly supported it.[63] In contrast to republicans who had been supportive of previous revolutions, they suggested, those of the 1870s had the best interests neither of the working class nor of democracy at heart. By drawing attention to republicans'

---

[61] See, for example, *Le Prolétaire*, 16 December 1882; 'Infamies politiciennes', *Le Prolétaire*, 20 January 1883. For more on opposition between more moderate republicans and Communards, see S. Hazareesingh, *Intellectual Founders of the Republic: Five Studies in Nineteenth-Century French Republican Political Thought* (Oxford: Oxford University Press, 2005. First published, 2001), p.209.

[62] '[N]'oubliez pas que ... Gambetta lui-même n'a cessé de glorifier l'ex-armée bonapartiste d'avoir inondé Paris ... du sang des fédérés de la Commune!' G. Lefrançais, *Un Communard aux électeurs français* (Geneva: publisher not specified, 1875), p.7. For more on politicians' hypocrisy, see C. Beslay, *1830–1848–1870: Mes souvenirs* (Neuchâtel: Imprimerie James Attinger, 1873), p.470; B. Malon, *La troisième défaite du prolétariat français* (Neuchâtel: G. Guillaume Fils, 1871), p.510.

[63] 'Les responsabilités devant l'histoire', *Le Prolétaire*, 18 March 1879. See also H. Rochefort, 'Le blâme platonique', *L'Intransigeant*, 18 March 1881.

support (whether tacit or otherwise) for the forces that had suppressed the Commune, revolutionaries thus cast doubt upon republicans' progressive credentials.

Such criticism was not targeted only at republicans. By focusing on the violence of government forces during the Semaine Sanglante, revolutionaries also called into question the moral fibre and the suitability of Moral Order politicians such as MacMahon for the highest political offices. While, unlike Clemenceau or Gambetta, these men were unconcerned with appearing truly republican, they staked their reputation on their ability to preserve peace and order. The Commune called into question their ability to do so. Whereas in the past leaders such as Napoleon III had successfully kept revolution and the army in check for decades, in spring 1871 the government had lost control of the situation in Paris not once, but twice. Like their republican opponents, then, the Commune had also proved these politicians to be lesser than their predecessors. While the Communards may, as Malon admitted, not have been up to the situation they found themselves in, neither, they suggested, was anyone else.[64]

In this context, revolutionaries' constant vocalisation and visualisation of the Commune acted as a form of political engagement. Both moderate and radical republican politicians and newspapers during this period were keen to forget the Commune or place it firmly in the past, along with what was often deemed their complicity in the violence of its final week.[65] The abundance and content of violent accounts of the Commune directly contradicted this quest for oblivion. Constantly highlighting radical and moderate complicity in the Versailles reaction acted as a way for writers of violent interpretations to attempt to reduce rising popular support for the Third Republic and claw back some of the good will they had lost during the Commune, using the Semaine Sanglante to question first the moral credibility and then the republican values of those in power.[66] By remembering the Commune in terms of its violent failure, revolutionaries attempted to shift public focus away from their own failings during March–May 1871 and onto the violent and often extra-legal actions of their opponents. While the Communards' actions may have been violent or destructive, its opponents had committed even worse acts. The

---

[64] Malon, *La troisième défaite*, p.177.

[65] See, for example, *Le Tricolore* (Paris), 1 June 1871. For a radical republican advocation of 'political amnesia', see C. Pelletan, *Questions d'histoire: le comité central et la Commune* (Paris: Lagny, 1879), pp.186–187 and Pelletan, *La Semaine de mai*, p.406. For a revolutionary accusation of this, see *Les Droits de l'homme* (Paris), 3 November 1876.

[66] See also *Le Travailleur* (Geneva), May 1877, p.11.

Commune's lasting significance, they suggested, lay not in what it had to say about the revolutionary movement, but in the ways in which it visualised the failings of those in power.

The emphasis on the Semaine Sanglante, though, was more than simply a way in which to criticise the French political class, and writers also employed it in their attempts to begin to rebuild a united revolutionary community.[67] As we have seen, hostile writers and publications made frequent reference to the factional divisions that had riven the Commune. In 1874, for example, *Paris-Journal* observed that '[a]fter three years, the Communards, who have been fighting amongst themselves right from the beginning, are as disunited as it is possible to be.'[68] In contrast to these undeniable divisions, the violence of the Semaine Sanglante had been an experience shared by all Communards. Indeed, in his *Souvenirs*, Lefrançais claimed that divisions between the minority and the majority had disappeared during this final week.[69] Focusing on the Commune's violent end rather than its beginning or its duration, then, was seen as reconstitutive. It acted as a way for revolutionaries to attempt to move past the divisions that had been both accentuated and created by the Commune. By concentrating on a trauma that they had all shared and could all actively condemn, writers constructing this interpretation were able to gloss over both their differences and their failings during spring 1871, depicting themselves as above all victims of the Versaillais.

Moreover, by reconstituting their community on this basis, writers emphasised the continued need for revolutionary action. At a commemorative banquet in London in March 1880, revolutionaries sought to transform resentment at the way in which the Commune had fallen into concrete political action, arguing that the coming revolution must be conceived of as 'absolute revenge ... for the defeat of 1871'.[70] The Blanquist pamphlet 'Aux Communeux' stated similar sentiments more explicitly:

---

[67] For a contemporary discussion of the unifying benefits of violence, see E. Renan, *Qu'est-ce qu'une nation? Conférence faite en Sorbonne, le 11 mars 1882* (Paris: Calmann Levy, 1882), p.27.

[68] 'Après trois ans, les communards ... sont aussi désunis qu'il est possible de l'être'. *Paris-Journal* (Paris), 21 March 1874. APP, BA429/1409.

[69] Lefrançais, *Souvenirs d'un révolutionnaire*, p.419.

[70] 'La Révolution droit être une revanche absolue ... de la défaite de 1871.' 'Le 18 Mars à Londres: le banquet des réfugiés', *Le Prolétaire*, 3 April 1880. See also 'Un anniversaire', *Le Prolétaire*, 22 May 1880; 'La Semaine de sang', *Le Prolétaire*, 22 May 1880; 'La semaine sanglante', *Le Prolétaire*, 26 May 1883.

We still see the endless assassinations of men, women, and children; the throat-cutting that caused rivers of the People's blood to run through the streets ... We see the wounded buried along with the dead; we see Versailles, Satory, the pontoons, the penal colony, and New Caledonia. We see Paris and France bowed under terror, continuous oppression ... Communards of France, Exiles, let us unite against the common enemy; let everybody, according to their ability, do their duty![71]

Remembering the Commune as violence, then, was not simply an attempt to reconstitute a revolutionary community or a tool for criticising those in power. Rather, such deaths acted as a motivational tool; an obligation.

Contrary to realist interpretations, this was not an obligation to continue the Commune's ideas. Indeed, as we have seen, these were often actively overlooked. Instead, in interpretations that privileged violence, this obligation was to the dead. While it went without saying that such martyrs had died for a cause, in violent interpretations that cause quite literally *went without saying*. It was not clearly defined. Instead, dying, and the manner of the Communards' deaths, were what was important. By attempting to rebuild a community on a foundation of shared trauma, writers who focused upon violence sought to galvanise their readers in the face of successive governments who sought – in various ways – to eradicate revolutionary action from French public and political life. Using the Commune's violent end acted as a way to remind supporters of the continued need for revolution, and to begin to rebuild some of the public support they had lost in 1871. Death during the Commune was not a subject to be avoided; rather, it was conceived of as the creator of future revolutions.

Finally, it should be noted that while these interpretations were extremely different, there remained considerable similarities. Despite their varying focuses, realist and violent accounts were far from mutually exclusive. It was entirely possible for the Commune to have been both intellectually motivated and to have met a violent end. Both, moreover, shared a common aim in the promotion of revolutionary unity.[72] In 1885, for example, Vaillant urged his readers,

---

[71] 'Nous voyons encore ces assassinats sans fin, d'hommes, de femmes, d'enfants; ces égorgements qui faisaient couler à flots le sang du Peuple dans les rues ... Nous voyons les blessés ensevelis avec les morts; nous voyons Versailles, Satory, les pontons, le bagne, la Nouvelle-Calédonie. Nous voyons Paris, la France, courbés sous la terreur, l'écrasement continu ... Communeux de France, Proscrits, unissons nos efforts contre l'ennemi commun; que chacun, dans la mesure de ses forces, fasse son devoir!' 'Aux communeux', at p.422.

[72] For a similar suggestion about unity amidst the discord, see C. Rihs, *La Commune de Paris (1871): sa structure et ses doctrines* (Paris: Éditions du Seuil, 1973. First published in Geneva, 1955), p.10.

In marching towards this new world of equality, of justice, and of science, towards this radiant future, let us not forget that even more than the resistance of the enemy, the divisions, the want of organisation of our forces, are the principal obstacle to our action. On this day, when appealing to all proletarians, to all the soldiers of the Revolution and of Socialism, we celebrate the revolutionary struggles and the Commune of 1871, let us pledge ourselves by the memory of those who then fell for the cause of the people that the coming struggle shall find us ready, united and resolute.[73]

Furthermore, the theoretical tools that they employed in order to bring about this unity were often also the same. Writers in both interpretations, for example, went to great lengths to shift popular focus and responsibility for the Commune away from the Communards and onto either the state or the French political class more broadly. While both interpretations sought to restore ownership of the Commune to those who they perceived to be its rightful guardians (in other words, themselves), simultaneously revolutionary writers were concerned with removing agency from the Communards, and taking the Commune out of revolutionary control. It is therefore necessary to remember that there were many fundamental similarities between these different interpretations.

IV

This attachment to the Commune, whether in the form of its ideas or its end, has often been seen as symptomatic of the increasing marginalisation of French revolutionaries and their ideas during this period. In his 1981 *Cult of the Revolutionary Tradition*, Patrick Hutton, for instance, drew a sharp line between Blanquist commemoration and useful or productive revolutionary action, arguing that

> From the time of the Commune, the Blanquists passed from their role as activists in a revolutionary movement to another as ideologists of the cult of the revolutionary tradition.[74]

This shift, he argued, signified a withdrawal from conspiratorial or active politics. In this post-Commune landscape, revolutionaries 'passed the frontier into that imaginary land wherein they could fulfill the aspirations of their aesthetic reverie free of the intrusion of harsh realities'.[75] For

---

[73] É. Vaillant, 'Vive la Commune!', p.1.
[74] P. Hutton, *The Cult of the Revolutionary Tradition: The Blanquists in French Politics, 1864–1893* (Berkeley: University of California Press, 1981), p.36.
[75] Ibid., p.169.

Hutton, attachment to the Commune was a sign of increasing anachronism. The Commune was a decisive break in the history of French revolution, after which activists were either integrated into one of the Third Republic's various republican groupings (whether the Radicals, or either of Ferry or Léon Gambetta's more moderate factions[76]) or drifted towards an intellectually distinct Marxist international socialism. While individual actors may have continued to be involved in revolutionary action, the Commune brought the revolutionary movement as it had existed until this point to an end.[77] In this reading, following the fall of the Commune revolutionaries hoping to remain relevant were forced to make a distinct choice between republican nationalism and international socialism.

Yet French revolutionary thought on the Commune from this period provides scant support for the thesis of decisive change. As we have seen, writings on the Commune certainly did not indicate that ex-Communards were amenable to integration into more mainstream republican parties. Neither did they signify a conscious shift towards Marxian socialism. The revolutionary movement's relationships with Marx and his ideas were extremely complex, and this entanglement shall be fully addressed in Part III. For the purposes of this chapter, though, it suffices to observe that Marx's interpretation of the Commune was not well received. While some sections of the revolutionary movement certainly accepted the classification of the Commune as a socialist dawn,[78] this was far from universal, and those more fully endorsing the views expressed in *The Civil War in France* were often verbally attacked.[79] Indeed, some writers actively sought to distance themselves from any association with communism.[80]

As we have seen, French revolutionary ideas on the Commune (particularly those in the 'realist' school of interpretation) often intersected with those of Marx, however this did not signify a definitive shift towards or integration into a Marxist position. Indeed, with its emphasis on the importance of the Commune's ideas, the realist interpretation was arguably a direct contradiction of Marx's account and a challenge to his characterisation of the Commune as intellectually irrelevant. The

---

[76] For a breakdown of these distinctions, see R.P Tombs, *France 1814–1914* (London: Routledge, 1996), pp.442–443.

[77] See also F. Furet, *La Révolution de Turgot à Jules Ferry* (Paris: Hachette, 1988), p.489.

[78] 'Le 18 Mars', *L'Égalité* (Paris), 18 March 1880; 'La Commune', *Le Prolétaire*, 18 March 1882; 'Le dix-huit mars', *Le Citoyen* (Paris), 19 March 1882; G. Deville (ed.), *Le Capital de Karl Marx* (Paris: Henry Oriol, 1883), p.58.

[79] *Le Prolétaire*, 21 October 1882. See also Rihs, *La Commune de Paris (1871)*, p.19.

[80] Beslay, *Mes souvenirs*, p.390; *La Fédération* (London), 24 August 1872, 31 August 1872.

suggestion that French revolutionary thought on the Commune during this period was indicative of a wholesale or even widespread shift towards Marxism is thus highly unsatisfactory. Communard and French revolutionary thought on the Commune may have been a response to Marx, but it was certainly not an endorsement of his views.[81]

The continued revolutionary focus on the Commune during this period, then, was neither a sign of their increasing detachment from meaningful action and thought, nor a sign of the inevitable ascendance of a Marxian revolutionary ideology. Instead, it is more productive to think of it as an attempt to remain visible and involved in French affairs. Expressing ideas through the medium of a contentious subject like the Commune was a way for exiled revolutionaries to guarantee themselves wide exposure. Moreover, their direct experience and unique defence of it enabled them to maintain an independent position in French politics in spite of their physical absence, demonstrating that while '[t]he Revolution was defeated, Thiers was not a victor.'[82]

In international revolutionary circles, Communard and French revolutionary attempts to establish and maintain an autonomous yet viable identity for themselves also centred upon recollections of the Commune. Indeed, it could be said that revolutionary thought on the Commune during this period represented an effort to preserve or recapture both the status and the identity that French revolutionaries had enjoyed prior to the events of spring 1871. While different authors within the revolutionary movement attempted to fashion a variety of identities, nonetheless the aim of creating a distinct yet viable revolutionary position and the use of the Commune in order to do so were common features of all these texts.

V

The idea of the Commune, then, opened many doors for revolutionaries during the 1870s and early 1880s. Yet at the same time there remained significant limitations to its possibilities. Even during the Commune's short life, its participants had never really been united by anything other

---

[81] For similar criticisms of the idea of the Commune as a communist phenomenon, see J. Plamenatz, *The Revolutionary Movement in France 1815–1871* (London: Longmans, 1965. First published, 1952), pp.156–157; M.P. Johnson, *The Paradise of Association: Political Culture and Popular Organisations in the Paris Commune of 1871* (Ann Arbor: University of Michigan Press, 1996), p.12.

[82] 'La Révolution était vaincue, mais Thiers n'était point vainqueur.' Arnould, *Histoire populaire et parlementaire*, vol.2, p.19.

than its existence. Composed of a variety of different revolutionary groups, the experiences of the Commune served primarily, as we have seen, to accentuate the differences between these factions. These demarcations continued to be of note after the Commune fell, and further deepened in exile during the 1870s, when many of these texts were produced and published. Surviving Blanquists predominantly fled to England, whereas former members of the minority headed for Switzerland.

These divisions were reflected in writing. In the *Histoire*, Arnould claimed that when he thought back to the Commune, 'I forget the minority and the majority',[83] however several pages later he directly contradicted this, confessing that he had lost many friends as a result of their decision to join a different faction.[84] Likewise, revolutionaries continued to trade personal insults over certain flashpoints during the Commune (for instance, the debate over whether or not it should have appropriated funds from the Bank of France) for years after its fall.[85] While many accounts of the Commune claimed that the divisions between majority and minority had disappeared at the first sign of danger in late May 1871, this was clearly not the case.[86] Accounts of the Commune from this period rather demonstrated that divisions that had been either created or deepened in spring 1871 had not disappeared in the ensuing years. The history of revolutionary thought on the Commune is thus one of fracture as well as of unlikely possibility.

As may be expected, the most significant of these divisions remained that between survivors of the Commune's majority and minority. For majoritarians such as Cluseret, Bergeret, and the London exile newspaper *La Fédération*, the Commune's disorganisation had been a 'fatal consequence of Proudhon's theory of anarchy'.[87] They contrasted Parisian political and intellectual advancement with 'the animals of France' who knew only how to follow,[88] and consequently suggested that the Commune both could and should have assumed national sovereignty.[89] Meanwhile, members of the minority such as Arnould and Malon celebrated the

---

[83] 'J'ignore s'il y a eu une minorité et une majorité'. Ibid., vol.3, p.92. [84] Ibid., vol.2, pp.95–96.

[85] See, for example, 'La Banque de France', *Le Citoyen*, 11 September 1882. For more on the debate during the Commune, see Tombs, *Paris, bivouac des révolutions*, p.189.

[86] Lefrançais, *Souvenirs d'un révolutionnaire*, p.419.

[87] 'Conséquence fatale de la fameuse théorie de Proudhon sur l'anarchie'. G.-P. Cluseret, *Mémoires du Général Cluseret*, 3 vols. (Paris: Jules Levy, 1887–1888), vol.1 (1887), p.4.

[88] Bergeret, *Le 18 Mars*, p.3.

[89] Cluseret, *Mémoires du Général Cluseret*, vol.1, p.38; É. Vaillant, 'Vive la Commune!', p.1.

Communards as 'sincere representatives of ... communal and social ideas',[90] and claimed that the Commune 'did not dream of governing France and, victorious, she would not have had any pretensions to do so'.[91]

Although revolutionaries claimed that the experience of the Commune had ultimately been a unifying one, their thoughts on it and opinions on what had constituted its successes and failures illustrated that this was far from the case. Competing conceptions of the Commune exposed not just minor disagreements, but the persistence of fundamental intellectual divisions on what the revolutionary movement was and what its ideas and goals should be. Revolutionary writings on the Commune of various hues thus not only exposed the divisions of the past, but also served to exacerbate them, both creating and highlighting intellectual fault lines and disagreements that would plague the movement in the coming years.

The frequent and insistent geographical focus on Paris also created tension. Although Paris remained the most famed uprising of spring 1871, communes had in fact been proclaimed in many other regional towns and cities. This was particularly true across the Midi, where larger towns had a long history of strong, organised republicanism. Both Lyons and Marseilles, at the time France's second and third largest cities, experienced uprisings, as did Toulouse, Le Creusot, and Narbonne.[92] The participants in these communes had also been punished (although not on the same scale as the Parisian Communards), yet their efforts in spring 1871 were often overlooked.[93] Malon, for example, devoted only one chapter of *Troisième défaite* to the provincial communes, while other writers barely mentioned them at all.[94]

Paradoxically, while exile physically united Communards from various different cities, it also brought such geographical tensions to the fore, driving a wedge between Parisian and provincial revolutionaries. A Préfecture informant in Geneva reported that such focus on the Parisian movement had caused unrest at a meeting, with exiles from other communes asking

---

[90] '[L]es représentants sincères des idées communales et sociales'. Malon, *La troisième défaite*, p.179.
[91] '[E]lle ne songea pas à gouverner la France, et, victorieuse, elle n'eût élévé aucune prétention à cet égard'. Arnould, *Histoire populaire et parlementaire*, vol.3, p.95; see also p.55; p.128; p.144. For more on municipal liberty, see *Qui vive!* (London), 20 October 1871.
[92] L.M. Greenberg, *Sisters of Liberty: Marseille, Lyon, Paris and the Reaction to a Centralized State, 1868–1871* (Cambridge, MA: Harvard University Press, 1971), pp.9–12.
[93] For more on provincial communes, see Greenberg, *Sisters of Liberty*; M. César, *1871. La Commune révolutionnaire de Narbonne* (Sète: Éditions singulières, 2008); J. Girault, *Bordeaux et la Commune. 1870–1871* (Périgueux: Fanlac, 2009).
[94] Malon, *La troisième défaite*, pp.346–396.

In France in 1871, was there only the Paris Commune? Did Lyons, Marseilles, St. Étienne not declare before Paris? ... You cannot, therefore, specify the *Paris* Commune.[95]

As this oversight regarding provincial communes showed, revolutionary writings on the Commune exposed not just divisions within the movement, but also the shortcomings of attempts to regain their previous post-Commune position, as well as their persistent geographical myopia. Although writings on the Commune were theoretically of universal appeal, at the same time they manifested a multitude of continued practical differences between Parisian revolutionaries and their counterparts in regional urban centres.

While many of these divisions had been present in one form or another in the revolutionary movement for years, the changed circumstances following the Commune's fall drastically altered their import. As Lefrançais observed, '18 March ... distinctly reformulated the revolutionary question'.[96] It reformulated the question, though, in a way that only truly benefited survivors of the minority. This was partly a case of straightforward numerical advantage. Many well-known Blanquist Communards had lost their lives as a result of the Commune. The journalist Raoul Rigault, for example, was shot in the street during the Semaine Sanglante, while Théophile Ferré, who ordered the execution of the Archbishop of Paris Georges Darboy, was executed by firing squad in November 1871.

Most of the minority's most prominent members, however, had survived, and were generally more visible than survivors of the majority during the 1870s and 1880s. Interest in the ideas that members of the minority had espoused during the Commune, particularly the tradition of federalist socialism, declined sharply in the years after 1871. Its members and supporters, however, continued to be extremely active in French revolutionary circles. Indeed, key members of all of the most prominent revolutionary groupings of the post-Commune period including the Guesdists and the Possibilists had either belonged to or identified with this faction.

---

[95] 'En France en 1871, n'y a-t-il eu que la Commune de Paris? Est-ce que Lyon, Marseille, St Étienne ne l'ont pas proclamée avant Paris? ... Vous ne pouvez donc pas spécifier: Commune de Paris'. Intelligence report to the Préfecture de Police, Geneva, 3 October 1874. APP, BA432/1276.

[96] 'Le 18 Mars ... a nettement reposé la question révolutionnaire.' Lefrançais, *Un Communard aux électeurs français*, p.16.

Their dominance was especially noticeable in terms of publication.[97] As we have seen, the focus upon symbolic violence would come to predominate in late nineteenth- and twentieth-century writings on the Commune, at the same time as it was made more visible through increased commemoration. This trend was compounded by the publication around the turn of the century of several lengthy and extremely popular accounts of the Commune written by former Blanquists. In 1904, Gaston da Costa, one of the revolutionaries responsible for destroying Thiers's private mansion in May 1871, published his three-volume memoir, *La Commune vécue*. This was followed up between 1908 and 1914 by Maxime Vuillaume's *Mes cahiers rouges (souvenirs de la Commune)*.[98]

During the period immediately after the Commune, though, it was realist interpretations that flooded the market. Almost all full-length memoirs and evaluations of the Commune from this period were written by members of the minority who favoured the realist interpretation. They also controlled the majority of long-running socialist daily newspapers, affording them a high degree of control over the diffusion of revolutionary thoughts on 1871. This enabled former members of the minority to effectively emphasise specific parts of the Commune at the expense of others, and ensured that while the likes of Ferré were celebrated as martyrs, dead Blanquists were also widely blamed for the majority of the Commune's excesses.[99]

This numerical disadvantage was but a small part of the Blanquists' problems. During the Commune, the majority had dominated the decision-making process, and forced through resolutions like the decision to create a Committee of Public Safety. The majority's domination during the Commune had effectively exposed the impracticality of their political ideas. As the historian David Stafford has observed,

> the memory of the Commune discredited the old Blanquist ideas of the *coup de main*, of the revolutionary uprising in the streets, and instead forced attention on the need for organisation and discipline and the avoidance of premature action.[100]

---

[97] For a breakdown of the majority and the minority, see Arnould, *Histoire populaire et parlementaire*, vol.2, p.86.

[98] G. da Costa, *La Commune vécue ... 18 mars–28 mai 1871*, 3 vols. (Paris: Ancienne Maison Quantin, 1903–1905); M. Vuillaume, *Mes cahiers rouges au temps de la Commune* (Paris: Cahiers de la quinzaine, 1908–1914).

[99] J. Andrieu, *Notes pour servir à l'histoire de la Commune de Paris en 1871* (Paris: Payot, 1971), p.89.

[100] D. Stafford, *From Anarchism to Reformism: A Study of the Political Activities of Paul Brousse within the First International and the French Socialist Movement 1870–1890* (London: Cox & Wyman, 1971), p.22.

Meanwhile, members of the minority often attempted to downplay their responsibility for the Commune's failures by drawing attention to their relative lack of influence. Arnould, for example, stated that 'the minority . . . exercised no influence over the material march of affairs . . . We could be critics, but we were not obstacles.'[101]

Majoritarians, however, had no such escape route. Given their heavy involvement in its policies and administration, effectively the only way in which the Commune could remain a positive experience for Blanquists was by jettisoning most of the elements that had distinguished Blanquism from other forms of revolutionary thought, for instance strong centralised power and violent action. It was for this reason that the violent interpretation proved so popular with Blanquists, as it enabled them to divert attention away from their actions during the Commune whilst simultaneously reconstructing it as a unifying experience. Besides being physically outnumbered when it came to accounts of the Commune, then, Blanquists were also intellectually outgunned.

Blanquists also had particular problems learning lessons from the Commune. This was most visible in the case of revolutionaries' relationship with the peasantry. Paris had received little support from the rest of France during the Commune, with many in the provinces considering it an attempt by the capital to arbitrarily impose its will upon the country. At the same time, Communards had thought little of the countryside. Indeed, this disregard and failure to elicit broader support would later come to be considered one of the Commune's greatest failings. The experiences of 1871 thus demonstrated the need for revolutionaries to reach outside both Paris and urban regional centres to the countryside. As Henri Lefebvre noted in his classic *Proclamation de la Commune*, one of the most effective ways to do this was through a language of federation.[102]

This situation conferred a distinct advantage upon former members of the minority. Certainly, many of these actors also remained largely unconcerned with the provinces.[103] Yet federation and municipal liberty had occupied a central role in their ideas during the Commune, and they were

---

[101] '[L]a minorité . . . n'exercait aucune influence sur la marche matérielle des événements . . . Nous pouvions être des critiques, nous n'étions pas des obstacles.' Arnould, *Histoire populaire et parlementaire*, vol.3, pp.27–28.
[102] H. Lefebvre, *La proclamation de la Commune, 26 mars 1871* (Paris: Gallimard, 1965), p.154.
[103] See, for example, Malon, *La troisième défaite*, p.75.

able to emphasise this in their retrospectives.[104] *Le Prolétaire*, for example, stressed that in terms of

> *municipal liberties*, they [the Communards] wanted complete decentralisation. In this way, hostilities between Paris and the provinces would cease, communes would govern themselves, and all towns in France would rally to federate in order to defend the Republic.[105]

L'Égalité and other papers also frequently published details of 18 March celebrations in the provinces.[106] Such rhetoric, though, was clearly inimical to both the long-standing Blanquist veneration of Paris and their favoured organisational structure of small cells of activists.[107]

Blanquists, effectively, were unable to learn from the Commune's mistakes, for in the changed circumstances of the 1870s, their ideas *were* the mistakes. Geographical and ideological divisions remained much the same as they had in the run up to and during the Commune, but this was not symptomatic of stasis within the revolutionary movement. The circumstances in which revolutionaries were operating had changed drastically around them, and this slowly altered the purchase and credibility of their ideas. Whereas thinkers from the minority were able to use their lack of influence and the circumstances of March–May 1871 to transform the Commune into a positive learning experience and even a vindication of their ideas, these very same ideas marginalised Blanquist elements of the revolutionary movement. Even as revolutionaries used the Commune to project an image of unity, their accounts exposed the fallacy of such claims.

The thesis, advanced by Hutton, that commemoration of the Commune was not particularly beneficial to revolutionaries during this period, then, is likely correct. Contrary to his suggestion, though, this was not because commemoration or violent interpretations of the Paris Commune themselves were inherently flawed.[108] Indeed, as we have seen, theoretically they were incredibly effective, enabling revolutionaries to divert

---

[104] Ibid., p.535; G. Lefrançais, *République et Révolution: de l'attitude à prendre par le prolétariat en présence des partis politiques* (Geneva: Imprimerie Ve Blanchard, 1873), pp.21–22; *Le Travailleur*, January–February 1878, p.4; quotes on universalism and federation in an intelligence report to the Préfecture de Police, Geneva, 14 March 1880. APP, BA433/2960.

[105] 'Relativement aux *libertés municipales*, ils voulaient la décentralisation la plus complète: de cette manière, la cessation de l'antagonisme entre Paris et la province, le gouvernement de la commune par la commune, et la fédération de toutes les villes de France solidarisées pour la défense de la République.' 'L'anniversaire du 18 mars 1871', *Le Prolétaire*, 18 March 1879.

[106] 'Le 18 mars en province', *L'Égalité*, 23–26 May 1880; 'Anniversaire du 18 mars', *Le Citoyen & La Bataille* (Paris), 19 March 1883; 'Le 18 mars à Nice', *Le Citoyen & La Bataille*, 29 March 1883; 'Le banquet', *Le Citoyen & La Bataille*, 13 May 1883.

[107] 'Aux communeux', at p.421.   [108] Hutton, *The Cult of the Revolutionary Tradition*, p.36.

attention towards the state's actions in May 1871 and gloss over their own failings. By privileging these memories of violent shared trauma, revolutionaries aimed to begin to both internally reconstruct a united revolutionary community, and simultaneously regain some of the external, popular support they had lost during the Commune. While the Blanquists may have practiced 'a politics of anniversary remembrance', as Hutton terms it, this need not necessarily have been a problem.[109]

Rather, these writers' problems derived largely from the effectiveness of their realist counterparts. Writers interpreting the Commune in the 'realist' fashion identified in Chapter 1 were simply better able to take advantage of the situation that revolutionaries found themselves in following their 1871 defeat. Former members of the minority were able to go further than majoritarian accounts and embrace not only the final, bloody week of the Commune, but its entire two-month duration, both acknowledging and appearing to take responsibility for their mistakes. Likewise, while the focus on violence may have enabled Blanquists to gloss over their own political, intellectual, and administrative shortcomings, simultaneously the realist accounts of the likes of Arnould, Lefrançais, and Andrieu unearthed and exposed the Blanquists' central role in the Commune's failure. Realist writers were thus able to define the Commune not only as a tragic event, but also as an occurrence of considerable intellectual significance. In doing so, they established the Commune as a foundation upon which to begin to build a carefully theorised and viable alternative to both the Third Republic as it currently stood and the international socialist movement in a way that the Blanquists could not.

*****

The historian Philippe Darriulat has claimed that '[t]he hundred days that followed [18 March] are well known to us all.'[110] This, however, has not historically been the case. Whilst the image of the Commune was near ubiquitous in the twentieth century, its participants and their ideas have been strangely absent from history. Yet this historiographical absence was not synonymous with a lack of thought. Indeed, revolutionary ideas on the Commune in the years immediately following its fall were abundant. Like its later counterpart, the immediate historiography of the Commune was dominated by two interpretations. One, the realist, focused upon

---

[109] Ibid., p.11.
[110] 'Les cent jours qui suivent nous sont bien connus.' P. Darriulat, *Les patriotes: la gauche républicaine et la nation 1830–1870* (Paris: Éditions du Seuil, 2001), p.278.

precision, personal experience, and heavy contextualisation of 18 March in order to begin to reinvest the Commune with intellectual import. The other, the violent, ignored the Commune's ideas and its duration, focusing instead on the shared experience of its violent end in an attempt to obscure the mistakes that many revolutionaries had made in spring 1871.

Much as twentieth-century interpretations of the Commune shared a belief in what the Commune was and where its significance lay, the two revolutionary interpretations from our period also shared a similar conviction. French revolutionary thought on the Commune during the 1870s and early 1880s had two interconnected aims: to establish a united French revolutionary identity that was at once politically viable and distinct from both its French and international rivals, and to begin to regain some of the support they had lost during the Commune. Likewise, many of the devices used in order to achieve these intellectual aims were extremely similar. Both realist and violent writers, for example, attempted to relieve the Communards of responsibility for the events of spring 1871. Again, they both did so primarily by shifting public focus to the actions of the Government of National Defence, French politicians more generally, and the Versailles army.

This attachment to the Commune was indicative of neither creeping anachronism nor the poverty of French revolutionary thought. Rather, it constituted an active and pragmatic choice. For revolutionaries cast adrift in the uncertain political circumstances of the period – exile, Moral Order, Opportunist republicanism – the Commune proved a life raft as they battled to remain relevant, and to reorient themselves and their ideas. Yet even as revolutionary writers managed to repurpose this defeat, their ideas on the Commune both emphasised and created deep intellectual divisions and personal grievances that would mark the revolutionary movement for years to come. As a unifier and a foundation upon which to rebuild revolutionary identities and ideas, the Commune was fractious and fragile.

This early historiography of the Paris Commune was not at all indicative of the directions that interpretations of 1871 would later take. The realist accounts most popular immediately after the Commune's fall were very much products of their time and place. The reconstruction of the Commune as an intellectually significant event was, as we have seen, only truly beneficial to a small group, and even here its utility was ultimately limited. The 1880 amnesty granted revolutionaries greater access to both the French public and the means by which to reach them. As the decade progressed, the arenas in which revolutionaries were able to test or implement their ideas multiplied, and the need to define themselves through the

Commune consequently decreased. By the end of the decade, a violent Commune that visualised a dark underside to Opportunist republicanism was more useful to its former participants. Whilst revolutionaries between 1871 and 1885 of course also commoditised the Commune, their thought on the subject was often in marked contrast to the interpretations that would later become dominant.

Contemporary revolutionary thought on the Commune thus directly contradicts the idea that the Commune very quickly became 'the Commune as legend'.[111] Rather, the Commune, as Robert Tombs has argued, 'left various possible memories'.[112] Although moving towards a more purely symbolic interpretation by 1885, for the majority of this period, revolutionary thought on the subject was heterogeneous and undefined. Buffeted by the changeable and uncertain circumstances that followed the *année terrible* of 1870–1871, contemporary revolutionary thought on the Commune shifted and swirled in a variety of different directions.

This thought cannot be characterised using later neat assignations of 'left' and 'right', or even the labels that are commonly used to distinguish different revolutionary groups during the late nineteenth century, such as 'socialist', 'nationalist', or 'anarchist'. Rather, Communard and French revolutionary thought on the Commune during this period was all of these things at once, often in the ideas of individual writers and publications. In order for the Commune to become an 'event' or a 'legend', it was necessary to achieve some form of closure. During this period, however, no such closure existed. The Commune was still a lived (and living) experience, and its meaning and structure were unclear.

Nevertheless, as the foundation upon which many revolutionaries sought to rebuild their ideas after 1871, accounts of the Commune touched upon many points that were central themes in revolutionary thought during the period 1871–1885. What exactly was the relationship between French revolutionaries, Marx, and Marxism? How would future revolutions relate to those of the past? Did revolutionary change necessitate violence? If so, how should activists go about achieving and justifying this under a republican government? If not, how would they distinguish themselves from these republicans? How would exile, and especially deportation, affect revolutionaries' ideas about who they represented? It is to these questions, amongst others, that we now turn.

---

[111] Johnson, *The Paradise of Association*, p.276.
[112] Tombs, 'How bloody was *la semaine sanglante*', at p.703.

PART II

Revolution and the Republic

CHAPTER 3

The French Revolutionary Tradition

The Paris Commune had left revolutionaries battered and bruised. Its survivors were scattered across the globe, and the events of spring 1871 had exposed and deepened the intellectual cracks within the revolutionary movement. Yet the Commune did not, as has previously been suggested, lead to the movement's dismemberment. Rather, in the years that followed 1871, a broad array of French revolutionaries actively and vocally strove to preserve a sense of unity, emphasising above all the solidarity and fraternity that their experiences had engendered. Through their recollections of the Commune and the revolutionary experience more broadly, they aimed to lay – or rebuild – the foundations of a movement that was at once intellectually autonomous and politically viable in the changed circumstances of the new Third Republic.

Yet how, precisely, did activists in the immediate post-Commune period envision a future revolution and their role in bringing it about? In an 1876 pamphlet, *Aux travailleurs manuels de France: partisans de l'action politique*, François Dumartheray offered a classic response to this question, writing,

> Now let us look at what is needed in order to be a revolutionary: most importantly, one must be persuaded that contemporary society is not and cannot be anything other than a constant affront to humanity. It is our duty to topple it, and any means for doing so are acceptable.[1]

A revolution's aim, he suggested, could be nothing less than a complete *bouleversement*, or reordering of society and contemporary social mores. In terms of the revolution's praxis, these changes were likely to be effected suddenly: society was to be *culbutée*, or 'knocked down', rather than

---

[1] 'Voyons maintenant ce qu'il faut être pour être révolutionnaire: il faut d'abord être persuadé que la société actuelle n'est et ne peut être qu'un outrage constant à l'humanité, et qu'il est de notre devoir de la culbuter: et pour cela, tous les moyens sont bons'. F. Dumartheray, *Aux travailleurs manuels de France: Partisans de l'action politique* (Geneva: publisher unknown, 1876), p.12.

81

gradually reformed. The revolutionary would play a crucial role in events, instantiating social change directly through their actions. In their quest to do so, they were, Dumartheray portentously suggested, licensed to use 'any means' necessary. Dumartheray identified as an internationalist and an anarchist, helping to establish the Fédération française anti-autoritaire in 1877 and co-founding *Le Révolté* with Peter Kropotkin two years later. His conception of revolution and revolutionary action, however, was reminiscent of the vision and tactics deployed so effectively by activists in the first French Revolution, and replicated in subsequent revolutions across Europe throughout the nineteenth century. Almost a century after its onset in 1789, the reach and influence of the French Revolution upon contemporary activists remained prodigious.

Historians working on revolution during this period have, as a result, overwhelmingly approached the subject through the prism of the French Revolution and revolutionary history. Scholars have devoted a vast literature to elaborating the use that both revolutionaries and republicans made of the French Revolution during the early Third Republic, exhaustively detailing their intellectual, political, and aesthetic debts to the revolutionaries of 1789, 1793, 1830, and 1848.[2] Indeed, it is '*only* in the light' of the Revolution, the likes of Robert Gildea claim, that modern French history can be understood.[3] The elucidation of these connections between successive generations of French political actors is undoubtedly fruitful. Yet the sheer abundance of work on tradition and the strength with which historians have emphasised its importance has given the impression that

[2] The literature on this subject is vast. See, for example, A. Gérard, *La Révolution française: mythes et interprétations (1789–1970)* (Paris: Flammarion, 1970); F. Furet, *La Gauche et la Révolution française au milieu du XIXe siècle: Edgar Quinet et la question du Jacobinisme 1865–1870* (Paris: Hachette, 1986); G. Best (ed.), *The Permanent Revolution: The French Revolution and Its Legacy 1789–1989* (Chicago, IL: University of Chicago Press, 1988); S. Hazareesingh (ed.), *The Jacobin Legacy in Modern France: Essays in Honour of Vincent Wright* (Oxford: Oxford University Press, 2002). See also J.F. Stone, *Sons of the Revolution: Radical Democrats in France 1862–1914* (Baton Rouge: Louisiana State University Press, 1996); R. Gildea, *Children of the Revolution: The French, 1799–1914* (London: Allen Lane, 1998). The focus on tradition has been particularly strong in work on revolutionaries. See, for example, R. Soltau, *French Political Thought in the Nineteenth Century* (London: Ernest Benn Limited, 1931), p.xvii; C. Willard, *Socialisme et communisme français* (Paris: Armand Colin, 1978. First published 1967), p.8; P.H. Hutton, *The Cult of the Revolutionary Tradition: The Blanquists in French Politics, 1864–1893* (Berkeley: University of California Press, 1981), p.3; P.H. Hutton, 'The role of memory in the historiography of the French Revolution', *History and Theory* 30 (February 1991), 56–69; M. Crapez, *La Gauche réactionnaire: mythes de la plèbe et de la race* (Paris: Berg International Editeurs, 1997), p.15; J. Moreau, *Les socialistes français et le mythe révolutionnaire* (Paris: Hachette, 2003), p.26.
[3] R. Gildea, *The Past in French History* (New Haven, CT: Yale University Press, 1994), p.61. Emphasis mine.

revolution in France during the nineteenth century was understood exclusively in this light and on these terms.[4]

At the same time, historians have often concluded that in the 1870s, revolutionary action ceased to play a meaningful role in French political life. Eugen Weber, for example, argued that the 'revolutionary quest' became 'increasingly eccentric to real life and real politics' during this period.[5] Others, including Samuel Bernstein, Conor Cruise O'Brien, and Philippe Darriulat, have drawn a similar distinction, suggesting that from 1871 onwards, activists faced a choice between viable revolution and loyalty to French traditions.[6] While attachment to the Revolution may have remained strong, in other words, simultaneously it reduced revolutionaries during this period to an ever-increasing political irrelevance. What had once been their great strength was now a sign that meaningful revolutionary action in France was over. Indeed, many revolutionaries, it is suggested, tacitly accepted this new state of affairs.[7]

Part II argues that this was not the case. Activists did not conceive of revolution solely in terms of recent French history, and neither did they regard revolutionary action as a thing of the past. Through a comprehensive reassessment of the various contexts in which the word 'revolution' was used during this period, it will become clear that activists were both broader and more proactive when it came to their thought on revolution than has previously been suggested. While the French tradition was important to revolutionaries during this period, interpretations like Dumartheray's were unusual rather than archetypal. By this period, the majority of revolutionaries had long ceased to regard the French Revolution as a paradigm for revolution. Rather than being an attempt to compile a revolutionary toolkit, their writings on France's revolutionary past were primarily concerned with negotiating the shape of contemporary society, and the new French Republic in particular.

It is rather to other contexts that we must look for activists' ideas about the future of revolution. Through the 1870s and early 1880s, activists drew

---

[4] J. Jennings, *Revolution and the Republic: A History of Political Thought in France since the Eighteenth Century* (Oxford: Oxford University Press, 2011), p.390.

[5] E. Weber, 'The nineteenth-century fallout', in Best, *The Permanent Revolution*, 155–181, at p.171. See also E. Jousse, 'La construction intellectuelle du socialisme réformiste en France, de la Commune à la Grande Guerre' (unpublished PhD thesis, Sciences-Po, 2013), p.174.

[6] S. Bernstein, *The Beginnings of Marxian Socialism* (New York: Russell & Russell Inc, 1965), p.xxi. See also C. Cruise O'Brien, 'Nationalism and the French Revolution', in Best, *The Permanent Revolution*, 17–48, at p.46; P. Darriulat, *Les patriotes: la gauche révolutionnaire et la nation 1830–1870* (Paris: Éditions du Seuil, 2001), p.281.

[7] See, for example, Hutton, *The Cult of the Revolutionary Tradition*.

upon more than simply French history when discussing revolution, regularly discussing it in the context of various other traditions and temporalities. More specifically, activists regularly defined revolutionary action as both an apocalyptic or religious experience and an irrepressible force of nature, consequently decentring or parochialising recent European experiences of revolution. In doing so, activists hoped to affect a widespread redefinition and rejuvenation of the concept of revolutionary action, and as a result ensure that it remained an active part of French political and social life in the irrevocably changed political circumstances of the Third Republic.

This reappraisal of French thought on revolution after 1871 is also significant for our understanding of revolution in nineteenth-century Europe more generally. While this interpretation of revolution served activists particularly well during the immediate post-Commune period, it cannot simply be classed as a response to the disaster of 1871. Rather, a broad and expansive definition of revolution had been a feature of radical thought since long before the failure of the Paris Commune. Although the specific circumstances and formulations of the 1870s and early 1880s differed from those of earlier periods, the ways in which activists thought about social transformation, revolution, and its place in French and European society did not appreciably change between the 1840s and the mid-1880s. In other words, there existed significantly more continuity in revolutionary thought during the second half of the nineteenth century than has previously been imagined.

This chapter begins this reappraisal by reevaluating revolutionary interactions with French revolutionary history and tradition. In order to do so, it draws upon a vast array of sources and primary materials that have customarily been used to determine activists' thoughts on revolution, the French Revolution, and their place in it. These include a number of full-length works such as Arthur Arnould's 1877 *L'État et la Révolution*, Gustave Lefrançais's 1873 *République et Révolution*, and Charles Beslay's 1873 *1830–1848–1870: mes souvenirs*, as well as articles from contemporary newspapers across the revolutionary spectrum, including *La Patrie en danger*, *L'Intransigeant*, and *La Fédération*.[8] In order to accurately delineate the breaks and continuities in characterisations of revolution across the

---

[8] A. Arnould, *L'État et la Révolution* (Lyons: Éditions Jacques-Marie Laffont et Associés, 1981. First published, 1877); G. Lefrançais, *République et Révolution: de l'attitude à prendre par le prolétariat en présence des partis politiques* (Geneva: Imprimerie Ve Blanchard, 1873); C. Beslay, *1830–1848–1870: Mes souvenirs* (Neuchâtel: Imprimerie James Attinger, 1873); *La Patrie en danger* (Paris), September 1870–March 1871.

nineteenth century, this material has also been compared to relevant revolutionary, radical, and moderate republican work on the Revolution from a broader period: roughly the 1840s to 1885. This includes seminal works such as Victor Hugo's *Quatre-Vingt-Treize*, and the collected writing and speeches of Louis Auguste Blanqui from 1848 to his death in 1881.[9]

The chapter demonstrates that on the subject of French revolutionary history, revolutionaries in the post-Commune period were both more pragmatic and more proximate to the ideas of other republicans than has previously been assumed. Although activists referred frequently to the events of the recent revolutionary past, these references revealed very little about their ideas on the shape of future revolutions. Activists during this period did not view the Revolution as a paradigmatic event or a blueprint for future action, and actively attempted to distance themselves from efforts to create a static and prescriptive 'French revolutionary tradition'. Rather than as a toolkit for future revolutions, activists used revolutionary history and tradition to meditate on the shape of contemporary society. In particular, their interactions with French history reflected revolutionaries' attempts to navigate the new French Third Republic, and to negotiate changes to the republican vision outlined by the Opportunists in the 1870s and legislated for in the early 1880s.

This disavowal of the links between revolutionary action and the revolutionary tradition was the result of several factors. Partly, it represented a response to the success of moderate republican efforts to lay claim to the French Revolution and 'bring it to an end' after 1871. It was not, however, solely a product of these circumstances. Rather, activists had been attempting to dissociate revolutionary action from revolutionary history in this way for some time, invoking the Revolution as a call to action only in times of significant national crisis. In this respect, revolutionary uses of the recent French past were in fact similar to those of radical republicans such as Georges Clemenceau and Victor Hugo. Far from differentiating or setting them apart from other republicans during this period, revolutionary interactions with the recent French past demonstrated that considerable intellectual and rhetorical similarities between

---

[9] V. Hugo, *Quatre-Vingt-Treize* (Paris: Imprimerie J. Claye, 1874). For Blanqui, see, for example, L.A. Blanqui, *L'éternité par les astres* (ed.) L. Block de Behar (Geneva: Éditions Slatkine, 2009. First published, 1872); L.A. Blanqui, *L'armée esclave et opprimée; suppression de la conscription enseignement militaire de la jeunesse armée nationale sédentaire* (Paris: Au bureau du journal *Ni dieu ni maître*, 1880); L.A. Blanqui, *Critique sociale*, 2 vols. (Paris: Félix Alcan, 1885).

revolutionary and radical republicans persisted for years after their divergence during the Paris Commune.

I

In the 1870s, the chain of events set off by the French Revolution in 1789 were more than mere history. Generations across Europe in the nineteenth century grew up, as it were, in the shadow of the French Revolution. The continent was marked for decades afterward by its successes and failures, its descent into tyranny, dictatorship, and empire, and the sheer number of people lost in the Revolutionary Wars. This phenomenon was particularly acute in France. The agonies and ecstasies of the 1790s, from the proclamation of the First Republic to the execution of the King, many aristocrats, and the architects of the Revolution themselves, loomed large in national consciousness. The subsequent revolutions of 1830 and 1848, meanwhile, and the regime changes that they ushered in, remained lived events for much of the population. It is thus not surprising that during the early Third Republic, France's revolutionary past was very much still present and alive in public discourse and public memory.

In radical circles, veneration of the Revolution had been common practice for much of the nineteenth century. Successive generations of revolutionaries turned to the French past in search of guidance, evoking both the language and the symbolism of the Revolution, and employing practical techniques pioneered by their eighteenth-century predecessors. This tradition found most meaningful form in the revolutions of 1830 and 1848, but was also evident in the proliferation of political clubs, banquets, and secret societies across France. Radicals outside of France also picked up on this 'revolutionary toolkit'. In 1895, Friedrich Engels, for example, noted that in 1848,

> in so far as our conception of the conditions and the course of revolutionary movements are concerned, we were all subject to the prevailing historic experience, notably that of France.[10]

Over the course of the nineteenth century, the Revolution became a paradigmatic event for radicals seeking to effect meaningful social and political change in Europe. Indeed, attempts at revolutionary upheaval

---

[10] F. Engels, 'Preface' (1895), in K. Marx, *The Class Struggles in France, 1848–1850*, (trans.) H. Kuhn (New York: New York Labor News Co., 1924. First published in German, 1850), 1–30, at p.6. See also G. Stedman Jones, *Karl Marx: Greatness and Illusion* (London: Allen Lane, 2016), p.281.

became so commonplace that writers such as Victor Hugo fantasised about a future in which 'there will be no more events'.[11]

Perhaps unsurprisingly, historians have often assumed that revolutionaries in the 1870s and early 1880s held similar beliefs about the Revolution's paradigmatic qualities. In *Les socialistes français et le mythe révolutionnaire*, for example, Jacques Moreau suggested that French socialists in the post-Commune period had

> lived through 1870–1871, their parents remembered 1848 and even 1830, and the memory of the Great Revolution was less than a hundred years old. When they spoke of revolution, it was an event of this kind that they envisaged.[12]

In *The Cult of the Revolutionary Tradition*, Patrick Hutton likewise placed the French Revolution at the centre of certain activists' thought and action, arguing that positioning themselves as the authentic guardians of a 'French revolutionary tradition' was central to the Blanquists' attempts to recover from the Commune.[13] While addressing very different groups of activists, these historians have thus come to similar conclusions regarding the importance of the Revolution. As generations of activists had before them, it is suggested, revolutionaries in the period after the Paris Commune continued to regard the French Revolution as a paradigmatic event. The Revolution, in other words, was central to their understanding of what a revolution was.

It is certainly true that activists made frequent reference to the Revolution.[14] Events, meetings, and congresses were swathed in its regalia, from

---

[11] R.P. Tombs, *France 1814–1914* (London: Routledge, 1996), p.86.

[12] 'Les militants du POF avaient vécu 1870–1871, leurs parents avaient connu 1848, voire 1830, et le souvenir de la Grande Révolution n'était vieux que de moins d'un siècle. Quand ils parlaient de révolution, c'est à un événement de cette nature qu'ils songeaient.' Moreau, *Les socialistes français et le mythe révolutionnaire*, p.26. See also Jennings, *Revolution and the Republic*, p.390; F. Furet, *Interpreting the French Revolution* (trans.) E. Forster (Cambridge: Cambridge University Press, 1981). First published in French, 1978), p.5; C. Rihs, *La Commune de Paris (1871): sa structure et ses doctrines* (Paris: Éditions du Seuil, 1973. First published in Geneva, 1955), p.11; M.P. Johnson, *The Paradise of Association: Political Culture and Popular Organisations in the Paris Commune of 1871* (Ann Arbor: University of Michigan Press, 1996), p.281.

[13] Hutton, *The Cult of the Revolutionary Tradition*, pp.14–15; p.166.

[14] See, for example, intelligence report to the Préfecture de Police, Geneva, 26 September 1876. Archives de la Préfecture de Police (APP) BA432/1989; J. Bergeret, *Le 18 mars: journal hebdomadaire* (London and Brussels, 1871), pp.31–32; G. Lefrançais, *Étude sur le mouvement communaliste à Paris en 1871* (Neuchâtel: Imprimerie G. Guillaume Fils, 1871), p.340 and p.356; 'Preface to the second edition' (1896), in P.-O. Lissagaray, *Histoire de la Commune de 1871* (Paris: Maspero, 1967. First published, 1876), p.15; 'Le 18 Mars', *L'Égalité* (Paris), 18 March 1880; B. Malon. 'La réserve révolutionnaire', *L'Intransigeant* (Paris), 1 December 1883; H. Rochefort, 'Les entrailles de Jules Ferry', *L'Intransigeant*, 30 June 1884.

busts of Marianne, the republican personification of Liberty and Reason, to the red caps of liberty worn by revolutionary insurgents including the *sans culottes*.[15] Newspapers, meanwhile, daily reaffirmed their connections to the revolutionary tradition, carrying the revolutionary calendar and titles nostalgic for the great subversive journals and pamphlets of the 1790s.[16] Between 1871 and 1885, for instance, seven separate newspapers were given some permutation of the title *Le Père Duchesne*, after the famed newspaper edited by the radical journalist Jacques Hébert between September 1790 and his execution in 1794.[17] Activists during this period thus went to considerable lengths to link themselves to the political culture of late eighteenth-century France – a time and a place where revolutionary policies and ideas had dominated the political landscape. Wherever the contemporary revolutionary turned in the 1870s, whether they were at a political meeting, in a café, or at home reading the news, they were likely to stumble across the Revolution.

Upon closer inspection, however, it is difficult to locate a definitive link between these references to the Revolution and ideas on revolutionary action. In the *Revue socialiste* in 1880, for instance, Benoît Malon recommended that his readers draw inspiration from their eighteenth-century predecessors. Yet at the same time, it was unclear precisely which of the many eighteenth-century revolutionaries he was referring to, what form this inspiration should take, or what exactly they should inspire activists to do.[18] Similarly, a wealth of writers repeatedly described workers as 'the Fourth Estate'.[19] The phrase clearly recalled Emmanuel Joseph Sieyès's influential 1789 pamphlet *Qu'est-ce que le Tiers État?* and represented an

---

[15] 'Quatrième congrès national-socialiste-ouvrier', *L'Émancipation* (Lyons), 20 November 1880.

[16] For more on the revolutionary calendar, see S. Perovic, *The Calendar in Revolutionary France: Perceptions of Time in Literature, Culture, Politics* (Cambridge: Cambridge University Press, 2012).

[17] *Le Vrai Père Duchêne* (Paris), March 1871; *La grande colère du Père Duchêne* (Paris), March–May 1871; *Le fils du Père Duchêne illustré* (Paris), April–May 1871; *Le Père Duchêne: journal des honnêtes gens* (Paris), June–July 1876; *Le Père Duchêne* (Sèvres), June–August 1878; *Le Père Duchêne illustré* (Paris), December 1878–January 1879; *Le Père Duchêne: journal quotidien*, August–September 1885. For more on this, see Crapez, *La Gauche réactionnaire*, p.28.

[18] B. Malon, 'Les Partis ouvriers en France', in *La revue socialiste* 5 (Paris, 5 May 1880), 257–269, at p.268; B. Malon, 'L'économie politique du Conseil municipal de Paris', *L'Intransigeant*, 1 January 1882.

[19] '[L]e Quatrième État'. Intelligence report to the Préfecture de Police, 24 February 1881 (Lyons). APP Ba199/476; Arnould, *L'État et la Révolution*, p.69; J. Guesde, *Services publics et socialisme* (Bordeaux: Imprimerie E. Forastié, 1883), p.4; J. Guesde, 'L'opportunisme ouvrier', *L'Égalité*, 10 February 1878; 'L'anniversaire du 18 mars 1871', *Le Prolétaire* (Paris), 18 March 1879; 'Étude sociale', *Le Prolétaire*, 25 October 1879; 'Aux Travailleurs!', *Le Prolétaire*, 17 January 1880; V. Marouck, 'Les socialistes en France', in *La revue socialiste* 2 (20 February 1880), 108–112, at p.111; Malon, 'Les Partis ouvriers en France', p.266; J. Guesde, 'République et socialisme', *L'Émancipation*, 31 October 1880.

attempt to associate themselves with a long national revolutionary tradition.[20] At the same time, such references did not reveal any clearly defined ideas about the shape or future of revolution. While mentions of the Revolution may have been plentiful, then, they were also vague.

Other revolutionaries were more explicitly indecisive about the revolutionary tradition and their place in it. In his 1874 *Idée libertaire dans la Commune de 1871*, for example, Gustave Lefrançais distinguished the Paris Commune from all other nineteenth-century French revolutions, asserting that 'the movement of 18 March 1871 has nothing in common with the political revolutions that have occurred since 9 Thermidor' – the date of Maximilien Robespierre's fall in 1794.[21] Yet several years later in an 1878 article in *Le Travailleur*, he readily likened the Commune to the June Days of 1848, during which a workers' uprising in Paris had been suppressed by the republican National Guard. The similarities between the two, he averred, were 'striking'.[22] Like Malon and those discussing the Fourth Estate, Lefrançais certainly had a favourable view of the Revolution, and was clearly mindful of his own relationship to it as a contemporary revolutionary activist. Again, like Malon and others, though, it was not clear precisely what this relationship was.

Insofar as it is possible to determine any links between tradition and future revolutionary action, the associations were overwhelmingly negative. In the final volume of his *Histoire populaire et parlementaire de la Commune*, Arthur Arnould cast a critical eye over the past ninety years of French history. Whilst they had been memorable, he observed dispassionately, France's revolutionary upheavals had also been overwhelmingly unsuccessful:

> after six Revolutions in less than a century, a beheaded king, four others dead in exile, and three Republics, the people in France are no more advanced than they were on day one, and find themselves always on the

---

[20] E.J. Sieyès, *Qu'est-ce que le Tiers État?* 3rd edn (Paris: publisher unknown, 1789).

[21] '[L]e mouvement du 18 mars 1871 n'avait aucun rapport avec les révolutions politiques qui l'avaient précédé depuis le 9 thermidor'. G. Lefrançais, *L'idée libertaire dans la Commune de 1871* (Cahiers de contre-courant 66, April 1958. First published, 1874), p.18. See also Intelligence report to the Préfecture de Police, Geneva, 28 February 1878. APP, BA433/2297; Intelligence report to the Préfecture de Police, Paris, 7 September 1879. APP, BA433/2764; G.-P. Cluseret, *Mémoires du Général Cluseret*, 3 vols. (Paris: Jules Levy, 1887–1888), vol.2, p.265.

[22] '[S]aisissante'. G. Lefrançais, 'Juin 1848: les Républicains bourgeois devant la République sociale', *Le Travailleur* (Geneva) 2:1 (January–February 1878), p.32. See also 'Un anniversaire', *Le Prolétaire*, 18 March 1882. Compare also 'Notre abstention', *Le Prolétaire*, 24 July 1880; 'Juillet 1789', *Le Prolétariat* (Paris), 11 July 1885.

cusp of a new Revolution, which will be as sterile as the others if we do not finally get ourselves out of this rut.[23]

Not only, then, were certain members of the revolutionary movement unsure as to their thought on the Revolution, but others were actively hostile towards the precedent it set, explicitly expressing scepticism about the Revolution's exemplary value and its achievements. Far from an example to be emulated or venerated, for the likes of Arnould, France's recent revolutionary history was rather evidence of what contemporary activists should seek to avoid.

These ambiguous interpretations, moreover, cannot be slotted into a conventional narrative of competing revolutionary traditions. From the 1820s onwards, even partisans of the Revolution came to accept that at least two competing revolutionary traditions existed. One positioned the Revolution as a triumph of liberal values. It emphasised the achievements of 1789, such as the publication of the *Déclaration des droits de l'homme et du citoyen*, whilst condemning or eliding the excesses of its later phases.[24] The other, on the contrary, embraced the violence of 1793, the radicalism of the Montagnards, and venerated figures such as 'Gracchus' Babeuf, who in 1796 led a revolt that aimed to install a proto-socialist egalitarian government. It was to the tradition of 1793 that many nineteenth-century revolutionaries, including the Italian conspirator Filippo Buonarroti and Louis Auguste Blanqui, adhered, and to which it has been suggested that the revolutionaries of the post-Commune period belonged.[25]

Yet in fact, revolutionaries during this period expressed scepticism of all stages of the Revolution. Assessing the record of 1793 in 1884, for example, *Le Prolétaire* asked: '[i]t defeated Europe, erased federalism, decapitated the reaction, and seemed victorious; and then what?'[26] Such sentiments in fact reflected a continuation of many revolutionaries'

[23] '[A]près six Révolutions en moins d'un siècle, après un roi guillotiné, quatre autres morts en exil, après trois Républiques, le peuple en France, n'est pas beaucoup plus avancé qu'au premier jour, et se trouve toujours à la veille d'une nouvelle Révolution qui sera aussi inféconde que les précédentes, si on ne sort enfin de l'ornière.' A. Arnould, *Histoire populaire et parlementaire de la Commune*, 3 vols. (Brussels: Imprimerie A. Lefevre, 1871), vol.3, p.124. See also S. Lacroix, 'De 1792 à 1876', *Les droits de l'homme* (Paris), 22 September 1876; H. Rochefort, 'Retour à l'ancien régime', *L'Intransigeant*, 18 August 1883; 'Le 31 Octobre 1870', *Le Prolétariat*, 25 October 1884.

[24] For an example, see F.A. Mignet, *Histoire de la Révolution française* (Brussels: Aug. Wahlen et Compagnie, 1824).

[25] See, for example, Hutton, *The Cult of the Revolutionary Tradition.*

[26] 'La force', *Le Prolétariat*, 13 December 1884. For more criticisms of early revolutions, see Lefrançais, *L'idée libertaire dans la Commune de 1871*, p.6; B. Malon, 'Un chapitre de la genèse propriétaire à propos du 14 juillet', *Le Prolétaire*, 15 July 1882; 'Amnistie!', *Le Prolétariat*, 12 July 1884.

attitudes during the Commune itself. As Robert Tombs has noted, Communards sought forcefully to dissociate their revolution from the violence of the 1790s, and even publicly burnt the guillotine.[27] While public doubts and criticisms as forceful as *Le Prolétaire*'s remained unusual, their presence – especially in such widely read publications – is nonetheless instructive. Activists' criticisms of the Revolution were notably not confined to 1789 and its earlier stages. Rather, they were considerably more comprehensive in their scope, stretching into the 1790s, and even to 1793 itself. As we have seen, radicals throughout the nineteenth century had rejected specific stages of the Revolution. Many revolutionaries in the period after the Commune, however, adopted a different approach, refusing to draw lessons or inspiration from any part of the Revolution at all.

Ambivalence about the Revolution's instructive value, moreover, was widespread across the revolutionary movement. It was particularly prevalent among socialists and federalists, who frequently complained, for example, that the Commune's reverence for the Revolution had been one of its gravest failings.[28] Yet wariness of too great a dependence on the Revolution permeated even the most traditionalist parts of the movement. The Blanquist general Gustave Paul Cluseret lamented revolutionaries' inability to imagine a world beyond that which already existed, complaining that '[a]s soon as a fleeting triumph puts power in the hands of the people, they use it to reconstitute the past'.[29] Meanwhile, the London-based Blanquist newspaper *La Fédération* carefully rationed its references to the Revolution. Discussing a 'project for a socialist federation' in 1872, for example, it did not mention France's recent history even when

[27] R.P. Tombs, *Paris, bivouac des révolutions: la Commune de 1871* (trans.) J. Chatroussat (Paris: Éditions Libertalia, 2015. First published in English, 1999), p.354; Tombs, *France 1814–1914*, p.12.

[28] Arnould, *Histoire populaire et parlementaire de la Commune*, vol.2, p.83, see also pp.103–104; J. Andrieu, *Notes pour servir à l'histoire de la Commune de Paris en 1871* (Paris: Payot, 1971), pp.100–101. See also R. Urbain, 'Vae Victis', Fonds Lucien Descaves, International Institute of Social History (IISH), 1035, p.5; Lefrançais, *Étude sur le mouvement communaliste*, p.247 and p.277; Lefrançais, *République et Révolution*, p.8; 'Moralités révolutionnaires', *Les droits de l'homme*, 12 August 1876; C. Bouis, 'Demain', *Le Citoyen* (Paris), 15 July 1882; P. Brousse, 'La force', *Le Prolétariat*, 13 December 1884; P.-O. Lisaagaray, 'La loi du drapeau', *La Bataille* (Paris), 4 June 1885.

[29] 'Aussitôt qu'un triomphe éphémère met le pouvoir aux mains du peuple, le premier usage qu'il en fait est de reconstituer le passé.' Cluseret, *Mémoires du Général Cluseret*, vol.2, pp.217–218; see also vol.1, p.38. See also Bergeret, *Le 18 mars*, p.9; 'La contagion cléricale', *L'Intransigeant*, 30 July 1880; J.H. Rochefort, 'Le blâme platonique', *L'Intransigeant*, 18 March 1881; M. Talmeyr, 'L'invraisemblable', *L'Intransigeant*, 24 January 1882.

discussing liberty and equality: ideas with a decidedly revolutionary heritage.[30] Ambivalence towards the Revolution was thus more than simply the preserve of a few publications or small parts of the revolutionary movement. Rather, it was widespread, and even the Blanquists distanced themselves from the idea that the French past should serve as a model for future revolution.

Activists' interactions with the French revolutionary past, in other words, were more complicated than has previously been suggested. During the nineteenth century, many revolutionaries and radicals drew heavily upon the history of the Revolution for inspiration on how to bring about meaningful social and political change. Despite previous suggestions, however, French revolutionaries from the immediate post-Commune period were not among them. Activists certainly made frequent reference to the Revolution and eagerly linked themselves to its political culture. Yet at the same time, they demonstrably did not conceive of the Revolution as a paradigmatic event, and even its greatest admirers did not seek to derive positive lessons on the future of revolutionary action from it. Indeed, many revolutionaries actively rejected attempts to define their own activities according to the terms of the French revolutionary past.

II

Rather than the nature of revolutionary action, activists' writings on the French revolutionary past were primarily concerned with the shape of the French Republic. As discussed in Part I, the first years of the Third Republic's existence were marked by political turmoil. Despite these initial uncertainties, however, by the end of the 1870s, the security of the Republican state was to all intents and purposes assured. Between February and July 1875, the Assemblée Nationale passed a series of constitutional laws concerning the organisation of the government and the Senate, endowing the Third Republic with a sound republican constitutional basis and a clearly defined political system. After a series of republican electoral victories, the Royalists lost their parliamentary majority in May 1877, bringing aspirations of a monarchical restoration to an end.[31] The death of Louis Napoléon, the Prince Imperial, in South Africa two years later similarly extinguished any hope of a Bonapartist restoration. By the end of the 1870s, France therefore had not only a republican constitution and a

[30] 'Projet pour une fédération socialiste', *La Fédération* (London), 28 September 1872.
[31] Tombs, *France 1814–1914*, p.438.

republican president in Jules Grévy, but also a moderate republican government.

Over the next five years, these republican governments passed a raft of reforming legislation. This began in 1881 with promulgation of the *loi sur la liberté de la presse*, which reversed years of press sanctions. The 1884 *loi Waldeck-Rousseau* legalised professional syndicates for the first time since 1791, while the *loi municipale* of the same year devolved greater decision-making powers to regions and communes. Republicans also legislated for significant social reform, passing the *lois Ferry* in 1881–1882, which mandated for the provision of free, universal, and secular education by the state, and repealing the ban on divorce in 1884. This, and the other legislation passed by these governments between 1879 and 1885, would later come to be seen as the cornerstone of French republican values. As a result, this period has been memorably described by Jean Leduc as one of *enracinement* and by François Furet and Mona Ozouf as one of *avènement*, in which not only the republic, but also republican values became fully embedded in French public life for the first time.[32]

For revolutionaries, the advent of an actively reforming Republic was a mixed blessing. Despite their criticisms of republicans who had failed to support the Commune, the majority of revolutionaries were themselves vocal republicans.[33] During the 1870s, many had cautiously supported radicals such as Gambetta in an attempt to protect the fledging Republic from the Moral Order regime.[34] In May 1874, for example, Henri Rochefort in the *New York Herald*

[32] J. Leduc, *Histoire de la France: l'enracinement de la République, 1879–1918* (Paris: Hachette, 1991); F. Furet and M. Ozouf (eds.), *Le siècle de l'avènement républicain* (Paris: Gallimard, 1993).

[33] For examples of revolutionaries identifying as republicans, see F. Pyat, *Lettre au peuple de Lyon* (London, 10 December 1875), p.7. Archives de la Préfecture de Police (APP) Ba429/1811/bis; Intelligence report to the Préfecture de Police, 22 February 1875 (Geneva). APP Ba432/1384; Intelligence report to the Préfecture de Police. 14 October 1877 (London). APP Ba429/2427; 'Le droit de respirer', *Le Citoyen & La Bataille* (Paris), 7 April 1883; H. Maret, 'De la lumière!', *Les droits de l'homme*, 8 March 1876; 'Aux républicains', *L'Égalité*, 26 November 1882; J. Guesde, 'Les étonnements de M. Clemenceau', *L'Émancipation*, 2 November 1880; H. Rochefort, 'Le choix d'un adjectif', *L'Intransigeant*, 16 August 1880; 'Meeting du Cirque d'Hiver', *L'Intransigeant*, 31 August 1885; 'Les voeux du *Prolétaire*', *Le Prolétaire*, 3 January 1880; 'Appel aux travailleurs', *Le Prolétaire*, 18 September 1880; 'Aux électeurs de M. Clemenceau', *Le Prolétaire*, 28 October 1882; 'Debout, l'atelier!', *Le Prolétariat*, 12 September 1885; V. Marouck, 'Les socialistes en France', in *La revue socialiste* (Paris) 2 (20 February 1880), 108–112, at pp.110–111; B. Malon, *La troisième défaite du prolétariat français* (Neuchâtel: G. Guillaume Fils, 1871), p.522; Lefrançais, *République et Révolution*, p.8; A. Regnard, *Études de politique scientifique: la révolution sociale, ses origines, son développement et son but* (London: No publisher given, 1876), p.50.

[34] See, for example, the unity displayed at Blanqui's funeral in 1881. For more, see D. Dodds, 'Funerals, Trials, and the Problem of Violence in Nineteenth-Century France: Blanqui and Raspail' (unpublished PhD thesis, University of Cambridge, 2010).

expressed the opinion that the prospect for the republicans is very bright ...
Thiers, he thinks, deserves great credit for his unswerving fidelity to the
Republic, and he (Rochefort) will do all he can to sustain him; but he
thinks Gambetta the best man for the Republic.[35]

Yet the moderate governments of the early 1880s were a long way from the
republican government that they had envisioned. As both Robert Tombs
and Sudhir Hazareesingh have observed, liberal and moderate republican
political positions converged considerably under the Second Empire, and
many young republicans like Gambetta and Ferry emerged in 1870 convinced of the value of liberal shibboleths such as parliamentary preponder-
ance and constitutional guarantees.[36] Such substantial ideological and
practical shifts remained unacceptable for many other republicans, from
revolutionaries to radicals such as Georges Clemenceau. Indeed, the
members of these governments were often pejoratively described as
'opportunists' on account of their perceived willingness to compromise
republican values in their quest for power.

Revolutionary writing on French history and the Revolution represented the revolutionaries' attempt to navigate these issues and negotiate
the shape of this new Republic and their place in it. Work on the Paris
Commune provides a particularly clear demonstration of this. As we have
seen, revolutionary work on the Commune was both plentiful and intellectually varied. History, moreover, played an important role in it.
Whether they had been personally involved in the Commune or not,
sympathetic writers were eager to provide the events and ideas of 1871 with
a long historical genealogy and prove that the 'idea of the Commune' was,
to quote Andrieu, 'as old as it is new'.[37] Revolutionary writing on the
Commune thus provides a particularly clear and self-contained example of

---

[35] 'Henri Rochefort', *New York Herald*, 29 May 1874, p.7.

[36] Tombs, *France 1814–1914*, p.73. For more, see S. Hazareesingh, *From Subject to Citizen: The Second
Empire and the Emergence of Modern French Democracy* (Princeton, NJ: Princeton University Press,
1998); S. Hazareesingh, *Intellectual Founders of the Republic: Five Studies in Nineteenth-Century
French Republican Political Thought*, 2nd edn (Oxford: Oxford University Press, 2005). First
published, 2001). For liberal praise of the Revolution, see, for example, É. Laboulaye, *Le parti
libéral: son programme et son avenir*, 4th edn (Paris: Charpentier, 1864), p.316. For more on the
Revolution's broad appeal, see Hazareesingh, *Intellectual Founders of the Republic*, pp.294–295.

[37] 'L'idée de la Commune, quoique beaucoup plus neuve, tant elle est vieille'. Andrieu, *Notes pour
servir à l'histoire de la Commune*, p.99. See also V. Marouck, 'Le Socialisme officiel sous la
Commune', in *La revue socialiste* 7 (5 June 1880), 330–336, at p.333; A. Arnould, *Histoire
populaire et parlementaire de la Commune de Paris*, vol.2, p.159; Andrieu, *Notes pour servir à
l'histoire de la Commune*, pp.154–155; Beslay, *Mes souvenirs*, p.7; B. Malon, *Exposé des écoles
socialistes françaises* (Paris: A. Le Chevalier, 1872), p.229; 'L'anniversaire du 18 mars 1871', *Le
Prolétaire* (Paris), 18 March 1879; 'Il y a cinq ans'. *L'Égalité*, 19 November 1882.

the ways in which activists conceived of the relationship between history, society, and contemporary social change.

In works in this genre, the Revolution and the revolutionary tradition played an important, but subordinate, role. While linking their current actions to the Revolution remained important, at the same time many writers also attempted to provide a longer historical genealogy for the Commune.[38] The international exile newspaper *Qui Vive!* traced the Commune's heritage back to the feudal 'revolutionaries' such as Étienne Marcel,[39] while Cluseret named 'Spartacus, Jan Hus, [Thomas] Munster, and all the others who, defeated, also pulled down the regimes that had defeated them' as inspirations.[40] The veteran revolutionary Charles Beslay, who had been involved in both the 1830 and 1848 revolutions as well as that of 1871, likewise compared the Commune to '[t]he slave revolts of antiquity'.[41] Thus while revolutionaries certainly mentioned the French Revolution in their work on the Commune, their historical reflections did not end at the late-eighteenth century. Rather, they also reached considerably further back into the past for their examples, often suggesting that they identified more closely with these than with their more immediate antecedents.

In doing so, revolutionaries sought to establish a theoretical distance between their current actions and those of other French activists since 1789. As we have seen, in both revolutionary literature and wider French political culture during this period, the French Revolution was principally characterised as a struggle for the provision of universally equal legal and political rights.[42] The earlier historical figures that revolutionaries chose to associate themselves with, on the other hand, were overwhelmingly associated with socially egalitarian or populist visions of society. Spartacus, for

---

[38] For examples of writers linking the Commune to the Revolution, see É. Vaillant, 'Vive la Commune!', *Commonweal* (London, April 1885), p.1; V. Marouck, *Les grandes dates du socialisme: juin 1848* (Paris: Librairie du Progrès, 1880), pp.2–3.

[39] *Qui vive!* (London), 12 October 1871. For more feudal references, see also Lefrançais, *Étude sur le mouvement communaliste*, p.393; Arnould, *Histoire populaire et parlementaire de la Commune*, vol.2, pp.48–49.

[40] 'Spartacus, Jean Huss, Munster et tant d'autres qui ont eu la leur [leur histoire], et dont la chute, par parenthèse, entraîna celle des régimes qui les avaient vaincus'. Cluseret, *Mémoires du Général Cluseret*, vol.1, p.10. See also Bergeret, *Le 18 mars*, pp.22–23.

[41] 'Les soulèvements des esclaves dans l'Antiquité'. Beslay, *Mes souvenirs*, p.472. See also B. Malon, *Spartacus, ou la guerre des esclaves* (Verviers: Imprimerie d'Émile Piette, 1876); Malon, *La troisième défaite du prolétariat français*, p.7.

[42] See for example Intelligence report to the Préfecture de Police, 11 September 1877 (London). APP Ba429/2406; Lefrançais, *République et Révolution*, p.21; 'Prudence!', *Le Prolétaire*, 8 December 1883.

example, had helped to instigate the Third Servile War, a slave revolt against the Roman Republic, while Étienne Marcel was renowned for his defence of Parisian craftsmen against the over-reaching power of the throne and the French state during the fourteenth century. Revolutionaries, therefore, were not simply seeking to link themselves to a version of society envisioned by revolutionaries in 1789. Indeed, far from tying themselves indiscriminately to the Revolution, they self-consciously aimed to provincialise it.

By providing a broader range of historical precedents, revolutionaries also outlined an alternative vision of liberty and equality. In order to be truly meaningful, they suggested, change could not confine itself to political or constitutional issues: it must also be social. This stood in direct contrast to the vision of equality advanced by the republican governments of the early 1880s. For the Opportunists, the path to a unified republican society lay in legislating for political equality and studiously ignoring conventional social distinctions. Gambetta, for instance, asserted that 'class is a bad word that I never use'.[43] While activists fulsomely discussed French revolutionary history in their accounts of the Commune, then, the subject of these discussions was demonstrably not the shape or future of revolutionary action. Rather, revolutionaries were discussing contemporary society and the shape of the French Republic, employing historical references both to suggest an alternative to the vision of society offered by moderate republicans and to legitimise their ideas.

Discussion of the Commune's patriotic roots likewise focused more on the Republic than on ideas of how a revolution should look. As discussed in Part I, revolutionaries frequently framed the Commune as an act necessitated by the danger that the fledgling Republic found itself in, and this regard for patriotism and for France was also reflected in their historical references.[44] *Qui Vive!*, for example, claimed that the ideas embodied in the Commune had originated in Gaul during the Roman occupation.[45] Descriptions of the Commune's French origins were often accompanied by parallel explorations of its opponents' foreign origins: Gambetta, whose father was from Genoa, was, Andrieu noted, of '*Italian origin*'.[46] Although the Commune might have represented the iteration of

---

[43] 'J'ai dit les nouvelles couches, non pas les classes: c'est un mauvais mot que je n'emploie jamais.' Quoted in P. Rosanvallon, *Le moment Guizot* (Paris: Gallimard, 1985), p.367.

[44] See, for example, Malon, 'Les Partis ouvriers en France', p.262.

[45] *Qui vive!*, 8–9 October 1871.

[46] '[D]'origine *italienne*'. Andrieu, *Notes pour servir à l'histoire de la Commune*, p.34. Emphasis original.

a potentially universal idea, revolutionaries remained keen to emphasise that it had also been a specifically French revolution.

Such sentiments reflected both the growing visibility and the stridence of patriotic nationalism in France during this period. While France's comprehensive loss in the Franco-Prussian War gave rise to many misgivings about the state of the nation, its humiliation at the hands of Germany also contributed to a renewed belief in both the supremacy of French ideals (elastically defined) and the necessity of retaining its status as a great continental and global power. Writing to Friedrich Engels in 1885, for example, Laura Lafargue noted that

> Nothing acts on the imagination and the feeling of Frenchmen like the sudden news of disaster in their wars abroad: the horror of want of work and food at home leaves them tame in comparison and indeed takes the heart out of them, while the fact that a few hundred Frenchmen have fallen on foreign battlefields will, at any time, sting them into madness.[47]

Revolutionaries were no exception to these sentiments. Reflecting on his years in exile, for example, the architect and ex-Communard Achille Ballière noted that while it was

> true that all people are brothers, . . . amidst all of these brothers, one always needs a place to rest one's head, and the preferred place is always of course in one's home country. Is it really living if one lives so far from his own, his *patrie*, the country where he was born, where he speaks the national language, far from the sites, the woods, the meadows, were he felt the first stirrings of his own thought?[48]

Revolutionaries' eagerness to burnish their credibility as defenders of the nation thus aligned with both the mood of many within the revolutionary movement and more widespread national sentiment.

The patriotic vision offered by revolutionaries in this writing, however, was again notably different. Rather than comparing themselves to classic French national figures, revolutionaries aligned themselves with historic

[47] 149: L. Lafargue to F. Engels, 1 April 1885 (Paris), in F. Engels, P. and L. Lafargue, *Correspondence*, 3 vols. (trans.) Y. Kapp (Moscow: Foreign Languages Publishing House, 1959), vol. 1, 279–280, at pp. 279–280.
[48] 'Les peuples tous des frères, c'est convenu . . . mais encore faut-il, au milieu de ces frères, une pierre pour reposer sa tête, et celle que l'on préfère est toujours celle qui se trouve au pays natal. Est-ce vivre que de vivre loin des siens, loin de sa patrie, loin de la contrée où l'on a ressenti les premiers élans de la pensée?' E.-A. Ballière, *La Déportation de 1871: Souvenirs d'un évadé de Nouméa* (Paris: G. Charpentier, 1889), p. 414. See also Intelligence report to the Préfecture de Police. 3 August 1877 (London). APP Ba429/2363; H. Rochefort, 'Merci!', *L'Intransigeant*, 15 July 1880; C. Bouis, 'Le 14 juillet', *L'Intransigeant*, 16 July 1880; H. Rochefort, 'L'invasion étrangère', *L'Intransigeant*, 6 September 1883.

failures. Writers frequently compared the official reaction to the Commune to the sixteenth-century Wars of Religion, branding the Semaine Sanglante a 'socialist Saint Bartholomew', in which the streets of Paris had run red with Communard rather than Huguenot blood.[49] The Albigensian Crusade, which all but eliminated Catharism in the Languedoc in the early thirteenth century, also proved a popular point of comparison. Referring to its infamous massacre and immolation by Catholic forces in 1209, for instance, Arnould accused Thiers of having 'made Paris into an Albigensian Béziers'.[50]

Alongside a social vision, revolutionary accounts of the Commune thus also offered their readers a kind of alternative patriotism. In linking the Commune to a series of French outcasts and historical 'losers' such as the Albigensians and the Huguenots, revolutionary writers attempted to establish an alternative French history of minority groups defeated by monolithic contemporary 'forces of order'.[51] In turn, this acted as a way for writers to encourage their readers to reflect on what it meant to be French. In contrast to the idea of a one and indivisible nation, they positioned the Commune, as well as their current activism, as a struggle for the right to express French – or indeed any – citizenship in plural ways. Again, while these references were clearly to historical revolutions and the French past, it was the Republic, rather than revolution, that they addressed.

Revolutionaries' writings on the Commune thus indicated the complicated nature of their relationship with both the Revolution and the new Third Republic. The particular ways in which they used history, and especially the Revolution, were neither new nor uncommon. Throughout the nineteenth century, numerous authors had used the Revolution to make broader historicophilosophical arguments about the nature of man and society, from liberals such as François Guizot to republicans including Adolphe Thiers and Jules Michelet, the socialist Louis Blanc, and

---

[49] '[S]aint-Barthélemy du socialisme'. Malon, *La troisième défaite du prolétariat français*, p.398; Andrieu, *Notes pour servir à l'histoire de la Commune*, p.141; Beslay, *Mes souvenirs*, p.6; 'Souvenons-nous!', *Le Prolétaire*, 18 March 1880; H. Rochefort, 'Le vrai Trinquet', *L'Intransigeant*, 14 January 1881; P.-O. Lissagaray, *Les huit journées de mai derrière les barricades* (Brussels: Au bureau du *Petit journal*, 1871), p.155. For another reference to the Wars of Religion, see Malon, 'Les Partis ouvriers en France', p.262. For a reference to the revocation of the Edict of Nantes, see P. Martine, *Souvenirs d'un insurgé de la Commune*, (ed.) J. Suffel (Paris: Librairie Academique Perrin, 1971), p.306.

[50] '[I]l a fait de Paris un Béziers au temps des Albigeois'. Arnould, *Histoire populaire et parlementaire de la Commune*, vol.3, pp.24–25; p.104. For another reference to the Albigensian crusade, see P. Lafargue, 'Blagues bourgeoises: la patrie', *L'Égalité*, 17 November 1884.

[51] See also E. Renan, *Qu'est-ce qu'une nation? Conférence faite en Sorbonne, le 11 mars 1882* (Paris: Calmann Levy, 1882), p.27.

conservatives such as Hippolyte Taine.[52] Although their ideas were often different, by using French history and the revolutionary tradition to discuss the shape of the Republic, revolutionaries were in fact acting in much the same way as these other authors. Rather than setting them apart from others or identifying them as arch revolutionaries, activists' treatment of French history during this period highlighted their methodological proximity to other parts of the French intellectual and republican communities.

Likewise, none of the historical references that activists used stood outside of revolutionary or enlightened traditions. Both pre-revolutionary and revolutionary figures had frequently used such references in their own writings, and this was especially true of those alluding to Catholicism's tendency for persecution. Condemnation of the treatment of Protestants and Cathars, for instance, was already an Enlightened trope before the Revolution.[53] Likewise, the Roman occupation of Gaul, and particular the general Flavius Aétius, often featured in debates on ethnicity and order distinction in the eighteenth century, which in turn inspired parts of Sieyès's *Qu'est-ce que le Tiers État?*[54] In drawing upon such references, revolutionaries were thus not attempting to separate themselves from the Revolution or the Republic entirely, or to construct an entirely different genealogy for their ideas. Indeed, the use of these references demonstrated both their deep knowledge of French history and republican theory, and their desire to play a part in both.

Yet although they were not unheard of, these references were esoteric. Rather than prioritising their connections to familiar years and events such as 1793, the storming of the Bastille, or the declaration of the First Republic, revolutionaries explicitly sought to attach themselves and their ideas to more unusual figures such as Aétius and the Cathars. While none of these references came from outside of French historical convention, they nonetheless picked at the vision of the Republic offered by the

---

[52] For more on using the Revolution as a historicophilosophical concept, see R. Koselleck, *Futures Past: On the Semantics of Historical Time* (trans.) K. Tribe (New York: Columbia University Press, 2004. First published in German, 1979), p.51. See, for example, F.P.G. Guizot, *Histoire de la civilisation en France depuis la chute de l'empire romain jusqu'à la Révolution française*, 4 vols., 2nd edn (Paris: Didier, 1840); A. Thiers, *Histoire de la Révolution française*, 10 vols., 9th edn (Paris: Furne et Cie, 1839. First published, 1823–1827); L. Blanc, *Histoire de la Révolution française*, 12 vols. (Paris: Langlois et Leclerc, 1847–1862); J. Michelet, *Histoire de la Révolution française*, 9 vols. (Paris: Chamerot, 1847–1853); H. Taine, *Les origines de la France contemporaine*, 5 vols. (Paris: Hachette, 1875–1893).

[53] See, for example, Jennings, *Revolution and the Republic*, pp.301–303.

[54] Sieyès, *Qu'est-ce que le Tiers État?*, pp.17–18.

Opportunists. By drawing attention to this history, they hoped to remind their readers of the complex and variegated nature of the French enlightened and revolutionary traditions, and open a conversation about how both society and the state should look in the Third Republic. Revolutionaries during this period, then, did not regard the recent French past as a militant toolkit that contained the answers for how to conduct future revolutions. Instead, as many French historians and theorists had done throughout the nineteenth century, they used the language of history to elaborate upon their beliefs on the nature of contemporary society and the shape of social change.

III

A more complex approach to the Revolution was not surprising given the changing status of both revolution and the Revolution in France during this period. By the end of the 1870s, as we have seen, the security of the Republican state was for all intents and purposes assured. Yet in spite of this, several powerful and influential sections of French society remained sceptical of both the Opportunists and the Republic itself. Specifically, both the Catholic Church and the army remained unconvinced of a Republic's ability to adequately represent their interests.[55] Both had been heavily involved in the Second Empire and regarded the advent of the Third Republic and subsequent rise of republican politicians as unwelcome developments. In particular, the army was horrified by radical republican support for ex-Communards, while the Church did not formally endorse the Republic until the 1892 encyclical *Au milieu des sollicitudes*. While the Republican state may have become legally and constitutionally secure in the second half of the 1870s, for many years, republicans' place at the centre of it was not.

The army and the Church's more substantive concerns about republican government derived from its persistent association with revolution and social upheaval. These issues were not entirely unreasonable, as prior to the *enracinement* of the Third Republic, France had never experienced a stable republican government. The First Republic was for many inseparable from the Terror, and the association between the two was actively promoted by both revolutionaries and the forces of order throughout the nineteenth

---

[55] J. Plamenatz, *The Revolutionary Movement in France 1815–1871* (London: Longman, 1965. First published, 1952), p.162; P. Nord, *The Republican Moment: Struggles for Democracy in Nineteenth-Century France* (Cambridge, MA: Harvard University Press, 1995), pp.247–249.

century.[56] Its power can be glimpsed in numerous texts. Gustave Flaubert, for example, bemoaned how this memory had haunted the Second Republic, writing in *L'éducation sentimentale* that in 1848 'the spectre of 93 reappeared, and the blade of the guillotine trembled in every syllable of the word Republic'.[57] Similarly in his 1873 *République et Révolution*, Lefrançais observed that

> For almost a century, Republic and Revolution have walked in tandem in our history and … people have come to believe that the more or less unforeseen arrival of the first must therefore lead to the revival and triumph of the latter.[58]

Satisfactorily resolving this situation was thus one of the most important tasks that advocates of republican government faced, both in opposition and after the Opportunists came to power.[59] On the one hand, republicans were anxious to pay the Revolution the respect they believed it deserved as the originator of modern European democratic rights. On the other, however, it was essential to reassure sceptical citizens and institutions that a truly republican state would ensure political, social, and economic stability rather than destroy it.

The Revolution played a central role in Opportunist governments' efforts to cement their political viability. Rather than seeking to distance themselves from France's revolutionary history, government republicans embraced it. Like revolutionaries, they eagerly swathed themselves in the symbolism of the revolutionary tradition. Claude Monet's *La rue Montorgueil à Paris: fête du 30 juin 1878* communicates these efforts, depicting a scene in which the contemporary enjoyment of 'peace and work' was explicitly linked to revolutionary history through the use of the tricolour flag.[60] Two years later in 1880, the government declared 14 July, the anniversary of the storming of the Bastille, a national holiday, and 1889 saw lavish celebrations for the Revolution's centenary.

---

[56] See, for example, M. du Camp, *Les convulsions de Paris*, 4 vols., 5th edn (Paris: Hachette, 1881), vol.2, p.1; p.40. Tombs, *France 1814–1914*, p.485. For forces of order, see Tombs, *Paris, bivouac des révolutions*, p.350. For revolutionaries, see Stedman Jones, *Karl Marx: Greatness and Illusion*, p.294, p.312.

[57] '[L]e spectre de 93 reparut, et le couperet de la guillotine vibra dans toutes les syllabes du mot République'. G. Flaubert, *L'éducation sentimentale: histoire d'un jeune homme*, 2 vols. (Paris: Michel Lévy Frères, 1870), vol.2, pp.94–95.

[58] 'Depuis bientôt un siècle, République et Révolution marchent de pair dans notre histoire et … le peuple en est arrivé à croire que l'avènement plus ou moins fortuit de la première doit forcément amener le réveil et le triomphe de l'autre.' Lefrançais, *République et Révolution*, p.6.

[59] Hazareesingh, *Intellectual Founders of the Republic*, p.297; Tombs, *France 1814–1914*, pp.73–74.

[60] C. Monet, 'La rue Montorgueil à Paris. Fête du 30 juin 1878' (1878, Musée d'Orsay).

The *Exposition universelle* even included a scale replica of the Bastille and its surroundings, enabling visitors to place themselves in the shoes of famous revolutionaries past.

This willingness to embrace the revolutionary past also had more direct political effects. After the fall of the Second Empire in September 1870, *quarante-huitard* veterans who had spent much of the last two decades in exile were welcomed back to France with open arms. Many, including Victor Hugo and the socialist Louis Blanc, swiftly returned to political life, once again taking up seats in parliament. The Opportunists' recognition of the Revolution was thus more than simply cosmetic. In the new Third Republic, former revolutionaries assumed positions of considerable influence and were transported to the heart of political power and national decision-making. The horrors of the Paris Commune, then, clearly had not put the Opportunists and their allies off the French revolutionary past. Indeed, during this period, the Revolution was promoted and celebrated on a scale not seen since the 1790s.

At the same time that they lauded revolution, though, these celebrations also historicised it. Republicans during this period demonstrably did not seek to draw any lessons for the future from the Revolution, but rather emphasised its historical character. It was during this period that historical study of the Revolution became professionalised for the first time, culminating in the creation of the first professorial chair in the history of the Revolution in 1886.[61] The Revolution, in other words, was now respectable. In promoting, even apotheosising, the events of 1789 to such a degree, republicans aimed to definitively tie the act of revolution to the historical event of the Revolution. In doing so, and by emphasising the Revolution's unique heritage and history, they hoped to demonstrate that revolution was an exceptional occurrence that neither could nor should be repeated: that French revolutions were a thing of the past.

Such rhetoric served a dual political purpose. On one hand, definitively tethering revolutionary action to the past rather than contemporary events rendered this rhetoric invaluable to republican attempts to reassure more conservative citizens that they also sought social and political stability. On the other, popularising the notion that the French Revolution was a unique event also served to deprive potential future revolutionaries of

---

[61] For more, see 'Augustin Cochin: The Theory of Jacobinism', in Furet, *Interpreting the French Revolution*, pp.164–204. For more on the professionalisation of history in the Third Republic, see I. Noronha-DiVanna, *Writing History in the Third Republic* (Newcastle: Cambridge Scholars Press, 2010).

political legitimacy. This specific interpretation of the Revolution thus enabled moderate republicans to simultaneously neutralise two diametrically opposed threats to the integrity of the Republic. Far from damaging the credibility of the Republican state, claiming ownership of the Revolution in this way was integral to moderate republicans' efforts to stabilise it and enhance its popularity.

This interpretation of the Revolution, moreover, emphasised that truly republican government was key to France's stability. In their discussions and celebrations of the Revolution, moderate republicans primarily emphasised the value of the 'liberal' Revolution, that is to say, the events and achievements of the period between 1789 and 1792. Given the violence of the Revolution's subsequent years, this made sense. Yet it also specifically tied both the termination of the Revolution and the socio-political instability it had engendered, as well as the ultimate realisation of its aims, to republican government. Gambetta, for instance, argued that only universal suffrage would bring the Revolution to an end, and described the radicals rather than Moral Order politicians as 'the true party of order in this country'.[62] It was republicans who had curtailed the president's power after the 16 May 1877 crisis, and it was the Opportunists who had brought an end to the upheaval and uncertainty caused by attempts at restoration – first by supporting the 1875 laws, and then in government themselves.

It was thus republicans, their ideas, and their tenure of power that kept revolution at bay. A republican state and a republican constitution, Opportunists argued, were not enough: the state must also be headed by a republican government. The specific conceptualisation of the Revolution promoted by the Opportunists and even the Radicals was therefore a warning as well as a reassurance, and an attempt to stabilise the position of truly republican government. Any other circumstances, they suggested, could bring about a reversal of the previous decade's progress and the relative political stability that France enjoyed during the early 1880s.

These attempts to reinterpret the Revolution were remarkably successful. The Third Republic, as David Todd recently suggested, was 'the regime which finally succeeded in ending the Revolution'.[63] Combined with the failure of the Commune, the rise of a government that was stable,

---

[62] '[L]e vrai parti de l'ordre dans ce pays'. Rosanvallon, *Le moment Guizot*, pp.364–365.

[63] D. Todd, *Free Trade and Its Enemies in France, 1814–1851* (Cambridge: Cambridge University Press, 2015), pp.232–233. Others, such as John Plamenatz and Philippe Darriulat, have not discussed the Revolution's end so explicitly, but have likewise used this period as a chronological terminus, decisively concluding their studies of the revolutionary movement in the early 1870s. See,

truly republican, and respectful of the French past brought traditional revolutionary action to an end: against a Republican state, the kind of revolutionary violence used by previous generations and advocated, as we have seen, by the likes of François Dumartheray was no longer considered politically legitimate. It was in the 'burning Paris' of May 1871, as François Furet memorably claimed in his 1988 *La Révolution de Turgot à Jules Ferry*, that 'the French Revolution said its goodbyes to History'.[64]

Revolutionaries were well aware of such attempts to use the Revolution to excise revolutionary action from French political life. *Le Prolétaire*, for example, railed against such efforts, branding the government 'bourgeois plagiarists of the past'.[65] So too were they aware of the growing popularity of this interpretation. Reviewing the stage premier of Victor Hugo's *Quatre-Vingt-Treize* in 1881, Gabriel Deville complained that

> The public love and respect [the Revolution]. They bow religiously before 'the immortal principles' inscribed in the *Declaration of the Rights of Man* without examining whether, for the immense majority, they are anything other than a trick of the eye.[66]

This period thus marked an important crossroads in the political rhetoric and culture of the revolutionary movement. Whereas it had previously been possible to justify revolutionary and anti-state action by calling upon the French past, after 1871 this was no longer the case. Not only had the crushing of the Commune drastically reduced the revolutionary movement, but the advent of a truly reforming Republic that embraced the heritage of the Revolution rendered the idea of violence against the state both illegitimate and undesirable.

It is in this context that activists' engagement with the Revolution and the revolutionary tradition during this period must be understood. Revolutionaries' own complicated engagement with the Revolution was central to their attempts to respond to the challenge of a republicanism that

---

for example, Plamenatz, *The Revolutionary Movement in France*; Darriulat, *Les patriotes: la gauche républicaine et la nation*.

[64] 'Dans ce Paris qui brûle, la Révolution française fait ses adieux à l'Histoire'. F. Furet, *La Révolution de Turgot à Jules Ferry* (Paris: Hachette, 1988), p.489.

[65] 'La guerre d'Afrique', *Le Prolétaire*, 23 April 1881. See also A. Lavy, 'Le 14 juillet', *Le Prolétaire*, 14–17 July 1880; H. Rochefort, 'Les nouveaux révolutionnaires', *L'Intransigeant*, 1 November 1885.

[66] 'Le public admire et respecte; il s'incline religieusement devant "les principes immortels" inscrits dans la Déclaration des droits de l'homme, sans examiner si, pour l'immense majorité, il y a là autre chose qu'un trompe-l'oeil.' G. Deville, 'Quatre-Vingt-Treize', *Le Citoyen*, 26 December 1881. See also Malon, *Exposé des écoles socialistes françaises*, p.230; Cluseret, *Mémoires du Général Cluseret*, vol.2, pp.217–218.

venerated the Revolution, but neither wanted nor needed to endorse revolution. Revolutionaries cautiously welcomed the installation of a stable republican government and the realisation of rights and ideals that they had long championed, and hoped to play a part in the new order. At the same time, however, they were also anxious to preserve their autonomy from other republicans and eager to promote the idea of a more social Republic.

In their interactions with French history and the revolutionary tradition, revolutionaries aimed to do just this. By publicly associating themselves with its imagery, activists attempted to reestablish their own connections to the recent French past and, if not wrest control of the Revolution from the government, then at least remind the population that its aims had been wider than those suggested. At the same time, situating the Revolution within a much broader historical genealogy enabled revolutionaries to deal with the unquestionable popularity of the Opportunists' interpretation. It served to weaken the idea that the Revolution was a unique and unparalleled event, whilst simultaneously positioning themselves and revolution as indispensable facets of contemporary French political life. Rather than a drift towards political irrelevance, then, activists' own interpretations of the Revolution and uses of French history were indicative of their attempts to respond to the changed circumstances – both political and intellectual – that they found themselves in after 1871.

IV

Yet although such ideas were politically advantageous in the new circumstances of the Third Republic, they were not solely a by-product of these circumstances. The abandonment of the Revolution as a paradigmatic event has often been framed by historians as a response to the fall of the Paris Commune and the *enracinement* of the Third Republic. Robert Tombs, for example, has suggested it was the myth of the Semaine Sanglante that discouraged future revolutionary action, giving 'an awful warning against future insurrection, so that even self-proclaimed heirs of the Commune had good reason not to overstep the mark between rhetoric and action'.[67] As we have seen, these circumstances certainly provide an explanation for the dominance of such an interpretation; however, this more complicated attitude towards revolutionary history and the French

---

[67] R.P. Tombs, 'How bloody was *la semaine Sanglante* of 1871? A revision', *The Historical Journal* 55 (September 2012), 679–704, at p.703. See also Tombs, *Paris, bivouac des révolutions*, p.368.

past had in fact been a feature of revolutionary thought since long before the fall of the Commune. The events of the 1870s, in other words, functioned more as a catalyst for this intellectual shift rather than a cause of it.

In order to demonstrate this, let us once again take a more specific example: the writing of Louis Auguste Blanqui. Born in 1805, by the 1870s, Blanqui was the elder statesman of the French revolutionary movement. For many revolutionaries active during this period, the Commune had been their baptism into revolutionary action. By contrast, Blanqui had been involved in revolutionary politics since the Restoration, joining the Carbonari – an international network of secret revolutionary societies – in 1824. As a result, he had been personally involved in many of the most important events in recent French revolutionary history. Blanqui was involved in two major revolutions in 1830 and 1848, and masterminded numerous smaller *attentats*, republican conspiracies, and demonstrations in the intervening years. These actions earned him substantial notoriety across the continent and long years in prison – famously, over half of his life. During the Paris Commune, revolutionaries considered Blanqui so symbolically important that they offered Thiers all of their hostages in exchange for his release.

In addition to his work as a revolutionary operative, Blanqui was also a theorist. Over the years, he had aired his ideas in a variety of media, including books, pamphlets, and proclamations. He wrote for numerous newspapers, including Pierre Leroux's *Globe* and the Saint-Simonian Prosper Enfantin's *Producteur*, and helped to popularise the practice of making politicised speeches from the dock during his numerous court appearances.[68] Rather than slowing down as he entered his later years, Blanqui's work rate increased. In the final decade of his life, he edited two newspapers and published two full-length texts – a type of publication that up until that point he had not substantively engaged with. Upon his death in January 1881, in other words, Blanqui had spent long years at the heart of the revolutionary movement and experienced almost everything that it had to offer. His work thus provides an unparalleled window through which to examine the shifting place of history and the Revolution in revolutionary thought over the course of the nineteenth century.

Perhaps as a result of his career, Blanqui has been widely considered by both contemporaries and later historians to be the 'archetypal' French

---

[68] For more on Blanqui's use of court appearances, see Dodds, 'Funerals, Trials, and the Problem of Violence in Nineteenth-Century France'.

revolutionary; steadfastly, even slavishly dedicated to the veneration of the Revolution and tending its 'tradition'.[69] Certainly, the Revolution was abundantly present in Blanqui's work. In an address to a workers' banquet in 1848, for example, Blanqui toasted '[t]o the Montagne of 93! To pure socialists, their true heirs!'[70] *La Patrie en danger*, the newspaper he edited from 1870 to 1871, frequently mentioned recent French history and vigorously endorsed the tradition that privileged its more radical years. In October 1870, it ran several articles on the Revolution within the space of two weeks, warning of the perils of Girondism and examining the links between 1792 and 1870.[71] Indeed, even the newspaper's title clearly invoked the Revolution, referring to a declaration issued by the Assemblée in 1792 that called on citizens to join the Revolutionary Wars to defend France and the cause of freedom.

Yet between the Commune and his death, Blanqui's writing on the Revolution and French history mirrored the patterns laid out earlier in this chapter. Blanqui's first full-length work, the 1872 *Éternité par les astres*, dealt explicitly with the subject of revolution, claiming that such change was structurally necessary in order to preserve a healthy society. Yet while *L'éternité par les astres* reaffirmed the need for revolutionary action, it framed it in entirely different terms. Rather than discussing it in the context of the French past, Blanqui approached revolution through the prism of cosmology. Indeed, *L'éternité par les astres* overlooked human history entirely. Blanqui, then, was clearly an admirer of the Revolution, and especially its later stages, but at the same time his work from the 1870s did not indicate a sustained commitment to it. Rather, in *L'éternité par les astres* he barely mentioned it at all, and even explicitly sought to decouple the two.

A similar tendency can be observed in his second full-length work from the period. The 1880 *L'armée esclave et opprimée* dealt more explicitly with human history, and with a subject that had a clear revolutionary pedigree: the perils of standing armies and the social benefits of a citizen militia.[72] Citizen soldiers had of course played a central role in France's recent

---

[69] See, for example, 137: P. Lafargue to F. Engels, 23 December 1884 (Paris), in Engels and Lafargue, *Correspondence*, vol. 1, 256–257, at p.257; Bernstein, *The Beginnings of Marxian Socialism in France*, p.12.

[70] 'A la Montagne de 93! Aux socialistes purs, ses véritables héritiers!' 'Toast de L.-A. Blanqui au banquet des travailleurs socialistes (2 décembre 1848)', in L.-A. Blanqui, *Œuvres complètes*, 2 vols. (ed.) A. Münster (Paris: Éditions Galilée, 1977), vol. 1, 217–228, at p.218.

[71] 'Le Girondisme', *La Patrie en danger*, 15–16 October 1870; '1792–1870', *La Patrie en danger*, 26 October 1870 and 30 October 1870.

[72] Blanqui, *L'armée esclave et opprimée*, p.30.

history, from the Revolutionary Wars to the Paris Commune, in which the Parisian National Guard had been heavily involved. Yet rather than connecting the issue to its recent French Revolutionary heritage, Blanqui situated it more broadly within the political and intellectual context of republicanism. When it came to standing armies and militia, he advised, contemporary activists should draw inspiration not from their French forebears, but from 'the grandeur of the famous Republics of antiquity' and America during the Civil War.[73] Where *L'éternité par les astres* overlooked French history in favour of other forms of revolution, in *L'Armée esclave et opprimée* Blanqui appeared interested in neither revolution nor the Revolution. The text focused primarily on the shape of republics, rather than on how to get there.

Yet even prior to the fall of the Commune, Blanqui linked his ideas on revolutionary action to French history far less than has conventionally been assumed. In 1850, for example, Blanqui wrote a short text on the mechanics of and the motivations for revolution. Despite being written well before the Third Republic's final 'extinction' of the Revolution, the text did not mention the French revolutionary tradition at all.[74] 'Sur la révolution' remained unpublished until 1885 but, as two pieces from 1851 demonstrate, Blanqui was not averse to publicly airing such sentiments. In the first, a toast written in February 1851 for a gathering of French exiles in London, he offered a damning indictment of radical reverence for the revolutionary tradition, remarking,

> As for the proletarians who let themselves be distracted by ridiculous strolls in the streets, planting trees of Liberty, and the sonorous oratory of lawyers ... Well what do they have to look forward to? First, the holy water, then slanders, and finally, a hail of bullets – and poverty always![75]

Rather than moderating his tone, Blanqui redoubled such sentiment in the follow-up piece (which, incidentally, was reprinted by *L'Égalité* in June

---

[73] Blanqui, *L'armée esclave et opprimée*, pp.25–26. For further references to ancient republics, see pp.13–14 and p.18; for the American Civil War, see pp.16–17. Other prominent Blanquists such as Louise Michel later made similar suggestions. See H. Rochefort, 'Louise Michel et ses juges', *L'Intransigeant*, 1 April 1883.

[74] 'Sur la révolution (1850)', in Blanqui, *Œuvres complètes*, vol.1, 307–308, at pp.307–308.

[75] 'La France hérissée de travailleurs en armes, c'est l'avènement du socialisme. En présence des prolétaires armés, obstacles, résistances, impossibilités, tout disparaîtra. Mais pour les prolétaires qui se laissent amuser par des promenades ridicules dans les rues, par des plantations d'arbres de Liberté, par des phrases sonores d'avocats, il y aura de l'eau bénite d'abord, des injures ensuite, enfin, de la mitraille, de la misère toujours!' 'Avis au peuple (toast du 25 février 1851)', in Blanqui, *Œuvres complètes*, vol.1, 327–331, at p.331. See also 'Toast de L.-A. Blanqui au banquet des travailleurs socialistes (2 décembre 1848)', in ibid., vol.1, 217–228, at p.221.

1878).[76] On examining a broad chronological range of Blanqui's writings
and speeches, it thus becomes clear that he had been intentionally decoup-
ling the two since at least the 1850s. Although attempts to separate
revolution from the Revolution took on a particular urgency after the fall
of the Commune and the Opportunists' rise to power, then, they were not
solely a product of these circumstances. Rather, this had been a feature of
revolutionary thought for several decades before it became 'necessary'.

In fact, it is possible to divine an alternative pattern or tradition in
Blanqui's work. It appears that Blanqui's invocations of the Revolution
were linked to moments of national crisis or protest. His comparison of
contemporary socialists to the Montagnards, for example, came just a week
before the Second Republic's first and only presidential election.[77] The
more sustained use of the Revolution in *La Patrie en danger*, meanwhile,
coincided with the height of the Franco-Prussian War, during which
France had been invaded and Paris besieged by the Prussian army. Texts
that overlooked the Revolution, meanwhile, were overwhelmingly composed during periods of relative social and political calm: 1850 and 1851
before Napoleon III's coup, 1872, and 1880. Rather than a constant and
unwavering commitment to the Revolution, Blanqui's references to
French history reveal an alternative pattern. The sporadic moments at
which Blanqui evoked the Revolution as a call to arms throughout his
career appeared to be a reflection of the national context rather than of his
ideas on revolutionary action.

In this way, Blanqui's work formed part of a shared discourse used by
many other radical and moderate republicans. During the Franco-Prussian
War, in particular, many writers, theorists, and politicians turned to
emotive and patriotic rhetoric in an attempt to galvanise the population.[78]
Victor Hugo, for example, called upon all Frenchmen, 'rich, poor, worker,
bourgeois' to fight the Prussians for the sake of humanity and civilisation:

> Frenchmen, you will fight. You will devote yourselves to the universal
> cause, because France must be great in order for the world to be
> enfranchised ... because it is time to show that virtue exists, that duty
> exists, and that the *patrie* exists. You will not fail ... and the world will
> know by your example that while diplomacy is weak, the citizen is brave;
> that although kings exist, so too do peoples; that if the monarchical

[76] 'À propos des clameurs contre l'Avis du Peuple (avril 1851)', in ibid., vol.1, 332–335, at p.332.
[77] 'Aux clubs démocratiques de Paris (22 mars 1848)', in ibid., vol.1, 170–172, at p.172.
[78] See, for example, 'La circulaire de M. Jules Favre', *L'Electeur libre* (Paris), 20 September 1870.

continent eclipses itself, the Republic will shine forth and that if, for an instant, there is no longer a Europe, there will always be a France.[79]

In referring to the nation's revolutionary past, it was this rhetoric that publications like *La patrie en danger* aimed to engage in. Indeed, in its first issue Blanqui explicitly stated that '[i]n the presence of an enemy, parties and differences disappear.'[80] The purpose of Blanqui's references to the Revolution during this period was thus demonstrably not to foment internal discord or a new French revolution. Rather, they formed part of a patriotic myth that a diverse array of writers combined to create in order to promote widespread unity during a moment of extreme national crisis.

It is tempting to view contemporary activists' ambivalence towards the Revolution in the 1870s and early 1880s as a definitive shift in revolutionary thought and rhetoric. Prompted by the very visible failure of the Commune and the changed political context of the Third Republic, revolutionaries abandoned their previous commitment to 1789 in search of a more appropriate historical genealogy for revolution. These circumstances, as we have seen, undoubtedly contributed towards the intellectual decisions that activists made in this period, yet their attitudes towards the Revolution cannot be attributed entirely to the context. As Blanqui's work suggests, intellectual neutrality on the subject of the Revolution was a continuity of revolutionary thought rather than a significant change. By summer 1871, activists had not sought to systematically define revolution in terms of France's recent history for some time. Rather than a shift in thought, their ambivalence during the 1870s and early 1880s represented the continuation of a pattern. The pattern was simply different from what many historians have assumed.

Activists' belief in the continued valence of revolution as a political action, then, did not derive from the French revolutionary tradition. While revolutionary interactions with French history and the revolutionary tradition were plentiful, they did not take the form that historians have conventionally assumed. Neither were they indicative, as has often been

---

[79] '[R]iche, pauvre, ouvrier, bourgeois . . . Français, vous combattrez. Vous vous dévouerez à la cause universelle, parce qu'il faut que la France soit grande afin que la terre soit affranchie . . . parce qu'il est temps de montrer que la vertu existe, que le devoir existe, et que la patrie existe; et vous ne faiblirez pas . . . et le monde saura par vous que si la diplomatie est lâche, le citoyen est brave; que s'il y a des rois, il y a aussi des peuples, que si le continent monarchique s'éclipse, la République rayonne, et que si, pour l'instant, il n'y a plus d'une Europe, il y a toujours une France.' 'Victor Hugo au peuple français', *L'Electeur libre*, 18 September 1870.

[80] 'En présence de l'ennemi, plus de partis ni de nuances.' 'La patrie en danger', *La Patrie en danger*, 7 September 1870.

suggested, of activists' increasing separation from contemporary national politics. Although they routinely invoked both recent and more distant instances from France's revolutionary past, these texts were largely not concerned with defining revolution. In fact, the majority of activists worked hard to separate revolution as a political action from France's revolutionary past. It was rather the shape of the Third Republic that activists were occupied with in these texts, using France's revolutionary past as a tool to negotiate the shape of the new French state and their place within it.

Yet while this particular interpretation of French history was especially useful in the circumstances that revolutionaries found themselves in during the 1870s and early 1880s, it was not solely a product of them. As an examination of Blanqui's work across multiple decades demonstrates, revolutionaries had been using the French past in this way since at least the fall of the Second Republic. In this respect, revolutionaries during this period were similar to many other radical and moderate republicans: while their ideas and their specific interpretation of French history may have been different, the ways in which they used it were not. Rather than highlighting the differences between revolutionaries and other members of the republican community, in fact their use of French revolutionary history primarily served to demonstrate their similarities.

CHAPTER 4

Rehabilitating Revolution

Revolutionaries during this period accepted that the French Revolution had come to an end. After the failure of 1848 and the Second Republic to bring about lasting or meaningful socio-political change, activists had begun to search for alternatives to the 'revolutionary toolkit' that they had previously relied on. This shift became more pronounced following the establishment of the Third Republic and the fall of the Paris Commune. The political events of the 1870s decisively reformulated the revolutionary question, rendering traditional revolutionary action and violence against the state neither practicable nor desirable – including, sometimes, to revolutionaries themselves.

Yet although revolutionary activists accepted that the Revolution had come to an end and took pragmatic steps to deal with this, they did not give up on the concept of revolutionary action entirely. Rather, activists during this period continued to believe that revolutionary action was very much still a viable political concept that was capable of expanding its appeal. Although the Revolution may have ended in 1871, this was not the only context in which activists conceptualised revolution. Their continued commitment to revolutionary action was to be found in these other contexts, namely religion and nature. Scholars have devoted considerable attention to these languages or definitions of revolution in the earlier nineteenth century, particularly the idea of revolution as a substitute for religion.[1] Whether as a result of the shifting political circumstances or the tight historiographical focus on the French tradition, however, their presence in the period after 1870 has been largely overlooked.

---

[1] See, for example. E. Berenson, *Populist Religion and Left-Wing Politics in France, 1830–1852* (Princeton, NJ: Princeton University Press, 1984); G. Stedman Jones, 'Religion and the Origins of Socialism', in I. Katznelson and G. Stedman Jones (eds.), *Religion and the Political Imagination* (Cambridge: Cambridge University Press, 2010), 171–189.

This chapter seeks to fill this historiographical lacuna. Far from being inconsequential, it argues that these contexts are crucial to understanding the ways in which activists conceived of revolution during this period. It demonstrates that activists sought out a variety of different languages and temporalities in an effort to broaden and rejuvenate their appeal following the fall of the Commune, defining revolution variously as a religious or transcendent experience and as a natural phenomenon. By defining revolution as a flexible and expansive phenomenon, activists hoped to demonstrate their attentiveness to the problems that 1871 had highlighted, both broadening their appeal and attracting new supporters, as well as satisfying convinced revolutionaries. Both of these languages of revolution and social change dated back to the mid-nineteenth century, and in drawing upon them, activists exposed their connections to both earlier radicals and their more moderate republican contemporaries. Yet while the languages of revolution that activists drew upon had not changed, both the circumstances and the ways in which they used them had, and they produced unintended effects and varied success.

The chapter is divided into two parts. The first part explores revolutionaries' attempts to expand their appeal outwards from Paris and regional cities to the French countryside by characterising revolution as a religious experience. This experiment ultimately ended in failure. Yet the willingness of increasingly atheistic revolutionaries to resurrect religious rhetoric demonstrated both their commitment to acquiring new support and their continued belief that revolution could be a viable political programme. The second part of the chapter discusses the definition of revolution as resulting from natural evolution rather than subjective will. It suggests that by presenting revolution in these terms, activists aimed to minimise the importance of their own recent failures, but more importantly to redefine revolution as the practice of everyday life. In the changed circumstances of the Third Republic, they believed, this broader revolution would be more accessible, appealing, and effective than traditional forms of action.

This chapter casts a wider net in terms of sources, broadening the scope out from those traditionally used to examine revolution. The 1870s and early 1880s saw revolutionaries such as the geographer Élisée Reclus deliver various public lectures on relevant subjects.[2] The chapter draws heavily upon the transcripts of these, as well as reactions to them in the

---

[2] É. Reclus, *La nouvelle géographie: la terre et les hommes*, 19 vols. (Paris: Hachette, 1876–1894); É. Reclus, *Évolution et révolution: conférence faite à Genève, le 5 mars 1880* (Geneva: Imprimerie jurassienne, 1880).

revolutionary press. In addition to works intended for a primarily revolutionary audience, the chapter also takes into account literature intended for wider dissemination, including pamphlets on revolution smuggled into France during the 1870s to the various newspapers established by revolutionaries outside Paris in the 1880s.[3]

I

In discussions of revolution after the events of 1871, religion played a prominent role. Descriptions of revolution in religious terms spanned the entire period and beyond, and could be found in the work of a diverse array of revolutionaries, from Blanquists to socialists from various groupings.[4] Immediately after the Commune's fall, for example, Jules Bergeret attempted to comfort readers of his pamphlet *Le 18 mars* by assuring them that acts of revolution, even if unsuccessful, were 'a sacred duty',[5] while Louis Auguste Blanqui likewise guaranteed in 1872 that revolution would bring salvation.[6] This religious lexicon, furthermore, covered every possible part of the revolutionary experience, with activists using it to condemn the revolution's enemies,[7] to contest disputes internal to the revolutionary movement,[8] and also to describe revolutionary life.[9] French revolutionary history, then, was not the only context in which activists discussed the idea

---

[3] For example, F. Pyat, *Lettre au peuple de Lyon* (London: *Courrier révolutionnaire*, 1875); A. Rocher, *La vie du Citoyen Jésus-Christ par le Citoyen Satan* (Geneva: Imprimerie V. Blanchard, 1875); *L'Émancipation* (Lyons, October–November 1880).

[4] *L'Ouvrier de l'avenir, organe des chambres syndicales et des associations ouvrieres* (Paris), 12 March 1871; H. Brissac, *Quand j'étais au bagne: poésies* (Paris: Derveaux, 1887), pp.v–vi.

[5] '[U]n devoir sacré'. J. Bergeret, *Le 18 mars: journal hebdomadaire* (London and Brussels, 1871), p.66.

[6] L.A. Blanqui, *L'éternité par les astres* (ed.) L. Block de Behar (Geneva: Éditions Slatkine, 2009. First published, 1872), p.114. See also É. Reclus, *Évolution et Révolution*, 6th edn (Paris: Imprimerie Habert, 1891. First published, 1880), p.47; 'Toast de L.-A. Blanqui au banquet des travailleurs socialistes (2 décembre 1848)', in L.A. Blanqui, *Œuvres complètes*, 2 vols. (ed.) A. Münster (Paris: Editions Galilée, 1977), vol.1, 217–228, at p.219.

[7] 'La contagion cléricale', *L'Intransigeant* (Paris), 30 July 1880; H. Rochefort, 'Capitulation', *L'Intransigeant*, 31 July 1880; H. Rochefort, 'Persécuteurs et persécutés', *L'Intransigeant*, 4 August 1880; H. Rochefort, 'Tout pour Belleville', *L'Intransigeant*, 23 April 1881.

[8] 'Les combles marxistes', *Le Prolétaire* (Paris), 7 October 1882. See also 'Pourquoi nous faisons une enquête?', *La Fédération* (London), 21 September 1872; 'Un candidat impossible', *Le Prolétaire*, 10 February 1883; 'Loriquet marxiste', *Le Prolétaire*, 29 December 1883; V. Marouck, 'Révolution – "Rrrrévolution!"', *Le Prolétariat* (Paris), 24 January 1885; 'Les Dangers prochains', *La Bataille* (Paris), 13 May 1885; B. Malon, *Le troisième défaite du prolétariat français* (Neuchâtel: G. Guillaume Fils, 1871), p.532; P. Brousse, *Le marxisme dans l'Internationale* (Paris: Imprimerie Nouvelle, 1882), p.8; J. Guesde, *Services publics et socialisme* (Bordeaux: Imprimerie E. Forastié, 1883), p.9.

[9] B. Malon, *Précis historique, théorique et pratique du socialisme* (Paris: Félix Alcan, 1892), p.iv.

of revolution, and in its place, many activists turned to the divine, reconceptualising revolution as a transcendent or religious experience.

The justification of revolution by faith had long been a prominent feature of revolutionary and radical thought in Europe.[10] In France, the relationship between the Revolution and the Catholic Church had historically been one of open hostility, characterised by strict sanctions upon religious property and personnel, and sporadic counter-revolutionary uprisings. During the 1830s and 1840s, however, some of this antagonism subsided, and revolutionaries came to enjoy increasingly cordial relations with liberal religious figures such as Félicité de Lamennais, the pioneer of 'social Catholicism'. This new spirit of rapprochement found particular expression in the thought of early socialists such as Henri de Saint-Simon and Charles Fourier, and in 1846, Étienne Cabet even claimed that socialism was 'the true Christianity'.[11]

Such rhetoric was exported into national politics in the late 1840s. As Edward Berenson has demonstrated in *Populist Religion and Left-Wing Politics in France*, many sought to present 'the world in terms of Christian moral principles' in order to bridge the political gap between themselves and the rest of France.[12] Religious language was particularly popular amongst radicals during the 1848 revolutions, and indeed as late as 1849 many revolutionaries professed themselves 'full of hope' about the Catholic Church.[13] In characterising revolution as a religious rather than an exclusively political or social experience, revolutionaries in the years after the Commune were thus not unusual. Rather, they drew upon an established and widely recognised trope of French radical thought.

Yet while revolutionaries in the post-Commune period regularly used religious language and analogies, there appeared to be little internal intellectual or linguistic consistency. Comparisons of the proletariat's suffering to that of Christ provide a particularly clear example of this. In his 1880 work *Le droit à la paresse*, for example, Paul Lafargue explicitly

---

[10] See C. Clark, 'From 1848 to Christian Democracy', in Katznelson and Stedman Jones (eds.), *Religion and the Political Imagination*, 190–213; J. Beecher, *Victor Considerant and the Rise and Fall of French Romantic Socialism* (Berkeley: University of California Press, 2001).

[11] J. Jennings, *Revolution and the Republic: A History of Political Thought in France since the Eighteenth Century* (Oxford: Oxford University Press, 2011), p.399. See É. Cabet, *Le vrai Christianisme suivant Jésus-Christ* (Paris: Au bureau du *Populaire*, 1846). For more on the relationship between socialism and religion, see Stedman Jones, 'Religion and the Origins of Socialism', 171–189.

[12] For more on radical and revolutionary uses of religion in the 1830s and 1840s, see Berenson, *Populist Religion and Left-Wing Politics in France*, p.xx.

[13] Clark, 'From 1848 to Christian Democracy', at p.191. Other activists such as Proudhon also frequently referred to revolution in moral terms. See K.S. Vincent, *Pierre-Joseph Proudhon and the Rise of French Republican Socialism* (Oxford: Oxford University Press, 1984), p.6.

compared contemporary workers to Jesus, describing their struggle for equality as a 'hard Calvary of pain'.[14] Only a year later, however, his colleague Jules Guesde used the same reference for a wholly different purpose, criticising what he saw as Léon Gambetta's messianic tendencies by describing him as 'Gambetta of Nazareth' and 'the Christ of Cahors'.[15]

Revolutionary uses of religion during this period were thus at once familiar and noticeably different from those of the 1830s and 1840s. The Christian socialists of earlier decades and the *démoc-socs* during the Second Republic had worked hard to present their ideas in the form of genuine religious principles and sustained analogies. During the 1870s and early 1880s, by contrast, revolutionaries were less intellectually consistent, less committed to precise analogies, and indeed often contradicted themselves. While drawing upon a long tradition, revolutionary uses of religion were thus qualitatively, if not quantitatively, different from those of earlier decades.

II

Revolutionaries' use of religion was particularly remarkable given the degeneration of the relationship between revolutionaries and religion since the early 1850s. It was in this period that, as Chris Clark has demonstrated, a coherent clericalism that 'did not simply rearticulate Catholic theological and moral positions but defended the church – under papal authority – as a social institution' emerged.[16] In France, this revival was inadvertently sparked by the Second Republic itself, whose relaxation of press restrictions enabled Catholics to print and publish content on a large scale for the first time in years. The Second Empire took up the cause of this resurgent clericalism and sought, like the first Napoleon, to heal the fractious relationship between the Church and the French state. These trends were exemplified by legislation such as the 1850–1851 *loi Falloux*,

---

[14] '[L]e dur calvaire de la douleur'. P. Lafargue, *Le droit à la paresse: réfutation du 'droit au travail' de 1848* (Paris: Henry Oriol, 1883. First published, 1880), p.49. See also Bergeret, *Le 18 mars*, p.72. Other authors placed themselves in the role of the devil. See, for example, Rocher, *La vie du Citoyen Jésus-Christ par le Citoyen Satan*; Méphisto, *Le diable rouge* (Paris), 23 September–15 November 1879.

[15] J. Guesde, 'Les sauveurs de la bourgeoisie', *Le Citoyen* (Paris), 31 January 1882. See also G. Lefrançais, *République et Révolution: de l'attitude à prendre par le prolétariat en présence des partis politiques* (Geneva: Imprimerie Ve Blanchard, 1873), p.18; P. Brousse, *Le suffrage universel et le problème de la souveraineté du peuple* (Geneva: Imprimerie Coopérative, 1874), p.11.

[16] Clark, 'From 1848 to Christian Democracy', at p.195.

which promoted the provision of Catholic primary education. [17] Whereas prior to 1848 many in the Church in France had experimented with relatively liberal intellectual positions, after the revolution this changed. The Church emerged from the 1840s less flexible, more cohesive, and more confident, while under the Second Empire, both its power and its presence in French public life grew exponentially.

Unsurprisingly, in these circumstances, the relationship between revolutionaries and the Church soured. Faced with this resurgent clericalism, revolutionaries and radicals abandoned their previous attachment to religion en masse. In its place, many returned to the Revolution's secularising roots and became involved in the Free Thought Movement, which sprung up across Europe and North America in the mid-nineteenth century. This new, hardened attitude towards the Church would later be reflected in the Commune's legislation. Reflecting both their commitment to Free Thought and their opposition to the Second Empire's proximity to the Church, the Commune passed a raft of secularising legislation, including the provision of universal secular education and the separation of church and state. [18]

Although the Communards' laws were thrown out following their defeat, revolutionaries maintained their connections to Free Thought. [19] Louis Barron, for example, wrote in 1880 that Communards deported to New Caledonia continued to affirm their commitment to Free Thought even 'in their hour of death and under the menace and insinuations of the priest', [20] while revolutionaries such as Paul Brousse and Louise Michel continued to attend Free Thought meetings in Paris well into the 1880s.

[17] For more on the *loi Falloux* and education in France under the Second Empire, see R.D. Anderson, *Education in France, 1848–1870* (Oxford: Clarendon Press, 1975).

[18] For more on the importance of secularisation during the Commune, see R.P. Tombs, *Paris, bivouac des révolutions: la Commune de 1871* (Paris: Éditions Libertalia, 2014. First published in English, 1999), p.205.

[19] See, for example, Intelligence reports to the Préfecture de Police, March 1877 (London). Archives de la Préfecture de Police (APP) Ba429/2152 and 2156; Advertisement, 'Dr. A. Regnard will deliver a lecture (in French) on "l'athéisme" on Friday March 23, 1877' (London). APP Ba429/2157; P.-O. Lissagaray quoted in an intelligence report to the Préfecture de Police. 1 December 1877 (London). APP Ba429/2494; E. Lebeau, *Périssent dieu et la prêtraille!* (Geneva: Imprimerie coopérative, 1872), p.11; 'Qui nous sommes', *Le Prolétaire*, 23 November 1878; 'De l'instruction religieuse', *Le Prolétaire*, 16 August 1879; Groupe d'études sociales de Bordeaux, 'Matérialisme et libre pensée', *Le Prolétaire*, 12 June 1880; M. Talmeyr, 'L'arbre qu'on n'arrachera pas', *L'Intransigeant*, 12 April 1881; E. Massard, 'La bourgeoisie et le patriotisme', *Le Citoyen*, 25 September 1882.

[20] 'La société de la presqu'ile Ducos, celle de l'ile des Pins étaient des sociétés de libres-penseurs, d'athées, assez convaincus pour affirmer, même au moment de mourir, sous la menace et l'insinuation du prétre, leur négation de l'absolu divin.' Quoted in L. Barron, 'La déportation et les déportés, 1871–1880', *La philosophie positive* (July–August 1880), 41–66, at p.45.

Blanquists, meanwhile, celebrated their rejection of the Church with secular fêtes, at which *L'Intransigeant* recorded Henri Rochefort performing several 'civil baptisms'.[21] Revolutionaries' and radicals' attitude towards religion thus significantly changed between 1848 and 1871. Whereas the religious terminology of the 1840s reflected a genuine willingness and desire amongst radicals to cooperate with Catholics, and even the Catholic Church, during the early Third Republic this was certainly not the case.

In fact, revolutionary opposition to religion became increasingly pronounced over the course of this period. This derived partly from the unabashed Catholicism of many of the Royalist politicians who ruled France in the early 1870s and in 1875, for example, permitted the Church to establish universities.[22] It received another boost with the secularising legislation passed by the Opportunists in the early 1880s, such as the 1881–1882 *lois Ferry*, which partially repealed the *loi Falloux* and mandated the provision of universal, secular primary education.[23] In doing so, the government met a demand that had long been central to revolutionary thought, and this had a notable impact upon activists' rhetoric. While some continued to engage in familiar anticlerical battles,[24] during the debate and promulgation of the *lois Ferry* many also began to declare themselves opposed to all religions, faiths, and rituals.[25] In 1883, for example, the Marxist journalist Gabriel Deville criticised the Free Thought Movement and their rituals as simply another form of religion, writing disparagingly of

[21] For Free Thought meetings, see J. Lalouette, *La Libre Pensée en France 1848–1940* (Paris: Éditions Albin Michel, 1997), pp.55–56. For civil baptisms, see 'Fête de la libre-pensée', *L'Intransigeant*, 9 August 1881.

[22] R.P. Tombs, *France 1814–1914* (London: Routledge, 1996), p.17; p.138.

[23] For more on education provision and the Third Republic, see M. Ozouf, *L'école, l'église et la République 1871–1914* (Paris: Éditions Cana, 1982).

[24] 'La contagion cléricale', *L'Intransigeant*, 30 July 1880; H. Rochefort, 'Capitulation', *L'Intransigeant*, 31 July 1880; H. Rochefort, 'Persécuteurs et persécutés', *L'Intransigeant*, 4 August 1880; 'Un état catholique: la Nouvelle France', *L'Intransigeant*, 26 December 1880; H. Rochefort, 'Tout pour Belleville', *L'Intransigeant*, 23 April 1881; 'Les religieuses et leur emploi industriel', *L'Émancipation*, 17 November 1880; P. Brousse, 'L'Église et l'État', *Le Prolétariat*, 29 August 1885; P. Brousse, 'De l'enseignement public', *Le Prolétariat*, 5 September 1885; P. Brousse, 'Sus à l'Église!', *Le Prolétariat*, 13 November 1885.

[25] H. Rochefort, 'L'enlèvement des crucifix', *L'Intransigeant*, 23 December 1880; A. Crié, 'Conversion inutile', *Le Citoyen & La Bataille* (Paris), 6 December 1882.

Our noisy anti-clericals, ridiculous amateurs with civil baptisms and other rites, who imagine that they are detaching civil society from all mystical and mystifying attachment by eating an *andouillette* on Good Friday.[26]

While it is possible, even likely, that sections of the revolutionary movement had always held these views, during this period they began to promote their unqualified opposition to faith and belief more stridently. In particular, many activists were opposed to the traditional connection of revolution with religion. In 1870, Blanqui described 'religious *tartuferie*' as 'the most infernal of all' vices, promising that it would be eliminated in a future society,[27] and even revolutionaries interested in religion expressed concerns about connecting the two. Benoît Malon, for example, had devoted several articles in revolutionary almanacs and the *Revue socialiste* to religion and religious morality, yet in 1872 he argued that revolutionaries' use of and belief and religion in 1848 had been one of their greatest failings. 'Everything', he noted disdainfully,

> was drowned in a dire mysticism; France was imagined as the *Christ Nation*, Jesus himself as the *first representative of the people*. They saw progress in *religious unity*, and association was to be at once communist and *communionist*; fraternal and *Eucharistic*.[28]

Revolutionaries, then, left their readers in little doubt about their opinions on describing revolution in religious terms. Not only were they fully aware of the historical connection between the two, but they were also deeply

---

[26] 'Nos bruyants anti-cléricaux, ridicules amateurs de baptêmes civils et austres rites, qui s'imaginent dégager la société civile de toute attaché mystique et mystificatrice en mangeant une andouillette le vendredi saint'. G. Deville (ed.), *Le Capital de Karl Marx* (Paris: Henry Oriol, 1883), pp.41–42. See also G. Deville, 'Rien que le Concordat', *Le Citoyen*, 1 December 1881; P. Lafargue, 'Liberté, Égalité, Fraternité', *L'Égalité* (Paris), 18 August 1880; G. Deville, 'La question religieuse', *L'Égalité*, 11 December 1881; 'L'ordre révolutionnaire', *L'Égalité*, 22 October 1882.

[27] 'Le jugement deviendra l'apanage commun . . . et la tartuferie religieuse, la plus infernale de toutes, ne sera plus qu'un souvenir historique, souvenir d'étonnement et d'horreur'. L.A. Blanqui, 'Le communisme, avenir de la société' (1869–1870), in *Critique sociale*, 173–220, at pp.186–187. See also É. Reclus, *Evolution and Revolution* (London: International Publishing Company, 1885), p.7. Note that a reference to religion and socialism at this point does not appear in French versions of the text until the publication of Reclus's much-extended *L'évolution, la révolution, et l'idéal anarchique* (Paris: P.-V. Stock, 1898), at p.126.

[28] 'Le tout était noyé . . . dans un funeste mysticisme; la France était envisagée comme la *nation-christ*, Jésus lui-même comme le *premier représentant du peuple*; on voyait le progrès dans *l'unité réligieuse*, l'association devait être à la fois communiste et *communioniste*; fraternelle et *eucharistique*'. B. Malon, *Exposé des écoles socialistes françaises* (Paris: Imprimerie de Lagny, 1872), p.230. For examples of Malon's interest in religion, see B. Malon, *L'Almanach du Peuple pour 1873* (Saint Imier: Propagande Socialiste, 1873), p.27; B. Malon, 'Les Morales religieuses', *La revue socialiste* (Paris, 1885), 923–931; 986–1006; 1076–1099. For another example of activists mocking religious revolutionaries, see 'Révolution – "Rrrrévolution!"', *Le Prolétariat*, 24 January 1885.

averse to it. Previous revolutionaries' commitment to religion, they suggested, was more than a weakness. It had been their Achilles' heel.

In *The Man on Devil's Island*, Ruth Harris delineated a complex picture of *fin-de-siècle* France in which spirituality (if not religiosity) permeated a variety of unexpected social groups and *milieux*.[29] The revolutionary movement during the 1870s and early 1880s, however, was not one of these places. Revolutionary uses of religious language to describe revolution, then, did not simply fail to reflect their own beliefs. Rather, such uses were diametrically opposed to revolutionaries' beliefs regarding religion, and this state of affairs became increasingly clear over the course of the period. While the association of revolution with religion was not an unfamiliar one, it thus nonetheless made little sense within the context of the contemporary revolutionary movement. Unlike the Christian socialists and *démoc-socs* of the 1830s and 1840s, revolutionary activists during the early Third Republic neither had faith of their own nor were willing to work with the Church and other religious figures. Rather, they were actively opposed to religious belief, and specifically to the association of revolution with religion. Indeed, it was arguably this opposition that explains the loose character of their work, which used religious terminology to describe revolution, but simultaneously sought to distance it from any systematic religious ideas.

III

Given these attitudes, it is tempting to dismiss activists' uses of religion as unimportant, and they have certainly received only scant scholarly attention.[30] In fact, however, religious comparisons formed a central part of activists' rhetoric on revolution. Revolutionaries, as we have seen, had lost a great deal of support as a result of their actions during the Commune, and the subsequent reprisals had further reduced their numbers. More worrying for many, however, was the realisation that in fact they had never enjoyed any kind of widespread national support. This was especially concerning as France during this period remained largely rural. By 1900, only 20 per cent of the population lived in cities with populations of over

---

[29] R. Harris, *The Man on Devil's Island: Alfred Dreyfus and the Affair that Divided France* (London: Allen Lane, 2010), p.373.

[30] Berenson, for example, mentions Opportunist uses of religious language during this period, but not revolutionaries'. See Berenson, *Populist Religion and Left-Wing Politics in France*, p.230. See also D. Ligou, *Histoire du socialisme en France (1871–1961)* (Paris: Presses Universitaires de France, 1962), p.53.

20,000, and the countryside consequently exercised considerable political power.[31] Indeed, historically, any revolutionary or politician seeking to effect significant political or social change had required the support of the countryside in order to succeed.[32]

Despite issuing numerous appeals for solidarity, only a few other cities had briefly risen up in support of the Commune. The majority of the country, meanwhile, regarded the Communards (not without reason) as authoritarians bent upon imposing Paris's wishes on an unwilling population. This experience had a profound effect upon the ways in which revolutionaries conceived of their place within the French population. The Commune's latent unpopularity forced them – as republicans had been forced after 1848 – to confront the fact that they were not a vanguard acting on behalf of the entire population.[33] Rather, revolutionaries were a small group acting against the wishes of the national majority. As Malon observed in *L'Émancipation* in 1880, '[do] not be deceived ... there are not thousands or even hundreds of men resolved to sacrifice their lives for the Revolution'.[34]

Revolutionaries quickly came to regard this as one of the most serious problems they faced. In 1876, the politician Yves Guyot in *Les Droits de l'homme* argued that the success of revolution hinged upon revolutionaries' ability to broaden their appeal, correctly noting that

> the only revolutions that have succeeded in Paris have been those that were organised by everyone, provoked by a feeling of general indignation, and received ratification in the whole of France beforehand.[35]

Several years later, the Blanquist Alphonse Humbert likewise impressed upon readers of *L'Intransigeant* the importance of appealing 'not just [to]

---

[31] L. Page Moch, *Moving Europeans: Migration in Western Europe since 1650* (Bloomington: Indiana University Press, 1992), p.127.

[32] Tombs, *France 1814–1914*, p.25.

[33] For more on republicans and 1848, see Jules Ferry quoted in C. Gaboriaux, *La République en quête des citoyens: les républicains français face au bonapartisme rural (1848–1880)* (Paris: Presses de la Fondation Nationale des Sciences Politiques, 2010), p.135. For more republican and liberal attempts to broaden their appeal during the Second Empire, see S. Hazareeisngh, *From Subject to Citizen: The Second Empire and the Emergence of Modern French Democracy* (Princeton, NJ: Princeton University Press, 1998), pp.301–303.

[34] 'Que nos amis ne s'y trompent pas: dans l'état actuel des choses, ce ne sont pas quelques centaines ou mêmes quelques milliers d'hommes, décidés à sacrifier leur vie pour la Révolution'. B. Malon, 'Une discussion', *L'Émancipation*, 15 November 1880.

[35] '[L]es seules révolutions qui aient réussi à Paris ont été celles qui, organisées par tout le monde, provoquées par un sentiment d'indignation générale, avaient reçu d'avance leur ratification dans toute la France.' Y. Guyot, 'La psychologie du 10 août', *Les droits de l'homme* (Paris), 12 August 1876.

our political co-religionists', but to 'the entire country'.[36] Whereas prior to 1871, revolutionary writers had been more or less content to cater to the ideas and preferences of their traditional core Parisian support base, the Commune's clear lack of widespread appeal prompted a tactical shift. Clearly, the zeal of convinced revolutionaries was not enough on its own. Rather, if revolutionaries aspired to political relevance and success, they had to broaden their geographical focus and win the support of sizeable parts of the French population.

In the years that followed, creating and disseminating a vision of the future that appealed to these audiences became a principal concern of the revolutionary movement. In exile in the 1870s, activists directed considerable effort towards smuggling revolutionary literature and propaganda into areas of France outside of Paris. Various factors facilitated this expansion into the countryside. During the 1860s, the government significantly relaxed restrictions on publishing and selling printed goods, abolishing a licensing system that had outlawed the selling of books outside of cities.[37] New technologies, meanwhile, made mass printing at low prices possible, and improvements in national infrastructure facilitated the transportation of such literature around the country: 17,000 km of railroad were built in 1870 alone.[38] Revolutionaries took full advantage of these changes, particularly in the Midi, and often achieved considerable success.[39]

Following the 1880 general amnesty, revolutionaries sought to consolidate these efforts. Capitalising on the boom in the regional newspaper market that had taken place since 1860, activists established a number of regional newspapers,[40] to which many celebrated revolutionary theorists contributed articles.[41] The famed Blanquist Édouard Vaillant returned to

---

[36] 'Ce ne sont pas seulement leurs [the orators of the socialist party] coreligionnaires politiques qui les en doivent féliciter ... c'est la patrie tout entière.' A. Humbert, 'Avènement du socialisme', *L'Intransigeant*, 11 March 1882. See also 'Réunions socialistes publiques' (London, 1878). APP Ba430/3502.

[37] F. Barbier, 'The publishing industry and printed output in nineteenth-century France', in K.E. Carpenter (ed.), *Books and Society in History: Papers of the Association of College and Research Libraries Rare Books and Manuscripts Preconference* (New York: R.R. Bowker Company, 1983), 199–230, at p.221.

[38] For new technologies, see C. Bellanger, *Histoire générale de la presse française*, 5 vols. (Paris: Presses universitaires de France, 1969–1976), vol.3 (1972), p.140. For transport, see Barbier, 'The Publishing Industry and Printed Output in Nineteenth-Century France', at p.201.

[39] A. Dowdall, 'Narrating *la Semaine Sanglante*, 1871–1880' (unpublished MPhil dissertation, University of Cambridge, 2010), pp.14–20.

[40] Bellanger, *Histoire générale de la presse française*, vol.2 (1969), p.318.

[41] See, for example, *Le Forçat* (Lille); *L'Exploité* (Nantes); *L'Émancipation*; 91: P. Lafargue to F. Engels, 7 January 1884 (Paris), in Engels, P. and L. Lafargue, *Correspondence*, vol.1, 162–164, at p.163.

his hometown of Vierzon in the centre of France in order to oversee his,[42] while in 1880 Malon informed Paul Lafargue that 'you will never see me in Paris, but always in the breach in the provinces'.[43] Revolutionaries during this period, then, did more than simply recognise the catastrophic effects of the Commune's (and their own) lack of broad national appeal. They also actively attempted to rectify the situation, implementing a variety of practical measures, from smuggling propaganda to establishing newspapers aimed, in the words of *Le Prolétaire*, at unifying 'the workers of the towns and the countryside'.[44]

Religion was central to these efforts. In 1882, the journalist and playwright Lucien-Victor Meunier in *Le Citoyen & La Bataille* observed that '[t]he country is Catholic – very Catholic.'[45] In the 1876 French census over 98 per cent of the population remained listed as Catholics and, although a proportion of this percentage were likely lapsed, Meunier was not wrong.[46] Construction projects such as the Sacré-Coeur Basilica – begun in 1875 and funded partly by public subscription – indicated the continued strength of Catholic feeling (and indeed the strength of opposition to revolution; the Sacré-Coeur was conceived of partly as expiation for the Commune).[47] Likewise, 1871 saw the establishment of the Cercles Ouvriers, a corporatist Catholic workers' association that by 1900 contained more members than all of France's socialist parties put together.[48] While this period was notable for the introduction of various secularising

---

[42] For the Blanquists, see P. Hutton, *The Cult of the Revolutionary Tradition: The Blanquists in French Politics, 1864–1893* (Berkeley: University of California Press, 1981), p.133.

[43] 'Si je rentre en France et si ma santé le permet, je vous promets qu'on ne me verra guère à Paris, mais toujours sur la brèche en province'. 10: Benoît Malon to Paul Lafargue, 18 May 1880 (Zurich), in E. Bottigelli and C. Willard (eds.), *La naissance du Parti ouvrier français: Correspondance inédite de Paul Lafargue, Jules Guesde, José Mesa, Paul Brousse, Benoît Malon, Gabriel Deville, Victor Jaclard, Léon Camescasse et Friedrich Engels* (Paris: Editions Sociales, 1981), 74–80, at p.76. See also A. Theisz, 'Le Congrès ouvrier du Havre', *L'Intransigeant*, 22 November 1880.

[44] 'Notre ligne de conduite', *Le Prolétaire*, 23 November 1878. See also J. Andrieu, 'The Paris Commune: A Chapter towards Its Theory and History', in *The Fortnightly Review*, vol.X (October 1871), 571–598, at p.581; A. Arnould, *L'État et la Révolution* (Lyons: Éditions Jacques-Marie Laffont et Associés, 1981. First published, 1877), p.105; É. Reclus, *Ouvrier, prends la machine! Prends la terre, paysan!* (Geneva: Éditions du *Révolté*, 1880); 'Notre ligne de conduite', *Le Prolétaire*, 23 November 1878; 'Les paysans et la révolution sociale', *Le Prolétaire*, 5 February 1881; P. Dervillers, 'La lutte de classe', *Le Prolétaire*, 25 December 1880.

[45] 'Le pays est catholique, très catholique'. L.-V. Meunier, 'Beautés du cléricalisme', *Le Citoyen & La Bataille*, 6 December 1882.

[46] Jennings, *Revolution and the Republic*, p.323.

[47] For more on the construction of the Sacré-Coeur, see D. Harvey, 'Monument and Myth', *Annals of the Association of American Geographers* 69 (September 1979), 362–381.

[48] Tombs, *France 1814–1914*, p.66.

laws, nonetheless there remained considerable strength of religious feeling amongst much of the population.

Even less devout citizens remained familiar with the Church's teachings. Pro-Catholic legislation such as the *loi Falloux*, which remained in place until 1880, ensured that a wide cross-section of the population during this period was educated by the Church. The number of pupils in school totalled 4.7 million in 1877 (a significant increase from the 2.9 million of 1840),[49] and in the mid-1870s, 30 per cent of boys and 70 per cent of girls in secondary education attended schools run by religious orders.[50] Despite the increasing acceptance of anticlericalism, religion, and especially Catholicism, thus continued to play a central role in French public and cultural life during the early Third Republic, even affecting the lives of citizens who professed no religious affiliation.

Revolutionaries were well aware of this.[51] By describing revolution in terms of religion, they hoped to appeal to broad and previously hostile swathes of the population. Authors of pamphlets that employed such language, such as *La vie du citoyen Jésus-Christ*, often explicitly stated that they were writing for religious audiences.[52] This tactic, revolutionaries hoped, would be especially useful in the countryside and amongst women, where they suspected religious feeling was particularly strong. Descriptions of revolution as a form of religion accordingly appeared particularly in literature bound for the provinces.[53] Revolutionary uses of religious language during this period thus had two interlinked aims. Firstly, by drawing upon familiar religious tropes and imagery, revolutionaries hoped to increase their national support, by reaching out to large sections of the population – especially in rural areas – that in 1871 had been hostile to their actions. Simultaneously, in the process of appropriating religious language in this way, activists also hoped to begin to neutralise the power of the Catholic Church, which they regarded as a powerful antagonist to

---

[49] Barbier, 'The Publishing Industry and Printed Output in Nineteenth-Century France', at p.201.
[50] Tombs, *France 1814–1914*, p.138.
[51] *Le Père Duchêne*, 2 June 1878 (Sèvres). See also E. Lebeau, *Périssent dieu et la prêtraille!* (Geneva: Imprimerie coopérative, 1873), p.1; Malon, *Exposé des écoles socialistes françaises*, p.230; A. Humbert, 'Tous cléricaux!', *L'Intransigeant*, 7 July 1881.
[52] Rocher, *La vie du citoyen Jésus-Christ par le citoyen Satan*, p.2.
[53] L.-V. Meunier, 'Beautés du cléricalisme', *Le Citoyen & La Bataille*, 6 December 1882. See also 'La contagion cléricale', *L'Intransigeant*, 30 July 1880; G. Deville, 'Religions et socialisme', *Le Citoyen*, 17 October 1881; G. Deville, 'Libre-pensée et socialisme', *Le Citoyen*, 5 April 1882; P.-O. Lissagaray, 'Prêtres filles', *Le Citoyen & La Bataille*, 26 December 1882; L.-V. Meunier, 'Petits papiers religieux', *Le Citoyen & La Bataille*, 4 April 1883.

revolution and social change. They sought, in other words, to replace the power of the priest with the power of revolution.

Despite their own aversion to it, religion was thus central to activists' thought on revolution during this period. Revolutionaries did not simply give up and turn inward upon themselves in the wake of the Commune. Rather, they continued to believe that revolutionary action was a viable political concept, responding to their failures in 1871 by considerably adapting both their tactics and their rhetoric on revolution in an effort to broaden their appeal. The use of religious language, they hoped, would demonstrate the scale of their belief in revolution, the intellectual compromises that they were willing to make for it, and their commitment to representing the views of the entire country. In terms of motivation, then, the revolutionaries of the 1870s and 1880s were in fact remarkably similar to the radicals and revolutionaries of the pre-1848 period. While their approach to and execution of religious characterisations of revolution differed considerably, the principal aim of the *démoc-socs* and post-Commune activists – to create a revolution capable of uniting the entire country – was broadly the same.

IV

While the aims of these revolutionaries may have been similar, the circumstances were vastly different. Rather than simply a return to the past, the Catholic revival of the 1850s and 1860s was, as Clark has observed, an extremely modern operation.[54] In France, the character of modern Catholic belief was perhaps best exemplified by the phenomenal success of Ernest Renan's 1863 *Vie de Jésus*, which depicted Jesus as a charismatic mortal rather than the Son of God and rejected the miracles of the Gospel.[55] Although the *Vie de Jésus* was censured by the Church, it nonetheless proved wildly popular. It quickly ran to eleven editions, and Renan continued to receive rapturous correspondence about it until his death in 1892.[56]

As Robert Priest has persuasively argued, occurrences such as the success of Renan's book delineate a complex and multifaceted picture of French

[54] Clark, 'From 1848 to Christian Democracy', at p.200.
[55] E. Renan, *Vie de Jésus* (Paris: Michel Lévy Frères, 1863).
[56] For the editions, see Jennings, *Revolution and the Republic*, p.371. For the correspondence and continued interest in the *Vie de Jésus*, see R.D. Priest, 'Reading, Writing, and Religion in Nineteenth-Century France: The Popular Reception of Renan's *Life of Jesus*', *Journal of Modern History* 86 (June 2014), 258–294.

Catholicism and religious belief in the second half of the nineteenth century. While under the Second Empire, the Church became progressively more powerful and didactic, at the same time French men and women were also increasingly 'prepared to look outside the traditional religious channels' in order to satisfy their spiritual needs.[57] Perhaps partly as a result of the success of the Second Empire's own educational reforms, from the 1850s onwards, many French citizens were more curious and independent in their religious belief and possessed a more sophisticated understanding of their own faith.

Revolutionary uses of religion during this period were thus based upon a fundamental misunderstanding of the nature of religious belief. Where revolutionaries conceived of religious citizens as slavish, homogenous devotees in need of enlightenment, in fact this was far from the case. They were ignorant not only of the significant geographical differences in religious practice across France, but also of the profound ways in which religious engagement had changed over the past few decades.[58] Religious belief, in other words, bore little resemblance to revolutionaries' perception of it.

The success of revolutionaries' efforts to broaden their appeal was consequently extremely limited. Many of the regional newspapers launched during this period failed to attract sustained readerships, and closed almost as swiftly as they had opened. Even Malon's Lyons-based *L'Émancipation*, which received substantial financial backing from Paris, folded after only a month. This failure was further reflected in poor electoral results outside of Paris;[59] indeed some revolutionaries were not just unable to accrue support, but actively repelled it. Jules Guesde's unpopularity was such, for example, that he was advised to abandon a proposed speaking tour of the Midi.[60] Although revolutionaries made a concerted effort to reach out to the countryside during this period, then, this effort was largely in vain. Actively and vocally disinterested in religion themselves, revolutionaries were either unable or unwilling to perceive the subtle shifts that had taken place in French religious thought and practice

---

[57] Priest, 'Reading, Writing, and Religion in Nineteenth-Century France', at p.292.
[58] For differences in religious practice, see Tombs, *France 1814–1914*, p.242.
[59] D. Stafford, *From Anarchism to Reformism: A Study of the Political Activities of Paul Brousse within the First International and the French Socialist Movement 1870–1890* (London: Cox & Wyman, 1971), p.204. See also R. Stuart, *Marxism at Work: Ideology, Class and French Socialism during the Third Republic* (Cambridge: Cambridge University Press, 1992), p.36.
[60] Stafford, *From Anarchism to Reformism*, pp.166–167. See also 23: Paul Brousse to Paul Lafargue, 24 April 1881 (Paris), in Bottigelli and Willard, *La naissance du Parti ouvrier français*, 111–113, at pp.112–113.

since 1848.[61] As a result, their use of religious language failed to reflect either the interests or the character of those to whom they were attempting to appeal.

This treatment of religion, moreover, was reflective of a broader lack of interest in France outside of Paris. Revolutionaries' regional newspapers, for example, rarely made an effort to engage with local issues, and often simply reprinted pieces prepared for the Parisian local press.[62] Articles on the rest of the country in Parisian newspapers, meanwhile, were few and far between, and many titles devoted more coverage to international issues than to the rest of France.[63] Indeed, in 1884, Henri Rochefort joked that 'the French only know geography by reputation'.[64] Other revolutionaries went further, and actively disparaged the countryside. In *Le 18 mars*, for example, Bergeret complained that

> the provinces [la province] bleat, wail, and screech; the provinces make the sign of the cross and go to sleep when the sun sets. The provinces have the sickness of potatoes: they are rotten from the roots.[65]

Activists theoretically recognised that broadening their support base (in other words, appealing to the countryside) was vital to the future well-being of revolution, and invested heavily in producing ideas and literature that they hoped would do so. At the same time, however, they remained fundamentally incurious about France outside of Paris, and this was reflected in the work they produced.

This palpable lack of interest, moreover, was visible across the entire revolutionary movement. Groups such as the Guesdists and the Blanquists had never invested significant time or effort in appealing to the country-side, a reflection of their belief in the need for a strong, centralised revolutionary state.[66] Possibilists and federalists, however, had placed

[61] Clark has suggested that this was also the case in the 1850s and 1860s. Clark, 'From 1848 to Christian Democracy', at p.200.

[62] Hutton, *The Cult of the Revolutionary Tradition*, p.134.

[63] For examples, see 'Correspondances: France', *Le Travailleur* 2:4 (Geneva) (April–May 1878), p.20; 'L'esprit républicain dans les campagnes', *Le Prolétaire*, 18 January 1879; 'Lettre d'un paysan', *Le Prolétaire*, 31 May 1879; series entitled 'Lettres d'un travailleur sur le mouvement ouvrier en province', *Le Prolétaire*, beginning 31 July 1880.

[64] 'Nous savons que les Français ne connaissent guère la géographie que de réputation'. H. Rochefort, 'Autre mensonge!', *L'Intransigeant*, 19 March 1884.

[65] '[L]a province bêle, miaule et piaille; la province fait le signe de la croix et se couche à la tombée du jour. La province a la maladie des pommes de terre: elle se gâte par la racine.' Bergeret, *Le 18 mars*, p.4. See also Blanqui, *Critique sociale*, p.202.

[66] See, for example, Deville, *Le Capital de Karl Marx*, p.15; 'Le collectivisme et la production agricole', *L'Égalité*, 23 December 1877; A. Theisz, 'Le mouvement social: la grève des mineurs de Denain', *L'Intransigeant*, 1 November 1880; 'La situation des communes', *Le Citoyen*, 20 April 1882; 193:

divestment from a centralised state at the centre of their political strategy both before and after the Commune.[67] Even many of these activists, though, displayed little genuine interest in the countryside. In *L'État et la Révolution*, Arhur Arnould, for example, expressed regret that 'all of France's large cities, all of its intelligent and revolutionary centres', had been 'obliged to tread water because there are 20 million farmers who have no idea of politics or society'.[68] Distaste for the wider French population, and for beliefs that did not align with those of the revolutionary movement, was not simply restricted to the work of those vocally uninterested in them, but rather lay at the heart of a broad range of revolutionary publications and ideas.

The relationship between socialism, revolution, and religion in French thought during the nineteenth century is a well-studied one. This scholarly attention, however, has tended to end with the defeat of 1848 and the clerical revival of the 1850s. As this section has demonstrated, though, such language underwent a pronounced revival during the 1870s and early 1880s as revolutionaries sought to redress the mistakes they had made during the Commune and broaden their national support base. From activists' commitment to accruing new support, we may infer that they remained committed to the idea of revolution as a viable political concept. The manner in which they went about it, moreover, demonstrated that revolutionaries were willing to significantly compromise their own beliefs in order to guarantee its survival. While the revolutionary movement may practically have remained a largely urban phenomenon, this was not for want of trying.

Simultaneously, however, the details of revolutionaries' religious language also exposed the limits of these ventures. They were appealing to a vision of the countryside that was, to quote Robert Stuart, based 'upon hope rather than theoretical or empirical insight'.[69] In characterising the

---

F. Engels to P. Lafargue (30 October 1882, London), in K. Marx and F. Engels, *Marx/Engels Collected Works* (trans.) R. Dixon et al., 50 vols. (London: Lawrence and Wishart, 1975–2004), vol.46 (1992), 351–352, at p.352.

[67] See for example P. Brousse, 'Liberté et égalité', *L'Émancipation*, 3 November 1880; P. Dervillers, 'La lutte de classe', *Le Prolétaire*, 25 December 1880; *Le Prolétaire*, 24 November 1883.

[68] 'C'est l'histoire de toutes les grandes villes de France, de tous les centres intelligents et révolutionnaires, obligés de marquer le pas sur la place, parce qu'il y a vingt millions de paysans qui n'ont encore aucune idée politique ou sociale.' Arnould, *L'État et la Révolution*, pp.129–130. See also Brousse, *Le Suffrage universel*, p.15; G. Lefrançais, *L'Idée libertaire dans la Commune de 1871* (Cahiers de contre-courant 66, April 1958. First published, 1874), p.17; A. Arnould, *Histoire populaire et parlementaire de la Commune de Paris*, 3 vols. (Brussels: Imprimerie A. Lefevre, 1878), vol.3, p.155.

[69] Stuart, *Marxism at Work*, p.400.

countryside as a reactionary, religious monolith revolutionaries exposed their inability to overcome their own prejudices. The language that revolutionaries used acted as a confirmation not of their desire for closer proximity with the countryside, but of their continued lack of interest in it. While activists promoted an inclusive notion of revolution, they were simultaneously unwilling to acknowledge that anybody other than them had anything valuable to contribute.

V

History and religion, then, both played a central role in activists' attempts to reshape revolution for post-Commune France. Yet despite their utility and importance, neither of these was of particular help to activists in one crucial area of politics: quotidian politics and the practice of everyday life. While placing revolution in such contexts could establish its theoretical importance or hopefully expand support for it, texts utilising both contexts spoke of revolution itself only in hypotheticals: the promise of future action, as opposed to tangible steps that its supporters could take in the present. In order to redress this, activists turned to a third definition of revolution as a natural law.[70] The association of revolution with science was widely discussed during the period. In 1885, Édouard Vaillant wrote that revolutionaries were 'marching towards [a] new world of equality, of justice, and of science',[71] while *Le Citoyen* devoted a long-running weekly column to explaining fundamental scientific principles.[72] Blanqui and Louise Michel also wrote extensively on the relationship between revolution and the natural world, although this work (especially Blanqui's *Éternité par les astres*) was largely overlooked by contemporaries and had limited public impact.[73]

Much like the other definitions activists assigned to revolution, the description of it in scientific terms was also popularised earlier in the

[70] For more on the pre-nineteenth-century history of science and revolution, see R. Koselleck, *Futures Past: On the Semantics of Historical Time* (trans.) K. Tribe (New York: Columbia University Press, 2004. First published in German, 1979), pp.45–46.

[71] É. Vaillant, 'Vive la Commune!', *Commonweal* (London, April 1885), p.1.

[72] 'La semaine scientifique', *Le Citoyen*, 9 December 1881; 16 December 1881; 23 December 1881; 6 January 1882; 13 January 1882; 20 January 1882; 27 January 1882; 3 February 1882; 10 February 1882; 17 February 1882; 3 March 1882; 10 March 1882; 24 March 1882; 31 March 1882; 24 May 1882.

[73] L. Michel, 'Notes encyclopédiques', vol.1 (2 vols.), Louise Michel: Fonds Moscou, International Institute of Social History, International Institute of Social History (IISH) 233:5/1, p.95; 'Les primitifs', *L'Intransigeant*, 28 October 1885; L.A. Blanqui, *L'éternité par les astres* (ed.) L. Block de Behar (Geneva: Éditions Slatkine, 2009. First published, 1872).

nineteenth century. Napoleon III's *coup d'état* and the failure of the Second Republic in December 1851 forced republicans to confront the failure of their own tactics. The messianic, romantic fervor that characterised much revolutionary and republican rhetoric in 1848 had effectively impelled citizens to the barricades and overturned the July Monarchy. Yet both the infighting and the indecision that plagued the Second Republic, and the election of Louis-Napoléon as President in December 1848, suggested that its ability to produce meaningful social and political change was limited. The year 1848, as we have seen, marked a parting of the ways between revolutionaries and religious rhetoric, but it also had a deeper effect, prompting a wholesale reassessment of the ways in which radicals and revolutionaries conceived of their own ideas, their place within society, and the way that they presented themselves to others.

Eager to prove that their political ambitions were not naïve or utopian, in the wake of 1848, defeated radicals across Europe began to search for alternative ways to define and present revolution, and alighted upon science and nature. In France, various radical and revolutionary theorists developed an interest in natural interpretations of human history and action. These included Gustave Flourens, a journalist who would later die during the Commune and the son of the physiologist and professor Jean Pierre Flourens. In 1863, Flourens delivered a series of lectures at the Collège de France on the subject of the natural history of man, which he later published as *L'histoire de l'homme*.[74] Although a rational being, man, Flourens claimed, was primarily an animal; a product of nature. As a result, his actions were therefore bound by the same laws that governed natural change, or progress.

By placing man and his actions within the context of natural history, Flourens and other activists aimed to redefine revolution entirely. Revolutions, they argued, were not brought about solely by human will, but also by natural processes such as evolution. As such, it was inevitable that they would ebb and flow just as natural life cycles did. Redefining revolution in this way enabled activists to diminish the significance not only of 1848's failure, but also the failure of individual revolutions in general. If it were an inevitable part of a longer process, then the failure of individual actions need not invalidate revolutionaries' ideas at the same time. The success of a revolution, in other words, must be quantified in terms of a longer process

---

[74] G. Flourens, *L'histoire de l'homme: cours d'histoire naturelle des corps organisées au Collège de France* (Paris: Imprimerie de E. Martinet, 1863–1864).

than simply a single *journée*. In fact, rather than obsolescence, the failure of one action heralded progress towards a larger and more significant goal.[75]

Revolutionaries' newfound interest in the natural world derived from several sources. The first was the publication in 1859 of the English biologist Charles Darwin's *On the Origin of the Species*.[76] As the first articulation of his theory of evolution and human understanding, the book proved an international sensation, and was censured and discussed in equal measure. In France alone, two different translations were made between 1862 and 1873, and four different editions of the book were published.[77] Discussions of Darwin in the French context were also frequently linked to the contentious scientific and philosophical debates around 'spontaneous generation', which reached their height between 1858 and 1864 in a series of exchanges between the naturalist Félix-Archimède Pouchet and the microbiologist Louis Pasteur.[78] By framing their ideas in terms of natural science, activists thus connected revolution to a language that was at once both pertinent and controversial.

Perhaps more importantly, though, revolutionaries' interest in science also arose directly from 1848; namely, from the relative success of the Positivists. Unlike other activists, the Positivists had not engaged in the mythological and messianic revolutionary promises that characterised much of the revolution's rhetoric. Their new social doctrine based upon the sciences had enabled them to more easily endure the failures of 1848–1851, and they were arguably the most active radicals of the 1850s. In gravitating towards a more scientific description of revolution, activists thus aimed to publicly demonstrate that they had learned the lessons of 1848, that they were no longer naïve about revolutions or

---

[75] For more on this widespread shift, see G. Stedman Jones, *Karl Marx: Greatness and Illusion* (London: Allen Lane, 2016), p.431; p.467. See also K. Ross, *Communal Luxury: The Political Imaginary of the Paris Commune* (London: Verso, 2015. First published in French, 2015), p.111.

[76] C. Darwin, *On the Origin of Species by means of Natural Selection, or the Preservation of Favoured Races in the Struggle for Life* (London: John Murray, 1859).

[77] C.R. Darwin, *De l'origine des espèces, ou des lois du progrès chez les êtres organisés* (trans.) C.-A. Royer (Paris: Guillaumin & Masson, 1862); C.R. Darwin, *De l'origine des espèces par sélection naturelle, ou des lois de transformation des êtres organisés* 2nd edn (trans.) C.-A. Royer (Paris: Guillaumin & Masson, 1866); C.R. Darwin, *De l'origine des espèces au moyen de la sélection naturelle, ou des Louis de transformation des êtres organisés* 3rd edn (trans.) C.-A. Royer (Paris: Guillaumin & Masson, 1870); C.R. Darwin, *De l'origine des espèces au moyen de la sélection naturelle, ou, la lutte pour l'existence dans la nature* (trans.) J.-J. Moulinié (Paris: Reinwald, 1873. First published in English, 1859).

[78] For more on spontaneous generation and this debate, see R. Fox, *The Savant and the State: Science and Cultural Politics in Nineteenth-Century France* (Baltimore, MD: Johns Hopkins University Press, 2012), pp.148–159.

politics, and that in the future they would be able to make any changes they wrought last.

In France, much of the support for this new definition of revolution came from the student population. Unlike primary and secondary education, universities had been left largely untouched by the Second Empire's reforms, and radical students quickly established themselves as some of the imperial government's most vocal opponents. This opposition often manifested itself as support for radical science,[79] and coalesced particularly around two overlapping groups: medical students and the student journalists of the *rive gauche*.[80] Many of these, such as Georges Clemenceau, Paul Lafargue, and Charles Longuet became leading figures in radical and revolutionary politics during the early Third Republic.[81] The revolutionary turn to science in the 1870s and early 1880s was thus not the result of completely novel theorisation, and neither could it be classified as a return to an older idea. Rather, it represented the continuation of a firmly established way of understanding revolution and social change; one that the revolutionaries of the early Third Republic, moreover, had been deeply personally involved in.

VI

The most widely discussed scientific concept during this period was undoubtedly evolution. Activists from across the revolutionary spectrum rushed to proclaim themselves 'evolutionist on the one hand, and revolutionary on the other',[82] indeed in 1880 Adhémar Lecler noted that

> Much has been said recently of *evolution* and *revolution*. There have been few conferences or speeches in which at least one, if not both, of these words has not appeared.[83]

---

[79] P. Nord, *The Republican Moment: Struggles for Democracy in Nineteenth-Century France* (Cambridge, MA: Harvard University Press, 1995), pp.31–32.

[80] For contemporary discussion of student involvement in radical politics, see B. Malon, 'Étudiants et prolétaires', *L'Intransigeant*, 22 February 1885. For further details, see Nord, *The Republican Moment*, pp.34–35; p.44.

[81] Bellanger, *Histoire générale de la presse française*, vol.2 (1969), pp.321–323.

[82] P. Dervillers, 'La foi s'en va', *Le Prolétaire*, 7 January 1883. See also J. Guesde, *Le collectivisme au Collège de France* (Paris: Henry Oriol, 1883), p.11; 'A nos lecteurs', *L'Égalité*, 18 November 1877; 'A propos des candidatures ouvrières', *Le Prolétaire*, 19 July 1879; B. Malon, 'Le droit de propriété et l'histoire', *L'Émancipation*, 10 November 1880; 'Le Parti ouvrier et l'État capitaliste', *L'Égalité*, 11 August 1880; 'Le parti socialiste', *Le Télégraphe*, 24 June 1881. APP Ba199/166.

[83] A. Lecler, 'Évolution – Révolution', *Le Prolétaire*, 28 August 1880.

In order to fully understand the ways in which activists during this period conceived of revolution, it is thus necessary to first understand their ideas of and interactions with evolution.

The fullest and clearest discussion of the relationship between evolution and revolution from this period is found in the work of Élisée Reclus. Born in 1830 to a French pastor, Reclus was educated at the University of Berlin under Carl Ritter, one of the founders of modern geography. Reclus himself went on to become an established geographer, well known and highly respected in international circles (as, indeed, did several of his brothers). His nineteen-volume magnum opus, *La nouvelle géographie universelle*, was published simultaneously in French and English between 1876 and 1894, and in 1892 he was awarded the gold medal of the Paris Geographical Society.[84]

As well as a geographer, Reclus was also an anarchist and a member of the Commune. He was banished from France in 1872, and after a short time in Italy, he settled in Switzerland, along with many Communards and other revolutionary exiles, including Georgi Plekhanov and Vera Zasulich, who emigrated from Russia in 1880. In the international exile community based in Geneva, Reclus found both a host of new collaborators and a large audience for his ideas. He took full advantage of these opportunities, editing, along with various other revolutionaries, the exile periodical *Le Travailleur* (see Chapter 8), and delivering frequent public lectures. While Reclus had certainly been active and well known in revolutionary circles prior to the Commune, the experience of exile significantly enhanced both his visibility and the level of his engagement. Indeed, both contemporaries and later historians have suggested that he was the exile community's 'moral leader'.[85]

On 5 March 1880, Reclus delivered a public lecture in Geneva entitled 'Évolution et Révolution'. In the lecture, he drew directly upon his academic work to highlight what he considered to be a contemporary political issue of pressing importance: the widespread misunderstanding and misuse of the concept of evolution. Over the course of the 1870s, Reclus suggested, the politicians, professionals, and industrialists of the Opportunists' *couches nouvelles* had become increasingly aware that neither the Commune's failure nor the establishment of the Third Republic had

---

[84] Reclus, *La nouvelle géographie universelle*.

[85] J.T. Joughin, *The Paris Commune in French Politics, 1871–1880*, 2 vols. (Baltimore, MD: Johns Hopkins University Press, 1955), vol.1, p.85. For a similar assertion by a contemporary, see Copy of a report to the Préfecture de Police, 15 February 1876. APP Ba432/1768.

brought an end to social discontent. Although Thiers had authoritatively declared socialism dead and buried in 1871, in fact both its disappearance and the relief it generated 'did not last'.[86] Fearful of the potential effects of future revolutionary challenges upon both their own livelihoods and the security of the Republic, politicians had alighted, with varying degrees of sincerity, upon evolution – or political reform – as an alternative to revolution. In present political discourse, Reclus noted, the two terms were 'constantly used ... as though their meaning were absolutely antagonistic'.[87]

By advocating political evolution, politicians drew self-consciously upon the memory of science's radical associations under the Second Empire, and often their own involvement in it.[88] In utilising the language of science, Reclus argued, politicians aimed to present their ideas as a 'third way' for French society: an alternative to both revolution and reaction that could potentially unite them both. This, it was hoped, would dissipate workers' anger at the persistent inequality of French social relations and with it, the potential for revolution. Whether their promises of gradual change were in good faith or not, the political use of evolution during this period was thus, according to Reclus, little more than another weapon in the war upon revolution and the well-being of the French working class. '[T]he word evolution', he claimed, 'serves but to conceal a lie in the mouths of those who most willingly pronounce it'.[89]

Yet contemporary revolutionaries, Reclus argued, were equally complicit in this state of affairs. While their social and political intentions were undoubtedly better, activists in the period after the Commune had also frequently juxtaposed the terms evolution and revolution. Following their break with radical republicans over the Commune, revolutionaries had too often turned their backs on political engagement and spurned the value of gradual change. Activists imagined that, in doing so, they were preserving the integrity of revolution. In fact, however, they were simply alienating the potential support of workers who – for whatever reason – did not want to commit themselves to violent revolution. '[I]f all the oppressed have not the temperament of heroes', Reclus reminded his audience, 'they feel their sufferings none the less'.[90] Activists, then, had effectively allowed

---

[86] 'Néanmoins, la joie causée par la disparition du socialisme n'a pas duré.' Reclus, *Évolution et Révolution*, p.6.

[87] '[I]ls sont plus d'une fois employés comme s'ils avaient un sens absolument opposé'. Ibid., p.3.

[88] Nord, *The Republican Moment*, pp.31–32.   [89] Reclus, *Évolution et Révolution*, pp.5–6.

[90] '[S]'ils n'ont pas le tempérament de héros, il n'en réfléchissent pas moins sur leurs intérêts.' Reclus, *Évolution et Révolution*, p.7.

politicians' definition of evolution to pass unchallenged, and had ceded control of science to their former radical and republican allies.

In fact, however, evolution was not an antidote to revolution, but its precursor. In one of his recent academic works, the two-volume 1868–1869 *La Terre*, Reclus argued that the evolution of the natural environment was not a process of peaceful, imperceptible change, but a cycle of 'destruction and renewal', in which gradual change prepared the way for sudden change, and vice versa.[91] The same, he suggested, was true of human society. While there had been no violent revolutionary upheavals since 1871, society was radically changing nonetheless:

> does not the great school of the outer world exhibit the prodigies of human industry equally to rich and poor, to those who have called these marvels into existence and those who profit by them? The poverty-stricken outcast can see railways, telegraphs, hydraulic rams, perforators, and self-lighting matches as well as the man of power can, and he is no less impressed by them. Privilege has disappeared in the enjoyment of some of these grand conquests of science. When he is conducting his locomotive through space, doubling or slacking speed at his pleasure, does the engine-driver believe himself the inferior of the sovereign shut up behind him in a gilded railway carriage, and trembling with the knowledge that his life depends on a jet of steam, the shifting of a level, or a bomb of dynamite? Without a doubt, he does not.[92]

While evolution and revolution often took different forms and moved at different speeds, their purpose – to effect change – was a shared one. It was not only the words, but also the concepts that 'closely resemble[d] one another'.[93] Indeed, they shared more than a common purpose. Rather, evolution and revolution were inextricably linked in a single cycle of progress: they were 'fundamentally one and the same thing'.[94] Evolution, Reclus argued, was thus a profoundly revolutionary concept, and an idea

---

[91] '[D]estruction et renouvellement'. É. Reclus, *La terre: déscription des phénomènes de la vie du globe*, 2 vols. (Paris: Hachette, 1877. First published, 1868–1869), vol.1, p.ii.

[92] 'Et la grande école du monde extérieur ne montre-t-elle pas également les grands prodiges de l'industrie humaine aux pauvres et aux riches, à ceux qui ont obtenu ces merveilles par leur travail et à ceux qui en profitent? Chemins de fer, télégraphes, beliers hydrauliques, perforatrices, allumettes à combustion spontanée, le malheureux voit toutes ces choses aussi bien que le puissant et son esprit n'en est pas moins frappé. Pour la jouissance de quelques unes de ces grandes conquêtes de la science le privilége a disparu. Menant sa locomotive à travers l'espace, en doublant la vitesse et en arrêtant l'allure à son gré, le mécanicien se croit-il l'inférieur du souverain qui roule derrière lui? Non sans doute.' Reclus, *Évolution et Révolution*, pp.13–14; see also p.18.

[93] 'Ces deux mots: Évolution, Révolution, se ressemblent fort'. Ibid., p.1.

[94] 'Au fond, elles ne sont qu'une seule et même chose'. Reclus, *Évolution et Révolution*, p.3. See also V. Marouck, 'Le socialisme officiel sous la Commune', in *La revue socialiste* 7 (5 June 1880), 330–336, at p.330.

that contemporary activists eager to remain politically relevant must embrace.

VII

The reaction to Reclus's lecture was immense. In the months after it was given, the lecture and its content were much discussed in revolutionary circles, both at meetings and in the revolutionary press.[95] The relationship between natural science and humanity had recently attracted significant interest in revolutionary circles. Friedrich Engels's 1877 *Anti-Dühring*, for example, addressed itself to this very subject.[96] Yet Reclus's lecture enjoyed a popularity all its own; indeed, it was arguably the single most popular French revolutionary text of this period. It was swiftly distributed in cheap pamphlet form in 1880 and proved extraordinarily successful, with a second edition appearing less than a year later.[97] An English translation soon followed and enjoyed similar attention, running to seven editions by 1891.[98] Indeed, the international popularity of *Évolution et Révolution* was such that in 1898 Reclus published a vastly extended and more theoretically detailed version entitled *L'évolution, la révolution et l'idéal anarchique*.[99] At a time when established revolutionary publications often experienced financial difficulties and fluctuating readerships, this popularity was truly remarkable.

Reclus's ideas had a particularly significant intellectual impact upon the French revolutionary movement in the early 1880s. Shortly after the lecture took place, *Le Prolétaire* had felt it necessary to provide a definition of evolution for unfamiliar readers.[100] By the mid-1880s, however, it occupied a central position in numerous revolutionary programmes, sitting alongside revolution itself as one of their key beliefs. Lecler in the Possibilist *Prolétaire*, for example, characterised evolution and revolution

[95] A. Lecler, 'Évolution – Révolution', *Le Prolétaire*, 28 August 1880.
[96] F. Engels, *Anti-Dühring: Herr Eugen Dühring's Revolution in Science* (trans.) E. Burns (Moscow: Progress Publishers, 1947. First published in German, 1877). See also Stedman Jones, *Karl Marx: Greatness and Illusion*, p.563.
[97] For the first edition, see above. For the second edition, see É. Reclus, *Évolution et révolution: conférence faite à Genève, le 5 mars 1880*, 2nd edn (Geneva: Imprimerie jurassienne, 1881).
[98] É. Reclus, *Evolution and Revolution*, 7th edn (London: W. Reeves, 1891. First published by International Publishing Company, 1885).
[99] É. Reclus, *L'évolution, la révolution, et l'idéal anarchique* (Paris: P.V. Stock, 1898). This version had itself run to at least six editions by 1910. For the sixth edition, see É. Reclus, *L'évolution, la révolution, et l'idéal anarchique* 6th edn (Paris: P.V. Stock, 1906).
[100] A. Lecler, 'Évolution – Révolution', *Le Prolétaire*, 28 August 1880.

as alternating parts of the same cycle,[101] while Casimir Bouis guaranteed readers of the Blanquist *Intransigeant* that society would improve

> For the natural, logical, irrefutable reason that the world turns, that everything progresses, and that everything obeys a kind of *fatality*, which is the uninterrupted evolution towards the good; the supreme goal of humanity.[102]

The Marxist *Égalité*, meanwhile, paid tribute to the role of railways in revolutionising economic relations, arguing that '[w]e do not live in lethargic times ... everything around us is shaking and faltering.'[103] Reclus's lecture was thus more than simply the clearest elaboration of revolutionary interest in evolution; it was arguably the source of wider revolutionary interest in it during this period. Although revolutionaries occasionally mentioned other theorists such as Darwin, it was Reclus's definition with which they were most familiar, and which they referred to the most.[104]

Given the extensive criticism meted out to the revolutionary movement in the lecture, it may seem surprising that they adopted its ideas so willingly. Yet in the circumstances that revolutionaries found themselves in, its ideas were particularly useful. Reclus's lecture redefined not only evolution, but also revolution, by embedding it in the natural processes he had observed in his capacity as a geographer. In this interpretation, human revolutions were not violent political events or even acts of will, but – as Flourens had suggested in 1863 – iterations of a much wider natural process. Their occurrence (or lack thereof) was thus inevitable, and their success or failure was beyond human control. Activists during this period hoped, like the defeated *quarante-huitards* in the 1850s and 1860s, to find definitive closure regarding the events of the Commune. By redefining revolution as a force of nature, they sought not to disown or hide their actions, but rather to place them in a wider context and, in doing so,

---

[101] A. Lecler, 'Évolution – Révolution', *Le Prolétaire*, 28 August 1880. See also Reclus, *Évolution et Révolution*, 6th edn, pp.59–60; *Le Travailleur*, May 1877, p.1; Arnould, *Histoire populaire et parlementaire de la Commune*, vol.1, p.24.

[102] 'Par cette raison naturelle, logique, irréfutable, que le monde marche, que tout progresse, et que tout obéit à une sorte de *fatalité* qui est l'évolution ininterrompue vers le bien, but suprême de l'humanité'. C. Bouis, 'Les deux républiques', *L'Intransigeant*, 30 August 1880. See also B. Malon, 'La reserve révolutionnaire', *L'Intransigeant*, 1 December 1883.

[103] '[É]branlé, chancelant'. 'Le possibilisme', *L'Égalité*, 5 February 1882.

[104] For references to Darwin, see Reclus, *Évolution et Révolution*, p.22; C. Bouis, 'Les deux républiques', *L'Intransigeant*, 30 August 1880; M. Talmeyr, 'L'athéisme clérical', *L'Intransigeant*, 13 May 1881; G. Deville, 'Darwin', *Le Citoyen*, 23 April 1882; Lafargue, *Le droit à la paresse*, p.vi.

demonstrate that their failure had been neither final nor unnatural. Revolution, in other words, was not dead; it had just been misunderstood.

The value of Reclus's revolution, moreover, was more than simply retrospective. It also made the practice of being a revolutionary in the post-Commune period considerably easier. For large parts of the nineteenth century, the life of a revolutionary had been characterised as one of sacrifice and ascetic devotion. By the time he died in 1881 Blanqui had spent over half of life in prison, while other revered figures such as Giuseppe Mazzini, the leader of the mid-century Italian revolutionary movement, had also emphasised the importance of sacrifice and individual will.[105] By the 1870s, the majority of French activists had distanced themselves from these more traditional models of revolution, yet participation in the revolutionary movement nonetheless still involved a substantial degree of dedication.[106] In 1878, for example, L'Égalité claimed that

> It is deceptive to tell the workers that their enfranchisement will be brought about by revolution without informing them of their duty and need to research the immediate goal of this revolution and the means by which this will be reached.[107]

Most commonly, this new dedication manifested itself in revolutionaries' increasing interest in and commitment to party organisation, which stipulated that militants follow and promulgate a strict party line.[108] Whether in the form of sacrifice or of political parties, however, the message remained the same: revolution was an exclusive activity that, compared to other political positions, required an unusual level of dedication and commitment.

---

[105] For more on Mazzini, see C.A. Bayly and E.F. Biagini (eds.), *Giuseppe Mazzini and the Globalisation of Democratic Nationalism 1830–1920* (Oxford: Oxford University Press, 2008).

[106] 'Ce qui nous sépare', *L'Égalité*, 10 November 1882. See also Andrieu, 'The Paris Commune', at p.574; Deville, *Le Capital de Karl Marx*, p.56; B. Malon, 'Les Partis ouvriers en France', in *La revue socialiste* 5 (5 May 1880), 257–269, at p.267; B. Malon, 'Le Droit de propriété et l'histoire', in *L'Émancipation*, 10 November 1880; 'La Révolution', *Le Prolétaire*, 19 February 1881; L. Picard, 'Le spectre maçonnique', *L'Égalité*, 11 November 1884.

[107] 'La politique socialiste', *L'Égalité*, 10 February 1878. Education provision was central to many revolutionary programmes. See, for instance, 'Réunion socialiste', *Petit Caporal*, 6 June 1880. APP Ba199/394; 'Programme', *Le Travail* (Saint-Ouen: Imprimerie Jules Boyer, 1879), p.2; B. Malon, 'Blanqui socialiste', in *La revue socialiste* 7 (July 1885), 586–597, at p.594. Many revolutionaries blamed the Commune's failure on workers' lack of education. See, for example, Intelligence report to the Préfecture of Police, March 1877 (London). APP Ba429/2151; Andrieu, 'The Paris Commune', at pp.579–580.

[108] 'Manifeste du Comité central électoral', *Le Citoyen*, 10 December 1880. APP Ba199/448; J. Guesde and P. Lafargue, *Le Programme du Parti Ouvrier: son histoire, ses considérations, ses articles* (Paris: Henry Oriol, 1883), pp.2–3; see also pp.46–47.

The characterisation of revolution as a natural event enabled activists to diminish the importance of this commitment. If revolution were a natural, inevitable, and holistic process, then every action constituted a revolutionary act.[109] Indeed, Reclus observed, '[i]n many a town where there is not one organised socialist group, all the workers without exception are already more or less consciously socialists'.[110] While determination, education, and organisation were undoubtedly useful, he implied, they were by no means necessary requirements for prospective revolutionaries. Where by defining revolution in terms of religion, activists sought to assume the absolute moral power of the priest and present revolution as a clearly defined lifestyle, with evolution the opposite was the case.

By presenting revolution as an inevitable force of nature, they removed the constraints that a revolutionary lifestyle had previously imposed upon its adherents. While people were entitled to live the life of a traditional revolutionary, and even potentially engage in violent action, it was by no means essential to the process of bringing about revolutionary social change.[111] This, activists hoped, would directly address what they believed to be a drain upon their numbers prompted largely by the rise of the Opportunists – an actively republican and reforming, less demanding alternative to the kind of social change traditionally promised by revolutionaries. By suggesting that, rather than demanding a life of dedication, being a revolutionary now required little in the way of sacrifice, activists aimed to remove the choice between ease and revolution and consequently render it a more attractive political prospect, both to novices and to former revolutionaries who may have drifted away from the movement.

Equally, this new definition of revolution also smoothed activists' own reintegration into French political life. As well as heeding Reclus's advice to take potential 'shy radicals' more seriously, revolutionaries began to reassess their own level of participation in public life. After the fall of the Commune revolutionaries had, as Reclus observed, largely withdrawn from more mainstream politics, horrified by the lack of support politicians had shown the Commune and convinced that it had nothing to offer them. In this, revolutionaries' own hand had partly been forced by exile and deportation, which physically removed them from the French political

[109] Reclus, *Évolution et Révolution*, p.18.
[110] '[D]ans telle ville où n'existe pas un seul groupe de socialistes organisés, tous les ouvriers sans exception sont déjà des socialistes plus ou moins conscients'. Reclus, *Évolution et Révolution*, p.8; p.13; p.17. See also G. de Greef, *Eloges d'Élisée Reclus et de Kellès-Krauz* (Gand: Société coopérative *Volksdrukkerij*, 1906), p.39.
[111] De Greef, *Eloges d'Élisée Reclus et de Kellès-Krauz*, p.43.

arena until 1880. At the same time, many activists spent the 1870s suggesting that their followers in France also abstain from national politics.[112] Yet this policy of non-intervention had its limits. It had been justifiable from exiled revolutionaries forced to observe French politics from the outside as the Moral Order politicians that had repressed the Commune ruled France and worked towards a restoration. Following the Opportunists' accession to power and especially after the general amnesty, however, it began to look increasingly outdated and counterproductive.

Accordingly, towards the end of the 1870s revolutionary ideas on political participation underwent a significant public shift. As Le Prolétaire observed, 'all or nothing politics' usually led to 'nothing at all'.[113] Following their return to France in 1880, revolutionaries became increasingly involved in mainstream politics.[114] A significant number of revolutionary and socialist candidates stood and achieved relative success in the 1881 legislative elections, although it would be another decade before a socialist deputy was elected. Indeed, by 1883 even Marxists such as Deville had thrown their full weight behind political participation and reform, arguing that '[t]o grant reforms is to arm us; it is to strengthen us against our adversaries, who become weaker as we become stronger. The appetite grows with eating'.[115]

Taking up elected office, in other words, was once again presented as an acceptable step towards meaningful social change rather than as a

---

[112] See, for example, G. Lefrançais, Un Communard aux électeurs français (Geneva: publisher not specified, 1875); F. Dumartheray, Aux travailleurs manuels de France: Partisans de l'action politique (Geneva, 1876), p.4.

[113] 'Encore l'union socialiste', Le Prolétaire, 19 November 1881.

[114] Arnould, L'État et la Révolution, p.199; F. Borde, Le collectivisme au congrès de Marseille (Paris: Delaporte, 1880), pp.19–20; Guesde and Lafargue, Le Programme du Parti Ouvrier, p.53; Deville, Le Capital de Karl Marx, p.36; 105: Paul Brousse to César de Paepe, 11 February 1884 (Paris), in C. de Paepe, Entre Marx et Bakounine: Correspondence (ed. B. Dandois) (Paris: Maspero, 1974), 245–249, at p.246; See also 'A propos des candidatures ouvrières', Le Prolétaire, 19 July 1879; 'Peuple, prends garde!', Le Prolétaire, 8 January 1881; 'Notre programme', La Révolution sociale: organe anarchiste (Saint-Cloud), 12 September 1880; 'Liberté, Égalité, Fraternité', L'Égalité, 18 August 1880; 'Réformes et révolution', L'Égalité, 7 November 1882; P. Brousse, 'Liberté & égalité', L'Émancipation, 3 November 1880.

[115] 'Accorder des réformes, c'est nous jeter des armes, c'est nous render plus forts contre nos adversaires devenant plus faibles à mesure que nous le sommes moins. L'appétit vient en mangeant.' Deville, Le Capital de Karl Marx, p.55. See also E. Digeon, Droits et devoirs dans l'anarchie rationnelle (Paris: Fayard, 1882), pp.12–13; 'La liberté sous la République', Le Prolétaire, 14 June 1879; 'Une candidature nécessaire', Le Prolétaire, 10 February 1883; 'Du pouvoir exécutif', Le Prolétariat, 22 August 1885; C. Bouis, 'Le 14 juillet', L'Intransigeant, 16 July 1880; H. Rochefort, 'Les plagiaires', L'Intransigeant, 6 October 1880. See also M. Talmeyr, 'Le vote universel', L'Intransigeant, 12 January 1881; A. Humbert, 'Flouerie électorale', L'Intransigeant, 26 July 1881; 'La Cohue nationale: élection du Président de la République', La Bataille, 30 December 1885.

traitorous activity. There is significant evidence to suggest that, even in the depths of their horror at morally bankrupt politicians, revolutionaries retained faith in the transformative potential of well-run electoral politics.[116] In terms of their public recommendations, however, this interest in mainstream contemporary French politics represented a complete about-face from their political stance during the 1870s. Reclus's redefinition of revolution as the practice of everyday life, however, enabled activists to argue that, while different, their new stance was no less revolutionary, thereby smoothing both this public theoretical *volte face* and revolutionaries' return to France.

Despite its vocal criticisms of the revolutionary movement during the 1870s, Reclus's evolutionary thesis proved popular because it enabled revolutionaries to deal more effectively with the shifting political landscape of the early 1880s. It has previously been suggested that Reclus's vision of revolution and future society was by definition exclusive of other forms of political organisation and the structures of contemporary French life.[117] In fact, however, it served to bring them back into alignment. By positioning revolution as an inevitable force of nature rather than an act of will, Reclus and other activists both broadened and generalised its meaning, creating a revolution more attuned to the relatively stable political conditions in France during the early 1880s. According to this definition, any action could be a revolutionary action, enabling activists to make significant alterations to their tactics and to accommodate a variety of different opinions and approaches without compromising either their unity or their status as revolutionaries. Revolutionaries thus did not give up on the idea that revolutionary action had a political future after the Commune. Rather, they sought to redefine what it meant to be a revolutionary in terms more applicable to their contemporary contexts.

At the same time, however, it must be noted that evolution was not a miracle cure. While this definition of revolution permitted many ideas and

---

[116] Although their circumstances meant that they had few practical avenues for expressing it, revolutionaries had, to a much greater extent than previous historians have allowed, remained interested in politics and political participation after the Commune and throughout the 1870s. See, for example, B. Malon, *L'Internationale: son histoire et ses principes* (Lyons: Extrait de la *République républicaine*, 1872), p.25; Arnould, *L'État et la Révolution*, p.198; 'Congrès annuel de la Fédération jurassienne', *L'Avant-Garde*, 12 August 1878 (La Chaux-de-Fonds); 10: Benoît Malon to Paul Lafargue, 18 May 1880 (Zurich), in Bottigelli and Willard, *La naissance du Parti ouvrier français*, 74–80, at p.76; 'Le chaos parlementaire', *Le Citoyen*, 2 February 1882; 'Notre politique', *L'Égalité*, 18 November 1877. See also 'La question économique et la question politique', *L'Égalité*, 2 June 1878; 'Organisez-vous', *L'Égalité*, 30 June 1878; Digeon, *Droits et devoirs dans l'anarchie rationnelle*, p.33.

[117] Ross, *Communal Luxury*, p.5; p.108.

actions, it was defined by none of them. In the sense that it broadened revolution's meaning and scope, and rendered it more appealing, this was its great virtue. In doing so, however, it also essentially stripped revolution of any specific meaning, potentially leaving both the French population and revolutionaries themselves unsure of what precisely they stood for. In fact, this trade-off – of rendering revolution at once more palatable and less clearly defined – was, as their historical and religious, as well as their scientific definitions of revolution suggest, characteristic of activists' thought on the subject as a whole during this period.

*****

In his seminal 1979 work *Futures Past*, the German historian Reinhart Koselleck observed that, for the contemporary reader,

> The semantic content of the word 'revolution' ... ranges from bloody political and social convulsions to decisive scientific innovations; it can signify the whole spectrum, or alternatively, one form to the exclusion of the remainder.[118]

'Revolution', in other words, is a broad linguistic church that is capable of accommodating various different meanings and interpretations. These different interpretations can, in turn, be deployed successively, in varying combinations, or all at once. As the previous two chapters have demonstrated, French revolutionaries in the years immediately after the Commune also conceived of revolution in these terms.

Previous work on this subject has focused primarily upon the ways in which contemporary activists interacted with the French Revolution and its subsequent tradition. As Patrick Hutton observed, the Revolution has continued 'to serve as a touchstone to which ... historians have returned countless times'.[119] This has led historians to interpret 'revolution' in the 1870s and early 1880s as a concept bounded by the frameworks of 1789 and its successors, and thus hopelessly anachronistic in the changed circumstances of the new Republican state. Activists continuing to advocate for revolution in the new political landscape of the Third Republic, and especially after the Opportunists' rise to power in the late 1870s, have consequently been classed as out of touch, excessively nostalgic, and increasingly extraneous to national political life.

---

[118] Koselleck, *Futures Past*, p.44.
[119] P.H. Hutton, 'Vico's Theory of History and the French Revolutionary Tradition', *Journal of the History of Ideas* 37 (April–June 1976), 241–256, at p.252.

Activists' ideas on revolution after 1871, however, were more complex and varied than this focus suggests. While revolutionaries certainly made frequent reference to recent French history, and the Revolution in particular, these references were largely unconnected to their thoughts on revolution itself. In fact, far from seeking refuge in a 'revolutionary tradition', they actively sought to disentangle revolution as a political concept from its previous French iterations. Rather than the future of revolution, it was the shape of the French Republic to which activists addressed themselves in such discussions. Using both recent and more distant national history, revolutionaries sought to simultaneously reaffirm their patriotism and outline an ideal Republic that was subtly but significantly different from that negotiated and legislated for by the Opportunists in the 1870s and early 1880s.

Activists in this period therefore recognised the ways in which the last few years had altered the political valence of the revolutionary tradition: that in a meaningful sense, the French Revolution had, in François Furet's evocative words, 'said its goodbyes to History' in the 'burning Paris' of May 1871.[120] Yet they also did more than passively observe this shift. In addition, activists' uses of French history during this period demonstrated the effort that they went to in order to adapt to this new reality, separating the idea of revolution as a political action from the history of its recent French iterations. In doing so, they sought to leave open the possibility that it could continue to function as a viable political position, even in the irrevocably changed circumstances of the Third Republic.

While the Commune may have heralded 'the defeat of a certain idea of revolution', it thus did not signal the end of revolution's relevance as a concept.[121] Rather than a cult to the past, activists remained committed to the idea that revolution was politically viable. This was evidenced in the variety of ways that they attempted to redefine it in the years after the fall of the Commune. Chief among these were the definitions of revolution as a religious experience and as a naturally occurring phenomenon. By couching revolution in the language of religion, revolutionaries attempted to expand their influence outwards from their traditional bases of Paris and large urban centres to the countryside and, in doing so, demonstrate both their regard for the provinces and their ability to learn from the problems

---

[120] 'Dans ce Paris qui brûle, la Révolution française fait ses adieux à l'Histoire'. F. Furet, *La Révolution de Turgot à Jules Ferry* (Paris: Hachette, 1988), p.489.
[121] 'Ce fut par conséquent la défaite d'une certaine idée de la révolution'. Tombs, *Paris, bivouac des révolutions*, pp.434–435.

of the Commune. These schemes frequently fell short in their application, and served to demonstrate instead the extent to which many revolutionaries' attitudes had remained the same. Yet nonetheless, they also served as evidence of both activists' continued belief in the viability of revolution, and the lengths that they were willing to go to in order to guarantee its future.

At the same time, activists also sought to redefine revolution in scientific and natural terms. From the late 1870s onwards, various revolutionaries, particularly Élisée Reclus and his associates in Geneva, attempted to place revolution in a context broader than French, or even human, history, linking it to processes of natural evolution that Reclus had observed in his capacity as a geographer. Revolution, they argued, was a long, inexorable, organic process, in which long periods of non-violent development were just as important as more traditional moments of violent uprising. The purpose of defining revolution in this way was twofold. Retrospectively, it served to rationalise and minimise the implications of their own revolutionary failures, repackaging them as insignificant moments within a broader narrative of natural development.

More importantly, in defining revolution as an all-encompassing process, activists transformed it into the practice of everyday life. In this interpretation, even the smallest gestures became revolutionary acts. This version of revolution thus aimed to provide answers to the question of how revolution could survive in a democratic Republic. It not only required fewer sacrifices of its proponents than either more traditional revolution or organised socialism, but also dovetailed more seamlessly with the political landscape of the new French state. As a result, revolutionaries hoped that it would appeal to several different groups at once, converting radicals and republicans who had balked at the level of commitment revolution had previously required, and satisfying convinced activists returning from exile and eager to assimilate into French politics once again. By redefining revolution in these different and broader terms, in other words, revolutionaries hoped to rejuvenate it in ways that were more appropriate for the social and political circumstances of the new Third Republic.

The shape of this continued belief in revolution has a broader significance for our understanding of revolution in nineteenth-century France. Activists during the post-Commune period were not the first to attempt to broaden revolution's meaning in this way. Rather, it had been a feature of revolutionary and radical thought since at least the 1850s, when the radicals and revolutionaries defeated in 1848 had begun to search for new ways to define and present revolution in order to demonstrate that their political ambitions were neither naïve nor utopian. These attempts revolved in particular around science, nature, and evolution. While the formulations of the 1870s and early 1880s may have differed from those of the earlier period, the ways in which activists thought about revolution were in fact much the same. If there was a significant turning point at which French thought on revolution changed during the nineteenth century, this new and deeper understanding of revolution in the post-Commune period indicates that it was not 1871, but 1848. This post-Commune continuity, moreover, was not damaging to revolutionary ambitions, but rather a crucial factor in enabling them to adapt effectively to their new circumstances.

Finally, the shape of such thought also reveals more than simply activists' ideas on revolution: it also speaks to the relationship between revolutionaries, other republicans, and the Republic itself during the 1870s and early 1880s. As we have seen, it has commonly been assumed that a decisive parting of the ways between revolutionaries and other republicans occurred after 1871.[122] In historical terms, this is fairly unproblematic. These were two groups that made fundamentally different political choices during the Commune. In terms of values and principles, however, this separation was not so clear. On the one hand, revolutionaries' continued belief in the contemporary political and social relevance of revolution separated them from moderate and even radical republicans such as Georges Clemenceau in meaningful intellectual terms.

Yet on the other hand, activists' thought on revolution also reveals the many similarities that remained between them and other republicans. Their use of science to justify social change, for example, spoke to revolutionaries' and republicans' shared political apprenticeship in the student journals and medical associations of the 1850s and 1860s. Likewise, activists' interactions with the revolutionary tradition and French history displayed a more complicated relationship with the Opportunists' Republic than has previously been acknowledged. While the gap between revolutionaries and other republicans may have been very wide in 1871, towards the end of the decade and during the early 1880s this was no longer the case. As many historians have demonstrated, this was a period of

---

[122] Some historians even date this parting of the ways to 1848. See, for example, D. Moggach, 'New Goals and New Ways: Republicanism and Socialism in 1848/49', in D. Moggach and P. Leduc Browne (eds.), *The Social Question and the Democratic Revolution: Marx and the Legacy of 1848* (Ottawa: University of Ottawa Press, 2000), 49–69, at p.62.

intellectual fluidity, in which diverse republicans increasingly came together in order to defeat a common enemy.[123] A comprehensive treatment of revolutionary activists' thought on revolution in the post-Commune period reveals that they also remained a part of this wider republican community, even after the divergence of 1871.

---

[123] See, for example, Nord, *The Republican Moment*; S. Hazareesingh, *Intellectual Founders of the Republic: Five Studies in Nineteenth-Century French Republican Political Thought*, 2nd edn (Oxford: Oxford University Press, 2005. First published, 2001).

PART III

Marx, Marxism, and International Socialism

CHAPTER 5

Texts in Translation

The vision of a viable revolutionary movement was based on more than just memories. Activists continued to think creatively about revolution following the fall of the Commune, drawing upon a variety of old and new ideas in order to present a rejuvenated version of revolution. This version was, at least theoretically, simultaneously attuned to present European circumstances, able to account for past histories of both success and failure, and able to adapt to possible future eventualities. Yet it would be inaccurate to characterise revolutionaries as solely interested in renewing their old ideas and languages during this period. Activists also sought out entirely new ideas and associations, becoming heavily involved, for instance, in the International Workingmen's Association – an organisation that, prior to the Paris Commune, French radicals and revolutionaries had largely displayed little interest in.

It is the introduction of these new situations and ideas that historians have often suggested drove an insuperable wedge between the more explicitly socialist sections of the movement and irreparably damaged revolutionary unity. In 1872, tensions that had been boiling for months between different factions in the International Workingmen's Association burst into the open at the annual congress in The Hague. The Russian anarchist Mikhail Bakunin and his Swiss associate James Guillaume were expelled from the organisation after refusing to ratify a resolution moved by Marx, and established their own, rival International at St. Imier in Switzerland. Many French Communard exiles were caught up in the power struggle. Part III of this book addresses the suggestion that revolutionary thought during this period was irreparably divided along factional, ideological lines that mirrored these Marxist–anarchist divisions of the international socialist movement.

Rather than attempting to examine the structural and intellectual integrity of French socialism as a whole, Part III approaches the subject from a familiar but recently overlooked angle: French interactions with Karl Marx and Marxism. It is not my intention to suggest that either Marx or Marxism were unknown in France prior to 1871, for this was manifestly not the case. Marx, along with around 85,000 other Germans, had lived and worked in Paris in the early 1840s.[1] During this period, he had made considerable efforts to engage with French radicals, and he was well known in certain circles.[2] Despite these efforts, however, by 1871 he had not been widely read in France.[3] It was only during the period after the Commune that French socialists and revolutionaries first began to identify with Marx or self-define as Marxists on a meaningful scale.

As demonstrated in Part I, Marx's ideas on the Paris Commune found few champions in France or French revolutionary circles during this period. Yet the relationship between Marx and the French revolutionary movement extended far further, and was far more complicated than this single interaction might suggest. From the late nineteenth century onwards, the relationship has been defined by noisy claims of insurmountable difference. In November 1882, Friedrich Engels famously noted in a letter to Eduard Bernstein that frustration at the so-called French Marxists had recently led Marx to declare, '[c]e qu'il y a de certain c'est que moi, je ne suis pas Marxiste': 'what is certain is that I myself am not a Marxist'.[4] The message behind Marx's reported words seems loud and clear. French Marxism was at once dangerous and banal. It was neither to be trusted nor associated with. In fact, it could not really be called Marxism at all.

The study of Marx and Marxism in France during the early Third Republic has long suffered from remarks such as these. In his 1966 classic, *Marxism in Modern France*, the historian of socialism George Lichtheim dismissed the beginning of the 1880s as 'a dead loss' in terms of 'the implantation of socialist theory' in France: '[w]hat passed for Marxism in the 1880s . . . was at best an approximation and at worst a caricature . . . a mere parody'.[5] It was not until the late 1880s and early 1890s, and the rise of better-educated and more cultured theorists such as Jean Jaurès and

[1] G. Stedman Jones, *Karl Marx: Greatness and Illusion* (London: Allen Lane, 2016), p.144.

[2] See, for example, M. Rubel and M. Manale, *Marx Without Myth: A Chronological Study of His Life and Work* (Oxford: Basil Blackwell, 1975), p.243.

[3] Stedman Jones, *Karl Marx*, p.435.

[4] 195: F. Engels to E. Bernstein, 2–3 November 1882 (London), in K. Marx and F. Engels, *Marx/Engels Collected Works*, (trans.) R. Dixon et al., vol.46 (50 vols.) (London: Lawrence and Wishart, 1975–2004), 353, 358, at p.356.

[5] G. Lichtheim, *Marxism in Modern France* (New York: Columbia University Press, 1966), p.9. See also C. Willard, *Jules Guesde, l'apôtre et la loi* (Paris: Éditions ouvrières, 1991), p.50; M. Agulhon, *Marianne au pouvoir: l'imagerie et la symbolique républicaine de 1880 à 1914* (Paris: Flammarion, 1989), p.292.

Georges Sorel, he claimed, that Marx's ideas began to make an impact in France.[6] Lichtheim's French contemporaries, such as Claude Willard and Daniel Ligou, were somewhat more forgiving of early Third Republican socialists. In their opinion, Paul Lafargue and Jules Guesde especially deserved credit for introducing Marxist ideas into France and, in doing so, breathing life back into the French socialist movement after the fall of the Commune. Yet they also remained faithful to the spirit of Engels's disdain.[7] While Guesde and Lafargue may have saved French revolution- ary activism and introduced Marxism into France, they had also systemat- ically misunderstood Marx's thought.

More recent work on French socialism has adopted an alternative focus, but the perception that there were no 'true' French Marxists until the late 1880s has remained. Reacting against the characterisation of Guesde and Lafargue as the saviours of French activism,[8] numerous historians began in the last quarter of the twentieth century to unearth the contributions of other actors to the development of French socialism. B.H. Moss's *Origins of the French Labour Movement* examined workers' associations between 1830 and 1914, while David Stafford, Steven Vincent, and Edward Berenson have provided biographies of alternative socialist figureheads such as Pierre-Joseph Proudhon and Guesde and Lafargue's political opponents Paul Brousse and Benoît Malon. This work constructed a different genealogy of French socialism, in which Marx was of little importance, and no French revolutionary socialists, even the Guesdists, were 'really' Marxists. The explanation for French socialism's development and historical trajectory, they argued, was to be found not in the power of Marxism, but in a combination of its institutions and the continued appeal of a much longer, distinctly non-Marxist French tradition.[9] In Vincent's

---

[6] Lichtheim, *Marxism in Modern France*. For Jaurès, see p.11; for Sorel, see p.9.

[7] See D. Ligou, *Histoire du socialisme en France (1871–1961)* (Paris: Presses Universitaires de France, 1962), p.25; S. Bernstein, *The Beginnings of Marxian Socialism in France* (New York: Russell & Russell Inc, 1965. First published, 1933), p.148; C. Willard, *Socialisme et communisme français* (Paris: Armand Colin, 1978. First published, 1967), p.61; see also p.65; J. Boulad-Ayoub, 'Marx: Thinking the Revolution', in D. Moggach and P. Leduc Browne (eds.), *The Social Question and the Democratic Revolution: Marx and the Legacy of 1848* (Ottawa: University of Ottawa Press, 2000), 101–110, at p.101; P. Hutton, *The Cult of the Revolutionary Tradition: The Blanquists in French Politics, 1864–1893* (Berkeley: University of California Press, 1981), p.100. By 'the new socialism', Hutton means Guesde and Lafargue.

[8] See, for example, Willard, *Socialisme et communisme français*, p.56; J. Moreau, *Les socialistes français et le mythe révolutionnaire* (Paris: Hachette, 2003), p.37.

[9] B.H. Moss, *The Origins of the French Labor Movement 1830–1914: The Socialism of Skilled Workers* (Berkeley: University of California Press, 1976), p.xi, p.8, p.18; J. Plamenatz, *The Revolutionary Movement in France 1815–1871* (London: Longmans, Green and Co, 1952), p.177.

words, 'in the early history of French socialism, the role of Marxism was marginal'.[10]

Whilst they advance vastly different hypotheses, these bodies of literature are united by two beliefs. First, that there exists an 'authentic', definitive Marxism, and second that this true Marxism did not make it to France during the 1870s and early 1880s. As a result of these apparent certainties, none of the historians mentioned above has attempted to interrogate contemporary French understandings of either Karl Marx himself or the idea of Marxism (which are related, but by no means identical subjects). Neither have they fully explored why French activists were apparently so attracted or unattracted to either. French socialists have simply been decisively categorised as either Marxists or not. Although several historians, such as Vincent and Leslie Derfler, have hinted at more complex intellectual interactions with Marxism, they have not developed or expanded upon their observations.[11] Like Lichtheim's classic study, more nuanced work on French Marxism, such as Robert Stuart's *Marxism at Work: Ideology, Class and French Socialism during the Third Republic*, has focused almost exclusively upon the period from the late 1880s onwards.[12]

Part III addresses itself to this historiographical absence. Rather than trying to discern whether French socialists were 'real' Marxists or not, it attempts to approach Marx and Marxism in the early Third Republic with the historical sensitivity that has so far been reserved for studies of Proudhonism and Possibilist socialism.[13] It juxtaposes and examines a variety of published and manuscript sources, arguing that Marxian ideas and language featured both more frequently and in more nuanced ways in French socialist thought during this period than has previously been suggested. The ways in which socialists invoked and interacted with Marx and Marxism did not resemble in the slightest the sharply delineated orthodoxy that has conventionally been associated with it, and with French

[10] K.S. Vincent, *Between Marxism and Anarchism: Benoît Malon and French Reformist Socialism* (Berkeley: University of California Press, 1992), p.3 and p.74; E. Berenson, *Populist Religion and Left-Wing Politics in France, 1830–1852* (Princeton, NJ: Princeton University Press, 1984), pp.237–238; J. Jennings, *Revolution and the Republic: A History of Political Thought in France since the Eighteenth Century* (Oxford: Oxford University Press, 2011), p.405.

[11] L. Derfler, *Paul Lafargue and the Flowering of French Socialism, 1882–1911* (Cambridge, MA: Harvard University Press, 1998), pp.xiii–xiv; Vincent, *Between Marxism and Anarchism*, p.100.

[12] R. C. Stuart, *Marxism at Work: Ideology, Class and French Socialism during the Third Republic* (Cambridge: Cambridge University Press, 1992).

[13] K.S. Vincent, *Pierre-Joseph Proudhon and the Rise of French Republican Socialism* (Oxford: Oxford University Press, 1984), pp.206–207; D. Stafford, *From Anarchism to Reformism: A Study of the Political Activities of Paul Brousse within the First International and the French Socialist Movement 1870–1890* (London: Cox & Wyman, 1971), pp.5–6.

Marxism in particular. Rather, French interactions with Marx and Marxism during this period were diffuse and shifting, and had yet to become imbued with the doctrinal significance and rigidity that they would take on in the late 1880s.

In order to properly understand French Marxism, we must first understand how Marx appeared in France. This chapter examines Marx's involvement in French socialist thought and action. Drawing upon the French publications of his work and his personal interactions with French activists, it argues that, contrary to the standard view, Marx's ideas were widely available in France at this time through a series of translations that appeared from 1872. These translations presented a 'French Marx' that was subtly, but noticeably, different from both the German original and other versions, and whose ideas were more finely attuned to French circumstances.

The construction of this French Marx, moreover, was overseen and encouraged by Marx himself, who in translation was often willing to sacrifice the 'purity' of his ideas in order to broaden their appeal. Marx was thus not separate or distant from French Marxism, but neither was the increasing visibility of his thought in French workers' circles the result of a top-down or 'foreign' imposition. Rather, the creation of the French Marx was a constant process of collaboration and circulation between French activists, French circumstances, and Marx himself. The chapter concludes by contrasting the construction of the French Marx with his rigidity in the International Workingmen's Association, arguing that in order to fully understand the relationship between Marx and France during this period, scholars must combine the two.

This chapter draws upon primary sources across several languages. It focuses primarily upon the French versions of Marx's texts that were available during this period, and principally upon *Le Capital*.[14] In order to ascertain the precise character of the French Marx, these texts are compared and contrasted with their German originals. They are also placed in the context of Marx's specific work on France, including *The Class Struggles in France* and *The Eighteenth Brumaire of Louis Bonaparte*.[15] The chapter also makes use of abridged French versions of Marx's texts,

---

[14] K. Marx, *Le Capital* (trans.) J. Roy (Paris: Maurice Lachâtre, 1872–1875. First published in German, 1867).

[15] K. Marx, *The Class Struggles in France, 1848–1850* (trans.) H. Kuhn (New York: New York Labor News Co., 1924. First published in German, 1850); K. Marx, *The Eighteenth Brumaire of Louis Bonaparte* (trans.) T. Carver, in M. Cowling and J. Martin (eds.), *Marx's Eighteenth Brumaire: (Post) modern Interpretations* (London: Pluto Press, 2002. First published in German, 1852), 19–109.

specifically Gabriel Deville's 1883 *Le Capital de Karl Marx*.[16] In order to more fully understand the processes of translation and dissemination, these published works have been supplemented with the private correspondence of a number of individuals. These include Marx and his long-time collaborator Friedrich Engels, as well as figures more embedded in French socialist circles, including Laura Lafargue – a prolific translator of Marx's work, as well as his daughter and Paul Lafargue's wife.

I

The twenty-year period between the mid-1860s and his death in 1883 was the time in which Marx could be said to have truly arrived. His involvement in the International Workingmen's Association, plus his 1871 work on the Paris Commune, *The Civil War in France*, placed Marx at the heart of the international socialist movement. From 1872 onwards, this renown was further burnished by the widespread reissuing of the *Communist Manifesto*. In March, August Bebel and Wilhelm Liebknecht, the leaders of the German Social Democratic Party, were prosecuted for treason in a highly publicised trial in Leipzig. The *Manifesto* appeared as evidence for the prosecution in the trial, and brought a newfound general public awareness to its ideas.[17] Throughout the 1870s, Marx's reputation as the 'Red Terror Doctor' inspired hatred and adulation in equal measure, haunting monarchs and governments and inspiring the creation of a wave of new, explicitly 'Marxist' parties across Europe. France was no exception to this trend, as the establishment of the Parti Ouvrier Français in 1880 attests.

Surprisingly, given Marx's increasing visibility in French circles during this period, his work has been very little mentioned by historians. In the mid-twentieth century, Marx's work in French attracted considerable attention from philosophers and social scientists – most notably in the form of Louis Althusser's 1965 classic *Lire le Capital*, which reproduced discussions from a Marxist reading group staged at the Sorbonne.[18] A decade later, the radical sociologist Kevin Anderson published an article

---

[16] G. Deville (ed.), *Le Capital de Karl Marx* (Paris: Henry Oriol, 1883).

[17] G. Stedman Jones, 'Introduction', in K. Marx and F. Engels, *The Communist Manifesto* (ed.) G. Stedman Jones, (trans.) S. Moore (London: Penguin Books, 2002. First published in German, 1848), pp.16–17.

[18] L. Althusser, É. Balibar, R. Establet, P. Macherey, and J. Rancière, *Reading Capital: The Complete Edition* (trans.) B. Brewster and D. Fernbach (London: Verso, 2015. First published in French, 1965), p.5; p.11.

on the subject, although this has not been followed up by further work.[19] By contrast, the interaction between Marx's ideas and France during this period has attracted almost no attention from historians.

This has been due in large part, perhaps, to French socialists' own vocal claims about the difficulties of understanding Marx. On receiving the second volume of *Das Kapital* in 1885, for example, Paul Lafargue confessed that he, Jules Guesde, and Gabriel Deville were unable to understand it. They were, he confessed to Engels, like 'monkeys turning over and over nuts that they cannot crack'.[20] Lafargue referred not to a failure to comprehend Marx's theory, but to something more prosaic: a language barrier. In a later letter, Paul's wife Laura Lafargue again raised this issue, informing Engels that '[t]he book has been reverently *looked at* and handled by our prisoner [Lafargue] and his friends, one and all of whom are unable to *read* German.'[21] Whereas later French readers of Marx such as the legendary socialist leader Jean Jaurès and the philosopher Georges Sorel were versed in German and therefore able to access Marx's work in the original, the vast majority of French socialists in the 1870s and early 1880s were not. Given that Marx had only produced two texts in French by 1870,[22] access to his original work during this period was highly limited in France.

Despite these complaints, though, French socialists showed little commitment to altering their situation. Both Guesde and Lafargue spent a number of years learning German, yet their inability to comprehend *Das Kapital* suggests that they failed to make any substantive progress.[23] Indeed, this was indicative of a broader disinclination amongst French activists towards interacting with foreign socialists on their own terms.

[19] K. Anderson, 'The "Unknown" Marx's *Capital*, Volume 1: The French Edition of 1872–1875, 100 Years Later', *Review of Radical Political Economics* 15 (1983), 71–80. Terrell Carver has also discussed issues of translation, although in a different context. See T. Carver, 'Marx's *Eighteenth Brumaire of Louis Bonaparte*: Democracy, Dictatorship, and Class Struggle', in P. Baehr and M. Richter (eds.), *Dictatorship in History and Theory: Bonapartism, Caesarism, and Totalitarianism* (Cambridge: Cambridge University Press, 2004), 103–127, at pp.122–123.

[20] 159: P. Lafargue to F. Engels (Sainte-Pélagie, 12 July 1885), in F. Engels, and P. and L. Lafargue, *Correspondence*, 3 vols. (trans.) Y. Kapp (Moscow: Foreign Languages Publishing House, 1959–1960), vol.1, 296–299, at p.296.

[21] 160: L. Lafargue to F. Engels (Paris, 18 July 1885), in Engels and Lafargue, *Correspondence*, vol.1, 299–301, at pp.299–300. Emphasis original. See also E. Jousse, *Réviser le marxisme? D'Éduard Bernstein à Albert Thomas, 1896–1914* (Paris: L'Harmattan, 2007), p.110.

[22] K. Marx, *Misère de la philosophie: réponse à La philosophie de la misère de M. Proudhon* (Paris: A. Frank, 1847); K. Marx, *Discours sur la question du libre-échange* (Brussels: Aux frais de l'Association démocratique de Bruxelles, 1848).

[23] See, for example, 70: F. Engels to L. Lafargue (London, 11 April 1883), in Engels and Lafargue, *Correspondence*, vol.1, 124–125, at p.125.

Lafargue, for instance, was born and raised in Cuba and spoke several languages fluently, including Spanish and Italian.[24] Yet at an 1866 meeting of the Central Council of the International Workingmen's Association, delegates apparently

> burst out laughing when Marx commented that Lafargue, who wanted to abolish nations and nationalities, had addressed them in French with the result that nine-tenths could not understand.[25]

As Part II demonstrated, French revolutionaries and socialists had long been committed to universal revolution. Yet both before and after their time in exile, they appeared unable and unwilling to engage with foreign socialists on anything but French terms. This lack of linguistic curiosity has perhaps been taken as indicative of intellectual indifference towards foreign thinkers and activists, including Marx, on the part of French socialists. Indeed, historiographical assumptions about French socialists' ambivalence to foreign ideas dovetail with other work that emphasises their preference for *franco-français* revolutionary traditions.

Yet although French access to Marx's writing was limited, it was far from non-existent. French translations of Marx underwent something of a boom in the period after 1871. The first volume of *Capital* appeared in instalments from 1872 to 1875, and an abridged version followed in 1883.[26] *The Civil War in France* first became available in French in 1871, and the *Communist Manifesto* followed in 1872.[27] Major new translations of each appeared in the 1880s.[28] Lafargue's best-selling abridged version of Engels's *Anti-Dühring*, entitled *Socialisme scientifique et socialisme utopique* (which Sorel would later describe as the catechism of modern Marxism[29]) was also first published in 1880.[30] In addition, serialisations of *Misère de la philosophie* and the *Communist Manifesto* further appeared in the long running and widely read Guesdist daily

---

[24] For Italian, see Derfler, *Paul Lafargue and the Flowering of French Socialism*, p.34.

[25] Rubel and Manale, *Marx Without Myth*, p.217.

[26] Marx, *Le Capital*; Deville, *Le Capital de Karl Marx*.

[27] For *The Civil War in France*, see Marx and Engels, *MECW*, vol.22 (1985), p.666. For the *Communist Manifesto*, see C. Willard, *Le socialisme de la renaissance à nos jours* (Paris: Presses universitaires de France, 1971), p.50.

[28] Derfler, *Paul Lafargue and the Flowering of French Socialism*, p.21.

[29] M. Angenot, *Les grands récits militants des XIXe et XXe siècles: religions de l'humanité et sciences de l'histoire* (Paris: L'Harmattan, 2000), p.134. For a similar assertion from Karl Kautsky, see Stedman Jones, *Karl Marx: Greatness and Illusion*, p.560.

[30] 'Socialisme utopique et socialisme scientifique', *La révue socialiste* (Paris) 3–5, March–May 1880.

newspaper *L'Égalité*, ensuring that Marx's work reached an even broader audience.[31] This publishing boom may have been a result of Marx's work on the Commune, which had a significant impact in France, or of French socialists' increased contact with (and subsequent interest in) him through the International Workingmen's Association. Regardless of the precise reason, though, French translations of Marx became progressively more available during this period.

Marx therefore had the potential to be of far more than merely symbolic importance for socialists in late nineteenth-century France. Historians have often implied that Marx's ideas and his work were largely inaccessible to French socialists before the late 1880s, and are therefore of little historical relevance.[32] Unable to speak German, it is suggested, French socialists during this period had no way of accessing Marx's thought. In *Le marxisme dans les grands récits*, Marc Angenot branded the 'doctrine of Karl Marx' 'apparently inaccessible' to French socialists,[33] while Edward Berenson described it as 'an alien and largely inscrutable dogma'.[34] In fact these texts have been banished to such dark recesses that historians are rarely even concerned with verifying simple facts such as when they first appeared in French.[35]

French socialists during this period, though, were neither unable nor unwilling to read Marx. In fact, quite the opposite was true. Although the French population's access to the original texts may have been circumscribed, French translations of Marx vastly increased during this period. This granted French readers both meaningful access to Marx's thought and the chance to engage with him as a philosopher and social critic for the first time. Marx, in other words, was more than simply a figurehead in French socialist circles during this period. He was also an intellectual figure, and his texts were of considerable importance.

[31] 'La misère de la philosophie', *L'Égalité* (Paris), 7 April 1880. *The Communist Manifesto* appeared in 1882; see Willard, *Jules Guesde, l'apôtre et la loi*, p.45.

[32] For the suggestion that there was a lack of translations, see, for example, Derfler, *Paul Lafargue and the Flowering of French Socialism*, p.21; Willard, *Le socialisme de la renaissance à nos jours*, p.50. Indeed, he disagrees with his own position; see Willard, *Socialisme et communisme français*, p.62; Vincent, *Between Marxism and Anarchism*, p.71; C. Willard, *Jules Guesde, l'apôtre et la loi* (Paris: Éditions ouvrières, 1991), p.46; Jousse, *Réviser le marxisme?*, p.110.

[33] '[A]pparemment inaccessible'. M. Angenot, *Le Marxisme dans les grands récits: essai d'analyse du discours* (Paris: L'Harmattan, 2005), p.18.

[34] Berenson, *Populist Religion and Left-Wing Politics in France*, p.237.

[35] See, for example, Derfler, *Paul Lafargue and the Flowering of French Socialism*, p.21; Willard, *Le socialisme de la renaissance à nos jours*, p.50. Indeed, he disagrees with his own position, see Willard, *Socialisme et communisme français*, p.62. See also Vincent, *Between Marxism and Anarchism*, p.71; Willard, *Jules Guesde, l'apôtre et la loi*, p.46.

II

Importantly, French translations were not always identical to the originals. This is of course to a certain extent to be expected of any translation, yet in this case the changes were particularly notable. It is to some of these that I shall now turn. In order to provide a sufficiently detailed and comprehensive analysis, I shall focus upon one translation: that of the first volume of *Das Kapital*. It was this text in which translational changes were most prominent. Some were little more than simplifications,[36] or clarifications,[37] but others significantly altered the tone of some of the text's most well-known chapters.[38] Although the alterations constituted only a small percentage of the text as a whole, they were thus significant nonetheless. Given the centrality of issues of translation to this section, all relevant quotations will be provided within the text in their original language. These have been drawn from the 1872 German edition of *Das Kapital* and the 1872–1875 French *Le Capital*. English translations appear in the footnotes.

Originally published in German in 1867, the first French edition of *Das Kapital* followed five years later. The translation was carried out by Joseph Roy, who had previously translated Ludwig Feuerbach into French, and the work was published by Maurice Lachâtre.[39] A radical editor of some renown, Lachâtre had worked with various revolutionaries and socialists including Louis Blanc and the Blanquist journalist Félix Pyat, and had also been Louis Auguste Blanqui's first choice of editor for *L'éternité par les astres*.[40] *Le Capital* was originally published between 1872 and 1875 in instalments priced at 10 *centimes* each; a strategy that Lachâtre hoped would 'enable as many of our friends [the working class] as possible to get hold of' copies.[41] A complete version of the translated text was also published in 1875 to mark the end of the serialisation, with Marx carrying the costs for printing and materials.[42]

---

[36] Compare, for example, Marx, *Le Capital*, pp.28–29, and K. Marx, *Capital, Volume 1* (trans.) B. Fowkes (London: Penguin, 1990. First published, 1976), pp.164–165; Marx, *Le Capital*, p.29 and Marx, *Capital, Volume 1*, pp.166–167; Marx, *Le capital*, p.342 and Marx, *Capital, Volume 1*, p.929.

[37] Compare Marx, *Le capital*, p.341 and Marx, *Capital, Volume 1*, pp.927–928.

[38] Anderson, 'The "Unknown" Marx's *Capital*, Volume 1', at p.72.

[39] J. Siegel, *Marx's Fate: The Shape of a Life* (Princeton, NJ: Princeton University Press, 1978), p.368.

[40] See L.A. Blanqui to Mme. Barrelier, 3 January 1872, in L.A. Blanqui, *L'éternité par les astres* (ed.) L. Block de Behar (Geneva: Éditions Slatkine, 2009. First published, 1872),47–50, at p.50.

[41] 'Le mode de publication que nous avons adopté, par livraisons à dix centimes, aura cet avantage, de permettre à un plus grand nombre de nos amis de se procurer votre livre'. Marx, *Le Capital*, p.8.

[42] Rubel and Manale, *Marx Without Myth*, p.271.

Chapter 15 section 4, 'The Factory', provides the clearest example of the possible effects of these small changes. This section was central to the text's narrative of the development of capitalism and addressed a series of pressing contemporary concerns. It was here that Marx tackled the ways in which the modern industrial workplace had transformed the relationship between workers and their tools, delineating also the effects that this had had upon the labourer.

Marx was certainly not the first to address this subject matter. The potential effects of industrialisation upon labour had occupied theorists from across the political spectrum for much of the nineteenth century. The liberal political economist Charles Dunoyer, for example, concluded his 1825 survey of the relationship between industry and liberty in different societies with a consideration of 'the obstacles to liberty in the industrial regime, or the inevitable limits that it encounters in the nature of things'. In the 1839 *Organisation du travail*, meanwhile, Louis Blanc sought to reconcile industrial capitalism with more equitable working conditions.[43] As industrialisation spread and the pace of social change accelerated, it also became increasingly important at the level of policy. In Britain, for example, Parliament passed a series of Factory Acts, which were designed to regulate the working hours and conditions of industrial labour (particularly child labour) and established a national Factory Inspectorate. These acts were continuously debated and amended throughout the century as the subject matter continued to mutate, occupying and perplexing successive generations of politicians.[44]

Marx was pessimistic about the benefits of this type of legislation. Building upon the premises established in other work including the *Communist Manifesto* and his private notebooks (eventually published as the *Grundrisse der Kritik der Politischen Ökonomie* in 1939), he argued that technological advancements and the invention of machinery capable of performing the tasks of multiple workers had drastically reversed the roles of labour and labourer. Where once labourers had been the motor of industry, they had now been displaced by the machine. In modern production, 'the motion of the whole factory proceeds not from the worker but from the machinery'.[45] This, Marx argued, had exacerbated existing

---

[43] C. Dunoyer, *L'industrie et la morale considérées dans leurs rapports avec la liberté* (Paris: A. Sautelet, 1825); L. Blanc, *Organisation du travail*, 5th edn (Paris: Au bureau de la Société de l'industrie fraternelle, 1847. First published, 1839).

[44] For more on the Factory Acts, see W.R. Cornish and G. de N. Clark, *Law and Society in England, 1750–1950* (London: Sweet & Maxwell, 1989).

[45] Marx, *Capital*, Volume I, p.546.

social distinctions and created a situation of radical inequality. The reversal of momentum initiated by industrialisation meant that tasks could be performed by anyone. As a result, labour had become cheap, abundant, and, as a result, disposable. Meanwhile machines, which capitalists perceived to be responsible for vast increases in productivity, were assigned significant value. This in turn enabled their owners to accrue status, capital, and as a result power on a scale vastly disproportionate to their personal contribution. The factory brought together all of these elements on a large scale and under one roof. In doing so, it both represented industrial capitalism in its purest form and elevated it to a higher stage of development.

The effects of the factory upon the worker were, according to Marx, twofold. Professionally and economically, it reduced them to a state of dual servitude. Workers were now entirely reliant upon the factory owner and the machine they operated; the former for employment and the latter in order to produce the number of products required. Whereas '[i]n handicrafts and manufacture', Marx wrote, 'the worker makes use of a tool; in the factory, the machine makes use of him'.[46] Naturally, this economic state of affairs also had political implications. Within the walls of their factory, the owner exercised absolute power over their workers. In particular, the abundance of cheap labour meant they had the power to hire and fire at will without fear of consequences.

This untrammelled power meant that the owner was not just an employer, but also effectively a sovereign. The territory of this 'factory Lycurgus' took the form not of the supposedly democratic state outside its walls, but of a military dictatorship in which workers were 'the private soldiers and the N.C.O.s of an industrial army'.[47] The social composition of factories thus exposed both the limits and the hypocrisy of the bourgeois state. Inside the factory, the supposedly universal rights won in successive French revolutions were thrown aside. Outside, meanwhile, politicians genuflected to the capital that kept the economy running and sought only to preserve their own interests. Legislation such as the Factory Acts was thus powerless to stop this exploitation, for it had never been designed with workers' interests in mind.

Factories also affected workers' mental and psychological health. The original version of 'The Factory' emphasised the debilitating effects of industrial conditions at every opportunity. In order to acquire any level of proficiency at their new job as machine assistants, *Das Kapital* argued

[46] Ibid., p.548.   [47] Ibid., pp.549–550.

that the labourer must devote their entire life to familiarising themselves with a single machine:

> Alle Arbeit an der Maschine erfordert früzeitigen Einbruch des Arbeiters, damit er seine eigene Bewegung der gleichförmig kontinuirlichen Bewegung eines Automaten anpassen lerne.[48]

Yet this professional dedication, Marx claimed, yielded no individual benefit for the worker. Although the ghosts of old professional hierarchies often remained, in the factory all labour was unskilled labour. The routine and repetitive nature of life at machinery (indeed, at one machine) 'sondern seine Arbeit vom Inhalt',[49] and '[d]as Detailgeschick des individuellen, entleerten Maschinenarbeiters verschwindet'.[50] In the factory, it was impossible for the worker to derive any pleasure or individual benefit from their work. The work itself was meaningless, and all time in the factory was dead time. What's more, the dehumanising nature of this work also affected all other aspects of workers' lives. For the labourer, the factory was all-consuming, and the extreme state of their dependency had effectively reduced them to a part of the machinery. As such, no other life was possible outside of their work.

Le Capital certainly did not embrace factory labour, but its condemnation was less comprehensive. Here, machinery deprived work of its 'intérêt' rather than of its 'content' or its significance.[51] Similarly, the worker's particular skill did not vanish when confronted with the factory owner's power, but instead appeared 'chétive' in comparison.[52] In *Le Capital*, industrial labour was draining and demeaning, and it was certainly not stimulating or interesting. Yet the French translation stopped short of claiming that it was pointless or deprived of content. While the worker may have been disempowered, they nonetheless retained some form of skill. Equally, whereas *Das Kapital* asserted that in order to master a single machine children must subject themselves to it from an early age, the French translation observed rather that '[t]out enfant apprend très-facilement à adapter ses mouvements au mouvement continu et uniforme de l'automate.'[53] In outlining the worker's relationship to machinery,

[48] 'The worker must be taught from childhood upwards, in order that he may learn to adapt his own movements to the uniform and unceasing motion of an automaton'. K. Marx, *Das Kapital, Band 1*, 2nd edn (Hamburg: Verlag von Otto Meissner, 1872. First published, 1867), p.442.
[49] '[D]eprive[d] the work itself of all content'. Marx, *Das Kapital*, p.444.
[50] 'The special skill of each individual machine-operator . . . vanishes'. Marx, *Das Kapital*, p.445.
[51] Marx, *Le Capital*, p.183.   [52] '[M]eagre'. Ibid., p.183.
[53] 'Every child learns very easily to adapt their movements to the continuous and uniform movement of the automaton.' Ibid., p.182.

Le Capital's focus was thus significantly different from *Das Kapital*'s. While, for instance, child labour remained a terrible form of exploitation, *Le Capital* prioritised the worker's skill rather than their subjection. At the very least, in *Le Capital*, the two were not necessarily mutually exclusive.

A comparison of 'Der Fabrik' and 'La fabrique' thus reveals the potential that these changes had for significantly altering the text. In both German and French, *Capital* addressed the same questions and made the same broad points, yet the detail was subtly different and could appreciably change the tone of the text. The relationship between workers, factories, and machinery remained one of subjection and alienation, and in both versions the skilled worker was reduced to a state of dependency. In *Le Capital*, though, this process was both more complicated and less certain. Here, the worker retained skill and individuality, and although both were diminishing, the text gave no indication that either would be completely obliterated by further industrial development.

In *Le Capital*, the worker remained an entity separate from the machine they operated. This raised the possibility that they could both maintain private interests and a life outside of work and pursue workers' empowerment within the factory itself. Moreover, in highlighting workers' ability to quickly master machinery, the text even hinted that wage-labourers could potentially harness industrialisation for their own benefit. Whether it was indicative of a different attitude towards factory work in general or simply reflective of France's lesser stage of industrial development, *Le Capital*'s treatment of the subject was strikingly different. Where *Das Kapital* left very little room for movement or variation, in *Le Capital* the experience of industrial labour was less uniform, less exceptional, and more flexible. Within the factory of 'La fabrique', the worker retained multiple (if decreasing) options, as well as the ability to make independent decisions.

This more plural, or hesitant, approach was also present in other parts of the text. Discussing the development of capitalism in Chapter 26,[54] 'The Secret of Primitive Accumulation', Marx wrote in *Das Kapital* that it

> nimmt in verschiednen Ländern verschiedne Färbung an und durchläuft die verschiednen Phasen in verschiedner Reihenfolge. Nur in England, das wir daher als Beispiel nehmen, besitzt sie *klassische Form*.[55]

---

[54] In the German original, this is chapter 24.

[55] '[A]ssumes different aspects in different countries, and runs through its various phases in different orders of succession, and at different historical epochs. Only in England, which we therefore take as our example, has it *the classic form*'. Marx, *Das Kapital*, p.745. Emphasis mine.

The French translation proceeded in much the same fashion, but for one alteration. While such developments had as yet only occurred in England, *Le Capital* noted that 'tous les autres pays de l'Europe occidentale parcourent le même mouvement'.[56] On one level, Marx accepted in both versions of *Capital* that the form of capital's development would vary from country to country according to the particularities of its historical development.

The French version, though, was both more restrictive and more permissive. Note the difference in geographical application. Whereas *Das Kapital* attached universal relevance to England's path of development, *Le Capital* merely stated that 'tous les autres pays de l'Europe occidentale' would undertake this path. On the one hand, this alteration definitively tied France to a particular model of development. Yet on the other, it also opened up the possibility of some countries experiencing not just a different pace of development, but a different form of development altogether. As Gareth Stedman Jones has recently demonstrated, Marx had been privately gravitating towards an appreciation for primitive communes since the late 1860s,[57] yet he did not publicly come around to the idea until the early 1880s in the famous letter to Vera Zasulich. In French, however, there was no such transition, for the Marx of *Le Capital* had always been open to plural trajectories of historical development. Until the early 1880s, in other words, the French version of Marx was uniquely plural.

The Marx of *Le Capital*, then, was subtly but significantly different from the Marx of *Das Kapital*. While the changes made to the text in translation were rare and often little more than one word, they considerably altered the tone and the meaning of important sections of the text. These changes fashioned a Marx that was more permissive, more cautiously optimistic about the situation of the modern worker, and more overtly plural. Unlike in *Das Kapital*, in *Le Capital* Marx recognised the potential for industrialisation and individual self-worth to coexist, the potentially positive impact of large-scale machinery, and the possibility of different trajectories of historical progress. Thus while they may nominally have been engaging with the same work, Marx's French audience was in fact reading and interpreting a text that was notably different from the original. Given these discrepancies, in order to properly understand French engagement

---

[56] 'All other Western European countries will experience the same movement'. Marx, *Le Capital*, p.315. For another discussion of this, see Stedman Jones, *Karl Marx*, p.581.
[57] Stedman Jones, *Karl Marx*, pp.578–579.

with Marx's ideas during this period, a close examination of these translations is essential.

III

The French Marx, moreover, was not confined to *Le Capital*. Historians of
French Marxism eager to justify their lack of attention to these translations
have frequently argued that they were neither widely read nor widely
known during the nineteenth century, and are thus of little relevance.[58]
Let us take *Le Capital* as an example again. It certainly seems to have been
the case that *Le Capital* failed to reach its target audience. Indeed, Marx's
own postface to the 1873 German edition of *Das Kapital* suggested as
much. When discussing *Le Capital's* reception in France, he mentioned
only positivists such as Émile Littré, suggesting that it had failed to make
an impact on the desired working-class demographic.[59] This trend apparently persisted for some years. A decade later, Marx remarked to Engels
that 'it would now seem to be the fashion for French real or would be
"advanced" leaders' such as Georges Clemenceau to read *Le Capital*, but
again made no reference to workers.[60]

The precise reasons for this lack of attention are unclear, although there
are several possibilities. The intention of publishing *Le Capital* gradually in
serialised form had been that workers would be able to both afford and
digest it, however the commitment required to keep abreast of a three-year
serialisation was significant. Indeed, Marx had initially voiced concerns
about this before the translation began, writing in a letter to Lachâtre that

> the method of analysis that I have employed, which has never been applied
> to economic subjects before, makes reading the first chapters rather ardu-
> ous. I am worried that the French public ... will become discouraged if
> they cannot skip past them.[61]

---

[58] See, for example, Angenot, *Le Marxisme dans les grands récits*, p.18; Moreau, *Les socialistes français et le mythe révolutionnaire*, p.45.

[59] K. Marx, 'Postface to the second edition' (1873), in Marx, *Capital, Volume 1*, 94–103, at p.99.

[60] 187: K. Marx to F. Engels, 30 September 1882 (Paris), *MECW*, vol.46 (1992), 338–339, at p.339. The English socialist leader Henry Hyndman also read *Capital* in French. See Stedman Jones, *Karl Marx*, p.550.

[61] '[L]a méthode d'analyse que j'ai employée et qui n'avait pas encore appliquée aux sujets économiques rend assez ardue la lecture des premiers chapitres, et il est à craindre que le public français ... ne se rebute parce qu'il n'aura pu tout d'abord passer outre.' K. Marx to M. Lachâtre, 18 March 1872 (London), in Marx, *Le Capital*, p.7.

Moreover, the serialised *Le Capital* was published in Paris during the decade that most Communards were exiled from France, meaning that its initial audience was likely severely limited.

Yet this did not mean that workers were unfamiliar with either the text or its ideas. In the early 1880s, Gabriel Deville, a young socialist journalist and associate of Guesde and Lafargue, obtained permission from Marx to publish a short version of *Le Capital*, which would be more accessible to workers than a long, scholarly tome.[62] The resulting book, *Le Capital de Karl Marx*, first appeared in 1883. It retained the structure of the original work, but in a heavily abridged form, and was accompanied by a long preface. Written by Deville, this explained the text, situated it within Marx's other work, and outlined possible strategies for its practical implementation.[63] Despite several mentions of it in the correspondence of Marx's closest associates, *Le Capital de Karl Marx* has rarely even been mentioned by historians, let alone discussed.[64]

At the time, however, it enjoyed a high level of exposure. This included large advertisements in prominent workers' newspapers, such as Prosper-Olivier Lissagaray's long-running Parisian daily *Le Citoyen & La Bataille*.[65] In fact, *Le Capital de Karl Marx* was simply one example of a much wider contemporary socialist practice called 'workers' libraries'.[66] Under this scheme, significant dates and texts that were considered important to the development of socialism were abridged (where relevant), summarised, and sold as books, which were often also serialised in newspapers.[67] *Le Capital de Karl Marx*, then, was clearly not considered recondite or unusual at the time. Rather, it was packaged and marketed as a new addition to a popular contemporary practice, and likely enjoyed a similar exposure and readership to other workers' library titles.

The majority of changes made to *Le Capital* were also integrated into *Le Capital de Karl Marx*. In fact, Deville was vocal about his desire to retain the original French text's meaning and its 'very original physiognomy' as far as possible.[68] In sections such as 'La fabrique', the altered passages

---

[62] 160: L. Lafargue to F. Engels (Paris, 18 July 1885), in Engels and Lafargue, *Correspondence*, vol. 1, 299–301, at p.300.

[63] Deville, *Le Capital de Karl Marx*, pp.1–63.

[64] Brief mentions can be found at Rubel and Manale, *Marx Without Myth*, p.327; Angenot, *Le Marxisme dans les grands récits*, p.5.

[65] *Le Citoyen & La Bataille* (Paris), 25 March 1883.

[66] For a reference to this practice, see 'La Bible moderne', *Le Citoyen & La Bataille*, 6 November 1882.

[67] See, for example, V. Marouck, *Les grandes dates du socialisme: Juin 1848* (Paris: Librairie du Progrès, 1880).

[68] '[L]a physionomie si originale de l'ouvrage'. Deville, *Le Capital de Karl Marx*, p.7.

discussed above were reproduced verbatim.[69] Sections such as 'Le secret de l'accumulation primitive', meanwhile, were rephrased to aid comprehension, but nonetheless remained closer to the tone of *Le Capital* than *Das Kapital*.[70] The French Marx was thus not only demonstrably but also consistently different.

While it may have been true that few workers read *Le Capital*, it was therefore certainly not the case that either the text or Marx's ideas were unknown. Rather, as part of a concerted effort to democratise what were considered key texts and ideas, French workers had wide access to an abridged and simplified version. Indeed, the very inclusion of *Le Capital* in this strategy suggests that contemporary French socialist leaders placed great importance upon disseminating and raising awareness of Marx's thought. Equally importantly, *Le Capital de Karl Marx* preserved the unique character of the original French translation. The French Marx, then, was both widely disseminated and widely known.

From the durability of these translational changes, we may infer one final point: that they were intentional. Despite ample opportunity to detect and correct the discrepancies between the publications of the two volumes, *Le Capital de Karl Marx* repeated rather than reversed the alterations made to *Le Capital*. These were not simply mistakes or errors of translation. Instead, the changes made to the French version of *Das Kapital* were indicative of a concerted effort to construct a different Marx.

IV

Marx, moreover, was heavily involved in the alteration process. Dissatisfied with Roy's initial translations, Marx took on much of the work himself.[71] He deemed the French version 'almost [a] complete rewriting', and in fact this was the final edition of *Capital* that he personally supervised before his death.[72] Marx frequently drew attention to the changes he had made. In the 1875 French postface, for example, he suggested that *Le Capital* possessed 'a scientific value independent of the original and should be consulted even by readers familiar with the German'.[73] Indeed, he even

[69] Ibid., pp.192–195.   [70] Ibid., pp.309–311. See particularly p.309.

[71] K. Marx, 'Postface to the French edition' (1875), in Marx, *Capital, Volume 1*, p.105.

[72] 19: K. Marx to F. Sorge, 4 August 1874 (London), *MECW*, vol.45 (1991), 28–30, at p.28. See also
11: K. Marx to L. Kugelmann, 18 May 1874 (London), *MECW*, vol.45, 17–19, at p.17.

[73] Marx, 'Postface to the French Edition', in Marx, *Capital, Volume 1*, p.105. For a similar recommendation several years earlier, see Marx, 'Postface to the Second Edition', in Marx, *Capital, Volume 1*, at pp.94–95.

expressed the hope that the French edition, rather than either of the German ones, would serve as the basis for forthcoming translations in England, Italy, and Spain.[74] These translational changes, then, did not occur without Marx's permission or involvement. Rather, he personally oversaw the alteration process, implementing the changes himself and subsequently actively drawing attention to them.

Marx had in fact always accepted that such changes would be made. From *Le Capital*'s inception, he had been indifferent to questions of 'authenticity', concurring with Lachâtre that the primary aim of the French edition should not be to replicate the original word for word but to reach as many workers as possible. This, he claimed, was 'a consideration which to me outweighs everything else'.[75] Unlike their German counterparts, he noted, French readers were 'always impatient to come to a conclusion, eager to know the connection between general principles and the immediate questions that have aroused their passions'.[76] This different audience would, naturally, require a different text, and indeed Marx's principal criticism of Roy's work was that it was 'far too literal'.[77] Similarly, responding to Engels's criticisms of *Le Capital de Karl Marx* in 1885, Laura Lafargue reminded him that Deville had been 'encouraged to undertake the work by Papa himself'.[78] It has often been posited that Marx was unhappy with the alterations made to *Le Capital*, believing the translation to be 'inauthentic' to the spirit of the original.[79] This, however, was quite clearly not the case. As both his initial letters to Lachâtre and his reaction to the translation indicated, he was neither displeased with the French texts nor concerned with their 'authenticity'. Rather, he was alert to the need to alter the text for a French audience and encouraged efforts to do so.

Indeed, Marx had been planning this translation for some time. In January 1863, he notified Engels of plans to translate *Das Kapital* into French as soon as it was published in German:

[74] For Lachâtre's expression of this hope, see Lâchatre to Marx, in Marx, *Le Capital*; for Marx's, see 227: K. Marx to N. Danielson, 28 May 1872 (London), in *MECW*, vol.44 (1989), 385–386, at p.385.

[75] '[P]our moi cette consideration l'emporte sur toute autre'. K. Marx to M. Lachâtre, 18 March 1872 (London), in Marx, *Le Capital*, p.7.

[76] K. Marx, 'Preface to the French edition' (1872), in Marx, *Capital, Volume 1*, p.104.

[77] Rubel and Manale, *Marx Without Myth*, pp.273–274.

[78] 160: L. Lafargue to F. Engels (Paris, 18 July 1885), in Engels and Lafargue, *Correspondence*, vol.1, 299–301, at p.300.

[79] Rubel and Manale, *Marx Without Myth*, pp.273–274. For a similar assertion, see Angenot, *Les grands récits militants des XIXe et XXe siècles*, p.117.

Through Abarbanel, my wife made the acquaintance in Paris of a certain Reclus, who has some sort of a POSITION in economic literature, and also knows German. The said R. . . and a number of others, is willing to apply himself to my work. They have a Brussels publisher at their disposal.[80]

This plan was more than simply a fleeting distraction, and appeared in a number of Marx's letters from 1862 and 1863.[81] In fact, he suggested that the French translation would be also pivotal to the success of the German original. Writing to Ludwig Kugelmann of the plans in 1862, he confessed, 'I do not think we can count on its having any effect in Germany until it has been given the seal of approval abroad.'[82]

It has been suggested by several scholars that Marx began tinkering with translations and texts that he had already written only late in life. Both Jerrold Siegel and, more recently, Gareth Stedman Jones have intimated that this was a practice born of frustration or dejection, which Marx turned to only after it became clear that the social transformations he had predicted were not materialising.[83] Yet these plans for a French translation at the peak of his success demonstrate that this was not the case. The French translation of *Das Kapital* was more than simply a distraction or an afterthought. Rather, such a translation had been planned since long before either the original was finished or it became clear that Marx's social and economic predictions were not materialising. Translation, in other words, formed an integral part of Marx's project, and his plans for publishing and distributing *Das Kapital*.

Marx's attention to France's circumstances becomes particularly clear when comparing *Le Capital* with some of his other work on France. Part I of this book explored Marx's engagement with the Paris Commune, but France's previous revolutions, especially those of 1848, also featured prominently in his work. There were two particularly clear examples of this. The first, *The Class Struggles in France 1848–1850*, dealt with the revolutions of February and June 1848 and the Second Republic. The second, *The Eighteenth Brumaire of Louis Bonaparte*, examined the political, social, and economic circumstances that led to Louis-Napoléon

---

[80] 265: K. Marx to F. Engels, 2 January 1863 (London), in K. Marx and F. Engels, *MECW*, vol.41, 439–441, at p.439.

[81] See also 261: K. Marx to F. Engels, 24 December 1862 (London), in K. Marx and F. Engels, *MECW*, vol.41 (1985), 432–433, at p.433; 290: K. Marx to F. Engels, 22 June 1863 (London), in Marx and Engels, *MECW*, vol.41, 481–482, at p.482.

[82] 263: K. Marx to L. Kugelmann, 28 December 1862 (London), in Marx and Engels, *MECW*, vol.41, 435–437, at p.436.

[83] Siegel, *Marx's Fate*, p.368; Stedman Jones, *Karl Marx: Greatness and Illusion*, chapter 12: part 1, pp.535–540.

Bonaparte's election as President in December 1848 and his *coup d'état* three years later, which abolished the Second Republic and installed him as emperor.

Unlike *The Civil War in France*, neither of these texts was widely known in French circles at the time. The issue was, again, one of translation, as both were originally published in German. *Class Struggles* appeared as a series of articles in *Neue Rheinische Zeitung* in 1850, and *Eighteenth Brumaire* was published in an American newspaper in 1852. Somewhat surprisingly, neither had been translated into French by 1885. There is a small amount of evidence that some French activists had read *Eighteenth Brumaire*, but it is inconclusive, and the text was certainly not widely known, read, or referenced.[84] These two bodies of work – the French translations and the German texts on France – thus provide an excellent opportunity to directly compare Marx's treatment of similar subjects in different circumstances and for different audiences.

Let us take the issue of workers' and peasants' private property. In *Eighteenth Brumaire*, Marx assigned private property a central role in class development. Discussing the state of the contemporary French countryside, he asserted that '[t]he economic development of small-scale landed property has fundamentally turned round the relationship of the peasantry to the other classes of society.'[85] Attachment to their smallholdings adversely affected the social and personal economic development of the French peasantry, preserving them as 'a nation of troglodytes'.[86] At the same time, though, such property was also the motor of national economic development, producing a fortune in revenues from taxation. It was on these economic foundations that the bourgeois state was built and grew, and as a result it also forced the development of class consciousness.[87]

Fifteen years later in *Das Kapital*, Marx made a similar argument about property. Here, he defined workers' private property as 'the foundation of small-scale industry',[88] which was in turn 'a necessary condition for the development of social production and of the free individuality of the worker himself'.[89] In both of these texts, then, the acquisition of small-scale private property by peasants and workers was of central importance.

---

[84] See the reference to tragedy and farce in M. Talmeyr, 'Pour les Khroumirs', *L'Intransigeant* (Paris), 8 May 1881.
[85] K. Marx, 'The Eighteenth Brumaire of Louis Bonaparte', (trans.) T. Carver, in Cowling and Martin, *Marx's Eighteenth Brumaire*, 19–109, at p.103.
[86] Marx, 'The Eighteenth Brumaire of Louis Bonaparte', at p.103.
[87] Ibid., at p.104. See also Marx, *The Class Struggles in France 1848–1850*, p.47.
[88] Marx, *Capital*, Volume I, p.927.　　[89] Ibid., p.927.

As the basis for the development of both the modern means of production and the modern state, it was essential to the progress of capitalism, and the entrenchment and visualisation of class difference. Small-scale private property was consequently also responsible for inciting revolution and bringing about meaningful social change.

By the beginning of the Third Republic in 1870, though, it was clear that small-scale private property had neither revolutionised social relations nor politicised the masses in France. Historians such as Maurice Agulhon and Chloé Gaboriaux have comprehensively deconstructed the tired dichotomy of radical town and reactionary countryside,[90] yet as previous chapters have demonstrated, it would not be inaccurate to characterise relations between urban revolutionaries and the provinces in this period as strained.[91] Certainly, revolutionaries were largely unsuccessful at constructing a shared class consciousness between peasants and urban workers. The provinces had not responded to the Paris Commune's overtures in 1871, and neither were they receptive to revolutionaries' half-baked attempts to appeal to them via religious language in the years after. Clearly the peasantry had not been delivered, as Marx had hoped in *Eighteenth Brumaire*, 'at last into the arms of the proletariat'.[92]

Economic conditions also showed little sign of progression along the path that Marx had delineated. For decades after the publication of *Das Kapital*, the French economy remained fundamentally peasant-based and agricultural. In 1870, 69 per cent of the population still lived in the countryside.[93] Perhaps unsurprisingly, industry was comparatively rare, and by 1876 it occupied only 27.6 per cent of the national working population.[94] Indeed, industrial employment did not overtake the

---

[90] See, for example, M. Agulhon, *The Republic in the Village: The People of the Var from the French Revolution to the Second Republic*, trans. J. Lloyd (Cambridge: Cambridge University Press, 1982. First published in French, 1970), p.295; C. Gaboriaux, *La République en quête des citoyens: les républicains français face au bonapartisme rural (1848–1880)* (Paris: Presses de la Fondation Nationale des Sciences Politiques, 2010), p.144.

[91] For more on the hardening of this rhetorical division in the late Second Empire, see Gaboriaux, *La République en quête des citoyens*, p.244.

[92] Carver, 'Marx's *Eighteenth Brumaire of Louis Bonaparte*: Democracy, Dictatorship, and Class Struggle', at p.111.

[93] F. Barbier, 'The Publishing Industry and Printed Output in Nineteenth-Century France', in K.E. Carpenter (ed.), *Books and Society in History: Papers of the Association of College and Research Libraries Rare Books and Manuscripts Preconference* (New York : R.R. Bowker Company, 1983), 199–230, at p.200.

[94] Vincent, *Between Marxism and Anarchism*, p.68. See also Moss, *The Origins of the French Labor Movement*, p.18.

agricultural sector until well into the twentieth century.[95] Even within this sector of the economy, modern industrial working conditions were uncommon. France, for example, had few factories, and as late as 1892 there were only ninety-two factory inspectors in the whole country.[96] Whereas the British (and later German[97]) industrial sectors had expanded rapidly during the nineteenth century, and along lines similar to those that Marx had predicted, the same could not be said of France. By the late nineteenth century, it was evident that France was pursuing a significantly different path to industrialisation, and had undergone nowhere near as dramatic industrial and social transformations as some of its neighbours.[98]

In fact, even in areas of France that were highly mechanised, the conditions of industrial labour were markedly different from those elsewhere in Europe. These differences are illustrated particularly clearly by the town of Roubaix. Located close to the Franco-Belgian border and northeast of Lille, Roubaix had long been a regional centre for the production of wool and textiles. Over the eighteenth and nineteenth centuries, Roubaix's industry underwent profound change. This included widespread mechanisation and even the adoption of English industrial technologies in an effort to maximise production.[99] By the late nineteenth century, Roubaix had become renowned for its dynamism and willingness to embrace new technologies, and was widely regarded as one of France's only 'factory towns'. Unlike other areas of France, in other words, Roubaix appeared to be following the conventional path of industrialisation.

Yet despite the similarities between Roubaix and other industrial centres, there remained notable differences. Population growth in France increased far less than elsewhere during the nineteenth century, and essentially stagnated from the 1860s onwards, resulting in a relatively small workforce.[100] This advantage, plus the persistence of agricultural alternatives, placed French workers in a strong position when negotiating with business owners, and enabled them to secure significantly more concessions from employers than workers in other countries. In Roubaix, for

---

[95] F. Crouzet, 'The Historiography of French Economic Growth in the Nineteenth Century', *Economic History Review* 61:2 (2003), 215–224, at p.236; R.P. Tombs, *France 1814–1914* (London: Routledge, 1996), p.150.

[96] Tombs, *France 1814–1914*, p.156.   [97] Jousse, *Réviser le marxisme?*, p.107.

[98] For figures on migration to cities, see R. Trempé, 'Deuxième partie: 1871–1914', in C. Willard (ed.), *La France ouvrière: Histoire de la classe ouvrière et du mouvement ouvrier français*, vol.1 (Paris: Éditions sociales, 1993), 221–410, at p.245.

[99] L. Page Moch, *Moving Europeans: Migration in Western Europe since 1650* (Bloomington, IN: Indiana University Press, 1992), p.132.

[100] Crouzet, 'The Historiography of French Economic Growth in the Nineteenth Century', at p.237.

instance, wages in the mid-1880s were 65 per cent higher than in nearby Belgium.[101] Even in highly industrialised towns such as Roubaix, in other words, workers did not experience the same conditions as those in more urban and industrialised economies. Not only had the French workforce and economy remained largely agricultural, but in addition to this, the industrialisation that did take place assumed a very particular (and perhaps less disruptive) character.

In addition to these social and demographic conditions, France's capacity for industrial growth was further inhibited after 1871 by its loss in the Franco-Prussian War. In particular, the terms of the peace treaty signed with Germany imposed significant financial constraints upon France. Most immediately damaging was the cession of Alsace and Lorraine, which saw France instantly lose 8 per cent of its industrial capacity.[102] In the long term, however, the indemnity of 5 billion francs proved equally, if not more, punitive. This amounted to the equivalent of 2.5 years of the state's total budget, and essentially prevented France from recouping its losses by developing or investing in new infrastructure or industry.[103] The combination of global economic slowdown and these uniquely unfavourable conditions were reflected in French industrial production, which fell by a remarkable 15 per cent between 1874 and 1877.[104]

At the same time, this relatively slow transformation also reflected widespread attitudes towards industrialisation. Far from regarding their economy as inferior to those of more industrialised nations, the French public expressed satisfaction with both the agricultural sector and the protectionist policies necessary to maintain it.[105] Public opinion, for example, remained proud of the country's large peasantry throughout the nineteenth century, regarding it as a pillar of social and political stability.[106] Likewise, politicians from across the political spectrum looking to cultivate the support of the substantial peasant landowner class often,[107] as Chloé Gaboriaux has demonstrated, substantially adapted their policies and rhetoric in order to do so.[108] Revolutionaries and socialists in the early Third Republic, then, were both numerically in the minority and

[101] Page Moch, *Moving Europeans*, p.134. See also Crouzet, 'The Historiography of French Economic Growth in the Nineteenth Century', at p.238.

[102] Crouzet, 'The Historiography of French Economic Growth in the Nineteenth Century', at p.235.

[103] Tombs, *France 1814–1914*, p.159.   [104] Ibid., p.445.

[105] For more on the nineteenth-century debate around protectionism and free trade in France, see D. Todd, *Free Trade and Its Enemies in France, 1814–1851* (Cambridge: Cambridge University Press, 2015).

[106] Crouzet, 'The Historiography of French Economic Growth in the Nineteenth Century', at p.236.

[107] Page Moch, *Moving Europeans*, p.110.   [108] Gaboriaux, *La République en quête des citoyens*.

ideologically on the back foot. In this context, pronouncements about the transformative power of private property and the French peasantry would have appeared not only irrelevant, but also untrue.

By the time of *Le Capital*, Marx's thought on workers' private property in France had shifted to fit these circumstances and this readership. Whereas in other texts such property had been foundational to the historical development of capitalism, the Marx of *Le Capital* asserted instead that '[l]a propriété privée du travailleur sur les moyens de son activité productive est *le corollaire* de la petite industrie'.[109] This change, as Anderson has noted, effectively 'decentred' private property, removing it as a necessary factor of capitalist accumulation.[110] While, for the French Marx, private property may often have coexisted with small-scale industry, the former was neither essential nor foundational to the latter's development. This change catered directly to a French environment in which no widespread urbanisation had taken place, and which remained more divided by geography (in terms of urban–rural antagonism) than by class. It enabled French socialist readers to effectively detach their 'progress' from that of the rural population, engaging with Marx's ideas whilst simultaneously remaining anchored in their environment.

This comparison of French translations and work on France thus demonstrates that Marx was more than willing to adapt his ideas and texts to suit different temporal and geographical circumstances. The Marx presented in French translation, in other words, was not the same as the German Marx, and nor was he simply a different Marx: rather, he was a specifically *French* Marx. In order to fully understand the relationship between Marx and France during this period, it is necessary to study not just his texts *on* France, but those in translation as well.

Although the French example provides a very clear demonstration of this side of Marx, it was in fact indicative of a more general intellectual principle. Discussing the introduction of political economy into Germany, which he argued had no historic background for such ideas, Marx complained that

> The theoretical expression of an alien reality turned in their hands into a collection of dogmas, interpreted by them in the sense of the petty-bourgeois world surrounding them, and therefore misinterpreted. The feeling of scientific impotence, a feeling which could not entirely be

---

[109] 'The workers' private property is . . . the corollary of small scale industry'. Marx, *Le Capital*, p.341. Emphasis mine.

[110] Anderson, 'The "Unknown" Marx's *Capital*, Volume 1', at p.75.

suppressed, and the uneasy awareness that they had to master an area in fact entirely foreign to them, was only imperfectly concealed beneath a parade of literary and historical erudition.[111]

Many of Marx's actions during this period, particularly within the General Council of the International Workingmen's Association, belied his inability to act according to such ideas. Yet theoretically, at least, he was hostile to 'metaphysical' totalities and attempts to indiscriminately transpose ideas from one context to another. While he may have often failed to live up to such principles, it is nonetheless important to keep this parallel intellectual openness in mind.

It is certainly true that this openness and flexibility had limits. Although several other translations of *Das Kapital* were begun in this period, including a Russian version in 1872, Marx did not express a desire for bespoke translations or versions for all countries.[112] Indeed, as we have seen, he hoped that the French edition would serve as the basis for future translations in Italy and Spain.[113] These translations are thus indicative of a certain national hierarchy, based perhaps on which countries Marx regarded as more socially important, or where he thought his ideas were most likely to find an audience. While there may have been a specific French Marx, we must bear in mind that not all countries received such treatment. Yet even taking these qualifications into account, it remains nonetheless that Marx was considerably more intellectually flexible than has previously been thought.

This comparison should also lay to rest the concept of an 'authentic' Marx. As the juxtaposition of his French translations and his writings on France demonstrates, Marx's thought was not a monolithic, immutable, or ideologically coherent entity. While diverse texts and translations addressed many of the same issues – property, industrialisation, the development of capitalism – Marx's analysis and practical recommendations varied from text to text. Furthermore, Marx himself was deeply involved in the process of translating and adapting his work for different audiences; indeed, no changes were made without his knowledge or permission. As a result, different versions of Marx abounded during his lifetime, many of which were based directly on his texts. Marx, in other

---

[111] Marx, 'Postface to the Second Edition', in Marx, *Capital, Volume 1*, 94–103, at pp.95–96.
[112] For the Russian version, see Stedman Jones, *Karl Marx*, p.535.
[113] For Lachâtre's expression of this hope, see M. Lachâtre to K. Marx (undated), in Marx, *Le Capital*, p.8; for Marx's, see 227: K. Marx to N. Danielson, 28 May 1872 (London), in *MECW*, vol.44, 385–386, at p.385.

words, could be eminently intellectually (if not often politically) flexible. He cannot be reduced to a codified set of ideas, and there is no 'authentic' Marx to be found in his texts.

V

Previous historians of Marx in France have overlooked the significance of his French texts, and have therefore failed to perceive this flexibility. It has conventionally been assumed that the French Marx's character during this period was derived almost entirely from his involvement in the International Workingmen's Association.[114] This is not particularly surprising, for many French revolutionaries did come into contact with Marx in these circumstances.[115] As we saw in Part I, following the fall of the Paris Commune the majority of revolutionaries escaping death or arrest fled to either London or Geneva, remaining there until the 1880 general amnesty enabled them to return to France.[116] This was largely because neither Britain nor Switzerland extradited political refugees, but the two cities were also the International Workingmen's Association's main operational hubs in Europe.[117] Marx, the head of the General Council, resided in London. Meanwhile, Mikhail Bakunin, the charismatic Russian anarchist and Marx's principal intellectual and operational rival within the organisation, drew most of his support from the similarly anarchist Jura Federation, which was based in Switzerland and headed by James Guillaume.

The French government kept the International Workingmen's Association under close surveillance during the Commune.[118] In the recriminations that followed its fall, the Association was widely blamed in the European press for having instigated the revolution.[119] In fact, though, French interaction with (let alone membership in) the organisation had

---

[114] See, for example, Vincent, *Between Marxism and Anarchism*, p.71.
[115] See, for example, intelligence report to the Préfecture de Police, 31 December 1878 (London). Archives de la Préfecture de Police (APP) Ba430/3189.
[116] For information on the refugees in Geneva, see Vincent, *Between Marxism and Anarchism*, p.39. For numbers of refugees in London, see Stedman Jones, *Karl Marx*, p.540, fn20.
[117] K. Ross, *Communal Luxury: The Political Imaginary of the Paris Commune* (London: Verso, 2015). First published in French, 2015), p.92.
[118] Intelligence report to the Ministère de l'Intérieur, 13 May 1871 (Versailles). APP Ba439/5097; see also Ba439/5102-5103; Report to the Préfecture de Police, 28 May 1871 (Vienna). APP Ba439/5104; see also Ba439/5252. For lists of IWA members and their fates after the Commune, see APP Ba439/4860-4862.
[119] Both the press and the police continued to fear the International Workingmen's Assocation's influence after the fall of the Commune. For the press, see, for example, *Le Pays* (Paris), 31 March

been relatively minimal prior to the Commune. The Bonapartist police kept a close eye on its operatives in France from its inception in 1864, and in fact the Paris International Branch of the Association was closed in 1869.[120] Likewise, while some Communards were members of the International, the involvement of the Association itself was far less than the press later suggested. It was not until the Commune's fall and its participants' flight into exile that membership soared.

These new members, moreover, became heavily involved in International. The sheer numbers of exiles flooding in from France were immense: approximately 1,500 to London and 750 to Switzerland.[121] As a result, established factions within the organisation rushed to recruit groups of new French members, hoping that the boost in numbers would help to conclude decisions and arguments in their favour. Marx, for example, relied on the support of Blanquist exiles in his efforts to expel Bakunin and Guillaume at the 1872 Hague Congress.[122] French exiles were thus more than simply passive members of the International Workingmen's Association. Rather, partly as a result of their numbers, and in spite of their relative inexperience, they became heavily involved in both the dissemination of propaganda and the organisation's internal politics. This included the events at the congress in The Hague, which effectively brought the First International to an end (although it struggled on for several more years, all semblance of unity was broken in 1872). As David Stafford has observed, the 'political apprenticeship of all the founders of the French socialist movement was in the First International'.[123]

This experience clearly had a profound effect upon French socialism in the 1870s and early 1880s.[124] The International Workingmen's Association and French experiences within it continued to feature

---

1874. APP Ba439/5568; *Le Comtat* (Vaucluse), 16 August 1874. APP Ba439/5576. For official documents, see APP Ba439/5457; 5493.

[120] Stedman Jones, *Karl Marx*, p.508.

[121] For these estimates, see A. Dowdall, 'Narrating *la Semaine Sanglante*, 1871–1880' (unpublished MPhil dissertation, University of Cambridge, 2010), p.12.

[122] See, for example, J. Guillaume, *L'Internationale: documents et souvenirs (1864–1878)* (Paris: Société nouvelle de librairie et d'édition, 1905–1910); *Mémoire présenté par la Fédération jurassienne de l'Association internationale des Travailleurs à toutes les fédérations de l'Internationale* (Sonvillier: Au siége du Comité fédéral jurassien, 1873), p.192; M. Cordillot, *Aux origines du socialisme moderne: La Première Internationale, la Commune de Paris, l'exil* (Paris: Éditions de l'Atelier, 2010).

[123] Stafford, *From Anarchism to Reformism*, p.6. See also E. Jousse, *Les hommes révoltés: les origines intellectuelles du réformisme en France (1871–1917)* (Paris: Fayard, 2017), p.47; Moss, *The Origins of the French Labor Movement*, pp.73–74.

[124] For more on this, see L. Godineau, *Retour d'exil: Les anciens Communards au début de la Troisième République* (unpublished doctoral thesis, Université de Paris I Panthéon-Sorbonne, 2000), p.413.

prominently in revolutionary writings well after the organisation's official demise in 1876.[125] Its structure furnished socialists such as Benoît Malon with new ideas on party organisation and post-revolutionary society,[126] and a variety of groups attempted to claim its legacy as their own.[127] The experiences and knowledge that French socialists gained through their membership in this organisation were, therefore, extremely important to their later thought. This was in spite of significant official French efforts to minimise its impact. In the wake of the Commune, the 1872 *loi Dufaure* had banned the International Workingmen's Association from operating in France, hoping to curtail its power and influence on French radicalism. The exilic trajectories of revolutionaries fleeing reprisals, however, led them straight to the centre of the International's operations and its politics, ensuring that it nonetheless had a significant and very visible impact upon French socialist thought and French society through the period in question.[128]

The importance of these experiences to French socialism, and the centrality of the International Workingmen's Association to its historiography, has inflected the French Marx with a set of very distinct characteristics. In this context, Marx was principally an organiser rather than a philosopher or a social critic. Moreover, he was not a particularly successful organiser. He was instead an egotist; a purist who would rather dissolve a supposedly democratic international association than compromise on his vision for it. He was a shadowy background figure, an intriguer pulling strings from London. The French Marx has thus until now largely remained a *separate* Marx, and French Marxism a phenomenon that occurred without the involvement of, indeed perhaps even in spite of, Marx himself.

---

[125] See, for example, É. Reclus, *Évolution et Révolution*, 6th edn (Paris: Imprimerie Habert, 1891. First published, 1882. Speech first given, 1880), p.54. This was also the case with Marx and Engels, see Anderson, 'The "Unknown" Marx's *Capital*, Volume 1', p.78.

[126] See, for example, B. Malon, *L'Internationale: son histoire et ses principes* (Lyons: Extrait de la *République républicaine*, 1872), pp.12–13.

[127] For Guesdist attempts, see 'La voix de l'histoire', *Le Citoyen* (Paris), 5 August 1882; 'Les deux congrès', *Le Citoyen*, 14 October 1882. For Possibilist attempts, see 'État et anarchie', *Le Prolétariat* (Paris), 10 May 1884 and 17 May 1884; 'Les travailleurs de la main et les travailleurs du cerveau devant l'Internationale', *Le Prolétariat*, 7 June 1884 and 5 July 1884; 'La coalition révolutionnaire', *Le Prolétariat*, 26 September 1885; B. Malon, 'L'Internationale', *L'Intransigeant*, 21 February 1884.

[128] Some revolutionaries claimed that sections of the International Workingmen's Association continued to operate in France even after 1872, but while this is possible, the claims are unsubstantiated. See, for example, *Mémoire présenté par la Fédération jurassienne de l'Association internationale des Travailleurs*, p.262.

An analysis of Marx's texts in French translation significantly complicates this picture. Where in the International Workingmen's Association Marx was a rigid authoritarian, in French translation he was flexible rather than dogmatic. Furthermore, Marx was deeply involved in the creation of this textual French persona. Rather than simply brooding in his study in London and penning disgruntled letters to his correspondents, Marx took an active part in disseminating his own ideas, adjusting his work for different circumstances, and engaging with the historical and economic contexts of various different countries. While Marx was involved in this process, then, the French Marx was also decidedly not a set of ideas imposed from the top down. Rather, it was a process of collaboration between Marx, his French disseminators such as Lachâtre and Deville, and the French *milieu* itself. It is thus only by combining the history of Marx in the International Workingmen's Association and Marx's texts in French translation that we can hope to approach an understanding of the character of the French Marx.

CHAPTER 6

The Origins of Marxism in Modern France

The French Marx was extremely influential for a variety of French socialists during the 1870s and early 1880s, both as a public figure and as a source of ideas. This chapter moves from the writings of Marx himself to the internal mechanics of French Marxism, addressing the ways in which French socialists interacted with and used the ideas of the French Marx in their own work. As Chapter 5 demonstrated, this period has been largely overlooked in synoptic studies of Marxism in France. Those that do mention the Marxism of this period have often characterised it in two ways. Intellectually, it is suggested, French Marxism in the 1870s and early 1880s was ideologically immature and impure – a misunderstanding of the original.[1] Politically, meanwhile, it has been seen as the exclusive preserve of the Guesdists, or self-described French Marxists. In his 2007 *Réviser le marxisme*, for example, Emmanuel Jousse characterised French Marxism during this period as 'an ideology of exclusion, which served to establish [the Guesdists'] difference from and superiority over other schools'.[2]

This chapter argues that this is an inaccurate characterisation of French Marxism during the 1870s and early 1880s. French interactions with Marx and Marxism during this period were both broader and less prescriptive than has previously been suggested. A far wider range of French socialists and revolutionaries than simply the Guesdists made use of Marx, and neither ideological purity nor even accuracy was their aim. Through a broader examination of such interactions, this chapter suggests that Marx performed two functions for French revolutionary socialists during this period. Primarily, Marx's ideas functioned as a theoretical tool internal to the revolutionary movement. Numerous, and often opposing, groups of

[1] See, for example, G. Lichtheim, *Marxism in Modern France* (New York: Columbia University Press, 1966), p.9.
[2] 'Le marxisme porté par les guesdistes devient, de ce fait, une idéologie d'exclusion, qui sert à créer une différence et une supériorité sur les autres écoles.' E. Jousse, *Réviser le marxisme? D'Édouard Bernstein à Albert Thomas, 1896–1914* (Paris: L'Harmattan, 2007), p.111.

socialists, including the Guesdists, their rivals the Possibilists, and even the Blanquists, relied upon intellectual tools fashioned largely, if not exclusively, from elements of Marx's thought in order to think through and dispute a variety of contemporary social issues. In particular, many built upon the translational differences present in the French Marx, such as his more muted opposition to machinery and mechanisation, to advance their own theories on such matters as the right to work and the role of the state.

Simultaneously, Marx also served an external, rhetorical purpose. In wider French political circles, the same socialists employed the rhetoric of Marx and Marxism in a conscious attempt to marginalise themselves, re-establishing the boundaries between the revolutionary movement and more mainstream politicians even as their ideas became less recognisably 'revolutionary'. French socialists saw Marx's ideas as a useful language for working through pressing social problems rather than as a fixed doctrine: in fact, 'orthodox Marxism' did not exist during this period. These more complicated interactions were not only true of their interactions with Marx and Marxism; they also reflected the complex and shifting structures of the revolutionary movement as a whole, and revolutionary thought cannot simply be folded into the social and organisational history of French socialism.

The chapter shall focus upon the three most prominent revolutionary and revolutionary socialist groups in France at the beginning of the 1880s: the Guesdists, the Possibilists, and the Blanquists. It draws primarily upon the ideas and works of six theorists: the Guesdists Jules Guesde, Paul Lafargue, and Gabriel Deville; the Possibilists Paul Brousse and Benoît Malon; and of course Marx himself. The source material comprises a wide range of socialist and revolutionary books and pamphlets from the period, such as Lafargue's best-selling *Le droit à la paresse*, as well as these theorists' more collective enterprises, namely the Parisian daily newspapers *L'Égalité*, *Le Prolétaire*, *Le Citoyen*, and *L'Intransigeant*.[3] In an attempt to provide further context for these ideas and actions, the chapter also draws to a lesser extent upon the thought of other socialist and revolutionary theorists that were prominent during the period, such as Proudhon, Louis Blanc, Louis Auguste Blanqui, and Mikhail Bakunin. This printed material has been further supplemented by documentation from the International Working-men's Association and the anarchist Jura Federation – organisations in

[3] P. Lafargue, *Le droit à la paresse: réfutation du 'droit au travail' de 1848* (Paris: Henry Oriol, 1883. First published, 1880).

which, as we have seen, French revolutionaries were heavily involved during this period.

I

As the self-proclaimed French Marxists, it is the Guesdists who first spring to mind when one considers the relationship between Marx and French theorists during this period. They were certainly eager to reinforce this connection, frequently naming Marx as their intellectual inspiration and broadcasting their knowledge of his work. The group's principal newspaper, *L'Égalité*, for example, declared in 1882 that 'our scientific communism emanates from Marx's learned critique'.[4] Likewise, a year later, Deville cast doubt upon the Possibilists' intellectual competence, disdainfully observing that 'few of them have read Marx'.[5] As Chapter 5 demonstrated, the Guesdists were also heavily involved in shaping and disseminating the French Marx. It was Paul and Laura Lafargue, for example, who finally secured a French publisher for *Das Kapital*, after a decade of Marx himself promising to do so.[6] They also translated many other texts themselves, including the *Civil War in France* and Engels's *Anti-Dühring*, while Deville produced the abridged version of *Capital*. In 1884, Lafargue and Deville continued their efforts to broaden Marx's French audience, staging a series of public lectures on materialism and the development of capitalism (later published as cheap pamphlets) to explain what they considered to be key areas of his thought.[7] The Guesdists, then, were closely linked to the French Marx. Marx was not only their intellectual inspiration, but he also played a leading role in bringing his ideas to France.

The Guesdists' role in bringing Marx to the attention of French audiences has long been recognised. The nature of their intellectual interactions with his work, however, has not. Even the most recent work on this subject, Marc Angenot's *Le Marxisme dans les grands récits*, dismissed Lafargue as

---

[4] '[N]otre communisme scientifique sorti de la savante critique de Marx'. G. Deville, 'Il y a cinq ans', *L'Égalité* (Paris), 19 November 1882. See also P. Lafargue, 'Le déisme de M. Pasteur', *Le Citoyen* (Paris), 23 April 1882.

[5] '[P]eu parmi leurs dupes ont lu Marx'. G. Deville (ed.) *Le Capital de Karl Marx* (Paris: Henry Oriol, 1883), p.6.

[6] M. Rubel and M. Manale, *Marx without Myth: A Chronological Study of His Life and Work* (Oxford: Basil Blackwell, 1975), p.271.

[7] G. Deville, *L'Évolution du capital* (Paris: Henry Oriol, 1884); P. Lafargue, *Cours d'économie sociale: le matérialisme économique de Karl Marx* (Paris: Henry Oriol, 1884).

a literary, bohemian spirit, and mediocre orator who was little interested in questions of party organisation. His correspondence with his father-in-law indicates that he had great respect for the author of *Capital* but ... was completely out of his depth when it came to Marx's science.[8]

The idea that the Guesdists systematically misunderstood or misrepresented Marx has thus been surprisingly durable. While they have been recognised and even celebrated as disseminators of Marxism, intellectually they have been dismissed as incurious and dogmatic.[9] Yet this was clearly not the case. As a more detailed exploration of their work shows, the Guesdists both closely engaged with and built upon the ideas of the French Marx.

The clearest example of this can be found in the Guesdists' work on labour and industrialisation. This, as mentioned in Chapter 5, had been an issue of central concern for French theorists, and in particular French socialists, for some time. It found its ultimate realisation in Louis Blanc's 1839 *Organisation du travail*, which declared 'the right to work' a central principle of socialism, and ran to four editions between 1840 and 1847.[10] Following the 1848 revolution, Blanc became a member of the Provisional Government, and his ideas were put into practice in the form of the national workshop scheme, under which the state guaranteed work for unemployed citizens.[11] Various other French radicals and state critics, such as the anarchist Pierre-Joseph Proudhon also placed work at the centre of their philosophy.[12]

In the early 1880s, the Guesdists mounted a highly unusual challenge to the significance of work in French socialist ideas. The most familiar

---

[8] '[E]sprit littéraire et bohème, médiocre orateur, s'interesse-t-il peu aux questions d'organisation du Parti. Sa correspondance avec son beau-père indique qu'il respecte beaucoup l'auteur du *Capital*, mais ... qu'il est parfaitement dépassé par sa science.' M. Angenot, *Le marxisme dans les grands récits: essai d'analyse du discours* (Paris: L'Harmattan, 2005), pp.11–12. See also E. Berenson, *Populist Religion and Left-Wing Politics in France, 1830–1852* (Princeton, NJ: Princeton University Press, 1984), p.238.

[9] Jousse, *Réviser le marxisme?*, pp.110–111.

[10] See L. Blanc, *Organisation du travail*, 5th edn (Paris: Au bureau de la Société de l'industrie fraternelle, 1847. First published, 1839). For the number of editions, see D. Moggach, 'New Goals and New Ways: Republicanism and Socialism in 1848/49', in D. Moggach and P. Leduc Browne (eds.), *The Social Question and the Democratic Revolution: Marx and the Legacy of 1848* (Ottawa: University of Ottawa Press, 2000), 49–69, at p.50. For more on Blanc and the right to work, see J. Jennings, *Revolution and the Republic: A History of Political Thought in France since the Eighteenth Century* (Oxford: Oxford University Press, 2011), p.401.

[11] For Marx on this, see K. Marx, *The Class Struggles in France 1848–1850* (trans.) H. Kuhn (New York: New York Labor News Co., 1924. First published in German, 1850), p.59.

[12] See, for example, P.-J. Proudhon, *Qu'est-ce que la propriété? Ou, recherches sur le principe du droit et du gouvernement* (Paris: J.F. Brocard, 1840).

iteration of the Guesdists' position was Paul Lafargue's *Le droit à la paresse*. *Le droit à la paresse: réfutation du 'droit au travail' de 1848* first appeared in 1880 as a series of articles in the Guesdists' newspaper, *L'Égalité*, and was published as a book three years later. While *Le droit à la paresse* crystallised the Guesdists' thought, however, variations of the same idea appeared throughout their writing during the early 1880s, and in texts and articles authored by Guesde and Deville as well as Lafargue.[13]

For the Guesdists, industrialisation had transformed work from a right that must be secured and defended into one of socialism's greatest problems. The long hours of menial, repetitive labour demanded of modern workers were irreparably damaging for both the individual labourer and society as a whole.[14] Whereas workers could once take pride in their labour, as a result of industrialisation and the division of labour, this was no longer the case. Individually, *L'Égalité* observed, work was no longer a potentially fulfilling activity, but a trial to be endured that 'deprive[d] the worker of any joy'.[15] At the same time, industrial production also directly contributed to the decomposition of social frameworks that had structured society for hundreds of years, and allegedly underpinned the modern bourgeois state. Chief among these was the family. In order to meet its production targets, Lafargue claimed, the factory 'dragged the workmen from their hearths, the better to wring them and squeeze out the labour that they contained'.[16]

Workers, then, found themselves no longer in control of their lives. Modern labour was not emancipation, but deception: '[f]or the modern wage labourer, work is no longer liberty, as the bourgeois philosophers assured them that it was, but slavery; the workshop is forced labour.'[17] While the Guesdists devoted as much space to questions of labour as did

---

[13] 'Un vieux cliché', *L'Égalité*, 14 May 1882. For similar ideas, see also 'Un mal pour le bien', *Le Citoyen*, 2 October 1881; 'Patrons et ouvriers', *Le Citoyen*, 6 December 1881; 'Utopies réactionnaires', *Le Citoyen* 29 April 1882.

[14] For analysis of living standards, see, for example, P. Lafargue, 'Caractère fatidique des misères prolétariennes', in *L'Émancipation* (Lyons), 12 November 1880; 'Leur fête', *L'Égalité*, 14 July 1880; 'Le collectivisme et la production agricole', *L'Égalité*, 23 December 1877. For more on French living standards during this period, see D. Stafford, *From Anarchism to Reformism: A Study of the Political Activities of Paul Brousse within the First International and the French Socialist Movement 1870–1890* (London: Cox & Wyman, 1971), p.203.

[15] Liberté, Égalité, Fraternité', *L'Égalité*, 18 August 1880. See also 'Le Creusot', *L'Émancipation*, 1 November 1880.

[16] '[I]l avait arraché les ouvriers de leurs foyers pour mieux les tordre et pour mieux exprimer le travail qu'ils contenaient'. P. Lafargue, *Le droit à la paresse*, p.16.

[17] 'Le travail pour les salariés modernes n'est plus la liberté, comme l'assurent encore les philosophes bourgeois, mais l'esclavage; l'atelier est le bagne.' P. Lafargue, 'Le travail c'est l'esclavage', *Le Citoyen*, 24 July 1882. For further Guesdist comparisons of modern workers to slaves and serfs, see 'La lutte

other French socialists, their conclusions were markedly different. For the likes of Blanc and Proudhon, work guaranteed freedom from the state and the power to live autonomously. For the Guesdists, however, industrialisation and the consequent changes in working conditions it had wrought cancelled out these potential benefits. Rather than a guarantor of liberty, labour was now an active impediment to it. These impositions, moreover, would only increase over time as industry itself grew and expanded.

For the Guesdists, solutions based on a return to pre-industrial forms of labour were not the answer to the problems raised by industrialisation. Although industrialisation had drastically reduced the worker's quality of life, they argued, it was impossible to reverse the process. Lafargue, as we have seen, was concerned that factories were slowly eroding the framework of society. In Guesde's view, however, this process was already complete. Small and autonomous forms of society such as communes, he argued, had 'died' '[t]he day the steam of a locomotive appeared on the horizon'.[18] Neither were relatively undeveloped economies spared this fate. While France was less industrialised than its neighbours England and Germany, even the French peasant, Deville wrote,

> cannot content himself with producing for his own personal use: in order to buy the little he needs, to pay his taxes, to pay off his debts, he must produce in order to exchange, that is to say he must enter into competition with other producers.[19]

While traditional forms of social organisation such as the peasant smallholding may have persisted for a time, the invention of modern machinery had inalterably changed society. The parallel existence of this new, more efficient means of production had doomed its more traditional counterpart to eventual obsolescence. There could thus be no return, the Guesdists

---

de classes', *L'Égalité*, 2 June 1880; 'Si les électeurs savaient!', *Le Citoyen*, 16 October 1881; J. Guesde, 'L'Église et les radicaux', *Le Citoyen*, 23 November 1881; 'La féodalité commerciale', *Le Citoyen*, 6 January 1882; C. Bouis, 'Leur logique', *Le Citoyen*, 2 February 1882; 'Travail et capital', *Le Citoyen*, 27 February 1882; E. Massard, 'L'instruction bourgeoise', *Le Citoyen*, 24 March 1882; Lafargue, *Le droit à la paresse*, pp.13–14.

[18] 'L'autonomie devant la science et devant l'histoire', *Le Citoyen*, 24 November 1881. See also J. Guesde, 'Socialisme et paysan', *L'Émancipation*, 9 November 1880; 'L'Internationale bourgeoise et l'Internationale ouvrière', *Le Citoyen*, 13 March 1882.

[19] 'Le paysan ne doit pas se contenter de produire pour son usage personnel; afin d'acheter le peu dont il a besoin, de payer ses impôts, d'acquitter les intérêts de ses dettes, il doit produire pour échanger, c'est-à-dire entrer en concurrence avec les autres producteurs.' Deville, *Le Capital de Karl Marx*, p.14.

argued, to communal or artisanal labour.[20] Demanding the right to work was not part of the solution, but part of the problem, and contributed only to workers' continued enslavement.

For the Guesdists, it was through industrialisation rather than through work that labourers could achieve a better quality of life. In industrial Europe, Lafargue noted, the greatest privilege was not work, but leisure time, or 'the right to be lazy'. In an age of joyless work, it was only this that enabled the individual to develop his or her own personality and interests. He approvingly cited the ancient philosopher Xenophon's claim that 'work occupies all of one's time, leaving none for the Republic or one's friends',[21] and christened laziness the 'mother of the arts and the noble virtues'.[22] In previous eras, democratising the right to be lazy had simply not been possible, but the advent of large-scale production had changed this. Where previously, Deville wrote, the 'slavery of some' had been 'the condition of the wellbeing of the others; with machines, these iron slaves, the wellbeing of all is possible'.[23] Lafargue, meanwhile, fêted machinery as 'the saviour of humanity, the god who shall redeem man from the *sordidae artes* and from working for hire, the god who shall give him leisure and liberty'.[24]

Industrialisation, in other words, was not inherently bad; it was simply badly used. By turning modern machinery to the benefit of all rather than the benefit of the few, society could simultaneously produce all that it required and grant all of its citizens the right to enjoy leisure time and develop their individual interests. Industrialisation was thus not a process in need of reversal, but a blessing that could guarantee workers a better life than their predecessors had ever enjoyed. Whereas communal or artisanal labour provided workers only with job satisfaction, industrialisation could give them the power choose how they lived their lives. Rather than

---

[20] J. Guesde and P. Lafargue, *Le Programme du Parti Ouvrier: son histoire, ses considérations, ses articles* (Paris: Henry Oriol, 1883), p.77.
[21] '[L]e travail emporte tout le temps et avec lui on n'a nul loisir pour la République et les amis'. Lafargue, *Le droit à la paresse*, p.52.
[22] '[M]ère des arts et des nobles vertus'. Lafargue, *Le droit à la paresse*, p.49.
[23] 'L'esclavage des uns a été la condition du bien-être des autres; avec les machines, ces esclaves de fer, le bien-être de tous est possible.' Deville, *Le Capital de Karl Marx*, p.14. See also G. Deville, L'État de nature', *Le Citoyen*, 17 September 1882.
[24] '[L]e rédempteur de l'humanité, le Dieu qui rachètera l'homme des *sordidae artes* et du travail salarié, qui lui donnera des loisirs et la liberté.' Lafargue, *Le droit à la paresse*, p.54. See also 'Le travail c'est l'esclavage', *Le Citoyen*, 24 July 1882. For other iterations of this, see 'Un mal pour le bien', *Le Citoyen*, 2 October 1881; 'Patrons et ouvriers', *Le Citoyen*, 6 December 1881; 'Utopies réactionnaires', *Le Citoyen*, 29 April 1882; 'Ce qu'est le progrès social', *Le Citoyen*, 21 August 1882; 'Un vieux cliché', *L'Égalité*, 14 May 1882. See also 'Le Proudhonisme est le passé', *L'Égalité*, 20 April 1880; 'Liberté, Égalité, Fraternité', *L'Égalité*, 18 August 1880.

idealistically and misguidedly demanding a return to pre-industrial labour and the right to work, Guesdists encouraged workers to embrace modernisation and mould it to their own benefit. The worker, *L'Égalité* argued, should endeavour to 'become his own capitalist'.[25]

In contrast to the return to communal labour, this was both realistic and progressive. Although France was less industrialised than its neighbours such as Britain and Germany,[26] it was nonetheless a part of the global economy, and turning back the tide of industrialisation was both politically unlikely and economically impossible. By advancing a theory of industrialisation that did not demand the dismantling of large swathes of the increasingly industrial French economy, the Guesdists were able to position themselves as at once realistic and forward-looking: champions of modern industry, innovation, and industrial workers. These ideas yielded considerable practical success. From the mid-1880s onwards, the Guesdists captured the industrial working-class voting demographic, and the emerging 'red belt' around Paris as well as the industrial towns of the north like Roubaix became their electoral strongholds.

At the same time, this position set the Guesdists apart from their opponents in both French politics and socialist circles. The majority of European socialists, from the Possibilists to English activists such as William Morris, continued to define work as a potentially fulfilling activity and to privilege the demand for communal labour as a central principle of socialism.[27] Radical republican deputies such as Georges Clemenceau, meanwhile, had repackaged the ability to work as the characteristic of a superior, more evolved humanity.[28] Labour, of course, remained important in Guesdist thought. It was work, after all, that ensured society ran smoothly and thus guaranteed the right to be lazy.[29] For the Guesdists,

---

[25] '[I]l faudrait que le travailleur fût à lui-même son capitaliste'. 'Collectivisme et socialisme', *L'Égalité*, 14 July 1878.

[26] F. Crouzet, 'The Historiography of French Economic Growth in the Nineteenth Century', *Economic History Review* 61:2 (2003), 215–224, at p.237.

[27] For contemporary French socialist endorsements of the right to work, see A. Theisz, 'Le mouvement social: le programme de l'Alliance républicaine socialiste', *L'Intransigeant* (Paris), 16 November 1880; B. Malon, 'Le droit au travail', *L'Intransigeant*, 30 August 1884; P. Brousse, *Le Suffrage universel et le problème de la souveraineté du peuple* (Geneva: Imprimerie Coopérative, 1874), p.48; P. Brousse, *La crise: sa cause, son remède* (Geneva: Éditions du Révolté, 1879), pp.25–26. For more on Morris, see R. Kinna, *William Morris: The Art of Socialism* (Cardiff: University of Wales Press, 2000).

[28] 'Le travail c'est l'esclavage', *Le Citoyen*, 24 July 1882.

[29] J. Guesde, *Collectivisme et révolution* (Paris: Librairie des publications populaires, 1879), pp.15–16. See also J. Guesde, *Le collectivisme au Collège de France* (Paris: Henry Oriol, 1883), pp.14–15; 'Collectivisme et socialisme', *L'Égalité*, 14 July 1878.

though, work was a social obligation: a duty to be fulfilled rather than a right to be enjoyed.[30] Its purpose was to create the conditions for social equality and nothing more.

This solution was built explicitly upon foundations derived from the French Marx. As demonstrated in Chapter 5, in *Le Capital* Marx offered an alternative, marginally more optimistic assessment of factory labour than the relentless depiction in *Das Kapital*. In 'La fabrique', Marx was more open to the possibility that, under the correct conditions, industrialisation could be harnessed for the benefit of workers. Likewise, the French Marx had left room for workers to sustain interests and a life outside of work. This was more attuned to France's particular path of industrialisation, which included higher wages, fewer factories, and more extensive workers' rights, as a result of both the stagnating size of the national population and protectionist policies implemented by successive governments.

The Guesdists' solution to the problem of industrial labour built explicitly upon these foundations. Lafargue and Deville both referred regularly and directly to *Le Capital* in their own work.[31] They also used Marx's ideas as a springboard in their efforts to construct a theory that offered a distinct solution to the problem of social equality without unrealistically requiring the wholesale reversal of significant aspects of the contemporary economy. This set them apart from both radical republicans and other socialists, and enabled them to establish a stranglehold on large sections of the industrial north of France. The Guesdists, in other words, were more than simply passive disseminators of Marx's ideas in France. While they were central to the construction of the French Marx, they also interacted with his ideas, using them inventively to theorise new solutions to pressing social problems, and to establish a distinct position for themselves in French politics.

II

The Guesdists, though, were not the only French socialists to engage with Marx and his ideas in the 1880s. Largely as a result of the tortured history of the French workers' movement during this period, it has often been

---

[30] 'La question économique et la question politique', *L'Égalité*, 2 June 1878.
[31] For Deville, see *Le Capital de Karl Marx*. For Lafargue, see *Le droit à la paresse*, pp.32–33; P. Lafargue, 'Une page d'histoire' in *La revue socialiste* 8 (Paris, 20 June 1880), 365–370, at p.366; P. Lafargue, 'Recherches sur les origines de l'idée du bien et du juste', *Revue philosophique* 20 (Paris, 1885), 253–267, at p.254. For other Guesdist references, see, for example, 'Évolution – Révolution', *L'Égalité*, 18 February 1880.

suggested that the Guesdists were the only French admirers of Marx's work. In 1882, the nascent French workers' party, which had been established in 1880, split. From this split came two new parties: the Parti ouvrier français (POF), which was the preserve of the Guesdists, and the Fédération des travailleurs socialistes français (FTSF), who became known as the Possibilists. Where the POF insisted upon the necessity of revolution and momentous social change in order to achieve socialist aims and believed government to be a distraction, the Possibilists' ideas were closer to those of the Belgian public service socialist César de Paepe. Revolutionary and socialist aims, they argued, could be realised (or, at least, workers' lives could be considerably ameliorated) through effecting small, gradual changes at the local level and the conquest of power through elections.

The official rupture took place at the 1882 annual congress, but it followed at least a year of rising tensions over the organisation and doctrinal direction of the party. The friction and recriminations surrounding these events played out very publicly and viciously in the French radical press, with each group using their newspaper to attack the other.[32] *Le Prolétaire*, for example, memorably skewered Guesde as 'Torquemada in pince-nez'.[33] Indeed, by 1882 such insults had become so commonplace that neutral parties, from other newspapers to ordinary party members, often publicly begged both sides to desist.[34]

Eager to win support and prove the broader legitimacy of their position, both sides often reverted to the Marxist-anarchist language of the split in the International Workingmen's Association, in which so many French

---

[32] For more on this, see R.C. Stuart, *Marxism at Work: Ideology, Class and French Socialism during the Third Republic* (Cambridge: Cambridge University Press, 1992), pp.34–35. For Guesdist attacks, see 37: Paul Lafargue to Benoît Malon, November 1881, in E. Bottigelli and C. Willard (eds.), *La naissance du Parti ouvrier français: Correspondance inédite de Paul Lafargue, Jules Guesde, José Mesa, Paul Brousse, Benoît Malon, Gabriel Deville, Victor Jaclard, Léon Camescasse et Friedrich Engels* (Paris: Editions Sociales, 1981), 164–165, at p.164; 31: Paul Lafargue to the members of the *Égalité* and *Prolétaire* groups, 21 October 1881 (London), in Bottigelli and Willard, *La naissance du Parti ouvrier français*, 142–145, at pp.143–144; Guesde and Lafargue, *Le programme du Parti Ouvrier*, pp.121–122; 'Les deux congrès', *Le Citoyen*, 14 October 1882; 'L'autonomie', *L'Égalité*, 25 December 1881; 'Prolétariana', *L'Égalité*, 19 February 1882; 26 February 1882; 19 March 1882; 'L'automaniaquisme', *L'Égalité*, 28 May 1882; 'Le taux des salaires et le prix des marchandises', *L'Égalité*, 28 May 1882; 'Le communisme et les services publics', *L'Égalité*, 2 July 1882; 'Un mot d'explication', *L'Égalité*, 20 August 1882. See also 132: F. Engels to L. Lafargue, 23 November 1884 (London), in Engels and Lafargue, *Correspondence*, vol.1, 245–249, at p.247. See also 'Dernier mot', *Le Prolétaire* (Paris), 10 March 1883.

[33] 'Les combles marxistes', *Le Prolétaire*, 7 October 1882.

[34] 'Correspondance', *Le Prolétaire*, 14 January 1882; 'L'élection de dimanche', *Le Citoyen & La Bataille* (Paris), 9 March 1883.

socialists had been involved.[35] Rejecting de Paepe's suggestion that he and Jules Guesde shared the same fundamental principles, for instance, Paul Brousse argued, 'I do not understand how a man like you, who lived through the *International*, can still be taken in by the same schemers and the same schemes.'[36] Historians have often taken this language at face value, reading intellectual differences into party political issues and assuming that the Possibilists were either uninterested in or opposed to Marx's ideas.[37]

Certainly, there were aspects of both Marx's thought and his conduct towards which the Possibilists were actively antagonistic.[38] This was especially true when it came to questions of leadership and organisation. What Possibilists perceived as Marx's appetite for authority and his friends' willingness to indulge him attracted widespread ire.[39] Brousse, for example, criticised Engels's effusive eulogy at Marx's graveside in 1883, exclaiming that Marx 'was not God'.[40] Moreover, both Brousse and Malon worried that these tendencies had also taken root in the French socialist movement. Brousse, for instance, criticised Guesdism as 'not a system that disseminates its ideas, but one that imposes them'.[41] Similarly, in his Marx obituary Malon hinted at his unease with Marx's attitude to organisation and activism. Not wishing to speak ill of a dead man, he wrote, he would

[35] For use of this language, see P. Brousse, *Le marxisme dans l'Internationale* (Paris: Aux bureaux du journal *Le Prolétaire*, 1882), p.32. See also 'A bas le masque!', *Le Prolétaire*, 16 September 1882; *Le Prolétaire*, 21 October 1882; 'Les dessous de la coterie marxiste', *Le Prolétaire*, 3 March 1883; 'Possibilistes, impossibilistes et anarchistes', *Le Prolétariat*, 3 January 1885; 31: Lafargue to the members of the *Égalité* and *Prolétaire* groups, in Bottigelli and Willard, *La naissance du Parti ouvrier français*, 142–145, at pp.143–144.

[36] 'Je ne comprends pas qu'un homme qui a vécu comme toi *L'Internationale*, tu puisses encore être le dupe des mêmes intrigants et des mêmes intrigues.' 105: Paul Brousse to César de Paepe, 11 February 1884 (Paris), in C. de Paepe, *Entre Marx et Bakounine: Correspondence* (ed. B. Dandois) (Paris: Maspero, 1974), 245–249, at pp.248–249. Emphasis original.

[37] M. Angenot, *Les grands récits militants des XIXe et XXe siècles: religions de l'humanité et sciences de l'histoire* (Paris: L'Harmattan, 2000), p.108; E. Jousse, *Les hommes révoltés: les origines intellectuelles du réformisme en France (1871–1917)* (Paris: Fayard, 2017), p.378; L. Derfler, *Paul Lafargue and the Flowering of French Socialism, 1882–1911* (Cambridge, MA: Harvard University Press, 1998), p.26.

[38] K.S. Vincent, *Between Marxism and Anarchism: Benoît Malon and French Reformist Socialism* (Berkeley: University of California Press, 1992), p.94.

[39] See, for example, Brousse, *Le marxisme dans l'Internationale*, p.4; 'La coterie marxiste et l'élection du vingtième', *Le Prolétaire*, 24 February 1883; 'Loriquet marxiste', *Le Prolétaire*, 29 December 1883. For a similar observation, see B.H. Moss, *The Origins of the French Labor Movement 1830–1914: The Socialism of Skilled Workers* (Berkeley: University of California Press, 1976), p.110.

[40] 'Karl Marx', *Le Prolétaire*, 24 March 1883.

[41] Un 'système qui tend non à répandre la doctrine marxiste, mais à l'imposer'. Brousse, *Le marxisme dans l'Internationale*, p.7; see also p.31. See also 'Der Social-Demokrat', *Le Prolétaire*, 14 April 1883.

'concentrate exclusively on him [Marx] as a *savant* and a thinker'.[42] It was certainly true, then, that the Possibilists disliked large swathes of Marx's activity in the last years of his life. Their misgivings, in addition, largely corresponded to the issues that had led to both the split in the International Workingmen's Association in 1872 and the division of the French workers' party a decade later.

Yet the Possibilists did not reject Marx completely. Marx made regular appearances in Possibilist publications including *Le Prolétaire*, their principal newspaper, and was also regularly quoted by both Brousse and Malon.[43] More importantly, the Possibilists' praise of Marx did not end with the 1882 split. Following Marx's death in March of the following year, Brousse praised him as 'a powerful thinker, and in the area of economic analysis and criticism ... unparalleled'.[44] Likewise, while Malon disputed Marx's interpretation of the Commune,[45] simultaneously he lauded him as 'the most eminent of contemporary socialists',[46] and 'the abundant source from which most of [modern workers' socialism] is drawn'.[47] The Possibilists' relationship with Marx, then, was not simply one of distance and disapproval. While they certainly rejected aspects of his thought and behaviour, equally Possibilist writers praised Marx as an important and original thinker. That they continued to do so even as tensions within the French socialist movement were at their height attested both to the strength of their affinity for Marx and to how widespread and widely accepted these sentiments were.

---

[42] '[N]ous nous en tiendrons ... pour ne nous occuper exclusivement que de savant et du penseur'. B. Malon, 'Le socialisme de Karl Marx', *L'Intransigeant*, 23 March 1883.

[43] B. Malon, *La question sociale: histoire critique de l'économie politique* (Lugano: J. Favre, 1876), p.216; B. Malon, *Le nouveau parti* (Paris: Derveaux, 1882), vol.1, p.43; 'De l'action sociale', *Le Prolétaire*, 18 January 1879; 'La grève', *Le Prolétaire*, 3 January 1880; 'Comédie parlementaire', *Le Prolétaire*, 7 February 1880; B. Malon, 'Évolution et ploutocratie', *L'Intransigeant*, 29 November 1881; B. Malon, 'La dépression', *L'Intransigeant*, 20 June 1884. For a Possibilist reference to Engels, see P. Dervillers, 'Un drole d'historien', *Le Prolétaire*, 18 September 1880.

[44] 'Karl Marx', *Le Prolétaire*, 24 March 1883. See also Brousse, *Le marxisme dans l'Internationale*, p.3 and pp.13–14; Brousse, *La crise: sa cause, son remède*, pp.6–7.

[45] See Chapter 1.

[46] Le 'plus célèbre des socialistes contemporains'. B. Malon, 'Karl Marx', *L'Intransigeant*, 17 March 1883.

[47] 'Elle n'est pas le *Credo* du socialisme ouvrier moderne; mais elle en est la source abondante où il a le plus puisé'. B. Malon, 'Le socialisme de Karl Marx', *L'Intransigeant*, 23 March 1883. See also B. Malon, 'Les Partis ouvriers en France', in *La revue socialiste* 5 (5 May 1880), 257–269, at p.260; B. Malon, 'Réponse à une question', *L'Émancipation*, 11 November 1880; Malon, *La question sociale*, p.216; Malon, *Le nouveau parti*, vol.1, p.43. For a similar sentiment from another thinker, see E. Halpérine, 'Karl Marx', in *La revue socialiste* 3 (March 1885), 238–245, at p.240; E. Fournière, 'Essai sur l'évolution socialiste', in *La revue socialiste* 5 (May 1885), 427–437, at p.428.

Although the Possibilists effusively praised Marx's thought in general, he and his ideas were less visible in their own work. Unlike the Guesdists, Possibilists rarely explicitly mentioned Marx, and an extended comparison between the two groups is therefore not possible. There were nonetheless several areas in which the Possibilists' ideas intersected with Marx's. Their belief in the social value of intermediary bodies such as communes, for example, was similar to Marx's late acceptance of the revolutionary potential of the commune.[48] There remained, however, significant points of difference on where this model could be applied and what its precise role should be. Furthermore, in these areas the Possibilists continued to draw heavily upon other thinkers, most notably Proudhon's ideas on federalism.[49]

My intention, though, is not so much to argue that the Possibilists embraced Marx with open arms, but simply to demonstrate that they could not accurately be termed *anti*-Marx. Rather, the Possibilists took a selective and non-committal approach to Marx and his ideas. They praised aspects of his thought – particularly his contribution to the understanding of capitalism – and criticised others, such as his ideas on leadership and organisation. If anything, these varied uses of Marx serve to demonstrate precisely how popular he was within French socialism during this period.

In fact, a selective approach to Marx was widespread in French revolutionary circles at the time. The Blanquists, for example, had long praised Marx. In 1869, Lafargue informed Marx that Blanqui 'has the greatest esteem for you'. According to Lafargue, Blanqui owned a copy of *Misère de la philosophie* (one of Marx's only texts in French at the time), which he routinely carried with him and frequently lent to associates.[50] They also continued to associate themselves with Marx after the fall of the Commune and throughout the period. The ex-Communard Albert Theisz, for example, quoted from *Le Capital* in *L'Intransigeant*, while the journalist and friend of Henri Rochefort, Maurice Talmeyr, appeared to be the only

---

[48] See, for example, A. Arnould, *L'État et la Révolution* (Lyons: Éditions Jacques-Marie Laffont et Associés, 1981. First published 1877), p.96; P. Brousse, 'Congrès annuel de la Fédération jurassienne', *L'Avant-Garde* (La Chaux-de-Fonds), 12 August 1878; P. Brousse, 'Liberté et égalité', *L'Émancipation*, 3 November 1880; *Le Prolétaire*, 15 April 1882.

[49] P.-J. Proudhon, *Du principe fédératif et de la nécessité de reconstituer le parti de la révolution* (Paris: Éditions Bossard, 1921. First published, 1863). For mentions of Proudhon, see 'Une faute', *Le Prolétaire*, 4 August 1883; 'Le "pays légal"', *Le Prolétaire*, 1 April 1885; A. Theisz, 'Le mouvement social: le programme de l'Alliance républicaine socialiste', *L'Intransigeant*, 16 November 1880; B. Malon, 'La révolution qui vient', *L'Intransigeant*, 12 August 1884. See also G. Lefrançais, *Un Communard aux électeurs français* (Geneva: publisher unknown, 1875), p.4

[50] Rubel and Manale, *Marx without Myth*, p.243.

French radical to have read the *Eighteenth Brumaire of Louis Bonaparte*.[51] Comparing recent French incursions into Tunisia with the Prussian invasion of France in 1870 in *L'Intransigeant*, he wrote that the sole difference between the two invasions was 'that the first was a tragedy and the second was nothing but a farce'.[52]

This regard was further evidenced in the Blanquists' political arrangements. Blanquist exiles in the International Workingmen's Association, for example, allied themselves with Marx and the General Council in the internal battles of 1872, and in the mid-1880s, the journalist Jules Vallès publicly aligned himself and his followers with the Guesdists. Indeed, in the 1885 elections, the two groups (plus candidates associated with Prosper-Olivier Lissagaray and his newspaper *La Bataille*) ran on a joint 'revolutionary' platform.[53]

At the same time, though, many of the same Blanquists rejected Marx's more contemporary ideas. In 1880, for example, *L'Intransigeant* declared '[w]e can heartily reaffirm that we have remained true to the principles that we fought for, and which can be found in the *formules* of the International'.[54] The principles *L'Intransigeant* referred to were the demands listed in the original programme of the International Workingmen's Association, which Marx himself had written in 1864. Subsequently, however, these had been removed and replaced by another Marx-authored manifesto. In declaring its allegiance to the 1864 principles, *L'Intransigeant* implicitly rejected the later version, thus simultaneously endorsing and refuting Marx's ideas.

Like the Possibilists, the Blanquists had a complicated relationship with Marx and his ideas. They accepted aspects of his thought, rejected others, and entered into political alliance with him – at times all at once. These Blanquist interactions with Marx also act as an additional reminder that French interactions with Marx during this period stretched beyond those

---

[51] A. Theisz, 'Le mouvement social: de la raison d'être du parti socialiste', *L'Intransigeant*, 12 October 1880; 27 October 1880.

[52] 'La seule différence entre l'invasion de 1870 et l'invasion de 1881, est que la première fut une tragédie, et que la seconde n'est qu'une comédie'. M. Talmeyr, 'Pour les Khroumirs', *L'Intransigeant*, 8 May 1881.

[53] 'Liste homogène', *Le Prolétariat*, 19 September 1885. See also 'Touchante fraternité', *Le Prolétaire*, 28 April 1883; '*La Bataille*', *Le Prolétariat*, 16 May 1885; 'Les candidats de la coalition révolutionnaire', *Le Prolétariat*, 3 October 1885.

[54] 'Nous pouvons hardiment affirmer que nous sommes resté fidèle aux principes pour lesquels nous avons combattu, et qui se resument dans les formules de l'Association internationale des travailleurs.' A. Theisz, 'Le mouvement social: conciliation', *L'Intransigeant*, 2 August 1880. For unfavourable Blanquist views of Marx, see 'Pourquoi nous faisons une enquête?', *La Fédération* (London), 21 September 1872; 'Karl Marx', *La Fédération* (London), 24 and 31 August 1872.

of the Guesdists and the Possibilists. French uses of Marx were not only not restricted to one group, but additionally, neither were they restricted to the explicitly 'socialist' sections of the revolutionary movement. Although Blanqui's ideas were often similar to those of French socialists, and many tried to claim him for socialism, this was not a term that Blanqui or his followers used to describe themselves. Blanquist interactions with his ideas therefore demonstrate that the scope of French interactions with Marx was wider, more inclusive, and more complex than has previously been allowed for.

Indeed, not even the Guesdists were interested in replicating Marx's shifting ideas point for point. While over time Marx had become increasingly amenable to the revolutionary potential of communes, for instance, the Guesdists continued to steadfastly deny that any form of commune could serve as a site for social change.[55] Even in non-industrialised areas such as rural parts of contemporary India, the Guesdists argued, communal living was conducive neither to social harmony nor to progress.[56] Indeed, not only was it powerless to bring about social equality, it was also actively injurious to the pursuit of it.[57] Much like their Possibilist and Blanquist counterparts, then, the Guesdists were also relatively flexible when it came to using Marx's thought. Although they may have drawn upon the French Marx more extensively and more visibly than other groups, their general approach to Marx's thought was largely the same. The Guesdists were not doctrinaires, and much like both the Possibilists and the Blanquists, they selected the elements of Marx that suited their own situation and ideas, while ignoring or rejecting others.

The use of Marx and his ideas by French revolutionaries and socialists during this period, then, was both widespread and reflexive. Rather than Marx being the intellectual property of one group, various groups used Marx in a variety of different ways, highlighting particular aspects of his thought and ignoring others. While mentions of Marx and Marxism were ever-present in French socialist thought during this period, 'Marxism' as a doctrine was thus nowhere to be seen. Instead, Marxism is perhaps better

---

[55] Guesde and Lafargue, *Le Programme du Parti Ouvrier*, pp.75–76; J. Guesde, *Collectivisme et révolution* (Paris: Librairie des publications populaires, 1879), p.14; J. Guesde, *Services publics et socialisme* (Bordeaux: Imprimerie E. Forastié, 1883), p.7; L'industrie individualiste', *L'Égalité*, 31 March 1880; 'Le Proudhonisme est le passé', *L'Égalité*, 20 April 1880; 'Protection et libre échange', *L'Égalité*, 11 February 1880; 'Victoire!', *L'Égalité*, 30 April 1882; 'Le communisme et les services publics', *L'Égalité*, 2 July 1882; 'La question des loyers', *Le Citoyen*, 16 June 1882.

[56] 'L'autonomie', *L'Égalité*, 25 December 1881; 8 January 1882.

[57] For a similar iteration of this view from Lafargue, see Lafargue, *Cours d'économie sociale*, pp.10–11. See also Deville, *L'Évolution du capital*, p.11.

characterised as a language, or a lexicon, which various French socialists drew upon in different ways. This lexicon enabled them to communicate with each other in a common language, and to articulate and discuss possible responses to some of the pressing social problems that France faced during this period.

III

This approach to Marx was not confined to France. In the 1870s, various European socialist parties began to employ a language of Marxism in a manner similar to that of French socialists. In the newly formed Germany, for example, the Socialist Workers' Party used Marx's ideas to establish a 'third way' between competing, and equally unpalatable, political strategies.[58] Marx was thus useful as more than simply a source of ideas for thinking through social problems. As industrialisation spread, this period witnessed a widespread internationalisation of the labour force. In Roubaix, for example, the majority of residents by 1886 were either Belgian migrants or Roubaix-born Belgians.[59] As a language to which all European socialists could subscribe, Marxism played a central role in uniting potentially disparate groups who increasingly coexisted side by side. It reaffirmed 'the links that must unite socialists all over the globe and all workers in the goal of social emancipation, solidarity, and concord'.[60]

This was especially important for French socialists. Following their return to France in after the 1880 general amnesty, the language of Marxism acted as a way of maintaining their connection to the international revolutionary socialist movement that so many had been involved with in exile. As their wide coverage of international affairs and increasing use of foreign references suggested, these were connections that they were keenly interested in both preserving and publicising.[61] As well as helping to maintain French socialists' connections to Europe, this new, shared

---

[58] G. Stedman Jones, *Karl Marx: Greatness and Illusion* (London: Allen Lane, 2016), p.559.
[59] L. Page Moch, *Moving Europeans: Migration in Western Europe since 1650* (Bloomington: Indiana University Press, 1992), p.133.
[60] 'Fête internationale', *Le Prolétaire*, 23 September 1882. See also 'Les trades unions et le Parti ouvrier', *Le Prolétaire*, 25 November 1882.
[61] 'L'autonomie', *L'Égalité*, 25 December 1881. See also P. Lafargue, 'Les cités ouvrières', *L'Égalité*, 23 July 1882. For parallel attempts to link themselves to foreign theorists, see 'Galérie socialiste', *L'Égalité*, 16 June–13 August 1880; 'La révolution en Europe', *Le Prolétaire*, 9 October 1880; B. Malon, 'Le socialisme en Angleterre', *L'Intransigeant*, 21 October 1884; 'Le socialisme devant le Reichstag: extraits du discours du citoyen Liebknecht', *Le Prolétaire*, 29 March 1879; F. Borde, *Le collectivisme au congrès de Marseille* (Paris: Delaporte, 1880), p.12; J. Delaporte, 'Le renversement de la loi des salaires', in *La revue socialiste* 9 (5 July 1880), 392–399, at p.397; M. Dommanget, *Auguste*

language of Marxism played a crucial role in sustaining a sense of shared purpose amongst various different socialist groups after the collapse of their organisational framework with the dissolution of the International Workingmen's Association in 1876.

Yet, French uses of Marx cannot be explained solely in terms of the European socialist movement. Although they had spent much of the 1870s in exile in Europe, by the end of 1880 the majority of French socialists and revolutionaries had returned to France. In 1881, the Opportunist government passed the *loi sur la liberté de la presse*, which significantly relaxed press restrictions and would later come to be seen as one of the cornerstones of French republican legislation. This enabled revolutionaries to publish freely (or at least with fewer impediments) for the first time since 1872. By the early 1880s, the majority of French socialists were both resident and publishing in France once again, and their primary audience was also French. As socialists did not operate in a vacuum, in order to understand their uses of Marx during this period, it is crucial to situate these within French, as well as European, contexts.

The French general public during this period was perhaps uniquely ill disposed towards Marx. As we have seen, his work on the Paris Commune and actions in the International Workingmen's Association had attracted widespread condemnation from French audiences. As a Prussian of Jewish descent, though, his personal background also marked him out as an unpopular figure. Anti-Semitism, both latent and active, was widespread in a variety of French circles during this period.[62] This would boil over several years later in Dreyfus Affair, but it had been common in French writing and public discourse for decades. Both the July Monarchy and the Second Empire were regarded by contemporaries as notably philosemitic regimes, and critics – including socialists – often employed anti-Semitic tropes in their attacks on them. The utopian socialist Alphonse Toussenel's 1847 *Les juifs rois de l'époque*, which argued that the French economy was controlled by a cartel of 'alien' Jewish bankers, was a typical example.[63]

Blanqui au début du IIIe République (1871–1880): dernière prison et ultimes combats (Paris: Mouton, 1971), p.133.

[62] R. Harris, *The Man on Devil's Island: Alfred Dreyfus and the Affair that Divided France* (London: Allen Lane, 2010). This was also the case in the revolutionary movement; see, for example, G. Tridon, *Du molochisme juif: études critiques et philosophiques* (Brussels: Édouard Maheu, 1884); N.L. Green, 'Socialist Anti-Semitism, Defense of a Bourgeois Jew and Discovery of the Jewish Proletariat: Changing Attitudes of French Socialists before 1914', *International Review of Social History* 30 (1985), 374–399.

[63] A. Toussenel, *Les juifs rois de l'époque: histoire de la féodalité financière*, 2 vols. (Paris: Imprimerie de Crapelet, 1847).

Indeed, traces of this can also be found in Marx's own work, particularly his 1844 *On the Jewish Question*.[64]

Perhaps more immediately and obviously palpable during this period were the pervasive French anti-German sentiments. These had been brought to the fore by France's definitive loss in the 1870–1871 Franco-Prussian War and compounded by the humiliating terms of surrender that visualised France's decline and Germany's ascendance. These included an indemnity of 5 billion francs and a victory parade through Paris. Indeed, it was partly outrage at these terms that caused the outbreak of the Commune. Resentment remained long after the parade and the Prussians had left Paris,[65] to the extent that it became legally defamatory to call someone a Prussian.[66] This resentment found political expression in *revanchisme*, a cross-party yearning for revenge against Germany that crystallised around persistent demands for the recovery of Alsace and Lorraine, which France had ceded to Germany in defeat in 1871.[67] Marx, then, aggrieved both dormant French prejudices and overt political sensibilities. Without even reading a word of his work, the French general public was disinclined to approve of him.

To refer to Marx in France was therefore to take a definitive political (or anti-political) stance. Certainly, as many historians have noted, socialist uses of Marx did very little for their public appeal.[68] Writing to Engels in 1882, Lafargue reported that *L'Égalité*'s circulation in Paris hovered around 5,000 copies. He contrasted this favourably with Lissagaray's *La*

---

[64] K. Marx, 'Zur Judenfrage', in A. Ruge and K. Marx, *Deutsch-Französische Jahrbücher* (Paris: Au bureau des Annales, 1844).

[65] See, for example, P. Darriulat, *Les patriotes: la gauche républicaine et la nation 1830–1870* (Paris: Éditions du Seuil, 2001), p.274. This was present in some revolutionary circles also. See, for example, H. Rochefort, 'Des preuves', *L'Intransigeant*, 28 July 1883. Revolutionaries also mocked the then Minister of the Interior Pierre Waldeck-Rousseau for his 'Teutonic' last name. See, for example, 'Iterum crispinus', *L'Intransigeant*, 28 June 1883; H. Rochefort, 'La République en Espagne', *L'Intransigeant*, 4 January 1884.

[66] R.P. Tombs, *France 1814–1914* (London: Routledge, 1996), p.51.

[67] For a revolutionary example of this, see V. D'Esboeufs, *La république telle que nous la voulons: programme révolutionnaire, politique, économique et social* (Geneva: Imprimerie J. Benoit et Ce, 1874), p.45.

[68] Moss, *The Origins of the French Labor Movement*, p.8; p.18; Stafford, *From Anarchism to Reformism*, p.167; Vincent, *Between Marxism and Anarchism*, p.100; K.S. Vincent, *Pierre-Joseph Proudhon and the Rise of French Republican Socialism* (Oxford: Oxford University Press, 1984), p.231; C. Willard, *Jules Guesde, l'apôtre et la loi* (Paris: Éditions ouvrières, 1991), p.40; S. Bernstein, *The Beginnings of Marxian Socialism in France* (New York: Russell & Russell Inc, 1965), p.93. For a contemporary iteration of this, see 33: Friedrich Engels to Eduard Bernstein, 25 October 1881 (London), in Bottigelli and Willard, *La naissance du Parti ouvrier français*, 148–155, at p.150.

Bataille, which he claimed had sold between 2,000 and 3,000 copies in its heyday.[69] Even accounting for the likely optimism of Lafargue's estimates, these figures were far higher than anything achieved by the ephemeral revolutionary newspapers of the early 1870s. Indeed, *L'Égalité*'s and *Le Prolétaire*'s sheer durability evidenced a sustained core of support. Yet in a Parisian population of several million, these numbers were still not particularly impressive.

While their use of Marx was not directly or solely responsible for this, it nonetheless suggests that socialists during this period did not gain widespread support. In the legislative elections of 1889, for example, the Guesdists won only 0.24 per cent of the vote share, or 25,000 votes.[70] As a German of Jewish descent Marx was certainly not the obvious choice with which to re-launch a political career in early Third Republic France. While French socialists may have used him in much the same way as their European counterparts, the national social, political, and cultural context significantly altered the import of such associations. In France during this period, Marx could not act as a 'middle road' in the way that he could for, for instance, German socialists. Although such connections many not have been unique to French socialists, their determination to advertise them was nevertheless remarkable.

In fact, this antipathy seems to have been precisely the point. Rather than attempting to combat or ignore Marx's marginality, French socialists embraced it. Guesdists, Possibilists, and Blanquists all made much of the symbolic and intellectual links between Marx and contemporary French revolutionaries such as Proudhon and Blanqui.[71] In *Le Capital de Karl Marx*, for example, Deville claimed that

---

[69] 63: P. Lafargue to F. Engels (Paris, 24 November 1882), in Engels and Lafargue, *Correspondence*, vol.1, 110–115, at p.113. Engels would later claim that *Le Citoyen* sold 25,000 copies over a summer. See 195: F. Engels to E. Bernstein, 2–3 November 1882 (London), in K. Marx and F. Engels, *Marx/Engels Collected Works* (trans.) R. Dixon et al., 50 vols. (London: Lawrence and Wishart, 1975–2004), vol.46 (1992), 353–358, at p.356.

[70] Jousse, *Réviser le marxisme?*, p.107.

[71] For Proudhon, see, for example, P. Brousse, 'La grève comme moyen de propagande et de groupement', in *La Bataille* (Paris), 17 May 1882. For Blanqui, see 'Blanqui socialiste', *L'Égalité*, 26 May 1878; B. Malon, 'Blanqui socialiste', *L'Intransigeant*, 8, 9, and 11 June 1885; B. Malon, 'Blanqui socialiste', in *La revue socialiste* 7 (July 1885), 586–597, at p.597, p.589. Marx also equated Blanqui with communism. See Marx, *The Class Struggles in France*, p.174. See also P. Rosanvallon, *The Society of Equals* (trans.) A. Goldhammer (Cambridge, MA: Harvard University Press, 2013. First published in French, 2011), pp.79–80. The relationships between Marx and other theorists has often been seen as one of opposition. See, for example, Bernstein, *The Beginnings of Marxian Socialism in France*, pp.46–47; p.93; G. Lichtheim, *Marxism in Modern France* (New York: Columbia University Press, 1966), p.11; P. Thomas, *Karl Marx and the Anarchists*, 2nd edn (London: Routledge, 2010. First published, 1980); R. Soltau, *French Political Thought in the*

The great revolutionary Auguste Blanqui in France and Marx in Germany are the first to have affirmed that an *entente* is not possible and that social renovation will be accomplished not with or by the bourgeoisie, but against the bourgeoisie.[72]

Marx was further located within wider traditions of radicalism, both geographical and temporal. Guesde, for example, likened Marx and the Guesdists to historic 'communist' predecessors including Plato, Tommaso Campanella, and Thomas More,[73] while Malon found class struggle in texts as diverse as the *Declaration of the Rights of Man* and the *Manava Dharma Sastra*.[74] Socialists, then, were well aware of Marx's unloved position in French public discourse. Rather than attempting to ignore it or overcome it, however, they embraced it, emphasising through these connections the many ways in which Marx (and by association they themselves) was unacceptable to contemporary French society.

In particular, French socialists emphasised their connections to Germany. As Emmanuel Jousse has noted, French militants had been sympathetic to German social democracy since at least 1870, when Bebel and Liebknecht protested against the Franco-Prussian War.[75] In 1882 in *L'Égalité*, for instance, Guesde explicitly linked French and German socialism, arguing that 'collectivism and communism are six of one and half a dozen of the other'.[76] From the 1880s, German domestic policy also presented an immediate practical challenge to French businesses and industrialists, in the form of the beginnings of social insurance legislation (health insurance in 1883 and accident insurance in 1884). An 1884 letter from Lafargue to Engels indicates that the Guesdists were intent on capitalising upon this and their German associations. Recounting a meeting in Roubaix, Lafargue noted that the factory owners present

---

Nineteenth Century (London: Ernest Benn Limited, 1931), p.287; L. Derfler, *Paul Lafargue and the Founding of French Marxism 1842–1882* (Cambridge, MA: Harvard University Press, 1991), pp.175–176; p.184.

[72] 'Le grand révolutionnaire Auguste Blanqui, en France, et Marx, en Allemagne, sont les premiers à avoir affirmé qu'une entente n'était pas possible, et que la rénovation sociale se fera, non avec ou par la bourgeoisie, mais contre la bourgeoisie.' Deville, *Le Capital de Karl Marx*, p.55.

[73] 'La Commune', *L'Égalité*, 26 March 1882. See also 'Galerie socialiste', *L'Égalité*, 16 June–13 August 1880; *Bulletin de la Fédération jurassienne*, 8 October 1876.

[74] Malon, *Le nouveau parti*, vol.2, p.15. See also A. Blanqui, *Critique sociale* (Paris: Félix Alcan, 1885), p.48.

[75] Jousse, *Réviser le marxisme?*, p.117.

[76] '[C]ollectivisme et communisme c'est bonnet blanc et blanc bonnet'. J. Guesde, 'Collectivisme et communisme', *L'Égalité*, 5 February 1882. See also B. Malon, 'Étudiants et prolétaires', *L'Intransigeant*, 22 February 1885.

were infuriated by the enthusiasm which greeted the reading of the address from the Germans; they called us Prussians, told us to go and hold our congress in Berlin: it is a great pity that Liebknecht or Bebel was not present; they would have been cheered by the workers, who shouted the more loudly 'Long live Germany! Long live the German Socialists!' the more the employers yelled 'Down with Germany!' from the bourgeois section present.[77]

Again, French socialists were acutely aware of the pervasive anti-German sentiments in France. Rather than avoiding these associations, though, they emphasised them, using German unpopularity to reinforce their own position as radical, anti-establishment figures.

In this quest, Marx, the most visible and widely known of German socialists, was extremely useful. In this particular context, then, for French socialists Marx was not particularly special or unique. Moreover, their intent when publicising to their connections to him was not to proselytise or advertise his ideas in any sustained or distinctive fashion. Marx was simply one theorist in a long line of radicals that stretched from Plato to the present day. Rather, these particular uses of Marx were dictated primarily by the French context. In the contemporary French political, social, and cultural climate, Marx – the German Jewish socialist – represented the zenith of prejudice and marginality, and this was why he was so useful.

French socialists' aim in publicising their associations with Marx was not to appeal to the French general public, but to preserve their traditional support base. As demonstrated in Part II, preserving revolutionary support had become increasingly difficult for French socialists following the fall of the Paris Commune. The repressive legislation that immediately followed the Commune, such as the 1872 *loi Dufaure*, left traditional revolutionary action next to impossible, and the subsequent foundation of a moderate, reforming Republic rendered it deeply undesirable to many. In this climate, many revolutionaries had significantly altered their definition of revolution. They shed the deep engagement with modern French revolutionary history that they had pursued during the *année terrible*, and sought out new and more appealing ways to conceptualise and package revolution.

The decision of French socialists to enter electoral politics further altered their policies and ideas. Where previously, revolutionaries had

---

[77] 104: P. Lafargue to F. Engels, 10 April 1884 (Paris), in Engels and Lafargue, *Correspondence*, vol.1, 191–194, at pp.191–192. See also 172: P. Lafargue to F. Engels, Paris (13 November 1885), in Engels and Lafargue, *Correspondence*, vol.1, 318–319, at p.318.

demanded the overthrow of contemporary society, candidates now pursued more manageable goals, such as seats on municipal councils and the reduction of working hours. Indeed, in 1880 even *L'Égalité* claimed that this was '[t]he sole aim of the proletarian revolution'.[78] The redefinition of revolution in terms of natural phenomena theoretically encompassed these shifts, presenting even small, quotidian actions as revolutionary. Nonetheless, this represented a significant shift from revolutionaries' previous positions. At the same time, the last few years of this period saw the rise of a new extremism in France in the shape of nihilist anarchism, and more traditional revolutionaries and socialists consequently lost their monopoly on violent anti-statist action.[79] French revolutionary socialists during this period, in other words, needed as much if not more help with maintaining their traditional support base as with appealing to the general public.

It was this French audience that socialists hoped their use of Marx would appeal to. Their embrace of Marx, then, did not constitute a failure to understand the country. In fact, French socialists' decision to publicise their affinity with him was based on a deep knowledge and understanding of the contemporary French context. Likewise, their use of Marx did not signal a withdrawal from French public life in favour of pan-European socialism, but rather a concerted effort to claim a marginal position within it. By utilising the language of Marxism in such a way, revolutionary socialists hoped to regain some of the marginal or anti-establishment status that was simultaneously so crucial to the ways in which they saw themselves as a distinct movement and being progressively eroded as both circumstances and their own *modus operandi* changed.

In a sense, then, Marx did serve as a way to delineate boundaries in French socialism, but not, however, in the ways that have been previously suggested. Marx was not the source of intellectual or political divisions within the revolutionary socialist movement. Rather, the language of Marx helped to preserve socialists' revolutionary credentials, demarcating the boundaries of the revolutionary socialist movement *as a whole*, and separating them from other actors in French politics.

---

[78] 'Liberté, Égalité, Fraternité', *L'Égalité*, 18 August 1880. See also 'Le Proudhonisme est le passé', *L'Égalité*, 20 April 1880; 'Un vieux cliché', *L'Égalité*, 14 May 1882; 'Ce qu'est le progrès social', *Le Citoyen*, 21 August 1882; Lafargue, *Le droit à la paresse*, p.49.

[79] For more on the anarchist movement in France, see J. Maitron, *Le mouvement anarchiste en France*, 2 vols. (Paris: François Maspero, 1975).

IV

The history of French Marxism during this period was thus far more complex and interconnected than has previously been suggested. While French activists toyed with labels such as 'Marxist' and 'anarchist',[80] these terms did not denote any meaningful intellectual identification or content.[81] As Brousse observed in 1882, '*Marxism* is not about being a partisan of Marx's ideas'.[82] In a letter to Engels in the same year, Lafargue similarly explained that

> in Paris the word anarchist is understood in a very different sense from that of 1871, and ... even the anarchists themselves do not agree on the meaning of the term. Many think like us. But it's a feather they like to wear in their hat. If it gives them pleasure, so much the better.[83]

The history of French Marxism thus cannot be folded neatly into the social, political, or organisational history of the workers' movement or the various groupings such as the Guesdists and the Possibilists.[84] The language of Marx and Marxism showed no regard for party political boundaries, and was to be found in the work of a wide variety of French socialists and revolutionaries during this period. The structure of parties and organisations cannot explain how this language of Marxism moved and spread.

---

[80] For use of this language, see Brousse, *Le marxisme dans l'Internationale*, p.32. See also 'A bas le masque!', *Le Prolétaire*, 16 September 1882; *Le Prolétaire*, 21 October 1882; 'Les dessous de la coterie marxiste', *Le Prolétaire*, 3 March 1883; 'Possibilistes, impossibilistes et anarchistes', *Le Prolétariat*, 3 January 1885; 31: Lafargue to the members of the *Égalité* and *Prolétaire* groups, in Bottigelli and Willard, *La naissance du Parti ouvrier français*, 142–145, at pp.143–144; 105: Paul Brousse to César de Paepe, 11 February 1884 (Paris), in de Paepe, *Entre Marx et Bakounine*, 245–249, at pp.247–249.

[81] Kristin Ross and Emmanuel Jousse make a similar, although not identical, claim that doctrinal differences during this period have been overdrawn. See Jousse, *Réviser le marxisme?*, p.107; K. Ross, *Communal Luxury: The Political Imaginary of the Paris Commune* (London: Verso, 2015). First published in French, 2015), p.108.

[82] 'Le *marxisme* ne consiste donc pas à être partisan des idées de Marx.' Brousse, *Le marxisme dans l'Internationale*, p.7. Emphasis original.

[83] 53: P. Lafargue to F. Engels (Paris, 19 June 1882), in Engels and Lafargue, *Correspondence*, vol.1, 85–87, at p.86. For more on the flexible nature of anarchism, see E. Digeon, *Droits et devoirs dans l'anarchie rationnelle* (Paris: Fayard, 1882), p.32; G. Lefrançais, 'A propos de "l'anarchie"', *Le Travailleur* (Geneva, February–March 1878), p.16; Copy of a report to the Préfecture de Police, 18 December 1873 (Geneva). Archives de la Préfecture de Police (APP) Ba431/923; Intelligence report to the Préfecture de Police, 3 April 1875 (Geneva). APP Ba432/1468.

[84] For suggestions that this was the case, see P. Gratton, *Les luttes des classes dans les campagnes* (Paris: Éditions Anthropos, 1971), p.34; D. Ligou, *Histoire du socialisme en France (1871–1961)* (Paris: Presses Universitaires de France, 1962), p.25 and p.98; Bernstein, *The Beginnings of Marxian Socialism in France*, p.148; Vincent, *Between Marxism and Anarchism*, p.74; C. Willard, *Socialisme et communisme français* (Paris: Armand Colin, 1978. First published, 1967), p.61; p.65.

While various groups all drew upon the language of Marx and Marxism, they did not do so identically. For the Guesdists, Marx was useful primarily as a theorist of industrial capitalism, while his later ideas on communal organisation were deeply unwelcome. The Possibilists, meanwhile, praised Marx's general contribution to the intellectual development of modern workers' socialism while criticising his attitude to organisation and authority. Finally, the Blanquists, by contrast, were eager to politically associate themselves with Marx and self-professed Marxists. With their fulsome praise of Marx's work from the 1860s, however, they implied that they rejected almost all of his later ideas. Indeed, on subjects such as the revolutionary potential of communes, various French socialists were able to violently disagree with each other while all drawing upon Marx's work. In using Marx's ideas, then, no group was attempting to faithfully recreate an 'authentic' Marx.

Marx and Marxism in late nineteenth-century France signified many things to many different historical actors at the same time. Approaching this subject matter in any way as the search for a defined French Marxism fails to capture not only its complexity, but the basic character of the ways in which French activists during this period interacted with Marx and his ideas. Previous historians have been correct in their assertion that there was no Marxism in France or French thought at this time. French socialists were indeed uninterested in propagating a doctrine of Marxism. These historians have been mistaken, however, in their reasoning as to why this was the case. Marxism was not non-existent because French socialists were incapable of understanding Marx and his ideas, or uninterested in them. In fact, as we have seen, French socialist and revolutionary interest in Marx was widespread. Rather, there was no Marxism in France during this period because at this point 'Marxism' as a distinct doctrine or a defined set of ideas simply did not exist.

*****

The years towards the end of this period would see the construction of precisely the kind of rigid Marxist orthodoxy that had not been prevalent in France during the 1870s and early 1880s. Following Marx's death in March 1883, the collection and dissemination of his work fell to close family and friends, many of whom took a different approach. In 1884, for example, Engels wrote to Laura Lafargue:

> Herewith the preface to the *Misère* by – Mohr [Marx] himself! Bernstein has rediscovered this old article which I have at once translated. Please, you

and Paul, to turn my translation into proper French and return it along with the original which belongs to the 'Partei-Archiv' at Zurich. There will only be a few more words required. But what will the French Public say to the rather unceremonious manner in which Mohr speaks of them? And will it be wise to give this true and impartial judgement at the risk that the Brousses say: *voilà le Prussien?* Anyhow, I should be very loth to soften the article down to suit *le goût parisien* but it is worth considering.[85]

This letter acts as both a physical and an intellectual demonstration of the ways in which the idea of Marxism changed and hardened towards the end of the period. For Engels, it was a science: a clearly defined and universally applicable set of ideas to be faithfully disseminated. This Marxism was altogether more systematic, less flexible, and more proximate to its common twentieth-century incarnation than that of the 1870s and early 1880s. While some theorists such as Karl Kautsky certainly continued to adopt a flexible approach to Marxism, many others shifted towards more orthodox positions.

Many of the French socialists discussed in this chapter were also involved in the later disavowal of flexible approaches to Marx. Reflecting on the state of French socialism over the previous twenty years in 1897, Paul Lafargue disparagingly observed that after reading *The Civil War in France*, many Communard exiles 'took themselves quite seriously as representing a socialism of which they did not know a single letter'.[86] Deville likewise would later apologise for his earlier work, remarking that '[w]e were learning socialism while we were teaching it to our readers, and it is unquestionable but that we were at times mistaken.'[87] The distance that Deville and Lafargue – the principal theoretical disseminators of Marx in France during this period – sought to place between themselves and French interactions with and interpretations of Marx from the 1870s and early 1880s has doubtless contributed to the perception of Lichtheim and others that Marx's ideas did not truly 'arrive' in France until later on.

In France, this more uniform, clearly defined, and polished Marxism also reflected the significantly changed political circumstances of the late

---

[85] 99: F. Engels to L. Lafargue, London (21 February 1884), in Engels and Lafargue, *Correspondence*, vol.1, 180–182, at pp.180–181.

[86] P. Lafargue, 'Socialism in France from 1876 to 1896', in *Fortnightly Review* (London, September 1897), cited in C. Tsuzuki, *The Life of Eleanor Marx, 1855–1898: A Socialist Tragedy* (Oxford: Clarendon Press, 1967), pp.33–34. See also P. Lafargue, 'Recherches sur les origines de l'idée du bien et du juste', *Revue philosophique* 20 (1885), 253–267, at p.254.

[87] Vincent, *Between Marxism and Anarchism*, p.72.

1880s. After the tumultuous 1870s, the early part of the 1880s had been years of relative political stability, exemplified by the enactment of progressive, republican legislation. At the same time, revolutionary socialists had only just begun to dip their toes in the waters of electoral participation, and many still regarded electoral campaigns primarily as wide political platforms upon which to test their ideas rather than in terms of contests to be won or seats to be defended. In this environment, socialists were relatively free to experiment with different ideas. In the latter half of the decade, however, both the rise of the nationalist General Ernest Boulanger and revolutionary socialists' increasing electoral success encouraged them to define their ideas and clarify their positions more strongly. As the examples above suggest, the Guesdists became increasingly territorial about their supposed guardianship of Marx's thought in France, while many Blanquists allied themselves with Boulanger, and the Possibilists embraced public service socialism.[88]

As a result of these factors, the relationship between Marx, Marxism, and French socialism in the early Third Republic has received very little sustained academic attention. Viewed through the lens of the later French Marxism, the thought of this period appears diffuse and confused. French socialists' relationship with Marx in the 1870s and early 1880s has been characterised as one of distance, disdain, and accidental misinterpretation.[89] It is certainly true that Marx, like Engels, frequently found French revolutionaries infuriating. In September 1882, he complained to Engels that 'the "*Marxistes*" and the "*Anti-Marxistes*"' had '*both* done their damndest to ruin my stay in France',[90] and several months later remarked with frustration:

> Difficult to say who is the greater – Lafargue, who pours out his oracular inspiration upon the bosoms of Malon and Brousse, or these two heroes,

[88] For the classic iteration of public service socialism, see C. de Paepe, *Les services publics, précédés de deux essais sur le collectivisme* (Brussels: J. Milot, 1895. First published, 1874).

[89] See, for example, R. Trempé, 'Deuxième partie: 1871–1914', in C. Willard (ed.) *La France ouvrière: Histoire de la classe ouvrière et du mouvement ouvrier français*, 2 vols. (Paris: Éditions sociales, 1993), vol.1, 221–410, at pp.301–302; Willard, *Socialisme et communisme français*; J. Moreau, *Les socialistes français et le mythe révolutionnaire* (Paris: Hachette, 2003), p.55; R.P. Tombs, *Paris, bivouac des révolutions: la Commune de 1871* (Paris: Éditions Libertalia, 2014. First published in English, 1999), p.365.

[90] 187: K. Marx to F. Engels (30 September 1882, Paris), *Marx/Engels Collected Works*, vol.46, 338–339, at p.339.

heavenly twins who not only tell deliberate lies, but deceive themselves into thinking that the outside world has nothing better to do than "intrigue" against them and, indeed, that everyone has the same cranial structure as the magnanimous twain.[91]

It is tempting to view all of Marx's interactions with France through this lens of frustration.

As this chapter has demonstrated, however, the relationship between Marx and French socialism was much more than these trivial facts and teleological assumptions suggest. French socialists during this period did not simply drift towards an orthodox and clearly defined party political Marxism, which they subsequently sought and failed to reproduce. Rather, the relationship was characterised by intellectual reflexivity, experimentation, and exchange. While Marx may have been frustrated by his French sons-in-law and their colleagues, he did not withdraw or keep his distance from French politics. He was both attuned to the specific socio-economic circumstances of the early Third Republic and sensitive to the need to tailor his own work for French audiences. Marx, moreover, was deeply involved in this process, creating, through the translation of his work, an alternative 'French Marx'.

French socialists in turn drew heavily upon this French Marx. A variety of different revolutionary groups, from the Guesdists to the Possibilists, and even the Blanquists, used aspects of Marx's thought as building blocks with which to create their own solutions to numerous contemporary social problems. Marx's ideas functioned not as orthodoxy to be faithfully replicated, but a language for discussing and working through their own ideas. At the same time, they also turned the language of Marxism outwards, using it simultaneously to connect with other European socialists and to maintain their marginal, revolutionary identity in France. The relationship between Marx, Marxism, and French socialism during this period was multi-layered and constantly changing: a process of collaboration between Marx, French activists, and the circumstances in which they found themselves. As Peter Ghosh has recently argued, it is perhaps more productive to conceive of the construction of ideologies in terms of a 'stream of ideas', in which a thinker, their context, and their reception – both

---

[91] 204: K. Marx to F. Engels (11 November 1882, Ventnor), ibid., vol.46, 374–376, at p.374.

contemporary and posthumous – all contribute to the ways in which their ideas are shaped and understood.[92]

This more intricate relationship was also reflective of the complex structure of the revolutionary movement as a whole. In 1879, *Le Prolétaire* observed the damage done to past political movements when they divided 'into distinct groups, each carrying a special name'. If the same were to happen to socialism, the paper warned, it could be 'fatal'.[93] It has often been assumed that cautious and conciliatory attitudes such as these were thrown to the wind in 1882 when the workers' party split at the St. Étienne Congress, bringing to a head years of tension, ideological differences, and factional infighting. As Part III has demonstrated, this was not the case. Despite the presence of clear intellectual differences and personal disagreements, the revolutionary movement was not hopelessly divided, either by the Paris Commune or by the newer ideas that many activists gravitated towards in the 1870s. Rather, at the same time activists – whether they called themselves Marxists, anarchists, Possibilists, or Blanquists – recognised these differences and noticeably struggled to ensure that the revolutionary movement – in thought, if not in practice – was neither defined nor consumed by them.

---

[92] P. Ghosh, 'Constructing Marx in the History of Ideas', *Global Intellectual History* 2 (2017) pp.124–168, at pp.150–151. See also L. Althusser, É. Balibar, R. Establet, P. Macherey, and J. Rancière, *Reading Capital: The Complete Edition* (trans.) B. Brewster and D. Fernbach (London: Verso, 2015. First published in French, 1965), p.5; T. Carver, 'Marx's *Eighteenth Brumaire of Louis Bonaparte*: Democracy, Dictatorship, and Class Struggle', in P. Baehr and M. Richter (eds.), *Dictatorship in History and Theory: Bonapartism, Caesarism, and Totalitarianism* (Cambridge: Cambridge University Press, 2004), 103–127, at p.109. The concept of 'resonance' suggested by David Todd is also similar. See D. Todd, *Free Trade and Its Enemies in France, 1814–1851* (Cambridge: Cambridge University Press, 2015), pp.236–237.

[93] 'Du danger des écoles', *Le Prolétaire*, 29 January 1879.

PART IV

Empire and Internationalism

Deportation, Imperialism, and the Republican State

In making use of the international language of Marxism and promoting the conception of revolution as a process embedded in natural phenomena, activists hoped to present a revised version of the revolutionary movement that was both intellectually unified and politically viable in local, national, and continental contexts.* Yet these ideas and values were not limited by the borders of Europe. The revolutionary journalist Gustave Flourens, for example, devoted much of his 1863 *Histoire de l'homme* to a racialised historical comparison between the development of Europe and other parts of the world.[1] In the later years of his life, Karl Marx assiduously studied North Africa and South Asian communes in search of alternative paths of social development, while the anarchist geographer Élisée Reclus used the *Nouvelle géographie universelle* to detail the physical similarities between different parts of the world.[2] Part IV of this book considers the reactions of ex-Communards to the 'imperial turn' of the French Third Republic in the 1870s and 1880s, and explores the role of colonialism, empire, and international questions in their thought.

In an article of June 1883, Antoine 'Tony' Révillon, a radical republican journalist and deputy for Paris's 20th arrondissement, expressed his desire that 'our sailors in Madagascar force respect for our flag through cannon

---

* An earlier version of some of these arguments can be found in J. Nicholls, 'Empire and internationalism in French revolutionary socialist thought, 1871–1885', *The Historical Journal* 59:4 (2016), 1051–1074.

[1] G. Flourens, *L'histoire de homme: cours d'histoire naturelle des corps organisés au Collège de France* (Paris: Imprimerie de E. Martinet, 1863–1864).

[2] 52: P. Lafargue to F. Engels, 16 June 1882 (London), in F. Engels, P. and L. Lafargue, *Correspondence*, 3 vols. (trans.) Y. Kapp (Moscow: Foreign Languages Publishing House, 1959), vol.1, 82–84, at p.83; É. Reclus, *La nouvelle géographie: la terre et les hommes*, 19 vols. (Paris: Hachette, 1876–1894). See also G. de Greef, *Éloges d'Élisée Reclus et de Kellès-Krauz* (Gand: Société coopérative *Volksdrukkerij*, 1906), p.32.

fire. Let our explorers create *comptoirs* in the Congo. Nothing could be more legitimate.'[3] France had long been a power abroad, colonising parts of the New World as early as the sixteenth century, and gradually expanding its influence across the Americas, the West Indies, West Africa, and South Asia during the seventeenth and early eighteenth centuries. More recently, it had claimed large parts of Algeria as its own, beginning with the invasion of Algiers in the last days of the Restoration in 1830.

Yet the beginning of the Third Republic marked a new phase in France's imperial expansion, and Révillon's article captured the spirit of many republicans' recently acquired imperial fervour. Despite initial successes, previous imperial exploits had often been defined by failure, whether the progressive loss of all but five of France's Indian territories, Napoleon's calamitous invasion of Russia in 1812, or the overthrow and execution of Maximilian I in Mexico in 1867, who had accepted the crown at Napoleon III's invitation. The Third Republic, however, approached imperialism with a renewed vigour and sense of purpose. Just as the Second Republic had when it declared Algeria an integral part of France in the 1848 constitution, the Third Republic looked to rescue empire from its royalist and Bonapartist connotations and invest it with a new meaning, conquering new territories, and in doing so, bringing glory to France and civilisation to far-flung countries. As David Todd recently observed, 'the advent of the Third Republic profoundly reshaped the nature of French imperialism'.[4]

For influential politicians and intellectuals alike, the establishment of an extensive empire and the dissemination of French ideas was not just a right, but a moral duty. In the 1882 preface to the second edition of *De la colonisation chez les peuples modernes* (originally published in 1874), the liberal economist Pierre Leroy-Beaulieu bemoaned France's diminished position in world affairs. With its population stagnating while those of Russia, China, and Germany grew, he asked,

> What is left of the great role that we played in the past? Of the influence – often decisive – that we exercised upon the direction of civilised peoples? Nothing but a memory, growing fainter every day.[5]

---

[3] 'Ce qui se passe', *Le Citoyen* (Paris), 10 June 1883.
[4] D. Todd, 'A French imperial meridian, 1814–1870', *Past & Present* 210 (February 2011), 155–186, at p.184.
[5] 'Du grand rôle qu'elle a joué dans le passé, de l'influence, souvent décisive, qu'elle a exercée sur la direction des peuples civilisés, que lui restera-t-il? Un souvenir, s'éteignant de jour en jour.' P. Leroy-Beaulieu, *De la colonisation chez les peuples modernes* 2nd edn (Paris: Guillaumin, 1882), p.viii. See also C. Charle, 'Préface', in C. Reynaud Paligot, *La République raciale: paradigme racial et idéologie républicaine (1860–1930)* (Paris: Presses universitaires de France, 2006), xiii–xxii, at p.xxi.

Fortunately, Leroy-Beaulieu wrote, '[o]ur country has a way of escaping from this inexorable decline: colonisation. For France, it is a question of life and death.'[6] France's own well-being was thus intimately tied to this mission, and imperialism represented a sign of faith in republican government. Both the regeneration of France and that of the world were inextricably linked to imperialism.

Sentiments such as these have in turn spawned a vast secondary literature on the connections between republicanism and empire in late nineteenth-century French politics.[7] Yet despite this conjuncture of republicanism and imperial fervour, one group of vocal republicans has been overlooked in the literature on French empire. Revolutionaries have been notable largely for their absence from studies of imperialism in the early Third Republic.[8] Other than several brief references to Henri Rochefort, Raoul Girardet does not touch upon revolutionaries in *L'Idée coloniale en France de 1871 à 1962*,[9] while other classic Francophone works such as Charles-Robert Ageron's *L'Anticolonialisme en France de 1871 à 1914* have tended to focus upon the period '[a]fter the anticolonial explosion of 1885' – a year often identified as a turning point in French attitudes towards imperialism.[10] While revolutionaries have appeared in more recent specialised literature, such as *Beyond Papillon*, Stephen Toth's study of French penal colonies and Matt Matsuda's *Empire of Love*, they have nonetheless remained absent from more general studies of French imperialism.[11]

---

[6] 'Notre pays a un moyen d'échapper à cette irremediable déchéance, c'est de coloniser ... La colonisation est pour la France une question de vie ou de mort'. Leroy-Beaulieu, *De la colonisation chez les peuples modernes*, p.viii.

[7] The most prominent example is A.L. Conklin, *A Mission to Civilize: The Republican Idea of Empire in France and West Africa, 1895–1930* (Stanford, CA: Stanford University Press, 1997).

[8] R. Aldrich, *Greater France: A History of French Overseas Expansion* (Basingstoke: Macmillan, 1996); Conklin, *A Mission to Civilize*; A.L. Conklin, S. Fishman, R. Zaretsky, *France and Its Empire since 1870* (Oxford: Oxford University Press, 2011).

[9] The closest Girardet comes are several mentions of Henri Rochefort. See R. Girardet, *L'Idée coloniale en France de 1871 à 1962* (Paris: Éditions de la Table Ronde, 1972), p.54; p.61.

[10] The first socialist text presented by Ageron dates from 1885. C.-R. Ageron, *L'anticolonialisme en France de 1871 à 1914* (Paris: Presses universitaires de France, 1973), p.38; pp.70–71. See also G. Manceron, *1885: le tournant colonial de la République: Jules Ferry contre Georges Clemenceau, et autres affrontements parlementaires sur la conquête coloniale* (Paris: La Découverte, 2007).

[11] M.K. Matsuda, *Empire of Love: Histories of France and the Pacific* (Oxford: Oxford University Press, 2005); S.A. Toth, *Beyond Papillon: The French Overseas Penal Colonies, 1854–1952* (Lincoln: University of Nebraska Press, 2006). See also C.J. Eichner, '*La citoyenne* in the World: Hubertine Auclert and Feminist Imperialism', *French Historical Studies* 32:1 (2009), 63–84.

Similarly, despite the increasing importance of empire in political rhetoric and metropolitan culture, scholars of the revolutionary movement have rarely engaged with imperialism.[12] The experiences of individual revolutionaries in the colonies have received only passing mentions in the work of historians such as Bernard Moss and James Lehning.[13] As previous chapters have demonstrated, the likes of Robert Stuart, Steven Vincent, Emmanuel Jousse, and Michel Cordillot have readily situated late nineteenth-century French revolution within an international context. Yet these studies have rarely looked beyond the West or the institutional boundaries of organisations such as the First International.[14] While for historians of the twentieth century, anticolonialism and socialism have often seemed natural bedfellows, for those of the nineteenth, revolutionary socialism and ideas of empire rarely collide. Indeed, this lack of extant literature may give the impression that no substantive link between the two existed.

What little work has been done on the relationship between revolutionaries and imperialism during this period has focused almost exclusively upon the mass deportations to New Caledonia that followed the fall of the Commune. This is both a fruitful and an illuminating avenue of study, which sheds light upon an often-understudied aspect of post-Commune revolutionary life. Yet the deep focus upon New Caledonia rather than ex-Communards' relationship to broader ideas of imperialism and colonialism has done little to dispel the idea that no such relationship existed. The emphasis of this body of work upon social history and reconstructing the quotidian life of Communards in New Caledonia has inadvertently further separated this experience from revolutionaries' intellectual activities. Their ideas on imperialism have thus been left unexamined.

Contrary to what this historiographical lacuna may suggest, though, French revolutionary thought in this area ranged far beyond the topic of deportation. Part IV explores French revolutionary ideas on empire and

---

[12] This is beginning to change. See, for example, Q. Deluermoz, *Commune(s), 1870–1871, une traversée des mondes au XIXe siècle* (Paris: Seuil, 2019).

[13] B.H. Moss, *The Origins of the French Labor Movement 1830–1914: The Socialism of Skilled Workers* (Berkeley: University of California Press, 1976), p.131; J.R. Lehning, *To Be a Citizen: The Political Culture of the Early French Third Republic* (Ithaca, NY: Cornell University Press, 2001), p.94.

[14] M. Cordillot, *Aux origines du socialisme moderne: la Première Internationale, la Commune de Paris, l'exil: recherches et travaux* (Paris: Éditions de l'Atelier/Éditions ouvrières, 2010); R.C. Stuart, *Marxism at Work: Ideology, Class and French Socialism during the Third Republic* (Cambridge: Cambridge University Press, 1992); E. Jousse, *Les hommes révoltés: les origines intellectuelles du réformisme en France (1871–1917)* (Paris: Fayard, 2017), p.12; Q. Deluermoz, 'The IWMA and the Commune: A Reassessment', in F. Bensimon, Q. Deluermoz, and J. Moisand (eds.), *'Arise Ye Wretched of the Earth': The First International in a Global Perspective* (Leiden: Brill, 2018), 107–126.

internationalism, and begins in turn to resituate these ideas within their wider patterns of thought. It approaches the subject from a dual perspective, examining both the form and content of deportees' thought as well as the work of revolutionaries who managed to escape arrest and deportation. It demonstrates that ideas of empire and internationalism were both more prevalent and more prominent in revolutionary thought at the beginning of the Third Republic than has previously been suggested. Far from being confined to New Caledonia and the deportees' experiences there, they were in fact both widespread in certain circles of revolutionaries that remained in Europe, and closely intertwined with other areas of their thought, becoming one of the principal channels through which they criticised the French state and, towards the end of the period, the Opportunist government.

This chapter looks at the place of empire and international questions in the deportees' thought. It draws upon a wide range of primary sources from both during and after the deportees' time in New Caledonia. This includes material produced by revolutionaries while in the South Pacific, including deportee newspapers such as *Le Parisien* and a wide selection of private correspondence between deportees in New Caledonia, including Louise Michel and Henri Messager, and their friends and family in Europe.[15] Indeed, this protracted correspondence often enables us to follow the arrested Communards from prison, through their trials in France and passage to New Caledonia in addition to their time there.

Following the 1880 amnesty, many deportees wrote and published memoirs of their experiences. These included renowned activists such as the journalist Henri Rochefort, the famed anarchist Louise Michel, and the future deputy and co-founder of the Section française de l'Internationale ouvrière (SFIO) Jean Allemane, as well as lesser-known Communards such as the architect Achille Ballière, who would later stand as a Boulangist candidate in the 1889 legislative elections.[16] The chapter also draws extensively upon these memoirs, using them to gain an insight into the ways in which returned deportees remembered and sought to make

---

[15] H. Messager, *239 lettres d'un Communard déporté: Île d'Oléron – Île de Ré – Île des Pins* (ed.) J. Maitron (Paris: Le Sycomore, 1979); L. Michel, *Je vous écrit de ma nuit: correspondance générale – 1850–1904* (Paris: Les Éditions de Paris, 1999).

[16] P. Grousset and F. Jourde, *Les condamnés politiques en Nouvelle-Calédonie: récit de deux évadés* (Geneva: Imprimerie Ziegler, 1876); O. Pain, *Henri Rochefort (Paris – Nouméa – Genève)* (Paris: Périnet, 1879); J. Allemane, *Mémoires d'un Communard, des barricades au bagne* (Paris: Librairie socialiste J. Allemane, 1880); A. Ballière, *La déportation de 1871: souvenirs d'un évadé de Nouméa* (Paris: G. Charpentier, 1889); Messager, *239 lettres d'un Communard déporté*; Michel, *Je vous écris de ma nuit*.

political use of their experiences. These sources have been further supplemented by contemporary French work on imperialism including Leroy-
Beaulieu's *De la colonisation chez les peuples modernes* and parliamentary
debates on the issue, as well as by newspapers from the various locations
that Communards visited in the years after 1871 including Australia and
the United States.[17]

Contrary to what has been suggested in the secondary literature, this
chapter establishes that the deportees in fact remained theoretically unconcerned with imperial and colonial questions. Their focus was instead the
French Republic, and revolutionaries primarily used their experiences of
deportation to criticise the established order, arguing that the sorry state of
French colonies exposed both Moral Order and Opportunist politicians as
unfit custodians of the Third Republic. Revolutionaries contrasted this
alleged failure with their own successful attempts to reconstruct a community in New Caledonia that was at once revolutionary and politically
viable. In doing so, they hoped to prove that even stable Republics had
lessons to learn from revolutionaries, and thus legitimise their renewed
participation in national political debates after the 1880 general amnesty
permitted them to return to France.

I

It is not surprising that deportation should form the basis for studies of the
relationship between revolutionary thought and French overseas expansion
during this period. Of around 35,000 citizens arrested and tried by the
military courts following the fall of the Commune, 4,253 were sentenced
to deportation.[18] Between 1872 and 1876, the new deportees were
shipped to New Caledonia, a constellation of islands in the South Pacific
about 2,000 miles to the east of Australia. Formally colonised by the
French in September 1853, New Caledonia functioned as France's principal penal colony from 1863 to 1896.[19] During this time, it accepted
22,315 prisoners, around 40 per cent of whom would die there.[20] The

---

[17] *New York Herald*, January–June 1874; *San Francisco Chronicle*, January–June 1874.
[18] A. Bullard, 'Self-Representation in the Arms of Defeat: Fatal Nostalgia and Surviving Comrades in French New Caledonia, 1871–1880', *Cultural Anthropology* 12 (May 1997), 179–212, at p.179.
[19] A.L. Bullard, *Exile to Paradise: Savagery and Civilization in Paris and the South Pacific, 1790–1900* (Stanford, CA: Stanford University Press, 2000), p.94.
[20] Forty per cent of this number would die in New Caledonia. I. Merle, 'The trials and tribulations of the emancipists: the consequences of penal colonisation in New Caledonia, 1864–1920', in R. Aldrich (ed.), *France, Oceania and Australia: Past and Present* (Sydney: University of Sydney/Department of Economic History, 1991), 39–55, at p.39.

Communard deportees thus contributed substantially to the penal colony's population. The average age of the deportees was 33, with the youngest aged 16 and the oldest aged 65.[21] Just twenty of the thousands were women.[22] There were several famous Communards among the deportees' numbers, including the journalist Henri Rochefort, several members of the Conseil de la Commune (the administration's governmental body), and Louise Michel, the so-called red virgin of Montmartre. The majority, however, had not been actively involved in either the administration of the Commune or efforts to spread its message.

Once in New Caledonia, the deportees were settled in one of three locations according to the severity of their crimes. The 400 convicted of criminal offences such as arson in addition to their political crimes were sentenced to forced labour in the colony's quarries and mines, and taken to the labour camp on Île Nou. The vast majority, having only been convicted of political crimes, were technically 'free' once they arrived in New Caledonia. Around 3,000, who had been convicted of insurrection but not of violence, were deposited in five 'communes' on the Île des Pins, while 900 who had been confined to cells during the voyage (likely due to convictions for using weapons) were placed in a limited area overseen by a prison warden on the Ducos Peninsula.[23] Of the 4,253 Communards deported to New Caledonia, almost 10 percent died in situ. Indeed, deaths were so frequent that the deportees constructed elaborate funeral rites,[24] and the Communard cemetery on the Île des Pins came to be known as 'the sixth commune'.[25]

These deportations caused an international sensation.[26] When, in 1874, Henri Rochefort and five other deportees made a sensational escape from New Caledonia under cover of night almost three years to the day after the outbreak of the Commune, international newspapers competed for access to the *évadés*. The *San Francisco Chronicle* reprinted Rochefort's signature on its front page, while the *New York Herald* considered sending a reporter to Australia in order to secure an interview as quickly as possible.[27] When

---

[21] J. Baronnet and J. Chalou, *Communards en Nouvelle-Calédonie: Histoire de la déportation* (Paris: Mercure de France, 1987), p.155.

[22] Ibid., p.93.   [23] Ibid.

[24] Grousset and Jourde, *Les condamnés politiques en Nouvelle-Calédonie*, p.25.

[25] Baronnet and Chalou, *Communards en Nouvelle-Calédonie*, p.339.

[26] See, for example, *L'Égalité* (Paris), 18 November 1877; E. Roche, '*Les légendes canaques* par Louise Michel', *L'Intransigeant* (Paris), 31 December 1884. 'Louise Michel!', *Le Prolétaire* (Paris), 29 November 1879; 'L'arrivée de Louise Michel et les exploits de la police', *Le Prolétaire*, 13 November 1880.

[27] 'Rochefort', *New York Herald*, 30 May 1874, p.3.

Rochefort returned to Europe several months later, the *Bulletin de la Fédération jurassienne* likened his arrival to 'the coming of a Messiah'.[28] The late nineteenth century also saw the publication of a raft of deportee memoirs, while Rochefort's escape was immortalised in paint by Édouard Manet not once but twice in 1880 and subsequently exhibited in the 1881 Salon.[29]

Deportation also carried significant political weight. The campaign for a Communard amnesty, which drew upon the deportees' situation in New Caledonia for much of its emotive power, haunted both the Moral Order and Opportunist Republican governments in the press and parliament during the 1870s. From soon after the Commune's fall, prominent republicans and radicals such as Victor Hugo, Camille Pelletan, and Alfred Naquet repeatedly drew attention to the Communards' plight, demanding more lenient punishments and even an amnesty. The campaign had very little concrete success until the late 1870s, but did serve to reunite radical republicans who had opposed the Commune with revolutionaries who had participated in it. In 1879, the Opportunist government began dispensing individual pardons, and on 11 July 1880 it grudgingly granted a full amnesty, shortly before an electoral campaign that the subject of the deportations had been forecast to dominate.[30]

Deportation placed the Communards on the frontline of colonial encounter. Although it had elsewhere condemned them for their moral depravity, the French government was keen to transform the Communards into colonial settlers, and the deportees' families were even offered free passage and encouraged to join them in New Caledonia.[31] They also made a number of foreign acquaintances, for New Caledonia at this time was home to at least four distinct communities. Alongside the Communard deportees, the islands were also inhabited by the indigenous Kanak population, as well as a large number of imported labourers from Asia and other parts of Oceania. The Communards, Kanaks, and labourers were also joined in New Caledonia by a variety of Algerian political prisoners, the largest group of which had been deported as a result of the 1871–1872

[28] '[C]omme la venue d'un Messie'. *Bulletin de la Fédération jurassienne* (Sonvilier), 20 June 1874.
[29] D. Armogathe, 'Le testament de Louise Michel', in L. Michel, *Souvenirs et aventures de ma vie* (ed.) D. Armogathe (Paris: La Découverte/Maspero, 1983), 11–20, at p.11.
[30] For more on opposition to the amnesty, see, for example, S. Hazareesingh, *Intellectual Founders of the Republic: Five Studies in Nineteenth-Century French Republican Political Thought* (Oxford: Oxford University Press, 2005. First published, 2001), p.155.
[31] Bullard, *Exile to Paradise*, p.93 and p.130; L. Barron, 'La déportation et les déportés, 1871–1880', *La philosophie positive* (July–August 1880), 41–66, at p.42.

Kabyle Rebellion.[32] This cultural and geographical diversity marked something of a change for the Communard deportees, whose world prior to 1871 had centred upon the fast-growing but ethnically homogenous urban metropolis of Paris. Abruptly, they found themselves deposited 10,500 miles from France, and thrown into contact with a wide variety of different cultures.

Perhaps as a result of these associations, many scholars who have researched deportation have attempted to divine a stance on overseas expansion in the deportees' thought. In *Déportations en Nouvelle-Calédonie* and *Communards en Nouvelle Calédonie*, the historians Germaine Mailhé, and Jean Baronnet and Jean Chalou, respectively, expressed disbelief that a sizeable proportion of the Communard deportees collaborated with the French colonial administration during a serious Kanak rebellion against colonial rule in 1878 that left several French citizens dead.[33] The deportees, it is implied, might have been expected to forgo national loyalty to the administration that was also oppressing them, in favour of a putative anticolonial or revolutionary solidarity with the Kanak rebels. In her study of the psychological effects of deportation, meanwhile, Alice Bullard has argued that initial Communard interest in cross-cultural interaction faded quickly after they reached New Caledonia, with the deportees ultimately coming to define themselves as 'French' through the affirmation of evolutionary hierarchies and insurmountable racial difference.[34] Studies of deportees in New Caledonia, then, have differed significantly in their approach and methodology, yet despite their differences these diverse authors have all been in agreement that strongly held views on empire and colonialism were characteristic of deportee thought.

It is certainly true that the deportees mentioned colonialism frequently, however their relationship to it was significantly more complicated than these previous approaches have suggested. In his *Mémoires d'un*

---

[32] For more on Algerian political prisoners in New Caledonia, see M. Ouennoughi, *Algériens et Maghrébins en Nouvelle-Calédonie: Anthropologie historique de la communauté arabo-berbère de 1864 à nos jours* (Algiers: Casbah Editions, 2008). For an example of Communards meeting the Algerian prisoners, see 120: Messager – Mère, Oléron, 17 June 1872, in Messager, *239 lettres d'un Communard déporté*, 163–164, at pp.163–164.

[33] Baronnet & Chalou, *Communards en Nouvelle-Calédonie*, p.333; G. Mailhé, *Déportations en Nouvelle-Calédonie des communards et des révoltés de la grande Kabylie (1872–1876)* (Paris: L'Harmattan, 1994), p.359. See also 'Débat: "La Commune: utopie ou modernité?"', in G. Larguier and J. Quaretti (eds.), *La Commune de 1871: utopie ou modernité?* (Perpignan: Presses universitaires de Perpignan, 2000), 407–424, at p.422.

[34] Bullard, 'Self-Representation in the Arms of Defeat', at p.205; see also at p.188.

Communard, Jean Allemane criticised not only indigenous colonial collaborators,[35] but also rebels against colonialism,[36] as well as colonialism itself.[37] Even Louise Michel, who has frequently been cited as the most sympathetic of the deportees to the Kanaks' subjection, fluctuated between anger at the injustice of colonial settlement and a belief that the Kanaks were child-like and in need of Western education.[38] This ambivalence should not be surprising. In her recent book, *Along the Archival Grain,* Ann Laura Stoler addressed the widespread 'flat' interpretation of the motivations of colonists and colonial officials. Far from conforming to paradigms of either 'ignorance' or 'acceptance' of imperial realities, she argued, European agents of and ancillaries to colonialism made their lives in a 'more complex psychic space' of 'tacit ambivalences and implicit ambiguities'.[39] Thus, it would be entirely possible for a deportee to decry, for example, both colonial settlement and the Kanak rebellion. Rather than a consistent and strongly held view, deportees often expressed many apparently conflicted thoughts on empire.

Indeed, it is not immediately clear that many of them gave extensive thought to the subject at all. Their references to colonialism notably contained frequent factual inaccuracies. In the case of the Algerian Kabyle deportees, Rochefort's collaborator Olivier Pain suggested that 'there are sincere republicans among them'.[40] In fact, the Kabyle deportees were largely aristocratic, and their rebellion had sprung partly from their refusal to submit to republican, as opposed to royal or imperial, authority.[41] Given that such mistakes were easily rectifiable and the deportees were elsewhere extremely concerned with factual and political accuracy,[42] they seem rather to indicate a lack of sustained intellectual interest in empire or colonial questions. While deportation may have introduced revolutionaries to a variety of other cultures, then, such a widening of geographic and cultural horizons did not necessarily prompt an increased interest in ideas of empire. Although they were certainly aware of imperialism, and indeed engaged in it in their role as 'colonial agents', it seems that it was not as

---

[35] Allemane, *Mémoires d'un Communard,* p.239.   [36] Ibid., p.426.   [37] Ibid., p.419.

[38] Contrast, for example, the 'egalitarian' attitude in Fonds Louise Michel Moscou, International Institute of Social History (IISH), 233, 5–2, p.4; p.17; with Michel, *Souvenirs et aventures de ma vie,* p.75.

[39] A.L. Stoler, *Along the Archival Grain: Epistemic Anxieties and Colonial Common Sense* (Princeton, NJ: Princeton University Press, 2009), pp.248–249.

[40] Mailhé, *Déportations en Nouvelle-Calédonie,* p.403.

[41] See Ouennoughi, *Algériens et Maghrébins,* pp.55–121; Mailhé, *Déportations en Nouvelle-Calédonie,* p.77; p.124.

[42] See, for example, 'Rochefort! Found At Last', *San Francisco Chronicle,* 23 May 1874.

central to either their experience or their thought as scholars have previously suggested.

II

Rather, it was to the French Republic that the deportees' thought often turned.[43] Deportees frequently used their experiences in New Caledonia as evidence that the incumbent government was unfit to rule France. Successive administrations in New Caledonia, particularly that of Charles Guillain, governor from 1862 to 1870, had implemented progressively stricter policies in an attempt to assert French control of the islands, and the deportees seized upon these actions.[44] Rochefort's newspaper *L'Intransigeant*, for example, wrote disparagingly that French colonial government 'is practically military dictatorship ... It considers settlers to be its subjects and treats them accordingly'.[45] Likewise, twenty-eight deportees penned an open letter to the Comités républicains de Paris, detailing at length the situation on the ground in French colonies, 'where the soldier reigns as absolute master, without serious control, and without real responsibility'.[46]

Such vocabulary and references were certainly colonial, yet the target of the criticism was clearly not colonialism itself. Rather, it was the metropolitan French government. For the twenty-eight deportees and for *L'Intransigeant*, French colonialism, with its pervasive culture of militarism and apparent suppression of liberty, was problematic because of its lack of democratic accountability or popular involvement. In other words, it contravened the values that they associated with French republicanism, and exposed whichever administration was currently in office, and by extension the Third Republic itself, as a government of ethical compromise.

---

[43] See, for example, 269: Louise Michel to Georges Clemenceau, 15 October 1879, in Michel, *Je vous écris de ma nuit*, p.254; H. Brissac, *Quand j'étais au bagne: poésies* (Paris: Derveaux, 1887), p.vi.

[44] B. Douglas, 'Conflict and Alliance in a Colonial Context: Case Studies in New Caledonia 1853–1870', *Journal of Pacific History* 15 (1980), 21–51, at p.31.

[45] '[N]os colonies d'outre-mer, livrées presque toutes à la dictature militaire. Là, règne sans conteste un fonctionnariat brutal ... qui considère les colons comme ses sujets et les traite en conséquence'. 'Ce qui se passe en Nouvelle-Calédonie', *L'Intransigeant*, 1 September 1880. For a similar criticism, see Ballière, *La Déportation de 1871*, pp.256–257.

[46] '[L]a colonie, où un soldat règne en maître absolu, sans contrôle sérieux, sans responsabilité réelle'. 'Appel adressé des transportés de la Commune aux Comités Républicains de Paris' (New Caledonia, s.d.), Fonds Lucien Descaves, International Institute of Social History (IISH), 135, p.5. See also H. Rochefort, 'Situation coloniale', *L'Intransigeant*, 8 July 1885.

The deportees' evaluations of colonial economy and production were similarly designed to highlight the failings of metropolitan government. As we have seen, economic advancement formed a central part of many colonial advocates' theories during the nineteenth century. The idea of a captive imperial market for French products was central to successive governments' decisions to put off painful economic reform,[47] while the promise of lucrative raw materials such as sandalwood and nickel formed a large part of the rationale for colonising places like New Caledonia.[48] Imperialism, in other words, was not simply a moral imperative, but also an economic one. Indeed, economic concerns were frequently considered more important. As Leroy-Beaulieu put it, '[t]he true life-force of colonisation is not emigrants, but capital'.[49]

Yet in reality, the deportees claimed, French colonies were not delivering the economic benefits that had been promised. In 1876, Paschal Grousset and Francis Jourde, two of the escaped deportees, wrote that in New Caledonia, '[c]ommerce and industry ... are subject to all the restrictions that the French military administration is so good at augmenting', suggesting that New Caledonia's status as a penal colony took precedence over its economic development.[50] The vast majority of men and resources, they claimed, were directed towards the running of prisons and camps.[51]

Settlers, on the other hand, were given little support. Many swiftly left New Caledonia for Australia, Tasmania, or New Zealand after failing to find regular work.[52] As Louise Michel noted, '[w]hen I was in New Caledonia, colonisation was nothing but a word.'[53] Rather than prioritising economic success and financial gain that could potentially benefit all French citizens, they argued, the authorities forfeited this in favour of

[47] R.P. Tombs, *France 1814–1914* (London: Routledge, 1996), p.159.

[48] Leroy-Beaulieu, *De la colonisation chez les peuples modernes*, p.viii.

[49] 'Le véritable nerf de la colonisation, ce sont plus encore les capitaux que les émigrants.' Ibid., p.vii.

[50] 'Le commerce et l'industrie y sont soumis à toutes les entraves que savent si bien multiplier les administrations militaires françaises.' Grousset and Jourde, *Les condamnés politiques en Nouvelle-Calédonie*, p.41. For similar criticisms, see *Lettres de la Nouvelle-Calédonie*, Fonds Louise Michel (IISH), 930; H. Rochefort, *L'Évadé: Roman canaque*, 2nd edn (Paris: Charpentier, 1880), p.3; J. Allemane, 'Braves gens!', *Le Prolétariat*, 1 November 1884. See also 'Nouvelle colonie', *Le Prolétariat*, 20 June 1885; Anon, *Les déportés civils de Gomen. Nouvelle Calédonie* (Paris: Imprimerie Nouvelle Association Ouvrière, 1871).

[51] Grousset and Jourde, *Les condamnés politiques en Nouvelle-Calédonie*, p.55. See also D. Shineberg, '"Noumea no good. Noumea no pay": "New Hebridean" Indentured Labour in New Caledonia, 1865–1925', *Journal of Pacific History* 26 (1991), 187–205, at p.187.

[52] Grousset and Jourde, *Les condamnés politiques en Nouvelle-Calédonie*, p.57.

[53] Michel, *Souvenirs et aventures de ma vie*, p.62. See also Barron, 'La déportation et les déportés, 1871–1880', at p.43.

secure prisons and party political interests. In contrasting their lived experiences of New Caledonia with the colonial lobby's claims, deportees sought to expose the government as duplicitous and dishonest: it was not the good of the Republic that they cared about, but rather the security of the present administration.

This, deportees noted, stood in stark contrast to British colonialism.[54] In his memoirs, for example, Achille Ballière contrasted Australia favourably with Senegal, remarking, upon his ship's arrival in Melbourne,

> For a moment I thought we were landing in Dover or Southampton. What a different from our arrival in the French colony of Senegal! Here, one was aware of civil life. Europe has rediscovered itself in this new continent, gaining strength and exuberance from it.[55]

In identifying the cause of this colonial economic stagnation as a combination of authoritarian power and neglect, deportees were able to use these seemingly remote problems to criticise the performance of the metropolitan government. Contrasting their own experiences with official claims about the profitability of imperialism, they called into question the current government's honesty, its suitability to lead the country, and its claims to have France's best interest at heart, casting doubt upon not only its loyalties but more importantly its capability.

This approach proved potent largely because of metropolitan Frances's own ambivalent attitude towards overseas expansion during this period. The colonial lobby became increasingly visible in France as this period progressed, with high profile enthusiasts taking up key roles in government and public life. In 1878, Leroy-Beaulieu took up the chair in political economy at the Collège de France, while Jules Ferry served in various capacities in different Opportunist governments between 1879 and 1885, including Prime Minister and Minister of Public Education. Yet in spite of this visibility, both the general public and many French politicians remained unconvinced of empire's value. Deputies from across the political spectrum dismissed imperial expansion as an attempt to distract from problems closer to home and draw eyes away from issues such as rising

---

[54] Others such as Tocqueville and Leroy-Beaulieu also made comparisons with British colonialism. For Tocqueville, see J. Pitts, *A Turn to Empire: The Rise of Liberal Imperialism in Britain and France* (Princeton, NJ: Princeton University Press, 2005), pp.219–226; for Leroy-Beaulieu, see Todd, 'A French imperial meridian, 1814–1870', at p.183.

[55] 'Un instant j'ai cru que nous débarquions à Dover ou à Southampton; quelle différence avec notre arrivée dans la colonie française du Sénégal: ici on sent la vie civile. L'Europe est venue se retremper dans ce continent neuf; elle y a gagné en exubérance et en force.' Ballière, *La Déportation de 1871*, p.177.

inequality in metropolitan society or the recent loss of Alsace and Lorraine to Germany.[56]

On the occasions that imperial matters did command national interest, they were usually not cast in a favourable light. Like the deportees, both parliament and the press used the empire to viciously attack the government. The most prominent proponent of this was the radical deputy Georges Clemenceau, who used his newspaper *La Justice* to argue that French overseas expansion 'left Bismarck master in Europe'.[57] Clemenceau also launched blistering attacks on members of the colonial lobby in the Chambre des Députés, and Ferry was eventually forced to resign as Prime Minister after Clemenceau brought down his government on imperial matters.[58] This negative interest, moreover, continued throughout the period of 'high imperialism' around the turn of the century: when shown a map of the world in 1905, Étienne Clémentel, the new Minister for Colonies, reportedly remarked 'I didn't know there were so many!'[59]

The public also remained largely unmoved and unwilling to leave the metropole to settle France's colonial acquisitions.[60] The 1872 Haussonville report, which had been commissioned to advise on the benefits of deportation, acknowledged this difficulty, noting that '[u]p until now, the Frenchman has not shown himself to be a colonist, but that is because he loves his hometown'.[61] Constructing a competent colonial bureaucracy consequently proved extremely difficult, and in 1887 over half of colonial bureaucrats were officially declared incompetent.[62] The problem of populating the colonies was further exacerbated by the political and military crises in metropolitan France in 1870–1871, which forced the sweeping withdrawal of troops from colonies such as New Caledonia.[63] Although imperialism had a high profile and France was accumulating possessions at

---

[56] For revolutionary iterations of this, see M. Talmeyr, 'Leur guerre', *L'Intransigeant*, 23 July 1881; 'Discours de M. Clemenceau', *L'Intransigeant*, 1 August 1885; 'Les naufrageurs', *Le Citoyen*, 12 November 1881; 'Gaspillage partout', *Le Citoyen*, 19 December 1881; 'La guerre!', *Le Citoyen*, 17 January 1882; 'La guerre d'Afrique', *Le Prolétaire*, 23 April 1881; 'Nouveaux exploits', *Le Prolétaire*, 12 May 1883; P. Brousse, 'La politique coloniale', *Le Prolétaire*, 18 July 1885; P. Brousse, 'Liquidation', *Le Prolétariat*, 28 November 1885. For more, see Conklin, Fishman, and Zaretsky, *France and Its Empire since 1870*, pp.67–68; Lehning, *To Be a Citizen*, p.136.

[57] Tombs, *France 1814–1914*, p.446.   [58] For more on this, see Manceron, *Le tournant colonial.*

[59] Tombs, *France 1814–1914*, p.207.

[60] J. Pitts, 'Liberalism and Empire in a Nineteenth-Century Algerian Mirror', *Modern Intellectual History* 6 (2009), 287–313, at p.302; p.312.

[61] 'Le Français ne s'est pas montré jusqu'à présent colonisateur, mais c'est par amour du clocher'. Quoted in Barron, 'La déportation et les déportés, 1871–1880', at p.42.

[62] Tombs, *France 1814–1914*, pp.208–209.

[63] Douglas, 'Conflict and Alliance in a Colonial Context', p.30.

an increasing rate during this period, few within France even had any opinions on empire, let alone first-hand knowledge of it.

This left France's hold on many of its colonies precarious at best. With many citizens unwilling to relocate to the colonies, French *colons* were often forced to rely heavily upon others to maintain their fragile supremacy. In New Caledonia, for example, the French administration relied almost entirely upon unstable treaties with various Kanak tribes to maintain their physical presence. Imported labour from East Asia, India, and elsewhere in Oceania, it hoped, would boost the colony's economic capacity.[64] So small was the free French presence on the islands that imported labour formed, as Dorothy Shineberg has noted, 'the backbone of the labour force available to both civil Administration and to private settlers up to almost the end of the nineteenth century'.[65] Indeed, even the penal authorities relied upon it.[66] Unlike their British counterparts, many French citizens during this period had little interest in empire, and were largely unwilling to leave the metropole. The consequent shortage of manpower in turn often put the country's possession of its colonies at severe risk.

This status quo inadvertently gifted the returning deportees a unique position in French politics. Few politicians or members of the public in France had any real experience of empire. By contrast, many of the deportees had spent the best part of a decade in a colony, and therefore had an intimate knowledge of it. Indeed, as the Haussonville report recommended, they had been expressly acting as agents 'in the service of France's larger colonial project'.[67] This apparent knowledge placed them in a unique position to influence what Matt Matsuda has called 'the "tides" of ideology and imagination that are so much parts of empire'.[68] While Ballière's comparison of Australia and Senegal – two extremely different colonies – was fairly meaningless, for example, few in France were in a position to know this. The voyage to New Caledonia and their experiences once there, in other words, furnished the deportees with unique

[64] R. Aldrich, *The French Presence in the South Pacific, 1842–1940* (Basingstoke: Palgrave Macmillan, 1990), p.162.
[65] Shineberg, '"Noumea no good. Noumea no pay"', at p.187.   [66] Ibid., p.187.
[67] Toth, *Beyond Papillon*, p.37. The torture inquiry, or Perin Inquest, ran from 1880 to 1881 and collected over forty depositions from Communard deportees. For more, see Bullard, *Exile to Paradise*, pp.244–245.
[68] Matsuda, *Empire of Love*, p.16. For later instances of socialists using anticolonialism as a form of political opposition, see Ageron, *L'anticolonialisme en France de 1871 à 1914*, pp.21–22.

knowledge (or at the very least, the appearance of knowledge) of a subject that was becoming increasingly important in French public life.

This translated into tangible political influence as well. The colonial lobby, anxious to increase its support, was eager to deflect criticism and present empire in the best possible light. The power that these circumstances gave the deportees can be glimpsed, for example, in the government's willingness to accede to an inquiry into torture in New Caledonia's penal colony, and in letters from deportees to politicians.[69] Reporting his own torture on Île Nou Jean Allemane, for example, warned the Minister for Colonies that

> if by some miracle, I see my complaint ignored, my moderation will transform into a tireless protest against all those who have let these acts – which every man of heart would declare cowardly and repugnant – go unpunished.[70]

In this exercise, few of the deportees' criticisms were original. Critiques of colonial militarism, for example, were also closely linked to broader revolutionary concerns about standing armies,[71] and unfavourable comparisons of French colonies to their British counterparts drew upon older insecurities about France's status in the world.[72] Both the desperation of metropolitan politicians to popularise empire during this period and the Communards' deep experience of it, however, combined to give these criticisms new weight and place the deportees in a powerful position upon their return to French politics.

Surprisingly, it was thus their time and distance away from France that provided the deportees' most successful point of entry back into metropolitan politics. Indeed, rather than shying away from their situation, the deportees forced deportation into metropolitan politics upon their return.[73] For the deportees, colonialism and empire were intellectual and political bargaining chips. They provided the easiest and most effective way for the deportees to regain prominence in French public life,

---

[69] For demands, see Grousset and Jourde, *Les condamnés politiques en Nouvelle-Calédonie*, pp.57–58.

[70] '[S]i par impossible, je me voyais débouter, ma modération se transformerait en une énergique et incessante protestation contre tous ceux qui auraient laissé des faits que tout homme de coeur doit déclarer lâches et infâmes.' Allemane, *Mémoires d'un Communard*, p.501.

[71] See, for example, L.A. Blanqui, *L'armée esclave et opprimée: suppression de la conscription enseignement militaire de la jeunesse armée nationale sédentaire* (Paris: Au bureau du journal *Ni dieu ni maître*, 1880), p.31.

[72] Todd, 'A French Imperial Meridian, 1814–1870', at p.162; p184. See also D. Todd, 'Transnational Projects of Empire in France, c.1815–c.1870', *Modern Intellectual History* 12 (2015), 265–293, at p.281.

[73] Grousset and Jourde, *Les condamnés politiques en Nouvelle-Calédonie*, p.6.

simultaneously rendering their time in 'the wilderness' relevant and offering another way in which to criticise the Third Republic. It was not so much the Kanaks who the deportees sought to define themselves in opposition to, but the authorities.

III

This focus was not surprising, given the government's own motivations for deportation. Deportation had been central to the government's handling of the aftermath of the Commune. The Semaine Sanglante had emptied the streets of Paris of revolutionaries in the last days of the Commune. Its arbitrary and apparently extra-legal nature, however, had alarmed both moderate republicans who had previously been unified with the Thiers administration in their condemnation of the revolution and even many of the Commune's staunchest opponents including, as Marx observed, 'the not over-sensitive London *Times*'.[74] Deportation provided a solution to this problem, enabling the government to deal with revolutionaries both comprehensively and legally. Enshrined in the penal code since 1791, it was a well-known sentence for political prisoners in nineteenth-century France, and enabled the government to semi-permanently empty Paris of revolutionaries whilst simultaneously emphasising the importance of the law and its own status as the law's responsible custodian. This was remarkably effective. As the former Communard and deportee Alexis Trinquet noted during the 1870s, 'they are so relaxed at the moment; no more revolts, no rebellions to worry about'.[75]

Yet deportation was more than just a convenient middle ground between death and liberty. The government also used it to ideologically isolate the Communards from the new Republican state. Although it had long been part of the penal code and was often delivered as a sentence, the physical deportation of prisoners from France – especially on such a large scale – was rare. Prior to the late nineteenth century, sentences of deportation had been largely nominal and even repeat offenders such as Blanqui had remained 'déporté sur place', or held for the duration of their sentence

---

[74] K. Marx, *The Civil War in France: Address of the General Council of the International Working-Men's Association* (London: Edward Truelove, 1871), p.15. See also D. Stafford, *From Anarchism to Reformism: A Study of the Political Activities of Paul Brousse within the First International and the French Socialist Movement 1870–1890* (London: Cox & Wyman, 1971), p.26.

[75] Michel, *Souvenirs et aventures de ma vie*, p.68.

in prisons in France.[76] The letters of Communards sentenced to deportation, such as Henri Messager, peppered with expectations of an imminent commutation or amnesty, indicated how unusual it was for the sentence to be carried out.[77]

Likewise, deportation was rarely used again after the Communard amnesty. The decision of almost all the Communards to return to France at the earliest possible opportunity (as well as their frequent return to revolutionary and radical political activity) visibly demonstrated the bankruptcy of the idea of the redemptive power of deportation.[78] While it remained on the statute books until 1960, it was deployed only in particularly serious cases such as treason and colonial rebellion. Alfred Dreyfus, for example, was deported to Devil's Island in French Guiana after his court martial and wrongful conviction for passing military secrets to the Germans in 1895, as were traitors during World War I. The decision to physically banish the prisoners from France thus communicated to even casual observers that the Communards' crimes were of exceptional gravity.

The details of their deportation further marginalised the Communards. The decision to intern the Communards in New Caledonia, which at the time was France's principal penal colony, brought the deportees into contact with transportees.[79] Whereas deportation had historically been a relatively respectable sentence, transportation (on the statute books since 1854) was for common criminals, who were widely perceived as social outcasts.[80] The Communard deportees were fully aware of this fact,[81] while Louis Barron, a bookkeeper and deportee, observed that 'the

---

[76] M. Winock, 'Communard et forçat', in Allemane, *Mémoires d'un Communard*, 7–21, at p.16. It is true that prior to the 1870s deportees often remained in France for want of a place to send them to, but neither increased colonisation in this period nor the sheer volume of Communards is satisfactory as a justification for their deportation. Although it remained in French law until 1960, deportation was rarely used again after the amnesty and then largely only for traitors and colonial rebels.

[77] See, for example, 30: Messager – Blanche, Île d'Oléron, 28 July 1871, 48–49; 168: Messager – Mère, 20 March 1873, 232; 173: Messager – Mère, Saint-Martin de Ré, 1 April 1873, 238–240, at p.239, all in Messager, *239 lettres d'un Communard déporté*.

[78] Bullard, 'Self-Representation in the Arms of Defeat', p.180.

[79] New Caledonia functioned as a penal colony from 1863 to 1897. During this period over 22,315 convicts were transported there. Merle, 'The Trials and Tribulations of the Emancipists', at p.39. See also S.A. Toth, 'Colonisation or Incarceration? The Changing Role of the French Penal Colony in *fin-de-siècle* New Caledonia', *Journal of Pacific History* 34 (1999), 59–74, p.59.

[80] Winock, 'Communard et forçat', at pp.8–9.

[81] 'Rochefort! Found at Last', *San Francisco Chronicle*, 23 May 1874.

deportation of 1871 was noticeably different from previous deport-ations'.[82] This association served much the same purpose as the govern-ment's decision to seize upon the image of the lawless *pétroleuse* and the Commune's connections with the First International in an effort to deny it revolutionary legitimacy. By linking the deportees to common criminals, they likewise aimed to eradicate sympathy for the Communards through exploiting fears of the 'criminal' working class that were widespread in Paris at the time.[83] In deporting the Communards to New Caledonia, the government hoped not only to ensure that they were deprived of political legitimacy and isolated from the state, but also to cut them off from French society altogether.

The Republican state was therefore very much at the centre of the government's motivations for deportation. The legal exclusion of the convicted Communards from France served as an effective means of eliminating vocal opponents to the new state and diverting attention from the Republic's own questionable activities during the last week of the Commune. The government's employment of deportation, though, was not merely fortuitous, but rather a visual demonstration and reaffirmation of official authority. Although nominally inclusive and egalitarian, the early Third Republic was very much a state, in the words of Giorgio Agamben, 'not founded on a social bond of which it would be the expression', but on the power of exclusion.[84] In a circular letter of 6 June 1871, for example, Jules Favre, the Minister for Foreign Affairs, stated that

> To detest [the events of the Commune] . . . and to punish them is not enough. It is necessary to seek out the germ of them and to extirpate it. The greater the evil, the more essential it is to take account of it . . . To introduce into laws the severities which social necessity demands and to apply these laws without weakness are novelties to which France must resign herself. For her, it is a matter of safety.[85]

Deportation was, as we have seen, only one of several ways in which successive governments sought to marginalise ex-Communards and assert

[82] 'La déportation de 1871 se distingue nettement des déportations précédentes, il importe de le faire observer.' Barron, 'La déportation et les déportés, 1871–1880', at p.44.

[83] Toth, *Beyond Papillon*, p.3; Bullard, *Exile to Paradise*, p.29.

[84] G. Agamben, *The Coming Community*, (trans.) M. Hardt (Minneapolis: University of Minnesota Press, 1993), p.86.

[85] J. Favre, in *Journal officiel de la République française* (Paris), 8 June 1871, 1259:1. Quoted in J.T. Joughin, *The Paris Commune in French Politics, 1871–1880*, 2 vols. (Baltimore, MD: Johns Hopkins University Press, 1955), vol.1, p.67. See also M.P. Johnson, *The Paradise of Association: Political Culture and Popular Organisations in the Paris Commune of 1871* (Ann Arbor: University of Michigan Press, 1996), p.284.

their own power. Nonetheless it was perhaps the most dramatic demonstration of both official authority and the lengths to which the Moral Order and Opportunist governments were willing to go to in order to maintain stability.

The deportees were well aware that this was the primary purpose of their sentence. Louise Michel, for instance, suggested that '[t]hey sent us to New Caledonia so that the enormity of their crime [during the Semaine Sanglante] would be lost in the enormity of the distance', while many others noted that negative associations continued to follow the Communards even after their return to France and their re-entry into mainstream politics.[86] Rochefort, for example, claimed

> It is agreed that we only came into the world in order to set it on fire and make it bleed. Up until now, it is we who they assassinated, slit the throats of, shot, and machine-gunned, from St Bartholomew's Day to the Commune, and from Admiral Coligny to Millière. Trinquet was on Île Nou for eight years and in double chains for thirty-four months. It doesn't matter. He was the persecutor. The moderates who tortured him in the *bagnes* have the right to speak of indulgences and pardons but he, who has been subjected to, suffered, and endured everything is forbidden from doing anything other than manning the barricades, from going for a walk unless he is holding an open petrol can in his hand ... he is not permitted to be either an honest man or a citizen who lives off his labour, and is obliged to carry a perpetual hatred in his heart. He should be walking around Belleville with a revolver in his hand, shooting an inoffensive passer-by every ten steps.[87]

Rehabilitation, in other words, was clearly not the point of deportation. Despite having served their punishment and received an amnesty,

---

[86] 'Ils nous ont envoyé en Nouvelle-Calédonie afin que l'énormité de leur crime disparaisse dans l'énormité de la distance'. *Lettres de la Nouvelle-Calédonie*, Fonds Louise Michel (IISH), 930. See also É. Vaillant, 'Vive la Commune!', *Commonweal* (London, April 1885), p.1.

[87] 'Il est convenu que nous ne sommes venus au monde que pour le mettre à feu et à sang. Jusqu'ici, c'est nous qu'on a assassinés, égorgés, arquebusés, mitraillés, depuis la Saint-Barthélemy jusqu'à la Commune, depuis l'amiral Coligny jusqu'à Millière; Trinquet est resté huit ans à l'île Nou; il a porté trente-quatre mois la double chaîne. N'importe! Le persécuteur, c'est lui. Les modérés qui l'ont torturé dans les bagnes ont le droit, eux, de parler d'indulgence et de pardon; mais lui, qui a tout subi, tout souffert, tout enduré, il lui est interdit de faire autre chose que des barricades, et de se promener sans tenir à la main une bouteille de pétrole toute débouchée ... il ne lui est permis d'être ni honnête homme, ni un citoyen vivant laborieusement de son travail. Son devoir est d'avoir au coeur une haine perpétuelle. Qu'il se promène dans Belleville un revolver au poing, et que tous les dix pas il le décharge sur un passant inoffensif'. H. Rochefort, 'Le vrai Trinquet', *L'Intransigeant*, 14 January 1881. See also 174: P. Lafargue to F. Engels, 19 November 1885 (Paris), in Engels and Lafargue, *Correspondence*, vol.1, 319–321, at pp.320–321.

Communards were unable to escape the negative associations of conviction and deportation.

Deportation was thus inextricably bound to the ways in which the government hoped to define their new Republican state. It reflected yet another attempt to symbolically bring the French Revolution to a close. By sending Communards en masse to New Caledonia, the state was not simply punishing individuals, but attempting to discredit all revolutionaries at the same time. Through deportation, successive Third Republic governments cast their revolutionary opponents as wholly alien to what France should aim to be, likening them to colonial subjects and criminals, and legally divesting them of both social and political agency. In contrast to this, the Third Republic depicted itself as France's protector, the sole arbiter of French values, and the true heir to the last century of French history. Indeed, it is perhaps for these reasons that many Republicans fought the granting of an amnesty for so long.

IV

The deportees, though, did not merely use their experiences of deportation to criticise the Third Republic. They also put details of their own lives in New Caledonia to theoretical use. Much attention has been given to both 'the enormity of the punishment' and the negative aspects of life in New Caledonia.[88] This, also, is unsurprising. Deportation was difficult and ex-Communards were not shy about documenting the hardships that they faced. Barron, for example, likened it to the 'long slumber of Epimenides', the Greek mythological character who reportedly fell asleep for fifty-seven years.[89] The deportees' professions of despair have been interpreted as evidence that their time in the South Pacific was profoundly traumatic: a 'void', to quote Bullard, in which 'the present appeared only as absence, as a tormenting reminder of what was missing'.[90]

Yet despite their vocal denunciation of 'the brutal administration',[91] deportee thought on New Caledonia was not wholly negative. Grousset

---

[88] L. Godineau, 'Retour d'exil: Les anciens Communards au début de la Troisième République' (unpublished doctoral thesis, Université de Paris I Panthéon-Sorbonne, 2000), p.513.

[89] 'La déportation fut pour eux un long sommeil d'Epiménide.' Barron, 'La déportation et les déportés, 1871–1880', at p.60.

[90] Bullard, 'Self-Representation in the Arms of Defeat', at p.193.

[91] Fonds Lucien Descaves (IISH), 135, pp.3–4. For contemporary examples of this, see 'Bulletin', *Le Travailleur* 1:4 (Geneva, August 1877), p.4; 'Discours des citoyens Paschal Grousset et Francis Jourde, ex-membres de la Commune de Paris, prononcés au banquet qui leur a été offert par des Républicains de San Francisco le 24 mai 1874', Fonds Lucien Descaves (IISH), 205, pp.6–7.

and Jourde, for example, claimed that while they experienced despondency in New Caledonia, they had nonetheless remained 'buoyed by that hope that never leaves a man'.[92] Following his release from the prison on Île Nou, Allemane similarly recalled living in a communal house on the Ducos Peninsula as 'one of my fondest memories'.[93] Indeed, some deportees even continued to maintain associations with New Caledonia after they had returned to France.[94] Whilst negativity and even trauma were indeed prominent in the Communards' portrayals of deportation, it is important to note that they were by no means the sole or even the primary focus of their writing on such matters.

Alongside their indictments of the penal and colonial administration, deportees highlighted their own attempts to build a community. During their time in New Caledonia, the deportees had, Barron argued, 'become veritable pioneers',[95] accomplishing 'prodigious feats'. In fact, they gave the lie to the oft-repeated adage that France is 'unable to colonise'.[96] Deportees on the Île des Pins – the location in which deportees enjoyed the most freedom – established theatre groups and several newspapers, such as *Le Parisien* and *Le Moniteur Calédonien*. They also embarked upon ambitious construction projects including a water tower and a memorial to the dead, the remains of which can still be seen today.[97]

These projects occupied the largely unemployed deportees,[98] but also, and more importantly, they suggested, helped to create new fraternal bonds. Recalling his arrival on the Ducos Peninsula, Allemane wrote that 'there were hands clasping ours, hugging us, even people that we didn't

---

[92] '[O]n était soutenu par l'espérance qui ne déserte jamais de l'homme'. 'Discours des citoyens Paschal Grousset et Francis Jourde, ex-membres de la Commune de Paris, prononcés au banquet qui leur a été offert par des Républicains de San Francisco le 24 mai 1874', Fonds Lucien Descaves (IISH), 205, p.6.

[93] '[C]e n'est pas là un de mes souvenirs les moins précieux'. Allemane, *Mémoires d'un Communard*, p.473.

[94] See, for example, 235: Messager – Mère, Île des Pins, 18 December 1875, in Messager, *239 lettres d'un Communard déporté*, 356–357, at p.357.

[95] 'Les déportés de l'île des Pins, devenus de véritables pionniers'. Barron, 'La déportation et les déportés, 1871–1880', at p.57.

[96] '[O]nt accompli des prodiges'; 'de n'être point capable de coloniser'. Ibid., at p.43.

[97] For an example of a play, see A. Pélissier, *Le Coq Gaulois* (Île des Pins, 1877), Fonds Louise Michel (IISH), 929. For newspapers, see *Le Raseur calédonien* (Île des Pins, 1877), Fonds Louise Michel (IISH), 937; *Le Parisien* (Île des Pins, 1878), Fonds Louise Michel (IISH), 934.

[98] Accounts differ on whether the Communards refused to work when it was offered (the government's and the administration's position), or whether they were eager to work but the opportunity was withdrawn in 1873 (the Communard position). Michel, *Souvenirs et aventures de ma vie*, p.44; Grousset and Jourde, *Les condamnés politiques en Nouvelle-Calédonie*, p.18.

know. We were all one family'.[99] Michel similarly emphasised that 'despite the divisions introduced among us by complete strangers [the penal authorities] ... the deportees had in no way forgotten their solidarity'.[100] By stressing this success in building communities, especially in what they had elsewhere described as such inhospitable conditions and under such punitive authorities, the deportees were attempting to turn their backs on the infighting that had very publicly plagued the revolutionary movement both before and during the Commune, and highlighted in Part I.[101] Deportation, then, was not only a negative experience, but also functioned as an important site of reconciliation for the deported Communards.

This reconstructed community did not merely exist in isolation, though, and deportees frequently attempted to embed it within French culture. Barron noted that the inability to enjoy 'the benefits of mutual learning and books' was one of the hardest privations that the deportees had to bear, and Louise Michel complained that the only 'culture' in New Caledonia was drinking hard spirits.[102] Perhaps in an attempt to compensate for this loss, deportees frequently discussed French cultural matters. *Le Parisien* made several references to Victor Hugo and Voltaire, as well as Diderot and D'Alembert.[103] Likewise, Ballière wrote that on the voyage to New Caledonia, the deportees discussed Alphonse de Lamartine, Alfred de Musset, and of course Hugo.[104] He was also eager to demonstrate that the deportees remained familiar with and engaged in contemporary French politics, noting that 'to pass time we discuss the political acts of Gambetta'.[105]

As Bullard has noted, in late nineteenth-century France, notions of social order carried immense weight, and revolution was widely associated

[99] 'Puis les mains s'étreignent; on s'embrasse, qu'on se soit ou non connu. N'est-on pas de la même famille: celle des vaincus?' Allemane, *Mémoires d'un Communard*, p.472.
[100] '[M]algré les divisions introduites parmi nous, par des gens complètement étrangers ... les déportés n'ont point oublié la solidarité'. 220: Louise Michel, published in the *Revue australienne*, in Michel, *Je vous écris de ma nuit*, 219–221, at p.220.
[101] See, for example, J. Allemane, *Mémoires d'un Communard*, p.237; 'Rochefort: His Lecture at the Academy of Music', *New York Herald*, 6 June 1874.
[102] 'Privés des bienfaits de l'enseignement mutuel et du livre, les déportés subirent dans toute sa tristesse démoralisante l'insupportable ennui de la solitude.' Barron, 'La déportation et les déportés, 1871–1880'. See also Michel, *Souvenirs et aventures de ma vie*, p.62.
[103] *Le Parisien*, 29 September 1878. Fonds Louise Michel (IISH), 934.
[104] Ballière, *La Déportation de 1871*, p.61. For further cultural references from deportees, see also H. Brissac, *Quand j'étais au bagne*, p.53.
[105] 'Entre temps, les jeux n'étant pas permis, on discute les actes politiques de Gambetta.' Ballière, *La Déportation de 1871*, p.19. For other examples of deportees engaging with the outside world, see *Le Raseur calédonien*, 11 February 1877; 22 April 1877. Fonds Louise Michel (IISH), 937; *Le Parisien*, 14 September 1878; 29 September 1878. Fonds Louise Michel (IISH), 934.

with the 'threat of a meaningless void'.[106] As demonstrated in Part II, the two became increasingly tightly linked as the Third Republic progressed and moderate republicans worked to exclude revolution from contemporary political discourse and place it firmly in the past. Much like the focus on evolution and religion, this interest in culture and self-improvement should be seen as part of revolutionaries' attempts to allay such fears. By demonstrating their familiarity with and interest in French culture and political life, the deportees aimed to show their similarity to 'ordinary' French citizens. As well as cohering as a movement, in other words, they also remained fully immersed in and attuned to the issues that concerned contemporary France. In contrast to the government's assertions that they were 'political savages', the deportees argued that they were as natural and credible a part of public life as the framework and personalities of the Third Republic.

The deportees were also eager to reassert their own republicanism, in fact using their expulsion from France to emphasise their commitment to republican values. Deportees often likened themselves to now-celebrated former political prisoners including 'Ledru Rollin, Louis Blanc, de Gent and many others'. These were, they noted, 'at the present moment the most honourable leaders of French democracy'.[107] Some even elevated their commitment to quasi-religious heights. Grousset and Jourde, for example, described the successive boatloads of republican deportees leaving for New Caledonia as ritual sacrifices made in order to 'appease the insatiable monster of monarchism'.[108] Despite the distance from metropolitan France and the treatment they had received in New Caledonia, the deportees implied, they had managed to retain, and perhaps even enhance, their republican values.

By contrast, the government was incapable of either constructing or maintaining a satisfactory republic even in France. Whereas distance, they suggested, had only augmented their values, it had exposed the government's ethics and republicanism as deeply flawed. Dwelling upon deportation thus functioned as a way for the deportees to reaffirm their

---

[106] Bullard, *Exile to Paradise*, p.271.

[107] 'Rochefort', *New York Herald*, 30 May 1874, p.3. For further comparisons, see 65: Messager – Blanche, Château d'Oléron, 17 October 1871, in Messager, *239 lettres d'un Communard déporté*, 92–93, at p.93. For more on these earlier exiles, see T.C. Jones, 'French Republican Exiles in Britain, 1848–1870' (Unpublished PhD thesis, University of Cambridge, 2010).

[108] 'Ces clairvoyants hommes d'Etat faisaient partir tous les trois mois pour les antipodes un convoy d'otages républicains, et croyaient apaiser par ces sacrifices périodiques l'insatiable minotaure monarchique'. Grousset and Jourde, *Les condamnés politiques en Nouvelle-Calédonie*, pp.54–55.

ideological proximity to the French nation, whilst simultaneously imbuing their years in exile with value. It enabled them to cast themselves as guardians of republican values and argue that, while they may have been outside the state, they nevertheless remained the ideological keepers of the republic and thus an essential part of French metropolitan life.

Indeed, the harmony created by deportation extended far beyond those in New Caledonia. Jean Joughin, for example, has noted the symbolic power of deportation and the propensity of other exiles to appropriate the deportees' experiences in New Caledonia or conflate them with their own.[109] The deportees themselves clearly recognised the symbolic, creative power of their experience, with Rochefort continuing to refer to other revolutionaries deported to New Caledonia as his '*co-déportés*' for years after his escape.[110] Paradoxically, the physical distance between the deportees and their counterparts in Europe and North America seemed to act as a unifying factor. The deportees did not jealously guard their experiences in New Caledonia, and many other revolutionaries displayed an affinity with it. Although intellectual differences remained and this unity proved ultimately fragile and temporary, deportation nevertheless provided a much-needed rallying point for disparate and dissatisfied French revolutionaries in the years after the Commune.

The cause of deportation further served to reunite revolutionaries with various republicans who had taken no part in the Commune. Rochefort's escape was funded by more moderate republicans, namely Victor Hugo, the writer and *salonnière* Juliette Adam (also a great Gambetta supporter), and her husband the senator Edmond Adam.[111] Parliamentary radicals such as Alfred Naquet, Georges Perin, and Camille Pelletan, meanwhile, heaped pressure on the government in the Chambre and coordinated large parts of the amnesty campaign.[112] Deportation, then, functioned as an important site of reconciliation and unification not only for the deported Communards, but also for their comrades in exile and

---

[109] Joughin, *The Paris Commune in French Politics*, vol.1, p.88. For an example, see *Le Travailleur* 1:5 (September 1877), p.32.

[110] 'L'Expulsion d'un français', *L'Intransigeant*, 17 November 1880; 'Le 18 mars', *L'Intransigeant*, 19 March 1884; H. Rochefort, 'Les assassins & la police', *L'Intransigeant*, 21 April 1885. For other instances of this, see 'La torture au bagne', *L'Intransigeant*, 10 December 1880. See also Alphonse Humbert's long-running series 'Les républicains au bagne', *L'Intransigeant*, 27 December 1880 onwards.

[111] 'European Life', *New York Herald*, 26 April 1874, p.8. For confirmation, see Matsuda, *Empire of Love*, p.121. For Rochefort's opinion on Juliette Adam, see H. Rochefort, '*La patrie hongroise*', *L'Intransigeant*, 30 September 1884.

[112] This campaign attracted significant support, both popular and political. For more, see Bullard, *Exile to Paradise*, p.244.

sympathisers in France. Much like their admiration for scientific progress, deportation was another subject on which revolutionaries and radicals found considerable common ground even after the 'break' of 1871.

V

In projecting such an image of newfound responsibility, it could be assumed that the deportees unconsciously carried out the government's professed aims for deportation. As Bullard has noted, moral regeneration lay at the heart of the government's rhetoric on deportation.[113] 'Once removed from the unhealthy atmosphere of large cities', the Haussonville report hoped,

> it will not take them [the deportees] long to understand that fighting the laws of society is as senseless as fighting the laws of nature. They will then be able to pour all of their energy into the work of social creation, whereas before it was consumed by their war against law and order.[114]

The natural paradise of the South Pacific, it was hoped, would prompt convicts to work extensively on the self and develop a sense of morality that was acceptable to the Third Republic. In doing so, they would be remade as functional citizens, capable of reintegrating into metropolitan society. Indeed, the idea of the deportees as responsible communitarians operating in adversity may certainly have appealed to the contemporary French mainstream.

Yet it also resonated with significant aspects of nineteenth-century radical thought. The scale of the deportation may have been unprecedented, but the idea of revolutionary and radical communities settling sparsely populated new lands certainly was not. From Charles Fourier's *phalanstères* to the Owenite communities of New Lanark and New Harmony, the idea of creating new communities based on revolutionary ideals was well established. As the likes of Omar Abi-Mershed and Jean-Louis Marçot have demonstrated, French radicals and socialists in the mid-nineteenth century (particularly Saint-Simonians) were consumed by the

---

[113] Ibid., p.93.
[114] 'Une fois soustraits à l'atmosphère malsaine des grandes villes, il ne leur faudra pas bien longtemps pour comprendre qu'il est aussi insensé de vouloir lutter contre les lois de la société que contre les lois de la nature, et ils déploieront alors dans leur oeuvre de création sociale toute l'énergie qu'ils ont consommée dans leur guerre contre l'ordre et les lois.' Quoted in Barron, 'La déportation et les déportés, 1871–1880', at p.42.

idea of settling Algeria.[115] Such ideas continued to enjoy broad popularity amongst revolutionaries in the late nineteenth century, and revolutionary newspapers often carried reports on contemporary utopian settlements, such as Étienne Cabet's Iowa Icariens and the Oneida Community in New York.[116]

The community created and lauded by the deportees in New Caledonia was thus not only designed to establish their suitability for public life, but was also a practical reinforcement of some revolutionary ideas on the government of the republic. By emphasising the apparent success of this self-governing, self-regulating society, the deportees directly challenged the form of government established by the Third Republic and offered a practical demonstration of the federalist contention made by the likes of Reclus that meaningful change was effected not at a national level by an increasingly centralised government, but from within the community and through small, everyday acts. If society were correctly attuned, then centralised government would be at best an unnecessary imposition and at worst, little more than dictatorship. At the very least, they indicated to other revolutionaries the potential for communal organisation to be a thorn in the government's side.

The idea of the deportees as saviours of the republic also seems to have enjoyed considerable popularity in France. Messager, for example, recalled that departing boats of deportees bound for New Caledonia were bade farewell by crowds on the dock and cries of 'Vive la Commune! Vive la République'.[117] Official reports appear to confirm these claims. Police accounts from the early 1880s, for example, recorded that public interest in the repatriation of deportees was high, and noted that large crowds proclaiming 'Vive la République!' gathered to welcome returning Communards as they disembarked from trains in Paris.[118] Significant parts of the population, in other words, seemed to share the conviction that the

---

[115] For the Saint-Simonians and Algeria, see O.W. Abi-Mershed, *Apostles of Modernity: Saint-Simonians and the Civilizing Mission in Algeria* (Stanford, CA: Stanford University Press, 2010); Ouennoughi, *Algériens et Maghrébins*, pp.63–67; J.-L. Marçot, *Comment est née l'Algérie française 1830–1850: la belle utopie* (Paris: Éditions de la différence, 2012).

[116] For the Icariens, see *Bulletin de la Fédération jurassienne*, 20 May 1877, pp.3–4; 'Le collectivisme internationale'; 'Ma commune', *Le Prolétaire*, 24 January 1880; É. Péron, 'Les communautés américaines', in *La revue socialiste* (Paris) 12 (20 August 1880), 493–501. For Oneida, see 'Visite au perfectionnistes d'Oneida', *Le Travailleur* 1:6 (October 1877), pp.16–20. For more on this, see Girardet, *L'Idée coloniale en France de 1871 à 1962*, p.17.

[117] 140: Messager – Mère, Saint-Martin de Ré, 7 October 1872, in Messager, *239 lettres d'un Communard déporté*, 189–190, at p.190.

[118] Godineau, 'Retour d'exil', pp.238–240.

exiles, rather than the government, represented a true version of the republic.

Such sentiments were also undoubtedly given traction by the Third Republic's own poor constitutional track record during the 1870s. As detailed in Part II, the Moral Order governments of the mid-1870s spent much of the decade attempting to restore the monarchy, and ultimately failed largely because the Bourbon and Orléans candidates could not come to an agreement over the succession. While Opportunist republicans vigorously opposed and ultimately put an end to these manoeuvres, their 1875 compromise with conservatives over the constitution remained unacceptable to certain more radical citizens. For many of those dissatisfied with the politics of the 1870s, it seems, the exiled Communards represented an alternative republic. The deportees were the most striking example of this, able to use their extreme isolation from France during the 1870s to reinforce revolutionaries' broader ideas about the republic and the place of revolution within it.

The focus on community as the basis for the republic, then, acted not only as a vindication of the Communards, but also as a vindication of the right to revolution. The deportees juxtaposition of the penal authorities that, 'far from attempting to moralise', only degraded,[119] with the community of revolutionaries in New Caledonia supplied a direct parallel with the contemporary French state and its adversaries. By emphasising their own ability to overcome such treatment and construct a successful community, the deportees offered a practical demonstration of revolutionary ideas about society. What the colonies needed, Barron argued, was

> an administration that is neither too militaristic nor too bureaucratic, which performs the fewest possible functions of 'government'. It should leave people to handle things in their own way, intervening only if they are in danger ... Centralisation is ruining our colonies as it ruined the metropole.[120]

French colonies, in other words, were in need of precisely the kind of revolutionary system established by Communard deportees in New Caledonia. Where the Commune had failed, New Caledonia demonstrated

---

[119] '[L]oin de chercher à moraliser'. Fonds Lucien Descaves (IISH), 135, pp.3–4.

[120] '[U]ne administration qui ne soit ni trop militaire ni trop bureaucratique, qui joue le moins possible le rôle de "gouvernement", laisse les gens se débrouiller à leur manière, sans intervenir dans leurs affaires, sinon pour leur porter secours à l'occasion, et sache enfin s'effacer à propos devant les administrations locales, au fur et à mesure qu'elles se constituent. La centralisation ruine nos colonies comme elle ruine la métropole.' Quoted in Barron, 'La déportation et les déportés, 1871–1880', at p.43.

not only that a revolutionary life was a viable alternative, but also that in order for the Republic to remain true to its professed values, it must preserve this element of society.

VI

Rather than a sustained interest in imperial expansion or settler colonialism, then, deportees' ideas on France and the structure of the state were demonstrative of the ongoing battle to define the French republic in the late nineteenth century. Instead of simply attempting to reinsert themselves back into the Third Republic upon their return, the deportees also used their experiences to contest what 'the French republic' was. Whereas the government increasingly conceived of 'the Republic' as a constitutional, legal, and territorially defined structure, the deportees used their writings on New Caledonia to contend that 'the republic' was a state of mind rather than a State. The twenty-eight deportees addressed their open letter to the citizens of France 'to your *republican sentiments*; your personal opinions on recent events; your conscience; your good faith', implying that it was faith rather than law that made a true republican.[121] A republic was not a specific form of government, it was the organic harmony of society correctly functioning – a set of ideals centred on virtue, sacrifice, and harmonious community life.[122] The deportees' reflections on their experiences thus acted simultaneously to cement their own place in the republic and as an affirmation of the persistent validity of the concept of revolution: if the republic were truly a set of values, its defenders must retain the right to protect it from any state, including the Republic itself.

Finally, it is also worth pointing out that the deportees' ideas on the republic were strikingly similar to many of those expressed by the Communards who remained in Europe. In particular, Communard exiles often made similar claims that those outside France constituted the 'real' republic. The 'true Paris', Guesde claimed, 'was no longer in Paris but abroad, in exile'.[123] While the deportees used their plight to condemn the government for what they deemed

---

[121] 'C'est à vos sentiments républicains, c'est à vos opinions personnelles sur les événements récents; c'est à vos consciences, à votre bonne foi, que nous adressons un suprême appel.' Fonds Lucien Descaves (IISH), 135, p.5. Emphasis mine.

[122] For more on republicanism as the good life, see S. Hazareesingh, *Political Traditions in Modern France* (Oxford: Oxford University Press, 1994), pp.65–97.

[123] 'Notre oeuvre', *L'Égalité*, 16 June 1878. For a similar claim about republican exiles during the Second Empire, see M. Talmeyr, 'Nos anciens', *L'Intransigeant*, 18 May 1883. See also 'Blanqui',

'crimes of *lèse-humanité*[124] (itself a throwback to liberal critics of colonialism in the first half of the nineteenth century[125]) and deemed it a 'Republican government without republicans',[126] Communard exiles in Europe scorned the National Assembly as an 'Assemblée des ruraux' that was 'driving the Republic to certain death'.[127] In studies of New Caledonia, scholars have tended to emphasise the isolation of the deportees from the political events of Europe and their separation from their comrades. While the deportees were extremely isolated, it is nonetheless worth bearing in mind that in some notable areas, there was – despite the distance – a remarkable unity of thought.

For the deportees, colonialism and imperialism did not represent independent or fully realised avenues of thought. Rather, they were intimately tied to ideas on the condition of France and their own position in French politics. Colonialism and empire were intellectual bargaining chips, providing an easy and effective means for the deportees to regain prominence in French public life, simultaneously rendering their time in the South Pacific relevant and justifying their continued political opposition to what was now at least nominally a republican government. Rather than assimilating into the Third Republic, deportees responded creatively to official efforts to use deportation to exclude them from the nation. Turning both their geographical isolation from France and their quotidian experiences in New Caledonia to their advantage, they used such experiences to construct an alternative republic that was both theoretically distinct from the Third Republic and politically viable. In this formulation, the deportees and France became 'the republic', while the government was transformed into an outsider. Empire was thus not so much peripheral to the deportees' thought, but rather part of a broader debate that was much more important to them: that on the nature of the state and the French Republic.

Le Prolétaire, 9 August 1879; H. Rochefort, 'Vengeance!', *L'Intransigeant*, 19 August 1885. See also the widespread claims that revolutionaries were 'the true France': 'A Monsieur Grévy, Président de la République', *Le Prolétaire*, 1 March 1879; 'Nommez Blanqui', *Le Prolétaire*, 29 March 1879; 'La guerre!', *Le Prolétaire*, 1 September 1883; G. Deville, 'Bourgeois & prolétaires', *Le Citoyen*, 4 November 1881; 'Un à compte', *L'Égalité*, 18 June 1882; B. Malon. 'La réserve révolutionnaire', *L'Intransigeant*, 1 December 1883.

[124] *Lettres de la Nouvelle-Calédonie*, Fonds Louise Michel (IISH), 930.

[125] J. Pitts, 'Republicanism, liberalism, and empire in post-revolutionary France', in S. Muthu (ed.), *Empire and Modern Political Thought* (Cambridge: Cambridge University Press, 2012), 261–291, at p.274.

[126] '[L]e gouvernement de la République sans républicains'. H. Rochefort, *Les Aventures de ma vie*, vol. 3, 5 vols. (Paris: Paul Dupont, 1896–1897), p.262.

[127] '*L'Assemblée des ruraux* ... qui conduit la République à une mort certaine'. 'Tribune libre', *Le Travailleur* 1:1 (May 1877), p.29.

CHAPTER 8

Exile and Universal Solidarity

While the deportees experienced colonialism firsthand in New Caledonia, it is to revolutionaries in Europe that one must look for more clearly elaborated thought on empire and internationalism.* The deportees' predicament likely helped widen awareness of these subjects. News from New Caledonia (usually in the form of letters from deportees) was regularly published in major revolutionary newspapers such as the *Bulletin de la Fédération jurassienne*, as well as the *London Times*.[1] As we have seen, exiles were often keen to associate themselves with the deportees' suffering, but their interest did not end at such opportunism. Rather, they went to considerable effort to publicise and keep up to date with their comrades' travails in New Caledonia.

Communard exiles also launched several highly coordinated efforts to aid their deported comrades. Those in London, for example, began a permanent subscription for the aid of the deportees in 1874,[2] supporting the venture through the organisation of public events and a tombola that

---

* An earlier version of some of these arguments can be found in J. Nicholls, 'Empire and internationalism in French revolutionary socialist thought, 1871–1885', *The Historical Journal* 59:4 (2016), 1051–1074.

[1] For the *Times*, see letter reprinted in *Le Courrier de l'Europe*, 30 March 1872. Fonds Louise Michel, International Institute of Social History (IISH) 939. *Bulletin de la Fédération jurassienne* (Sonvilier), 15 March 1874; 5 April 1874; 18 October 1874; 21 March 1875; 28 March 1875; 27 June 1875; 31 October 1875; 28 November 1875; 11 November 1877. See also 'Lettre d'un forçat', *Le Prolétaire* (Paris), 1 January 1879; 'Correspondance', *Le Prolétaire*, 12 April 1879.

[2] 'Souscription permanente, ouverte à Londres, pour les condamnés politiques à la Nouvelle Calédonie'. Archives de la Préfecture de Police (APP), Ba427/93; Intelligence report to the Préfecture de Police (London, 16 February 1877). APP Ba429/2128; 2314. For instances of its international advertisement, see, for example, *Le Travailleur* (Geneva) 1:1 (May 1877); *Bulletin de la Fédération jurassienne*, 9 December 1877.

were both nationally and internationally publicised.[3] With the help of exiles in Belgium, Switzerland, and America, by April 1877 the London committee had raised 6,000 francs.[4] Indeed, an agent from the Préfecture de Police in Paris claimed that the New Caledonia aid committee was the 'one organised group among the exiles in London'.[5] Clearly, then, New Caledonia and the plight of the deportees featured prominently in revolutionaries' actions and news sources during this period. This served to place them in close intellectual proximity with the empire, despite the fact that they were not living in it.

Yet revolutionary interest in international affairs was not confined solely to deportation and events in New Caledonia. Several large newspapers, for instance, published updates on South American socialists in Mexico and Uruguay,[6] while the *Bulletin* explored their links with the International Workingmen's Association and Swiss socialists in Berne.[7] Intelligence reports on exiles in Geneva and Belgium also contained details of links to foreign socialists in New York, and as far afield as China.[8] As well as keeping up to date with news of other socialists, revolutionaries also attempted to popularise their own ideas outside metropolitan France. The Possibilists' principal organ, *Le Prolétaire*, for example, was sold in Algeria.[9] Others, meanwhile, displayed even broader interests, and Benoît Malon devoted a long series of articles to world religions in the 1885 *Revue*

---

[3] For international publicity, see 'Tombola organisée à Londres au profit des condamnés politiques à la Nouvelle-Calédonie', *Le Travailleur* 1:5 (September 1877), p.32; *Bulletin de la Fédération jurassienne*, 28 January 1878; 23 September 1877. See also APP Ba429/2160; 2182; 2197; 2210; 2287; 2382; 2481; Ba430/3428. For its presence in the national news, see *Le Rappel* (Paris), 5 May 1877; *Le Radical* (Paris), 17 May 1877; *Le Figaro* (Paris), 18 October 1877; *La Patrie* (Paris), 22 October 1877; *Le Pays* (Paris), 24 October 1877; *La Lanterne* (Paris) 10 December 1877; *L'Égalité* (Paris), 12 May 1878.

[4] 'Tribune libre', *Le Travailleur* 1:1 (May 1877), p.30.

[5] Intelligence report to the Préfecture de Police (5 December 1878). APP, Ba430/3170.

[6] *Bulletin de la Fédération jurassienne*, 24 December 1876. See also 'Un Saint-Barthélemy au Mexique', *Le Prolétaire*, 11 December 1878; 'Bulletin politique', *Le Citoyen & La Bataille* (Paris), 7 May 1883; 'Les Chiliens fusilleurs', *L'Égalité*, 7 November 1882.

[7] *Bulletin de la Fédération jurassienne*, for similarities with the International, see 26 December 1875; for links to Berne, see 10 December 1876. For further references to non-Western issues, see 'Mouvement social', *L'Égalité*, 20 January 1878; E. Fournière, 'La question tunisienne', *Le Prolétaire*, 2 April 1881; 'Lettre d'Alger', *Le Prolétaire*, 7 May 1881; 'La Chine et les chinois', *Le Prolétariat* (Paris), 30 August 1884; 'Le Japon', *Le Prolétariat*, 13 September 1884; C. Bouis, 'Battez, tambours!', *Le Citoyen*, 21 July 1882. See also 'Le théatre de la guerre', *Le Citoyen*, 29 July 1882; 'La Chine actuelle', *L'Intransigeant* (Paris), 14 January 1885.

[8] Intelligence report to the Préfecture de Police (Belgium, 28 May 1876). APP Ba427/385; Intelligence report (Geneva, 16 January 1874). APP Ba432/953. For mention of Cluseret's visit to China, see Intelligence report to the Préfecture de Police (Geneva, 12 March 1873). APP Ba431/580.

[9] 'Correspondance algérienne', *Le Prolétaire*, 20 November 1880.

socialiste, exploring various 'religious moralities' including Buddhism and Confucianism.[10] While concerned with their compatriots in New Caledonia, French revolutionary interests thus ranged far wider than the South Pacific. The extra-European interests of revolutionaries who remained in Europe were broad and diverse in a way that those of the deportees were not.

Revolutionaries, moreover, were fully aware of the global importance and totalising nature of imperialism. During the 1877–1878 Russo-Turkish War, Britain became increasingly alarmed at Russia's growing influence in the Balkans and eastern Mediterranean, worried that it would jeopardise its routes to India. This prompted a year-long diplomatic and military crisis, with war only decisively averted in July 1878. Discussing this year of tensions, troop movements, and diplomatic manoeuvres, the Swiss exile periodical *Le Travailleur* claimed:

> In the presence of this great battle, all States feel the earth tremble beneath their feet: for them, it is about survival, and whether ... they take part or not, their destiny is no less in play on that immense battlefield.[11]

Indeed, by 1886 the Parisian daily *La Bataille* was arguing that '[i]n these times of industrial development, he who lives by the colony will die by the colony.'[12] In the French context, public interest in imperialism is often dated by historians to the 'tournant colonial' of 1885.[13] In fact, however, by the late 1870s Communard exiles and their European comrades were not only embedded within international intellectual networks, but also cognisant of the importance of empire and imperialism in a broader sense.

This chapter explores the presence of empire and internationalism in the thought of the French revolutionaries who managed to evade capture and deportation following the fall of the Commune. It encompasses the years

---

[10] B. Malon, 'Les Morales religieuses', *La revue socialiste* (Paris) (1885), 923–931; 986–1006; 1076–1099. For Buddhism, see Malon, 'Les Morales religieuses', at p.929. For Confucianism, see Malon, 'Les Morales religieuses', at p.997. For an early manifestation of these interests, see *L'Almanach du Peuple pour 1873* (Saint Imier: Propagande Socialiste, 1873), p.27

[11] 'En présence de la grande lutte, tous les États sentent la terre trembler sous eux: pour tous, il s'agit de l'existence, et que ... ils prennent ou non part à la guerre, leur destinée ne s'en joue pas moins sur l'immense champ de Bataille.' 'La guerre d'Orient', *Le Travailleur* 1:1 (May 1877), p.12. See also E. Vauquelin, 'Rule Britannia!', *L'Intransigeant*, 2 April 1883; B. Malon, 'La colonisation', *L'Intransigeant*, 3 October 1884; P. Lafargue, *Le droit à la paresse* (Paris: Henry Oriol, 1883. First published, 1880), pp.36–37.

[12] 'Par ce temps de développement industriel des peuples, quiconque se servira des colonies périra par les colonies.' 'Les anglais en Birmanie', *La Bataille* (Paris), 4 January 1886.

[13] For the wording, see G. Manceron, *1885: le tournant colonial de la République. Jules Ferry contre Georges Clemenceau, et autres affrontements parlementaires sur la conquête coloniale* (Paris: La Découverte, 2007).

both before and after the general amnesty, following the Communards through their years of exile from spring 1871 and back to France after 1880. The chapter adopts a broad definition of empire, which includes both the formal imperialism that became commonplace during the Third Republic and the informal expansion that characterised the period 1815–1870.[14] It shall focus upon past and contemporary European territorial empires in Asia, Africa, Oceania, and the Americas, but will not ignore events closer to home. Mindful that late nineteenth-century definitions of the 'civilised world' rarely stretched further east than Germany, it will also take into account events such as the Balkan Crisis that enveloped Eastern Europe, Russia, and the Ottoman Empire during the 1870s.

This chapter looks at empire and internationalism in the thought of revolutionaries who remained in Europe following the fall of the Commune. It demonstrates that it is here that we need to look for more clearly elaborated ideas on empire. As we can see from above, such questions, connections, and concerns peppered a wide variety of publications. In the interests of brevity and clarity, this chapter shall focus primarily upon the two journals in which these ideas were most systematically developed: *La Bataille* and *Le Travailleur*, the latter of which scholars have not previously examined.[15] Although published second of the two newspapers, *La Bataille*'s ideas on empire and internationalism were more conventional than *Le Travailleur*'s, and thus provide a more apposite basis for sustained analysis. It is this newspaper that shall be discussed first.

The chapter delineates two very different approaches to international questions through these two case studies. While both newspapers condemned imperial conquest on some level, they did so in different ways and with different aims in mind. Although it disapproved of current French efforts at imperialism, the more nationalist *La Bataille* approved in principle of efforts to spread French civilisation on a global scale. The more universalist *Le Travailleur*, meanwhile, rejected imperialism in principle and enjoined its readers to empathise with Europe's new colonial subjects.

The chapter then turns to assess the intellectual impact of these differing stances on imperialism. These two approaches had radically different implications for revolutionaries' wider thought. It shows that such themes

---

[14] For an elaboration of this broader definition, see D. Todd, 'A French Imperial Meridian, 1814–1870', *Past & Present* 210 (February 2011), 155–186, at p.160.
[15] The only reference to it comes in one footnote in D. Stafford, *From Anarchism to Reformism: A Study of the Political Activities of Paul Brousse within the First International and the French Socialist Movement 1870–1890* (London: Cox & Wyman, 1971), p.302, footnote 68.

were not extrinsic to the main body of revolutionary thought, but often closely imbricated with other ideas. As such, they frequently served to demarcate the limits and possibilities of some of the supposedly universal concepts examined in earlier chapters. *La Bataille*'s protectionism exposed limits to its supposedly universalist thought that had not been visible in purely Western contexts, while *Le Travailleur*'s stance was both consistent with its universalist claims and broadened the scope for revolutionary action, highlighting practical ways in which small groups of revolutionaries could bring about meaningful social change.

This chapter aims to explore French revolutionary ideas on empire and internationalism, and begin in turn to resituate these ideas within their wider patterns of thought. With these findings in mind, it also reflects upon a more methodological question: the use of empire as a category of historical analysis. In *By Sword and Plow*, Jennifer Sessions noted that domestic and imperial politics were often so 'intimately intertwined' in post-Revolutionary France that they 'became one'.[16] In the case of French revolutionary socialist thought at the beginning of the Third Republic, however, this intimate braiding of concerns did not end at the frontiers of the French overseas empire.[17] Revolutionary thought concerning the wider world was markedly not confined to meditations on or interactions with empire. Rather, it frequently transcended and disregarded imperial frameworks. This is both historically and historiographically striking. The nuanced interaction with such ideas serves to visualise the considerable ambiguities surrounding ideas on empire and the morality of conquest in a period of 'high imperialism'. Meanwhile, the frequency with which revolutionary socialists looked beyond the boundaries of empire raises questions about the utility of 'empire' and 'the colonial' as categories for analysing the multifarious ways in which Europeans interacted with the wider world during this period.

I

La Bataille was published daily in Paris under the editorship of Prosper-Olivier Lissagaray. A former Communard and author of the wildly popular *Histoire de la Commune de 1871* discussed in Chapter 1, Lissagaray was

---

[16] J.E. Sessions, *By Sword and Plow: France and the Conquest of Algeria* (Ithaca, NY: Cornell University Press, 2011), pp.324–325.

[17] For 'braided concerns', see U.S. Mehta, 'Edmund Burke on Empire, Self-Understanding, and Sympathy', in S. Muthu (ed.), *Empire and Modern Political Thought* (Cambridge: Cambridge University Press, 2012), 155–183, at p.166.

something of an intellectual hybrid. Perhaps intellectually closer to the Guesdists than the Possibilists, he had had extensive contact with Marx and his circle while in exile in England. Indeed, Marx and his youngest daughter Eleanor had assisted with the English translation of the *Histoire de la Commune*. Lissagaray, however, was a member of neither group. While close, his relationship with Marx was strained (Marx and his wife refused Eleanor and Lissagaray permission to marry), and Lissagaray and Paul Lafargue reportedly disliked each other so much that they would not even shake hands.[18]

His newspaper adopted a similarly independent stance. The first series of *La Bataille* ran from May 1882 to January 1886. Between October 1882 and May 1883, it merged with *Le Citoyen*, another long-running revolutionary socialist newspaper, to form *Le Citoyen & La Bataille*, but retained *La Bataille*'s staff and style. It was owned for at least the first year by the prominent republican journalist and novelist Lucien-Victor Meunier, and aimed primarily at socialist revolutionary members of the Parisian working class. It is impossible to determine newspapers' circulation figures during this period, as no comprehensive records were kept, however at the time Lafargue estimated *La Bataille*'s to have been between 2,000 and 3,000 copies.[19] In his seminal *Histoire de la presse française*, Claude Bellanger described *La Bataille* as a paper that enjoyed little success despite the talent of its editor, and Lafargue's circulation estimates certainly were not large compared to other revolutionary papers such as *L'Égalité* or *Le Prolétaire*.[20]

At the same time, though, they were not insignificant, and the length of the print run alone indicates a fairly substantial loyal readership. The paper appeared in broadsheet style and each issue boasted articles on a wide variety of subjects, indicating that Lissagaray was able to employ a considerable staff. Meunier, the registered owner, also wrote for the paper. *La Bataille*, then, was a far cry from the many ephemeral revolutionary newspapers of the early 1870s. While, again, it is impossible to precisely determine the interests of its readers, nevertheless articles on imperial matters featured regularly in *La Bataille*'s pages, thus exposing many Parisian workers to such concerns.

---

[18] G. Stedman Jones, *Karl Marx: Greatness and Illusion* (London: Allen Lane, 2016), p.545.
[19] 63: P. Lafargue to F. Engels (Paris, 24 November 1882), in F. Engels and P. and L. Lafargue, *Correspondence* 3 vols. (trans.) Y. Kapp (Moscow: Foreign Languages Publishing House, 1959), vol.1, 110–115, at p.113.
[20] C. Bellanger, *Histoire générale de la presse française*, 5 vols. (Paris: Presses universitaires de France, 1969–1976), vol.3 (1972), p.371.

At first glance, *La Bataille* appears to have adopted a critical attitude towards imperialism. Meunier, for example, praised Abdelkader, the Islamic scholar who struggled against the French occupation of Algeria for much of the nineteenth century, asking readers to 'consider him . . . not as an enemy, but a patriot!'[21] The paper also participated in the widespread condemnation of Jules Ferry during the Tonkin Affair.[22] In the final weeks of the 1884–1885 Sino-French War in Vietnam, Louis Brière de l'Isle, the commander-in-chief of French forces in Tonkin, telegraphed the French government informing them of several debilitating military retreats and requesting that reinforcements be sent 'as soon as possible'.

Brière de l'Isle's telegram provoked alarm and anger in France. Despite his assurances that the situation had improved, the public and press alike continued to believe that French troops had been needlessly sent into mortal danger. In the Chambre des Députés, Georges Clemenceau claimed Ferry had dishonoured France and dramatically accused the entire cabinet of treason in a speech that was widely reprinted in the press. The Affair brought down the government and effectively ended Ferry's ministerial career.

La Bataille gleefully joined in the widespread condemnation of Ferry, publishing several caricatures concerning his handling of the situation. Indeed, the paper had long questioned Ferry's actions in Indochina. The prime minister, they argued, was 'a true student of Pyrrhus'.[23] In an 1883 article addressed to the troops in Tonkin, Lissagaray offered a more in depth analysis of imperialism:

> You are in Tonkin to defend our Cochinchinese border. If you manage to maintain that, they will send you to China to defend our Tonkinese border, for in this time of fraternity one colony leads to another. If you conquer China, they will send you to Russia in order to defend our Chinese border, and then nothing will stop you being sent to Germany to ensure the safety of our possession of Russia.[24]

---

[21] '[C]onsidérons-le, non comme un emmeni, mais commune un patriote'. 'Abdelkader', *La Bataille*, 29 May 1883. Abd al-Qadir is better known in nineteenth-century European sources as Abdelkader or, as in the case of this article, Abd-el-Kader.

[22] For more on the widespread criticism of Ferry's colonial ventures, see T. Zeldin, *France 1848–1945: Politics and Anger* (Oxford: Oxford University Press, 1979), p.267.

[23] '[É]lève en droite ligne de Pyrrhus'. 'Aux troupiers du Tonkin', *La Bataille*, 12 December 1883.

[24] 'Vous êtes au Tonkin pour défendre notre frontière Cochinchinoise: si vous arrivez à vous y maintenir, on vous expédiera en Chine pour maintenir notre frontière du Tonkin: car, par ce temps de fraternité, une colonie amène l'autre. Si vous conquérez la Chine, on vous enverra en Russie pour préserver notre frontière chinoise, et rien ne s'oppose à ce qu'on vous mène en Allemagne pour nous assurer la possession de la Russie.' 'Aux troupiers du Tonkin', *La Bataille*,

For Lissagaray and *La Bataille*, contemporary French imperialism was a process of permanent and ever increasing acquisition with no discernible benefit. Moreover, imperialism echoed modern industrial exploitation, necessitating ever-increasing expansion that proved relatively safe for the elites or the capitalist but extremely dangerous for the worker – or, in the case of Tonkin, the army private. Not only, then, were Ferry's and the colonial lobby's immediate political decisions regarding imperial expansion regrettable, but for *La Bataille*, imperialism was apparently theoretically unacceptable from a socialist standpoint.[25]

French imperialism, however, was not only ineffective, but also actively detrimental to citizens' rights in the metropole. On the first Franco-Hova War (for *La Bataille*, 'the coup in Madagascar'), which marked the beginning of the French colonisation of Madagascar in 1885, Lissagaray asked the government:

> Why did [the Chamber] spend a month studying the pros and cons in your name just to change everything? What is the point of deliberations if they are not taken into account? Your parliamentary regime is nothing . . . if you cannot submit to the rulings that you yourselves pronounced. We were absolutely right to say that there can be no working with you. During the Empire public deliberations on matters of peace and war were nothing but a farce, and you are now showing us that the same can be said for the Republic.[26]

For *La Bataille*, as for the likes of Leroy-Beaulieu, imperialism and domestic politics were inextricably linked.

Unlike the colonial lobby's fantasies of civilising savages and advancing the economy, however, *La Bataille* argued that the government's bad decisions abroad were affecting both the colonies and France.[27] French imperialism was unacceptable as it involved political and ethical

---

12 December 1883. For a similar opinion, see H. Rochefort, 'Un vol sur la planche', *L'Intransigeant*, 15 March 1885.

[25] See also 'Colonies et travailleurs', *Le Citoyen & La Bataille*, 18 May 1883; 'L'Honneur du drapeau', *La Bataille*, 27 October 1884.

[26] 'Pourquoi donc a-t-elle pendant un grand mois étudié en votre nom le pour et le contre si c'est pour tout remettre en l'état? A quoi servent ses délibérations si vous ne devez pas en tenir compte? Votre régime parlementaire n'est donc qu'un jeu d'enfants, si vous ne savez pas vous soumettre aux règlements que vous avez vous-mêmes édictés.' 'Le coup de Madagascar', *La Bataille*, 24 December 1885.

[27] Highlighting the disconnect between French colonial practices and republican values was fairly common at the time. See, for instance, the criticism of missionaries in *La Bataille*, 5 January 1886; *L'Intransigeant*, 12 October 1882, Fonds Louise Michel (IISH), 939. See also J.P. Daughton, *An Empire Divided: Religion, Republicanism, and the Making of French Colonialism, 1880–1914* (Oxford: Oxford University Press, 2006).

compromises that were not only ineffective, but more importantly actively corrupted the political process and the French republic by infringing upon French citizens' democratic rights. Their opposition derived from the fear that imperial expansion gave reign to authoritarian tendencies incompatible with a French republic and republican values. French empire, in other words, remained a decidedly Bonapartist enterprise, and the government's actions abroad raised fears of authoritarianism at home.

Yet alongside these criticisms of the French colonial lobby, *La Bataille* also displayed a theoretical enthusiasm for imperialism. In August 1883, it spoke approvingly of the colonisation of Africa, noting that its 'importance' was 'happily, today understood by all intelligent citizens'.[28] Similarly, after the formal European division of Africa at the 1884–1885 Berlin Conference, it displayed no qualms about the European expropriation of African natural resources.[29] This colonial enthusiasm was also evident in *La Bataille*'s assessment of the British Empire. While an article on India, for example, suggested that the British were sowing the seeds of their own downfall, it also praised them as good (or efficient) colonists for having 'always known how to apply exactly the correct laws to suit the temperament, customs, religion, and indigenous civilisation of each of their individual colonies'. Regretfully, they mused, the French did not possess this skill.[30]

It is therefore necessary to distinguish between theoretical and practical opposition to imperialism. For Lissagaray and the paper's wider staff, the problem with French imperialism was that it was neither efficient nor democratically sanctioned. Yet although *La Bataille* heavily criticised the practice of French imperialism, this did not correlate to a corresponding theoretical opposition. Rather, as its articles on Britain suggested, *La Bataille* supported the right of Europeans to colonise, and disagreed merely with the French colonial lobby's ways of exercising this right.[31] French imperialism, in other words, was not bad because imperialism itself was bad. It was bad because in its current incarnation, it was damaging to

---

[28] 'L'importance de la colonisation en Afrique est, heureusement, aujourd'hui comprise par tous les citoyens intelligents.' 'La mer intérieure en Afrique', *La Bataille*, 8 August 1883.

[29] 'Les richesses de l'Afrique', *La Bataille*, 4 January 1886.

[30] '[L]es Anglais, avec un tact que malheureusement nous n'avons pas en France, ont toujours su appliquer à chacune de leurs colonies le régime qui convenait le mieux au tempérament, aux moeurs, à la religion, à la civilisation des indigènes.' 'Anglais et Indous', *La Bataille*, 12 May 1885.

[31] For a similar historical view, see C.J. Eichner, '*La citoyenne* in the World: Hubertine Auclert and Feminist Imperialism', *French Historical Studies* 32:1 (2009), 63–84, at pp.71–72; p.75.

France and the new Republic that revolutionaries felt they had worked so hard to establish and protect.

Indeed, *La Bataille*'s support for imperialism extended further than an abstract belief in its hypothetical possibilities. It argued that effective imperialism was not only desirable, but also vital to the maintenance of France's well-being. Discussing the colonial economy in December 1883, Lissagaray argued that, contrary to Leroy-Beaulieu's claims, colonisation did not make for ideal economic markets. 'There is', he suggested, 'a simpler way to sell our products than at the point of a bayonet, and that is to produce better.' However, he continued:

> If our domestic economy were better, if French industry could take up its tools and get itself once more to the level of other nations, if our taxes were better distributed, if our industry and commerce were not dependent upon the caprices of the railway bosses and their tariffs, *our deputies would not need to send you to Tonkin or anywhere else.*[32]

While Lissagaray accepted that colonisation in order to force the sale of French products was an unsatisfactory state of affairs, he did not suggest a termination of the practice. Rather, he argued that such action was necessary in order to protect French jobs and the French economy, and called for a reform of colonial practices to increase their profitability.

Lissagaray and his staff, then, were certainly critical of the form that the colonial lobby's (and in particular Ferry's) imperial policies took. Unlike the deportees, however, who employed imperial metaphors simply as a method for commenting upon domestic French affairs, *La Bataille* endorsed the theory and fact of imperial expansion as not only beneficial, but also necessary to the continued prosperity and international standing of France. Furthermore, while its journalists praised, for example, Abdelkader's patriotism, their 'positive' assessments of other cultures were not accompanied by a belief in the right to self-rule.[33]

These ideas on imperialism and its benefits were not unusual in radical and socialist circles. As David Todd demonstrated in *Free Trade and Its Enemies in France*, for example, French socialists had long displayed a

---

[32] 'Si notre économie intérieure était meilleure, si l'industrie française savait renouveler à temps son outillage et le mettre au niveau des autres nations, si nos impôts étaient mieux répartis, si notre industrie et notre commerce n'étaient pas livrés au caprice des chemins de fer maîtres de fixer les tariffs, nos députés n'auraient pas besoin de vous expédier au Tonkin ou ailleurs'. 'Aux troupiers du Tonkin', *La Bataille*, 12 December 1883. Emphasis mine.
[33] 'Anglais et Indous', *La Bataille*, 12 May 1885.

degree of ambivalence on such issues as free trade and protectionism.[34] *La Bataille*'s ideas were also relatively similar to the views of other contemporary radicals such as Hubertine Auclert, the radical feminist and founder of the society Le droit des femmes. In 1881, Auclert launched *La Citoyenne*, a monthly newspaper that campaigned for women's suffrage and endorsed expansive French republicanism as an agent capable of bringing about universal female enfranchisement.[35] For *La Bataille*, European superiority was never in doubt. It remained the only means by which to rule effectively and, combined with their concern for French workers, thus rendered imperial expansion (as for the colonial lobby) both a right and a moral duty.[36]

II

Le Travailleur took an altogether different view of European imperial expansion. Published in Geneva from May 1877 to May 1878, it was the product of collaboration between exiled anarchist and federalist revolutionaries of several nationalities, primarily French and Russian. As we have already seen, Geneva was at the time one of Europe's most prominent anarchist centres, located firmly within the anarchist Jura Federation's sphere of influence in the Swiss Jura and home to an international array of exiles. Unlike *La Bataille*, *Le Travailleur* appeared only once a month or bimonthly, and often acted as a vehicle for long-form essays. At the same time, however, it retained many of the trappings of a more regular newspaper, such as a letters page, and maintained links with the Jura Federation's main newspaper, the weekly *Bulletin de la Fédération jurassienne*.[37] Indeed, it was the collapse of the *Bulletin* in April 1878 that brought *Le Travailleur* to an end.

Le Travailleur dealt extensively with imperial and transnational subjects. The majority of these articles were written by either Élisée Reclus or his Russian colleague Lev Mechnikov. An anarchist geographer and

---

[34] D. Todd, *Free Trade and Its Enemies in France, 1814–1851* (Cambridge: Cambridge University Press, 2015), pp.224–225.
[35] Eichner, 'La citoyenne in the World', pp.71–72.
[36] See, for example, 'Raïatea', *Le Citoyen & La Bataille*, 25 October 1882. See also 'Question coloniale', *Le Citoyen & La Bataille*, 5 November 1882; see, for example, 'Le Tong-kin', *Le Citoyen & La Bataille*, 21 November 1882; 'Madagascar', *Le Citoyen & La Bataille*, 6 December 1882; 'Tong-king', *Le Citoyen & La Bataille*, 19 December 1882.
[37] The *Bulletin de la Fédération jurassienne* collapsed in April 1878, at which point *Le Travailleur* merged with Paul Brousse and Peter Kropotkin's *L'Avant-Garde* (Geneva). See Stafford, *From Anarchism to Reformism*, p.107.

sociologist, Mechnikov arrived in Switzerland in 1876 after several years of teaching Russian in Japan. He published a number of academic books, in addition to contributing to Alexander Herzen's *Kolokol* and Nikolai Chernyshevsky's *Sovremennik*, and collaborating with Reclus on the *Nouvelle géographie* and *Le Travailleur*.[38] Although Reclus and Mechnikov authored the majority of articles on imperialism, the editorial board was populated by Geneva's most prominent Communard exiles including Arthur Arnould and Gustave Lefrançais, all of whom supported the views expressed by their colleagues.[39]

Although it appeared some four to five years before *La Bataille*, *Le Travailleur* nevertheless expressed some of the same suspicions about the French empire. Addressing the problem of the limits of colonisation, the first issue worried that 'the dream of Universal Empire constantly plays on the minds of heads of State. The more they possess already, the greater fury of acquisition they have'.[40] A year later, an editorial highlighted the elite's exploitation of workers in the name of imperial wars. In an article on the 1877–1878 Russo-Turkish War, in which Russia made substantial territorial gains but at heavy human cost, *Le Travailleur* mockingly asked the Tsar,

> Aren't all the millions spent, all the men killed worth it for his glory? . . . of the three million humans born every year in his territories, he will always be able to find enough . . . cannon-fodder to sacrifice in his wars.[41]

It is thus possible to discern a certain degree of unity on empire amongst the deportees, *La Bataille*, and *Le Travailleur*. All three shared many of the same concerns – the exploitation of the worker, for instance, and the effects of imperialism upon Western governments. Most notably, all three were united in their opposition to the current form of French imperialism.

Unusually, though, *Le Travailleur* also raised a number of ethical objections to imperialism. Reporting on a communist revolt in Mexico in 1877, the periodical argued that colonial occupation and possession

---

[38] For more on Mechnikov, see J.D. White, 'Despotism and Anarchy: The Sociological Thought of L.I. Mechnikov', *The Slavonic and East European Review* 54 (July 1976), 395–411.

[39] *Le Travailleur*, 1:1 (May 1877), p.28; A. Arnould, *L'État et la Révolution* (Lyons: Éditions Jacques-Marie Laffont et Associés, 1981. First published 1877), pp.187–188.

[40] '[L]e rêve de l'Empire universel hante toujours les chefs d'Etat; plus ils possédent déjà, plus ils ont la fureur d'acquérir'. 'La guerre d'Orient', *Le Travailleur* 1:1 (May 1877), p.12.

[41] 'Combien a coûté cette guerre? Question naïve. Qu'importe à notre "petit père" le tsar? Tous les millions dépensés, tous les hommes tués, ne l'ont ils pas été pour sa gloire? . . . sur les trois millions d'êtres humains qui naissent chaque année dans ses domaines, il pourra toujours prélever . . . assez de chair à canon pour les faire mitrailler dans ses batailles.' 'Bulletin', *Le Travailleur* 2:2 (February–March 1878), p.2.

lacked legal legitimacy, asserting that the rebels 'wanted to reclaim the land that the whites had *stolen* during the conquest'.[42] Categorising the accumulation of land during the Spanish colonisation of the Americas as 'theft' suggested that for *Le Travailleur*, conquest was not a legitimate mode of acquisition, but a crime. Indeed, in the September 1877 issue, one of *Le Travailleur*'s journalists stated this categorically, writing: 'I do not believe that conquest can ever be justified.'[43]

This was an important theoretical distinction. Given the centrality of the moral right to conquest to justifications of late nineteenth-century imperialism, *Le Travailleur*'s opposition to it implied an opposition to the idea of empire itself, rather than simply to its current French iteration. *La Bataille*'s and *Le Travailleur*'s criticisms of French colonialism, then, were at once similar and fundamentally different. While many of their issues with the practical realisation of imperialism were the same, the basis for these criticisms was not. *Le Travailleur* recognised the problems with France's practical implementation of imperial ideas, yet it also called the legality of colonisation and imperialism in general into question. Its disavowal of French imperialism, in other words, was based also on a rejection of its theoretical foundation.

It was not only the right to conquest that *Le Travailleur* attacked, but also the credence of notions of Western superiority. For *Le Travailleur*, a variety of different cultures were just as advanced as those of Europe. In a study of Berber societies in Algeria, Reclus suggested that '[t]he political organisation of the Kabyles' was 'the ideal of democracy'.[44] Likewise, in an article on communism and socialism in China, Mechnikov wrote that '[w]hile in western Europe, labour associations remain the exception, they have been the rule for centuries in the far East.'[45] These other cultures were not merely equal to Europe's, though, *Le Travailleur* suggested, but often superior. Reclus, for example, claimed that 'utopia is already a reality

---

[42] 'Ils voulaient reprendre les terres que les blancs leur ont enlevées du temps de la conquête.' 'Dernières nouvelles', *Le Travailleur* 1:6 (October 1877), p.9. Emphasis mine. See also 'La guerre d'Orient', *Le Travailleur* 1:1 (May 1877), p.14.

[43] 'Je ne crois pas que la conquête puisse jamais être justifiée'. 'La solidarité chez les Berbères', *Le Travailleur* 1:5 (September 1877), p.17.

[44] 'L'organisation politique des Kabyles est l'idéal de la démocratie.' 'La solidarité chez les Berbères', *Le Travailleur* 1:5 (September 1877), p.19.

[45] 'Tandis que dans nos contrées de l'Europe occidentale les associations ouvrières sont encore l'exception, elles sont depuis des siècles la règle uniforme dans l'extrême Orient.' 'L'Internationale et les Chinois', *Le Travailleur* 2:3 (March–April 1878), p.24.

south of the Mediterranean' in Algeria, 'the promised land of association'.[46]

Such views were not historically unusual. In particular, the suggestion that Berber societies were cradles of democracy can be traced back to earlier perceptions of Kabyles as skilled practitioners of a republican or democratic form of socio-political organisation. As Jean-Louis Marçot has detailed in *Comment est née l'Algérie française*, French socialists of various hues had displayed an interest in non-Western forms of social organisation (particularly in Algeria) since at least the 1830s.[47] In fact, though, such subjects were widely discussed across the political spectrum in the mid-nineteenth century. Indeed, even Alexis de Tocqueville, an ardent defender of the French imperial project, echoed such views in his own writings on Algeria.[48]

By the 1870s, however, they were extremely rare, and most writers had shifted towards more racially prescriptive ideas of contemporary superiority. Plenty of European theorists still referred to non-Western societies. In the first paragraph of his seminal 1882 lecture *Qu'est-ce qu'une nation?*, for instance, Ernest Renan mentioned 'huge agglomerations of men in China, Egypt, and ancient Babylon' and 'the tribes of the Hebrews and the Arabs'.[49] Some, such as Henry Maine, even praised them, but *Le Travailleur*'s approach was subtly, but significantly, different.[50] As Karuna Mantena has demonstrated, non-Western cultures were typically praised as once-mighty civilisations that had long since atrophied or decayed, and were thus in need of European protection.[51] *Le Travailleur* specifically refuted these suggestions, arguing by contrast that non-Western civilisations such as China and Kabylia had retained their greatness.[52] For *Le Travailleur*, the future ideal society was not merely an expansion of European modernity, and neither did it involve a total rejection of modern societies: rather, elements of it were to be found everywhere.

---

[46] '[L]'utopie ... [est] la réalité au-delà de la Méditerranée'; 'L'Algérie ... la terre promise de l'association'. 'La solidarité chez les Berbères', *Le Travailleur* 1:6 (October 1877), p.15.

[47] J.-L. Marçot, *Comment est née l'Algérie française 1830–1850: la belle utopie* (Paris: Éditions de la différence, 2012).

[48] A. de Tocqueville, *Writings on Empire and Slavery* (ed.) J. Pitts (Baltimore, MD: Johns Hopkins University Press, 2000).

[49] 'Les grandes agglomérations d'hommes à la façon de la Chine, de l'Égypte, de la plus ancienne Babylonie; la tribu à la façon des Hébreux, des Arabes'. E. Renan, *Qu'est-ce qu'une nation? Conférence faite en Sorbonne, le 11 mars 1882* (Paris: Calmann Lévy, 1882).

[50] For more on Maine, see K. Mantena, *Alibis of Empire: Henry Maine and the Ends of Liberal Imperialism* (Princeton, NJ: Princeton University Press, 2010).

[51] Ibid., pp.56–88.　　　[52] *Le Travailleur* 1:5 (September 1877), p.21.

Notably, *Le Travailleur* went further than acknowledging parity between atomised Western and non-Western cultures. It also recognised connections and similarities. As one editorial argued:

> Questions of production and consumption are the same everywhere; mountains and oceans may delimit regions and determine the character and activity of the producers, but mountains and oceans do nothing more to change the situation of workers than artificial frontiers do. They are exploited everywhere.[53]

The universal power of the worker to determine their own destiny, then, superseded both national borders and the power of international markets. *Le Travailleur*'s journalists returned frequently to this theme, often implying that such similarities were not merely superficial, but deeply ingrained in a kind of universal workingman's consciousness. Describing a raid on a Chinese immigrant association in Southeast Asia, for example, the paper claimed that:

> the British police got their hands on the statutes of an extremely influential popular society. To their astonishment they recognised in them, in exactly the same terms, the language of our European labourers.[54]

By drawing attention to the deep similarities between Chinese and European labourers who had never met, *Le Travailleur* implied that socialism and its goals were both natural and universal. European and non-Western civilisations and cultures were not only equal, but more importantly they were fundamentally alike.

For *Le Travailleur*, solidarity was thus primarily based not upon nationality or civilisational superiority, but upon class and profession. In this matter, it positioned itself against the kind of interracial hostilities that had already broken out in cities with large immigrant populations such as San Francisco, declaring, for instance, that '[t]his terrible *yellow question* is a corner into which the bourgeois regime has pushed civilisation.'[55] As

---

[53] 'Les questions de production et de consommation sont les memes partout; montagnes et océans peuvent délimiter les régions et déterminer le caractère et l'activité des producteurs, mais pas plus que les frontières factices, montagnes et océans ne changent rien à la situation des travailleurs. Ceux-ci sont exploités partout.' 'Notre programme', *Le Travailleur* 1:1, (May 1877), p.2.

[54] '[L]a police britannique mit la main sur les statuts d'une société populaire très-influente, et c'est avec stupeur qu'on y reconnut, et Presque dans les mêmes termes, le langage de nos ouvriers d'Europe.' 'L'Internationale et les Chinois', *Le Travailleur* 2:3 (March–April 1878), p.28. See also 'La solidarité chez les Berbères', *Le Travailleur* 1:5 (September 1877), p.22.

[55] 'Cette terrible *question jaune* est une impasse dans laquelle le régime bourgeois accule la civilisation'. 'Quelques mots sur les associations chinoises', *Le Travailleur* 2:4 (April–May 1878), p.17. Emphasis

Reclus argued, universal workers' solidarity was not merely beneficial, but natural and inescapable:

> *Solidarity is no mere sentiment; it is a law of nature.* We have been mistaken in not considering the barbarians of Algeria as our brothers, and we have been victims of our own prejudices and egotism. It is against the Algerians that the men who would slit our throats did their apprenticeship in murder and arson.[56]

Universal proletarian solidarity, *Le Travailleur* argued, was thus the natural state of the worker, whereas the regional solidarities and protectionism of publications such as *La Bataille* were products of, rather than solutions to, exploitative industrial modernity.

In order to combat such manipulation, according to *Le Travailleur*, it was necessary for the worker to realise that 'the misery of one proletariat and another are the same' and unite:[57]

> Up until now, prejudiced labourers have taken out their anger on other unfortunate people. They have fought like gladiators in the arena *while the masters watch the massacre.* Labourer fights labourer. One trade fights another trade. Nations and races gut themselves over common boundaries. And now Chinese, Americans, and Europeans are meeting each other on the same battlefield. Will they massacre each other, snatching the bread from each other's mouths ... or will they, believing in the same ideas, unite and demand in common the integral product of their labour?[58]

---

original. See also 'L'Internationale et les Chinois', *Le Travailleur* 2:3 (March–April 1878), p.29; 'La théorie des races', *L'Égalité*, 14 May 1882.

[56] 'La solidarité n'est pas un simple sentiment, c'est une loi de nature. Nous l'avons méconnue en ne considérant pas les barbares d'Algérie comme des frères et nous avons été victimes de nos préjugés et de notre égoïsme. C'est contre les Algériens que nos égorgeurs avait fait leur apprentissage de meutre et d'incendie.' 'La solidarité chez les Berbères', *Le Travailleur* 1:5 (September 1877), p.22. Emphasis mine. For similar expressions of solidarity, see L. Dramard, 'En Afrique', *L'Émancipation* (Lyon), 22 November 1880; 'Les affaires d'Égypte et le Parti ouvrier', *Le Citoyen* (Paris), 31 July 1882; 'La défaite', *Le Citoyen*, 17 September 1882; 'Nos proconsuls en Afrique', *Le Prolétaire*, 22 July 1882; La férocité arabe!', *Le Prolétaire*, 9 September 1882; 'L'Angleterre, la France, et l'Égypte', *Le Prolétaire*, 1 March 1884.

[57] '[L]es misères de l'un et de l'autre prolétariat ont pu se reconnaître'. 'L'Internationale et les Chinois', *Le Travailleur* 2:3 (March–April 1878), pp.28–29. See also *Bulletin de la Fédération jurassienne*, 16 July 1876.

[58] 'Jusqu'à maintenant, les travailleurs lésés ont assouvi leur colère sur d'autres malheureux: ils ont combattu comme des gladiateurs dans une arène, tandis que les maîtres regardaient le massacre. L'ouvrier combat les ouvriers; un corps de métier lutte contre d'autres corps de métier; nations et races s'entrégorgent sur les frontières communes. Et maintenant, Chinois, Américains et Européens, se rencontrant sur le même champ de bataille, vont-ils se massacrer les uns les autres, s'arracher le pain dans la bouche ... ou bien, comprenant les mêmes idées, s'unissant dans une même volonté, sauront-ils s'associer pour revendiquer en commun le produit intégral de leur travail?' 'L'Internationale et les Chinois', *Le Travailleur* 2:3 (March–April 1878), p.31. Emphasis mine.

If solidarity were a law of nature defined along professional or class lines, then logically the international bourgeoisie were also united. Indeed, Reclus referred to this universal bourgeoisie in the same edition, demanding that the worker '[a]sk the conservative if he does not shout "Death! Death to the *communeux* of all countries!"'[59]

Given that both socialism and capitalism were universal phenomena, interracial hostilities and disputes between labourers were detrimental to the workers' cause everywhere. For Western workers to damage the interests of their non-Western counterparts was thus to be trapped in the masters' arena, too preoccupied with fighting each other to notice the true, common enemy. By failing to elaborate a viable alternative to the current system, they would strengthen the hand of their foe and perpetuate their own oppression. Imperial expansion may have superficially benefited the European worker by providing a captive market for their products and thus temporarily securing their jobs. Social revolution, however, could ultimately not be realised within such parochial boundaries.

It should be noted, though, that there remained limits to this proto-anticolonialism. While *Le Travailleur* opposed the exploitation of other cultures and nationalities, it nonetheless expressed support for what it called 'true colonisation' – a quasi-Lockean appeal for the proper use of land. Perhaps the most notable example was the cultivation of industry around esparto grass, a plant used in crafts that is native only to countries in the western Mediterranean such as Spain, Algeria, and Tunisia. Discussing the economic development that esparto cultivation prompted in Oran province in Algeria, Reclus argued '[t]rue colonisation is not a useless and costly displacement of population. It must bring new tools to a country, facilitating the exploitation of previously neglected products.'[60]

---

[59] 'Demandez au conservateur s'il ne criera pas: A mort! A mort! pour les communeux de tous les pays?' 'L'Internationale et les Chinois', *Le Travailleur* 2:3 (March–April 1878), p.30. This was a widely held opinion. See, for example, Congrès général de l'Association internationale des Travailleurs, *Manifeste adressé à toutes les Associations ouvrières et à tous les Travailleurs, par le Congrès général de l'Association internationale des Travailleurs tenu à Bruxelles du 7 au 13 Septembre 1874*, pp.5–6; J. Guesde, *Textes choisis* (ed.) C. Willard (Paris: Éditions Sociales, 1959), p.144; 'Les syndicats professionels'. *L'Égalité*, 9 July 1882; P. Lafargue, 'Blagues bourgeoises: la patrie', *L'Égalité*, 18 November 1884; M. Talmeyr, 'Rien pour la France', *L'Intransigeant*, 10 July 1881; J. Guesde, 'Nations et classes', *Le Citoyen*, 3 April 1882; P. Lafargue, 'Socialisme et patriotisme', *Le Citoyen*, 7 August 1882; J. Guesde and P. Lafargue, *Le programme du Parti Ouvrier: son histoire, ses considérants, ses articles* (Paris: Henry Oriol, 1883), p.90.

[60] 'La vraie colonisation n'est pas un inutile et coûteux déplacement de population. Elle doit apporter à un pays un outillage nouveau permettant l'exploitation de produits jusqu'alors négligés.' 'La solidarité chez les Berbères', *Le Travailleur* 1:5 (September 1877), p.24. This was a fairly regular criticism; for example, see also 'Tong-king', *Le Citoyen & La Bataille*, 11 December 1882. On

Moreover, despite its pleas for unity, *Le Travailleur* simultaneously retained a belief in the hierarchy of races. The Chinese, Mechnikov implied, were more 'productive' than Southeast Asians.[61] Likewise, it asserted that, with reference to Africa, '[o]ne should not compare [Algeria] to the virgin lands whose inhabitants are in an infant state. The Berbers have conserved the tradition of an old civilisation'.[62] It is also worth pointing out that, unlike other publications including *Le Citoyen* and *L'Intrasigeant*, *Le Travailleur* never provided column inches for colonial subjects to advance their own ideas.[63] While *Le Travailleur* may not have been 'imperialist' in the sense of advocating a concerted system of domination,[64] it must nevertheless be remembered that it was neither opposed to all forms of colonisation nor convinced of the equality of all races.

Le Travailleur was also by no means the first French publication to express ethical objections to empire. Like *La Bataille*'s protectionism, its views had historical precedent. Maximilien Robespierre, for example, had famously preferred principles over colonies; a preference that contributed to the decision to abolish slavery in French colonies in 1794. Likewise, Benjamin Constant's 1814 *De l'esprit de conquête* represented, as Jennifer Pitts has demonstrated, a 'sweeping denunciation of any policy of conquest as inappropriate to the modern era'.[65] In the early 1830s, meanwhile, the liberal scholar Hamdan Khodja had published the pamphlet *Le Miroir*, which made the first ethical case for complete French withdrawal from Algeria.[66] In many ways, *Le Travailleur* could be said to represent a return to earlier criticisms of conquest by the likes of Denis Diderot and Constant.[67]

Locke and colonialism, see D. Armitage, 'John Locke: Theorist of Empire?', in *Foundations of Modern International Thought* (Cambridge: Cambridge University Press, 2013), 114–131.

[61] 'L'Internationale et les Chinois', *Le Travailleur* 2:3 (March–April 1878), p.27.

[62] 'Il ne faudrait pas comparer ce pays aux terres vierges dont les habitants sont à l'état d'enfance. Les Berbères ont conservé la tradition d'une vieille civilisation.' 'La solidarité chez les Berbères', *Le Travailleur* 1:6 (October 1877), p.16. See also 'Correspondances: Paris', *Le Travailleur*, 1:2 (June 1877), p.22.

[63] For examples of this elsewhere, see 'Déclaration du Parti national égyptien' and 'La presse égyptienne', *Le Citoyen*, 17 August 1882; 'Manifeste en faveur d'Arabi', *Le Citoyen*, 23 August 1882; G.D. al-Afghan, 'Le Mahdi', *L'Intransigeant*, 8 December 1883; 'La Chine d'après un chinois', *Le Prolétariat*, 26 December 1885.

[64] For this differentiation, see Armitage, 'John Locke', at p.115.

[65] J. Pitts, *A Turn to Empire: The Rise of Imperial Liberalism in Britain and France* (Princeton, NJ: Princeton University Press, 2005), p.173. B. Constant, *De l'esprit de conquête et de l'usurpation, dans leurs rapports avec la civilisation européenne*, 3rd edn (Paris: Le Norment, 1814).

[66] On Khodja, see J. Pitts, 'Liberalism and Empire in a Nineteenth-Century Algerian Mirror', *Modern Intellectual History* 6 (2009), 287–313.

[67] D. Diderot, *Supplément au voyage de Bougainville*, (ed.) P. Jimack (London: Grant & Cutler, 1988). First published, 1772.

Where *Le Travailleur* departed from this tradition was its belief that progress must be brought about by unity and universal solidarity, rather than merely legal parity. Whilst for Constant and others, the good of the nation remained the principal concern, *Le Travailleur* advocated greater transnational affinity rather than national protectionism or isolation. For *Le Travailleur*, European imperialism represented a violation of natural law, and both the colonial stage and colonial actors were vital rather than ancillary to revolution. The rights of the worker and the rights of the nation were to be realised not through protectionism, but through truly international solidarity, and an anticolonial stance was thus both politically and ethically necessary.

III

Although they represented wildly different intellectual positions, at the heart of *Le Travailleur*'s, *La Bataille*'s, and the deportees' thought on contemporary imperialism lay a critique of industrial modernity. For those in power, they claimed, competition led only to insecurity, and consequently to further acquisition. Meanwhile, capitalists' determination to acquire workers' bodies and labour at the lowest possible price prompted interracial strife amongst the workers themselves.[68] This lack of solidarity in turn reduced all workers' prospects of winning concessions from their employers or achieving meaningful social change.

Indeed, this critique of industrial society was extremely widespread in contemporary French work on empire. In an article in the *Revue socialiste*, for example, the Blanquist Albert Regnard claimed:

> The civilised world is nothing but a great theatre of ills, filling the air with its ugly wailing ... Journey from country to country and ask from door to door: 'Does contentment reside here? Are you satisfied and happy?' Everywhere, people will reply: 'Carry on looking! We don't have what you speak of.'[69]

Contrary to the colonial lobby's claims, modernity and 'progress' as exemplified by the endless process of acquisition that was imperial

---

[68] 'Quelques mots sur les associations chinoises', *Le Travailleur* 2:4 (April–May 1878), p.19.

[69] 'Le monde civilisé n'est qu'une immense salle de malades qui remplissent l'air de leurs gémissements navrants et se tordent en proie à tous les genres de souffrances. Allez de pays en pays et demandez de porte en porte: "Le contentement habite-t-il ici? Etes-vous tranquilles et heureux?" Partout on vous répondra: "Cherche plus loin! nous n'avons pas ce dont tu parles!"' A. Regnard, 'Les Mensonges conventionnels de notre civilisation', *La revue socialiste* (1886), 697–706, at p.697. See also, for example, *L'Intransigeant*, 12 October 1882, Fonds Louise Michel (IISH), 939.

expansion, revolutionaries suggested, brought neither happiness nor social harmony. Even those who endorsed the supremacy of Western civilisation, such as *La Bataille*, were wholly unsatisfied with its current state. Although, as we have seen, French revolutionary thought during this period encompassed a variety of positions on empire, their basis was largely the same. All were concerned with how to improve the worker's lot, and all approached imperialism as a close relation or by-product of industrial modernity.

This engagement with imperialism was more successful for some than for others. *La Bataille*'s criticisms of the colonial lobby's policies were both strident and visible. It maintained a clear editorial line and addressed a diverse range of situations. The paper's protectionist stance, however, dulled the impact of its criticism. As opposed to *Le Travailleur*'s, *La Bataille*'s issues with French imperialism sprung ultimately from nationalist concern not for 'the worker', but exclusively for the *French* worker.[70] At a push, it advocated for the rights of the European worker. *La Bataille*, in other words, elaborated a hierarchy – far from unusual in revolutionary ideas on nations – in which France occupied the top spot, followed by Europe, and with the rest of the world bringing up the rear.

The visibly different circumstances in which the two papers appeared undoubtedly influenced these stances. *Le Travailleur* published prior to the amnesty in a likeminded community of international exiles, and positioned itself as a journal designed to provoke thought and discussion. *La Bataille* was targeted primarily at French (or Parisian) workers. It published daily, reacting immediately to events as they unfolded, and competing for readers in a crowded market of revolutionary socialist newspapers.[71] It was launched, moreover, in the midst of a terrible economic crisis. France's economy had been particularly hard hit by the global slowdown of the 1870s, and its woes were compounded by the spread in the 1870s and 1880s of epidemics such as silk-worm disease and phylloxera (which affected grape vines) that sent production and incomes into freefall.[72] In such circumstances, it is not surprising that *La Bataille* prioritised the protection of French jobs and markets.

---

[70] 'Colonies et travailleurs', *Le Citoyen & La Bataille*, 18 May 1883.
[71] For a discussion of the popularity of protectionism during this period, see P. Rosanvallon, *The Society of Equals* (trans.) A. Goldhammer (Cambridge, MA: Harvard University Press, 2013. First published in French, 2011), p.141.
[72] R.P. Tombs, *France 1814–1914* (London: Routledge, 1996), p.445; L. Page Moch, *Moving Europeans: Migration in Western Europe since 1650* (Bloomington, IN: Indiana University Press, 1992), p.115.

Yet although this context goes some way towards illuminating the reasons for *La Bataille*'s position on imperialism, such a stance nonetheless highlighted the limits of its supposedly universal values. The paper preached solidarity and universal equality, but in reality, this solidarity ceased at the borders of the West. It considered the rising 'moral level' of Hindus brought about by the introduction of English culture into India 'a danger'.[73] Likewise, it deemed British bankers' plans to finance Chinese industrialisation in 1886 'treason'. In retaliation, it suggested that British proletarians should 'string up the English financiers who gave the Chinese this loan from the doors of their banks' and pull the plug on Chinese production in order to protect the European worker.[74] *La Bataille*'s engagement with empire and international questions therefore effectively confined them to a national framework for social change, and visibly demarcated the practical limits to their professions of universal solidarity and fraternity.

This position with regard to the rest of the world was in fact extremely proximate to the colonial lobby's own. As we have seen, *La Bataille*'s (and indeed many other revolutionaries'[75]) opposition to contemporary French imperialism sprang from the conviction that the Third Republic was not doing imperialism properly. As Jennifer Pitts has argued in relation to liberal critics of French expansion under the July Monarchy, intellectual positions based wholly upon the well-being of France were ineffective, for they were ultimately derivative and could be easily undermined by changes in the government's colonial fortunes.[76] Such criticisms were thus highly unlikely to be sustainable over an extended period of time.

Neither did they offer anything new or unusual. *La Bataille*'s international thought, which focused solely on empire and its possible benefits for the metropole, effectively conformed to modern social standards, undermining claims that they offered a fresh alternative to the current order. Speaking from within the bounds of contemporary society, they were unable to offer an alternative to the binary colony–metropole paradigm established by the government's own ideas on imperialism.

---

[73] 'Anglais et Indous', *La Bataille*, 12 May 1885.

[74] '[P]endre aux portes de leur banque les financiers anglais qui émettront l'emprunt chinois'. 'Le milliard chinois', *La Bataille*, 5 January 1886.

[75] See, for example, 'Les naufrageurs', *Le Citoyen*, 12 November 1881; 'Gaspillage partout', *Le Citoyen*, 19 December 1881; 'L'alliance avec Arabi', *Le Citoyen*, 26 July 1882; Anon, *Les déportés civils de Gomen. Nouvelle Calédonie* (Paris: Imprimerie Nouvelle Association Ouvrière, 1871), pp.15–16.

[76] Pitts, 'Republicanism, Liberalism, and Empire in Post-Revolutionary France', in Muthu (ed.), *Empire and Modern Political Thought*, 261–291, at p.264.

Rather, *La Bataille*'s imperial and international thought represented a typical manifestation of Alice Conklin's assertion that faith in empire and the civilising mission was 'part of what it meant to be French and republican in this period'.[77]

Le Travailleur's interest in international affairs, by contrast, was truly transnational. For *Le Travailleur*, as for Albert Regnard, imperial exploits were nothing but the 'preoccupations of a decadent patriotism'.[78] The periodical warned its readers to beware of imperialism's apparent perks, urging them (as it urged the French government) to consider the less fortunate. Discussing the future, Reclus stated:

> The world has been made small by the network of railways and steamboats that cross it. Different peoples are more and more becoming neighbours, multiplying their points of contact ... From their diverse and even opposing elements, they will gradually form a new race *in which all races will be united.*[79]

Unlike for *La Bataille*, for *Le Travailleur* the world was defined not by borders, but by the increasing mobility and unity brought about by travel and technological innovation.

Le Travailleur encouraged the establishment of connections between a wide variety of national proletariats, and often discussed their own. In Oran, for example, the paper numbered a wide variety of nationalities amongst its associates including 'Spanish youths ... the sons of the French *proscrits* of 48', and 'young Kabyles who have remained in the towns and who know the European workers well'.[80] In promoting the establishment of transnational networks and overlooking national borders, *Le Travailleur* both enlarged and shrank the scope of politics and revolutionary action, reducing it to the figure of the individual worker. *Le Travailleur*'s worker was defined not by their country, but by their profession, forcing readers to

---

[77] A.L. Conklin, *A Mission to Civilize: The Republican Idea of Empire in France and West Africa, 1895–1930* (Stanford, CA: Stanford University Press, 1997), p.2. This position was similar to that of radical republicans as well as the colonial lobby. See, for instance, 'La guerre', *Le Citoyen*, 29 August 1883. See also Eichner, '*La citoyenne* in the World', at p.75.

[78] 'Ces préoccupations d'un patriotisme de décadence'. Regnard, 'Les Mensonges conventionnels de notre civilisation', at p.697.

[79] 'La terre se fait petite sous le réseau de chemins de fer et de bateaux à vapeur qui l'entoure; les peuples de plus en plus voisins les uns des autres, multiplient leurs points de contact; ils se rapprochent et se mêlent; de leurs éléments divers et même opposés, ils se préparent à former graduellement une race nouvelle où toutes les races se trouveront unies.' 'L'Internationale et les Chinois', *Le Travailleur* 2:3 (March–April 1878), p.30. Emphasis mine.

[80] '[L]es jeunes espagnols ... Les fils des proscrits français de 48 ... ainsi que les jeunes Kabyles qui sont restés dans les villes, et qui ont fréquenté les travailleurs européens.' 'La solidarité chez les Berbères', *Le Travailleur* 1:6 (October 1877), pp.15–16.

identify common ground between themselves and others and reflect upon the possibility of a universal common good.

In the sense that their interest in world affairs was more transnational than imperial, *Le Travailleur* was in fact similar to the deportees. Although they gave little sustained thought to imperialism and spent much of their time abroad in the South Pacific, the deportees' associations were not restricted to the territorial confines of New Caledonia. As we saw in the previous chapter, the deportees also briefly experienced an array of other countries on their voyages to and from the penal colony, including Senegal (colonised by the French in the 1850s[81]) and Australia. Indeed, Achille Ballière noted that he had almost 'made a world tour'.[82]

The 1874 *évadés* in particular encountered a wide variety of like-minded people. Two of the *évadés*, Paschal Grousset and Francis Jourde, addressed a banquet held in their honour by 'the Republicans of San Francisco' following their escape,[83] while Olivier Pain and Henri Rochefort met and discussed politics with a number of foreign radicals in New York. These included John Swinton, the Scottish-American journalist, trade unionist, and former chief editorial writer for the *New York Times*; Jeremiah O'Donovan Rossa, a member of the Cuba Five and architect of the Fenian dynamite campaign in the early 1880s; and several journalists from the *New York Herald*.[84] While the deportees spent the majority of their time in New Caledonia, then, it was not only in the South Pacific that cross-cultural encounters took place. For a number of them, especially of those who would later publish about their experiences, deportation proved to be a truly transnational affair.

This broadening of the deportees' geographical horizons also translated into a broadening of intellectual and cultural horizons. This was particularly evident in the deportees' private correspondence. In letters to his brother, for example, Raoul Urbain, a former member of the Conseil de la Commune,

---

[81] French territorial expansion into the mainland primarily occurred in the 1850s, although parts had been colonised prior to this period.

[82] '[F]ait le tour du monde'. E.-A. Ballière, *La Déportation de 1871: souvenirs d'un évadé de Nouméa* (Paris: G. Charpentier, 1889) p.125.

[83] 'Discours des citoyens Paschal Grousset et Francis Jourde, ex-membres de la Commune de Paris, prononcés au banquet qui leur a été offert par des Républicains de San Francisco le 24 mai 1874', Fonds Lucien Descaves (IISH), 205.

[84] O. Pain, *Henri Rochefort (Paris – Nouméa – Genève)* (Paris: Périnet, 1879), pp.614–615. For the *New York Herald*, see, for example, 'The Rochefort Manifesto', *New York Herald*, 2 June 1874; 'Rochefort's Manifesto', *New York Herald*, 3 June 1874.

addressed him by the Kanak word 'taio' (brother).[85] Louise Michel, as we saw in the previous chapter, complained about the lack of European culture in New Caledonia.[86] In order to compensate for this, she turned to indigenous Kanak culture, and often included traditional Kanak poems and stories in her extensive correspondence with Victor Hugo.[87]

These encounters had a still greater intellectual impact upon many deportees. Henri Rochefort's collaborator Olivier Pain, for example, expressed a kind of solidarity of the vanquished with the Kabyle deportees, describing them as 'pariahs that a merciless hand keeps here in defiance of all legality'.[88] Similarly, Jean Allemane declared of the Kabyles, 'I understood that these ... were, like me, the vanquished, and that they had been treated in the same way'.[89] Deportation, then, prompted a shift in how the deportees located themselves and their political actions in the world. While the deportees displayed little interested in engaging with the concept of empire, they were not insensible to their surroundings, and often interacted with other communities in New Caledonia. The encounters that took place as a direct result of deportation encouraged them to reach across cultural divides and identify similarities and solidarities between themselves and ostensibly very different peoples.

Furthermore, these new transnational revolutionary solidarities were increasingly reflected in their political thought and action. Following their return to Paris, many of the deportees began a campaign for the amnesty of Algerian political prisoners. In August 1880, Pain addressed a 1,500-strong meeting in Paris calling for a general amnesty,[90] and L'Intransigeant quickly took up the case of 'les Arabes', republishing open letters and articles on the Paris meeting from the republican French Algerian

[85] Letter from R. Urbain to E. Urbain, 12 November 1880, Fonds Lucien Descaves (IISH), 1050, p.15.

[86] L. Michel, *Souvenirs et aventures de ma vie* (ed.) D. Armogathe (Paris: La Découverte/Maspero, 1983. First published, 1905–1908), p.62.

[87] Louise Michel Papers (IISH) 21. For more use of Kanak culture by Michel, see Fonds Louise Michel Moscou (IISH) 233, 5–2, p.4; p.10; p.17.

[88] '[D]es parias qu'une main impitoyable détient au mépris de toute légalité'. Olivier Pain quoted in G. Mailhé, *Déportations en Nouvelle-Calédonie des communards et des révoltés de la grande Kabylie (1872–1876)* (Paris: L'Harmattan, 1994), p.403.

[89] 'J'ai appris que les arrivants [the Algerians] étaient, comme moi, des vaincus, et qu'ils étaient traités de la même façon'. J. Allemane, *Mémoires d'un Communard, des barricades au bagne* (Paris: Librairie Socialiste J. Allemane, 1880), p.190. See also 'Rochefort: His Lecture at the Academy of Music', *New York Herald*, 6 June 1874.

[90] Mailhé, *Déportations en Nouvelle-Calédonie*, p.403. See also *La Bataille*, 17 January 1886.

newspaper *L'Echo d'Oran*.[91] The deportees' lack of interest in colonialism or empire, then, was not reflective of xenophobia or unwillingness to work with foreigners or colonial subjects. Although their primary focus remained France and alliances continued to be made and broken largely on the basis of political benefit, similarly to *Le Travailleur*, deportees increasingly situated themselves within a wider, more transnational context.[92]

Crucially, while both the deportees and revolutionaries such as those at *Le Travailleur* involved themselves extensively with international actors and affairs, these engagements were not defined or bounded by the concept of 'empire'. It is of course possible, even likely, that revolutionary thought on empire and transnationalism ultimately often served to reinforce colonial hierarchies and the popularity of imperialism.[93] This, however, was often demonstrably not their objective. By expressing their admiration for other cultures and establishing connections with a wide variety of other nationalities, both *Le Travailleur* and the deportees radically undermined the theoretical basis of imperialism in the Third Republic, which dictated that France had a moral obligation to colonise and develop less civilised populations.

As Greg Dening has observed, '[b]eing different challenges definitions of what being civilised might be.'[94] The deportees' affinities with strangers – in particular colonial strangers – presented a direct theoretical challenge to the imperial system of hierarchies and assimilation. In highlighting these attributes, *Le Travailleur* provided hope to its readers that progress was possible outside the paradigm of contemporary European nation-states, turning the notion of the civilising mission and the 'co-operative emulation' that facilitated imperial expansion on its head.[95] If, as *Le Travailleur*'s examples suggested, European civilisation was not superior to all others, then far from civilising savages, European colonial expansion was retarding world progress

---

[91] 'L'Amnistie pour les Arabes', *L'Intransigeant*, 8 August 1880.
[92] 'Rochefort', *New York Herald*, 30 May 1874, p.3.; Pain, *Henri Rochefort (Paris – Nouméa – Genève)*, p.617.
[93] At times they did so explicitly. See, for example, P. Lafargue, 'La politique de la bourgeoisie', *L'Égalité*, 18 December 1881; 'La femme en Égypte', *Le Citoyen*, 16 August 1882; 'Où commence l'anthropophagie? Où finit-elle?', *Le Prolétariat*, 24 October 1885. Perhaps the clearest examples are to be found in revolutionary discussions of Chinese workers. See, for example, 'La liberté du commerce et le système protectionniste, jugés au pont [sic] de vue ouvrier', in *L'Avant-garde* (Geneva), 2 December 1878; 'Chinoiseries capitalistes', *Le Citoyen*, 4 October 1882; H. Brissac, 'Les chinois aux États-Unis', *Le Citoyen*, 11 April 1882; 'Encore les chinois', *Le Citoyen*, 12 April 1882.
[94] G. Dening, *Readings/Writings* (Melbourne: Melbourne University Press, 1998), p.158.
[95] Todd, 'A French imperial meridian', at p.162.

and the dissemination of worthwhile ideas.[96] To define oneself and ones' actions as transnational was thus to subvert the boundaries set by modern industrial society, whereas to be an imperialist was not.

In this sense, Le Travailleur's interest in international affairs reflected and enhanced their demands for a radical reordering of society. Japanese property ownership and Kabyle democracy provided ideals on which European society could hope to remodel itself. Like the deportees' ability to build a community in New Caledonia, Le Travailleur's unusual opposition to imperialism reinforced the vision of a decentralised society proposed by many of the Swiss exiles as an antidote to industrial modernity and centralised political power. Whereas La Bataille remained tied to national political questions, Le Travailleur's transnational solidarity and the radical possibilities it engendered enabled them not just to bypass contemporary political debates, but also to make a virtue of this marginality. Suggesting precisely this in one of the final issues of Le Travailleur, Reclus asked:

> And we socialist combatants, what are we in the face of these great States, these enormous machines of war and destruction? Puny insects, crushing ourselves beneath the wheels of the wagon as we try to stop it! How the great victors must despise us, and laugh from time to time at our efforts! We know, though, that they are not always calm. What's more, one has already been pushed to cries of terror. This is because all of their force can have no other possible result than suppression and destruction ... *All free thought, all true sentiment, all spontaneous effort are enemies of the State.*[97]

At the same time, this approach also contributed to Reclus's attempts to render revolution more universally accessible, as discussed in Chapter 4. By highlighting political and social systems currently in operation in other parts of the world as potential political models for a viable alternative society, revolutionaries directly contradicted the belief that all societies

---

[96] See also H. Brissac, 'N'oublions pas le but', *Le Citoyen*, 7 October 1881; 'L'Internationale bourgeoise et l'internationale ouvrière', *Le Citoyen*, 13 March 1882; M. Talmeyr, 'Pour les Khroumirs', *L'Intransigeant*, 8 May 1881; *Le Prolétaire*, 14 May 1881; 'La moralité bourgeoise et le commerce d'opium', *L'Égalité*, 16 June 1880; C. Bouis, 'Marchands d'hommes', *L'Égalité*, 6 November 1882; P. Lafargue, 'Le Congo', *L'Égalité*, 25 November 1882; J. Allemane, 'Ce qui se passe', *Le Prolétariat*, 30 August 1884.

[97] 'Et nous socialistes lutteurs, que sommes-nous en face de ces grands Etats, de ces énormes machines de guerre et de destruction? Pauvres insectes qui nous pressons sous la roue du char, comme pour en arrêter la marche en nous faisant écraser! Que les hauts triomphateurs doivent nous mépriser parfois et se rire de nos efforts! Et pourtant, nous le savons, ils ne sont pas toujours rassurés et plus d'un a déjà poussé des cris d'effroi. C'est que toute leur force n'a d'autre résultat possible que de supprimer et de détruire ... Toute pensée libre, tout sentiment vrai, tout effort spontané sont autant d'ennemis de l'Etat.' 'Bulletin', *Le Travailleur* 2:2 (February–March 1878), p.6. Emphasis mine.

must pass through a unilinear model of historical development (whether in the form of French revolutionary history, the civilising mission, or historical materialism). Rather, the revolution should take the form of a 'hydra of socialism', manifesting itself in different guises according to circumstance, and its work could therefore be begun everywhere immediately.[98] A transnational approach thus empowered small, marginal groups (such as revolutionaries during this period), enabling them to challenge the bases of government and society whilst not logically compromising other aspects of their thought.

*****

In *Readings/Writings*, Greg Dening observed of the twentieth-century academic:

> We make ourselves open to discoveries that are global as well as regional. Our ears become open to many conversations around the world. We have had our imaginations empowered by what Frantz Fanon wrote in *The Wretched of the Earth*, or EP Thompson in *The Making of the English Working Class*, or Oscar Lewis in *The Children of Sanchez*. We have had our imaginations empowered by Subaltern Studies, by Gender Studies, by Edward Said's *Orientalism*. We know that when we hear these voices, we don't clone them. We don't impose their understandings on our own like some template. No, we use them to enlarge our way of seeing. It is not our point to be faithful to them. We are in conversation with them. That makes our history global, if not in topic, then in discourse.[99]

Historians of political thought have traditionally been reticent to incorporate the non-West into their work, positioning Western actors and concerns at the centre of intellectual history, although recent work has begun to change this.[100] Yet while they may not have had access to Fanon, Thompson, or Said, historical actors in the nineteenth century operated in global contexts in much the same ways as their twentieth-century successors.

---

[98] '[L]'hydre du socialisme'. 'L'Internationale et les Chinois', *Le Travailleur* 2:3 (March–April 1878), p.30.
[99] Dening, *Readings/Writings*, p.216.
[100] For a discussion of this, see C. Goto-Jones, 'Comparative Political Thought: Beyond the Non-Western', in D. Bell (ed.), *Ethics and World Politics* (Oxford: Oxford University Press, 2010), 219–236. Recent work has begun to change this. See, for example, U. Mehta, *Liberalism and Empire: A Study in Nineteenth-Century British Liberal Thought* (Chicago, IL: University of Chicago Press, 1999); Pitts, *A Turn to Empire*; Mantena, *Alibis of Empire*; E. Rothschild, *The Inner Life of Empires: An Eighteenth-Century History* (Princeton, NJ: Princeton University Press, 2011); Muthu (ed.), *Empire and Modern Political Thought*; C.A. Bayly, *Recovering Liberties: Indian Thought in the Age of Liberalism and Empire* (Cambridge: Cambridge University Press, 2012).

European imperial exploits and technological advances ensured not only that people traversed the globe on a scale never seen before, but also that those who did not were increasingly connected to the world outside of their own country, whether through the press, the telegraph, or universal exhibitions.

Imperial and international concerns featured prominently in the thought of French revolutionaries at the beginning of the Third Republic. Although scholars have previously approached these themes almost exclusively through the writings of Communards deported to New Caledonia, they featured as much, if not more, in the thought of revolutionaries who remained in Europe. Whereas deportees overwhelmingly used their experiences in New Caledonia to comment on the state of the French republic and to reintegrate themselves into metropolitan political life, revolutionaries such as those at *La Bataille* and *Le Travailleur* offered more clearly elaborated ideas on empire and internationalism.

The divergent focus of these theories had radically different implications for revolutionary socialists' wider bodies of thought. Whereas *La Bataille*'s adoption of a conventionally republican imperialism highlighted the limits of their universalist discourse, *Le Travailleur*'s advocation of transnational affinities rather than imperial expansion logically cohered with and reinforced their ideas on social organisation and international solidarity, indicating that they were committed to finding a solution beneficial to workers not only in Europe but the world over. Situating revolutionary thought (indeed all thought) within these contexts is thus crucial to reaching a proper understanding of it in all its complexities. First, because revolutionaries saw themselves as operating within contexts considerably broader than the borders of the West, but second – and more importantly – because their interactions with the wider world served to highlight the limits and possibilities of ideas such as solidarity and fraternity that were central to revolutionaries' self-image: ideas that, from within a purely Western context, appeared universal.

It is possible to locate revolutionaries during this period within wider traditions of thought on empire. *La Bataille*, with its concern for the French state and its eagerness to bring what it perceived to be French values to the rest of the world, could be easily situated with the tradition of nineteenth-century liberal imperialist thought identified by the likes of Uday Mehta and Jennifer Pitts.[101] Indeed, all three groups drew upon well-established debates and ideas on empire. In particular, they drew

---

[101] Mehta, *Liberalism and Empire*; Pitts, *A Turn to Empire*; Mantena, *Alibis of Empire*.

upon languages elaborated in the 1840s – whether ambivalence about free trade, condemnation of colonial militarism, or regard for Kabyle society. As with their thought on revolutionary action, revolutionary ideas on empire and internationalism thus also illustrate a broader point about both the history of socialist thought and French political history. Namely, that there existed much greater continuity until the 1880s than has previously been assumed.

At the same time, *Le Travailleur* and to an extent the deportees could also be seen as an early example of yet another tradition, which the postcolonial scholar Leela Gandhi has termed the 'politics of friendship'. In her 2006 *Affective Communities*, Gandhi explored how select 'marginalised' Europeans around the turn of the century abnegated the privileges accorded to them by their nationality in favour of a radical solidarity with colonised subjects. In doing so, she argued, they opened up a space for anticolonialism in metropolitan intellectual and political life.[102] Anticolonialism in France during this period gained its most visible patron in July 1885 when Clemenceau attacked Ferry and the colonial lobby for seeking to proclaim 'the primacy of might over right'.[103] As this chapter has demonstrated, however, anticolonial ideas were present much earlier in French discourse, and were more deeply linked to older ideas, than has previously been thought. There was no grace period, in other words, in which anticolonial ideas were not present in French thought.

Yet we must also be careful with such associations. Whilst revolutionaries engaged extensively with the imperial experience, whether through deportation or through coverage of international issues, the concept of 'imperialism' itself remained vague in their thought. Certainly, as Stoler has suggested, the idea that historical actors either did not think about colonies or should have opposed them is a false antithesis.[104] In fact, the last two chapters cast doubt upon the supposed European 'certainty' regarding empire in the period of high imperialism.

---

[102] L. Gandhi, *Affective Communities: Anticolonial Thought, Fin-de-Siècle Radicalism, and the Politics of Friendship* (Durham, NC: Duke University Press, 2006).

[103] '[L]a proclamation de la primauté de la force sur le droit'. G. Clemenceau, 'Discours à la Chambre des deputes, 31 juillet 1885', at www.assemblee-nationale.fr/histoire/7ec.asp [last accessed, 27 August 2017].

[104] A.L. Stoler, *Along the Archival Grain: Epistemic Anxieties and Colonial Common Sense* (Princeton, NJ: Princeton University Press, 2009), pp.248–249. See also A.L. Stoler and F. Cooper, 'Between Metropole and Colony: Rethinking a Research Agenda', in F. Cooper and A.L. Stoler (eds.), *Tensions of Empire: Colonial Cultures in a Bourgeois World* (Berkeley: University of California Press, 1997), 1–56, at p.36.

None of the revolutionaries examined here had a clearly defined or delineated theory of empire. For the deportees, colonial examples provided a way to reflect on the republic, *La Bataille* remained primarily concerned with the fate of the French worker, and even in *Le Travailleur*, imperialism was subsumed by the larger issue of transnational solidarity – which was not necessarily anticolonial. Indeed, this tendency can be glimpsed in many socialist movements well into the twentieth century. Perhaps most notably it is seen in Leninism, in which colonialism was approached exclusively through the concept of economic imperialism, in other words as a form of monopoly. For revolutionaries, 'empire' was not a discrete category of thought. While empire was ever-present in their thought, it was rarely the sole object of it. Rather, it was inseparable from other concerns, both domestic and global.

The study of empire and internationalism, then, is both more and less than it has often been depicted as. Empire was at once intertwined with and absent from revolutionary ideas during the 1870s and early 1880s. Awareness of the ways in which Europeans in this period approached and interacted with the wider world is surely essential for understanding both the historical development and the limits and possibilities of such thought. This has long been realised by historians working on the non-Western world.[105]

At the same time, however, the very ambiguity and imbrication of ideas on empire highlights limitations to the utility of 'empire' and 'the colonial' as categories of analysis, and of their ability to capture the complexities of international and transnational thought. In the case of French revolutionaries in the early Third Republic, attempts to locate imperialism as either a central or a peripheral concern fail to elaborate the breadth of their engagement with questions concerning the wider world. International and transnational thought during this period transcended imperial frameworks. Though imperialism pervaded every area of revolutionary socialist thought, it cannot be isolated from broader concerns as they attempted to locate the limits of their struggle within local, national, and global contexts.

---

[105] See, for example, D. Chakrabarty, *Provincializing Europe: Postcolonial Thought and Historical Difference* (Princeton, NJ: Princeton University Press, 2000).

Conclusion

In late September 1873, an agent by the name of Laurentin filed a report to the Parisian Préfecture de Police. Based on his observance and infiltration of revolutionary circles, he provided a wide-ranging account of the movement, activities, and state of mind of the French exiles who had evaded arrest and settled in Britain following the fall of the Commune. The police, he concluded, had little cause for concern:

> time and exile have already done their work ... conflicts of interest, the dispersion of individuals, and the need to secure daily bread have all contributed to the break up of the group. All that remains are a few isolated individuals and extremely small groups, who are consumed by gossip and theories.[1]

This observation is characteristic of attitudes towards the French revolutionary movement since the fall of the Commune in May 1871. Historians and political actors alike have overwhelmingly depicted the Commune as a definitive turning point in modern history that ripped apart decades-old political alliances, gave birth to modern socialism, and finally brought the French Revolution to a close.

Its participants and their ideas, meanwhile, have been relegated to the side lines. Those fortunate enough to escape immediate death or arrest during the Semaine Sanglante found themselves depleted, defeated, and scattered to the corners of the globe. Their thought is assumed to have

---

[1] '[L]e temps et l'exil ont déjà fait leur œuvre ... l'opposition des intérêts, la dispersion des individus, la nécessité de pourvoir au pain quotidien, tout cela a concouru à rompre le faisceau; il ne reste guère que des individualités isolées ou de très-petits groupes, qui épuisent leur conversations dans des commèrages ou dans des théories.' Intelligence report to the Préfecture de Police, 24 September 1873 (Paris). Archives de la Préfecture de Police (APP) Ba428/1184. See also Intelligence report to the Préfecture de Police, 25 July 1873 (Geneva). APP Ba431/743; Intelligence report to the Préfecture de Police. 3 August 1877 (London). APP Ba429/2363; General report to the Préfecture de Police. 13 October 1877 (London). APP Ba429/2466; Intelligence report to the Préfecture de Police, 4 October 1878 (Paris). APP Ba430/3133.

followed a similar trajectory. Revolutionaries hoping to remain politically relevant, historians have suggested, abandoned their previous ideas wholesale and gravitated towards a series of powerful prefabricated orthodoxies such as Marxian international socialism or more moderate French republicanism in the form of the radicals or the Opportunists. Yet even these revolutionaries, historians claim, enjoyed little success. Intellectually, they were derivative and often actively incapable, misinterpreting the ideas of more sophisticated theorists such as Marx and Blanqui, while politically they were consumed by damaging factional infighting that alienated both current and potential supporters. These were years of stagnation and disarray, suspended between and dominated by the events of 1870–1871 and 1889.

As this book has demonstrated, this was not the case. The Paris Commune – extraordinary as it was – did not represent a rupture, and the French revolutionary movement did not collapse in the wake of its defeat. Rather than being overwhelmed by the new situations that they found themselves in, revolutionaries accepted and even embraced them. Whether exile and poverty in Europe and North America or imprisonment and deportation to New Caledonia, revolutionaries attempted to turn their circumstances to their advantage, establishing new relationships and unexpected alliances with a variety of international revolutionaries and radicals. In making these new connections, revolutionaries did not abandon their old ideas or submit to new orthodoxies as has been assumed. Rather, through a creative use of new ideas and the intensive redefinition of familiar concepts, they aimed to reconstruct a French revolutionary movement that was at once unified, autonomous, and politically viable. It was intellectual flexibility rather than orthodoxy or tradition that ensured the continued relevance of French revolutionaries and revolution in the years that immediately followed the fall of the Commune.

These ideas and this approach to revolutionary thought were reflective of the time in which they were expressed, and must remain situated within this context. By the late 1880s the flexible, collaborative approach that characterised revolutionary ideas and associations in the immediate post-Commune years had all but disappeared. This was the result not of a single large event, but of a constellation of more minor occurrences in the mid-1880s. Following Marx's death in 1883, Engels's promotion of a more systematic, doctrinaire Marxism encouraged French socialists to approach Marx's ideas as an orthodoxy to be owned or disowned rather than a language to be adopted and adapted. Events such as Olivier Pain's death (possibly at the hands of British agents) in Sudan in 1885 led many revolutionaries to adopt a more bellicose, nationalistic approach towards the wider world and international relations, while the poor showing of both Opportunist republican and revolutionary candidates in the 1885 legislative elections sent many in the direction of more populist (and often prejudiced) philosophies.

Events such as the Boulanger and Dreyfus Affairs and the establishment of the Second International undoubtedly encouraged revolutionaries to further solidify their shifting intellectual positions. Paul Lafargue, for example, played a central role in founding the Paris Congress of the Second International in 1889 and continued his campaign against what came to be known as 'reformist socialism'.[2] Others such as Henri Rochefort and Gustave Paul Cluseret, meanwhile, shifted towards what Zeev Sternhell has called the 'revolutionary right', increasingly espousing nationalist and anti-Semitic ideas, and throwing their weight behind the campaign against Dreyfus in the 1890s.[3] The shifts towards these sorts of positions, however, had arguably been put in motion several years beforehand by the events in the mid-1880s described above.

The fact that many of the ideas of this period were quickly replaced does not, however, mean that they were entirely unsuccessful or that these years were historically unimportant. Indeed, far from it. It was in the 1870s and early 1880s, of course, that many of the most influential actors in *fin-de-siècle* French leftist circles such as Paul Lafargue, Benoît Malon, and Jean Allemane did their political apprenticeship. Additionally, and more importantly, as suggested by Marx's commitment to properly engaging with French socialists, the abundant police reports cataloguing their every move, and the Opportunists' efforts to marginalise them, these revolutionaries were also taken seriously in the post-Commune period itself. In terms of French revolutionary thought these years were more than simply a stepping-stone or a holding period. Both nationally and internationally, revolutionaries continued to operate at the centre of political events, and in order to understand this period, we must have a proper understanding of their thought. Indeed, the fact that this flexible intellectual approach faded should also be seen a sign of its success: a sign that by 1885 activists had managed to re-establish an acceptable position for themselves in both French public life and international revolutionary circles.

---

[2] For more on reformist socialism, see E. Jousse, *Les hommes révoltés: les origines intellectuelles du réformisme en France (1871–1917)* (Paris: Fayard, 2017).

[3] Z. Sternhell, *La droite révolutionnaire 1885–1914: les origines françaises du fascisme* (Paris: Éditions du Seuil, 1978).

Although its defeat curtailed many of their activities in France, the Commune's surviving participants and its supporters were not disillusioned or crushed by the events of 1871. The majority were not surprised that the Commune was defeated, and as such they did not consider its defeat a significant blow to their ideas. Far from attempting to forget about the Commune, revolutionaries embraced it, publishing abundant memoirs and commemorative pieces that interpreted 1871 in a variety of ways. In terms of French politics, revolutionaries' constant references to the events of 1871 put both Moral Order and many republican politicians in an uncomfortable position, and acted as an attempt to discredit the widespread portrayal of both the Communards and revolution as forces external to modern civilisation. Revolutionaries' emphasis upon the importance of eyewitness testimony, meanwhile, acted as a direct challenge to Marx's attempts to coopt the Commune. Improbably, revolutionaries managed to transform their defeat into an opportunity, simultaneously using its memory to navigate the new circumstances in which they found themselves and to establish a foundation upon which to rebuild the idea of a unified French revolutionary movement.

Activists' attempts to reestablish the legitimacy of such an idea, however, were built upon more than simply the memory of revolutions past. Using a variety of different languages and temporalities, activists from across the revolutionary movement attempted to separate the concept of revolution from the history of the French Revolution and redefine it in broad, expansive terms. In an effort to guarantee their continued relevance, they created a more complex French historical genealogy for their politics and sought (unsuccessfully) to expand national support for revolution by recasting it in religious terms. Finally, using Reclus's definition of evolution, they returned to older definitions of revolution as an unstoppable force of nature in an effort to create a unified revolutionary identity prepared for the practice of everyday life and politics.

While in practice, the revolutionary movement may have remained a small, largely urban phenomenon, these ideas demonstrate that revolutionaries during this period did not simply fade into anachronism. They were not content to sit upon their laurels, and they did not jealously guard the epithet of 'revolutionary'. Rather, they continued to conceive of revolution as an active and viable political concept, and went to great measures to ensure that it remained so in the changed political, social, and cultural circumstances of early Third Republic France.

Neither, despite the clear presence of factions bearing names such as 'Marxist', were revolutionaries irreparably divided along ideological lines.

French activists did not simply adopt a pet theorist – whether Marx, Bakunin, or Proudhon – and draw exclusively and relentlessly upon their ideas. Rather, socialists across the revolutionary movement in this period utilised a broad array of theorists and ideas in order to create effective solutions to the pressing social problems they considered contemporary France to be facing. Neither Marx nor his thought, for example, was or was even considered to be the exclusive intellectual property of French Marxists such as Guesde and Lafargue.

This was not, however, a case of simple importation. In using and promoting their connections to Marx, French socialists did not introduce a complete and universally applicable 'Marxist doctrine' into France. French revolutionary ideas were always constructed in collaboration with other thinkers, and they were always reacting to more than just French events. As the French translation and subsequent abridgement of the first volume of *Das Kapital* suggest, Marx himself went to considerable efforts to create a specific 'French Marx' and adjust his ideas and language to what he thought a French audience might like to hear. French revolutionaries were thus not divided along hard ideological lines, for no intellectual orthodoxies existed.

Despite their heavy attention to national politics and organisations such as the International Workingmen's Association, French revolutionaries and their ideas demonstrably did not remain confined to Europe and the West. This period was marked by the highly publicised deportation of 4,500 ex-Communards to New Caledonia as well as the rise of a new kind of imperialism, and the effects of both were visible in revolutionary thought. In fact, imperial, colonial, and international concerns assumed a position of great importance in their thought during the 1870s and early 1880s, becoming one of the principal channels through which revolutionaries criticised both the French state and, towards the end of the period, the Opportunist government.

The success of these efforts was mixed. Reclus's and the deportees' uses of empire and internationalism were largely consistent with their wider bodies of thought, and it thus served to expand the reach and legitimacy of their declarations in favour of central revolutionary concepts such as solidarity and universal equality. Their opposition to imperialism both reflected and enhanced their broader opposition to the modern state system. For the likes of Lissagaray and *La Bataille*, on the other hand, the preoccupation with imperialism and the European worker exposed limits to their supposedly universal thought that had not been visible in purely French, European, and Western contexts.

This study, however, reveals more than simply the internal mechanics of French revolutionary thought. Through the elaboration and exploration of their flexible intellectual approach, it becomes clear that the 1870s and early 1880s were in fact a creative period for left politics more generally. As our explorations of revolution and Marxism made clear, intellectual flexibility was not restricted to revolutionaries in the early stages of their careers. In the last years of their lives, both Blanqui and Marx continued to seek out new ideas and new ways to adapt their own thought in the wake of the Commune.

Neither was it only the French revolutionary movement that thought in this way. Rather, Marx's flexible approach towards the translation of his work and socialists' use of his ideas as an international language suggest that the structure of the international socialist movement as a whole was more collaborative and less clearly defined than has previously been thought. Historians must in turn broaden their own approach to these questions. In order to fully understand why ideas such as Marxism spread, we must supplement the social and organisational histories of international socialism with attentive studies of its ideas, its texts, and their dissemination.

If the story of French revolutionaries within the international socialist movement was one of flexibility and collaboration, the same could also be said of French politics. The period after the fall of the Commune has often been seen as one in which defeated revolutionaries either integrated into more mainstream republican parties or separated themselves entirely from the Republic.[4] This, however, was not the case. As we have seen, under the Second Empire radicals, republicans, and revolutionaries often worked closely together, and although the Commune certainly had an impact upon these ties, they did not dissolve completely in 1871.[5] Many

---

[4] B.H. Moss, *The Origins of the French Labor Movement 1830–1914: The Socialism of Skilled Workers* (Berkeley: University of California Press, 1976), p.70; D. Stafford, *From Anarchism to Reformism: A Study of the Political Activities of Paul Brousse within the First International and the French Socialist Movement 1870–1890* (London: Cox & Wyman, 1971), p.251; M.P. Johnson, *The Paradise of Association: Political Culture and Popular Organisations in the Paris Commune of 1871* (Ann Arbor: University of Michigan Press, 1996), p.284; A. Dowdall, 'Narrating *la Semaine Sanglante*, 1871–1880' (unpublished MPhil dissertation, University of Cambridge, 2010), p.64. Hutton and Vincent similarly suggest that revolutionaries only began to take the Republic and French politics seriously again in the late 1880. See P.H. Hutton, 'The Role of the Blanquist Party in Left-Wing Politics in France, 1879–1890', *Journal of Modern History* 46 (June 1974), 277–295, at p.278; K.S. Vincent, *Between Marxism and Anarchism: Benoît Malon and French Reformist Socialism* (Berkeley: University of California Press, 1992), p.136.

[5] P. Nord, *The Republican Moment: Struggles for Democracy in Nineteenth-Century France* (Cambridge, MA: Harvard University Press, 1995), p.247. For a delineation of the more complicated political

revolutionaries including Arnould and Michel retained close ties with radicals such as Clemenceau.[6] Michel furthermore corresponded prolifically with Victor Hugo who also, along with Edmond and Juliette Adam, financed Rochefort's sensational escape from New Caledonia in 1874.[7]

These physical connections were reflected in their ideas. Revolutionaries, as has been demonstrated throughout this book, did not simply abandon their old ideas with the fall of the Commune. In theory, if not in practice, this meant that revolutionaries often continued to advocate for many of the same ideals and policies (for instance, secular education and republican government) as the radicals and the Opportunists. Although revolutionaries may have been excluded from the Republic for much of this this period, they were not entirely cut off from it, either physically or intellectually. In fact, while they certainly mistrusted French republican politicians and made this abundantly clear, on many issues they did not disagree with them. This period, then, was a more complicated story than one of increasingly confident and secure moderate republicanism, however complex that was. Revolutionary politics and positions did not disappear in 1871 and reappear only in the late 1880s and early 1890s. Rather, both revolution and revolutionaries continued to occupy a role in French public life through the 1870s and 1880s as well.

The position of the revolutionary movement was thus closer to other parts of the republican community than has previously been assumed. Despite their desire to preserve both their historical identity and a place for revolutionary opposition in French public and political life, activists during this period did not wish to bring down the Third Republic or even to offer a theoretical alternative to it. The advent of a real republic based on universal suffrage, secular education, and the marginalisation of the power of the Church without a domineering executive was a real achievement, and revolutionaries recognised it as such.

Their frequent criticisms of the Opportunists derived not from total opposition, but from revolutionaries' belief that they often failed to live up to their promises and ideals. Revolutionaries, in other words, were not

---

landscape during the Commune itself, see R.P. Tombs, *Paris, bivouac des révolutions: la Commune de 1871* (trans.) J. Chatroussat (Paris: Éditions Libertalia, 2014. First published in English, 1999), p.296.

[6] Intelligence report to the Préfecture de Police, 5 December 1879 (Geneva). APP Ba430/3263-64. Exiles also associated with more mainstream British radicals in London. See, for example, 'Les réfugiés à Londres' (1876). APP Ba429/1354.

[7] For Michel's correspondence with Hugo, see L. Michel, *Je vous écris de ma nuit: correspondance générale – 1850–1904* (Paris: Les Éditions de Paris, 1999).

angry with more mainstream republicans, but merely disappointed, and likewise they did not want to distance themselves from the Republic; they wanted to be a part of it.[8] Indeed, as we have seen, major theoretical disagreements, such as the one over deportation, arose only when revolutionaries felt that they were being excluded. Revolutionaries to a large extent saw themselves as a pressure group operating from within the theoretical boundaries of the Third Republic, rather than a direct practical or intellectual alternative to it.

In an effort to recover the Communards from the shadow of the modern revolutionary tradition and reconstitute them as historical actors with agency and ideas, this study has focused primarily on the years that immediately followed the Commune's fall. It has demonstrated that the production and dissemination of French revolutionary thought during this period was a complex process in which grandees such as Marx and Blanqui collaborated equally with anonymous pamphleteers, experimenting with new ideas and approaches, and attempted (with varied success) to alter their arguments to fit a variety of circumstances, rather than imposing or insisting upon intellectual orthodoxies. The French revolutionaries that supposedly solidified the revolutionary tradition, in other words, were not interested in tradition.

This study's findings thus also have broader implications for our understanding of the revolutionary tradition itself. As we have seen, revolutionaries in the post-Commune period were far from the first to have adopted this approach. Rather, from 1789 to the mid-1880s, successive generations of activists had sought to reinvent continuities with their predecessors, drawing upon new ideas to invest familiar terms such as equality and solidarity with fresh meanings more appropriate to their circumstances. This suggests that there was no fixed 'revolutionary tradition' in France during the nineteenth century: rather, there was a process of perpetual intellectual adaptation. It also highlights potentially fruitful avenues for further study regarding the nature of its other supposed adherents' commitment to it, and indeed whether it is productive to term it a 'political tradition' at all.

Several years after the spy Laurentin filed his report on the dissolution of the London exiles, another missive to the Préfecture noted that Prosper-Olivier Lissagaray had recently addressed a similar subject. Lissagaray noted the intellectual differences within the revolutionary movement,

---

[8] See, for example, M. Talmeyr, 'L'extrême gauche', *L'Intransigeant* (Paris), 4 November 1881.

but considered an open, experimental approach to ideas to be a benefit, rather than a disadvantage:

> we do not represent a particular school or theory. We hope for the development of all theories and all schools, for we are convinced that it is from diverse investigations [différentes recherches] that everyone may discern the most rational principles for attaining . . . Human Equality.[9]

The 1870s and 1880s were not years of introversion, stagnation, or defeatism in French revolutionary thinking, but of creativity and flexibility. This intellectual flexibility, moreover, was not a weakness, but revolutionaries' great strength. The period that immediately followed the defeat of France's last nineteenth-century revolution was one of deparochialisation in which revolutionaries' vision (if not always their reach) expanded increasingly outwards. This took in the French countryside, European revolutionary organisations, and far-flung parts of the world in search of new ideas with which to reformulate their historical identity and reconstitute a French revolutionary movement that was at once able to accept its past, function in the present, and prepare for the future.

---

[9] 'Groupés au hasard, nous ne représentons pas une école, une théorie particulière. Nous désirons le développement de toutes les théories, de toutes les écoles, persuadés que, dans les différentes recherches, chacun pourra discerner les principes les plus rationnels pour atteindre le but tracé à la Société: l'Egalité humaine.' 'Aux socialistes!', April 1877 (London). APP Ba429/2203. See also B. Malon, *Le nouveau parti*, 2 vols., 4th edn (Paris: Derveaux, 1882), vol.2, p.79; P. Lafargue, 'Le but du Parti ouvrier', *L'Égalité* (Paris), 18 June 1882.

Bibliography

ARCHIVAL MATERIAL
Archives de la Préfecture de Police, Paris

BA199
BA365–5
BA366–2
BA370
BA426–433
BA439
BA464
BA891
BA1516
DA168
DA185
DA186
DA249
DA250
DA295
DB421

International Institute of Social History, Amsterdam

César de Paepe Papers. 38; 137; 174; 181; 257; 302; 402; 403.
Constantin Pecqueur Papers. 190; 192194; 196–198; 200; 201; 204–206.
Fédération Jurassienne Archives. 7; 8; 45; 47; 48; 53; 54; 56–58; 63; 65; 68; 75;
    79; 115; 117; 119; 124; 148–153; 155; 156.
G. Brocher Papers. 2; 14; 20; 47; 92; 94; 97; 104; 109; 115; 125; 126; 128; 140;
    165–169; 173; 174; 176; 186.
Louis Auguste Blanqui Papers (Fonds Moscou).
Louise Michel Papers (Fonds Moscou).
Lucien Descaves Archives. 16; 29c; 50; 82; 89; 131b; 135; 138; 139; 144d; 166b;
    167; 169b; 189a; 205; 238; 239c; 260a; 262; 276; 277; 290b; 291; 413;
    426; 464; 465a; 611; 669; 670; 689; 690; 695–697; 700; 701; 704; 710;
    711; 728; 780; 783–785; 789; 796; 804; 812–815; 866; 867; 972; 984;

1035; 1042; 1046; 1050; 1051; 1084; 1086–1088; 1209; 1235–1238; 1242; 1244; 1569.
Lucien Descaves Archives – Louise Michel Section. 13; 21; 26; 32; 35; 43; 45; 48; 49; 160; 194; 337; 359; 469; 543; 569; 897; 899; 900; 906; 907; 918–924; 926–934; 936–944; 953; 958–962; 987; 1007; 1010; 1042; 1050–1054.
Paul Lafargue Papers (Fonds Moscou).

PRINTED PRIMARY SOURCES
Ephemeral Newspapers, 1870–1871

L'Affranchi (Paris), April 1871.
L'Ami du peuple (Paris), April 1871.
L'Avant-garde (Paris), March–May 1871.
Le Bonnet rouge (Paris), April 1871
Bulletin communal: organe des clubs (Paris), May 1871.
La Caricature politique (Paris), February–March 1871.
Le Châtiment (Paris), March–April 1871.
Le Combat (Paris), September 1870–January 1871.
La Commune (Paris), March–May 1871.
Le Cri du peuple (Paris), February–May 1871.
Diogène (Paris), March 1871.
La Discussion (Paris), May 1871.
Le Drapeau (Paris), March 1871.
L'Électeur libre (Paris), September–December 1870.
L'Estafette (Paris), April–May 1871.
Le fils du Père Duchêne illustré (Paris), April–May 1871.
La Flèche (Paris), April 1871.
La grande colère du Père Duchêne (Paris), March–May 1871.
L'Illustration (Paris), March 1871–March 1872.
Journal officiel de la Commune (Paris), March–May 1871.
Le Journal populaire (Paris), May 1871.
La Marseillaise (Paris), December 1869–July 1870; September 1870.
La Montagne (Paris), April 1871.
Le Mot d'ordre (Paris), February–May 1871.
La Nation souveraine (Paris), April–May 1871.
L'Ouvrier de l'avenir (Paris), March 1871.
Le Parisien (Ile des Pins), September 1878.
Paris-journal (Paris), May 1871.
Paris libre (Paris), April-May 1871.
La Patrie en danger (Paris), September–December 1870; March 1871.
Le Père Fouettard (Paris), 1871.
La Puce en colère 1–4 (Paris), 1871.
Le Républicain (Paris), May 1871.
Le Réveil du peuple (Paris), April–May 1871.
La Révolution (Paris), April 1871.

La Révolution politique et sociale (Paris), May 1871.
Le Salut public (Paris), May 1871.
Le Tricolore (Paris), May–June 1871.
Le Vengeur (Paris), February-May 1871.
Le Vrai Père Duchêne (Paris), March 1871.

Later Newspapers

L'Avant-garde (La Chaux-de-Fonds), 12 August–2 December 1878.
La Bataille (Paris), May-October 1882; May 1883–January 1886.
Bulletin de la Fédération jurassienne de l'Association internationale des travailleurs (Sonvillier), July 1872–December 1876.
La Chronique illustrée (Paris), September 1872; March 1873–September 1875.
Le Citoyen (Paris), October 1881–October 1882; May 1883–March 1884.
Le Citoyen & la Bataille (Paris), October 1882–May 1883.
Commonweal (London), April 1885–April 1886.
Le Cri du peuple (Paris), March–May 1885.
Le Diable rouge (Paris), October–November 1879.
Les Droits de l'homme (Paris), March 1876; May 1876; August–September 1876; November 1876; January 1877; March 1878.
L'Égalité (Paris), November 1877–July 1878; January–August 1880; December 1881–November 1882; October–December 1882; February 1883.
L'Émancipation (Lyon), October–November 1880.
La Fédération (London), August–September 1872; March 1875.
L'Intransigeant (Paris), July 1880–December 1885.
La Lanterne par Henri Rochefort (Geneva), January–April 1875.
Le Livre rouge (Saint-Germain), October–December 1877.
La Lutte (Lyons), April–July 1883.
La Lutte sociale (Lyons), September–October 1886.
Le Monde illustré (Paris), March–June 1871.
New York Herald (New York), January–June 1874.
Ni dieu, ni maître (Paris), November 1880.
Paris-Journal (Paris), March 1874.
Le Père Duchêne (Sèvres), 2 June–4 August 1878.
Le Père Duchêne: journal des honnêtes gens (Paris), June–July 1876.
Le Père Duchêne: journal quotidien, August–September 1885.
Le Père Duchêne illustré (Paris), December 1878–January 1879.
Le Prolétaire (Paris), December 1878–March 1884; April 1885.
Le Prolétariat (Paris), April 1884–December 1885.
Qui Vive! (London), October–November 1871.
La Révolution sociale: organe de la Fédération jurassienne (Geneva), October 1871–January 1872.
La Révolution sociale (Saint-Cloud), September–October 1880.
La revue socialiste, January-September 1880 (Saint-Cloud); January 1885–December 1886 (Paris).

San Francisco Chronicle (San Francisco), January–June 1874.
Le Temps (Paris), March–June 1871.
La Tenaille (Paris), August 1882–January 1883.
Le Travailleur (Geneva), May 1877–May 1878.

Other

Allemane, J., *Mémoires d'un Communard, des barricades au bagne*, Paris: Librairie Socialiste J. Allemane, 1880.

L'Almanach du Peuple, 5 vols., Saint-Imier and Le Locle: Propagande Socialiste, 1871–1875.

Andrieu, J., 'The Paris Commune: a chapter towards its theory and history', *The Fortnightly Review* X, October 1871, 571–598.

Notes pour servir à l'histoire de la Commune de Paris en 1871, Paris: Payot, 1971.

Anon., *Les déportés civils de Gomen. Nouvelle-Calédonie*, Paris: Imprimerie Nouvelle Association Ouvrière, 1871.

Arnould, A., *L'État et la Révolution*, Lyons: Éditions Jacques-Marie Laffont et Associés, 1981. First published, 1877.

Histoire populaire et parlementaire de la Commune de Paris, 3 vols., Brussels: Imprimerie A. Lefevre, 1878.

Bakunin, M., *Lettres à un français sur la crise actuelle*, publisher unknown, 1870.

Statism and Anarchy, trans. and ed. M. Shatz, Cambridge: Cambridge University Press, 1990. First published in Russian, 1873.

The Paris Commune and the Idea of the State, London: Centre International de Recherches dur l'Anarchisme, 1971. First published in German, 1878.

Marxism, Freedom and the State, trans. and ed. K.J. Kennafick, London: Freedom Press, 1950.

Ballière, E.-A., *La déportation de 1871: souvenirs d'un évadé de Nouméa*, Paris: G. Charpentier, 1889.

Barni, J., *Ce que droit être la République*, 3rd edn, Amiens: Imprimerie Alfred Caron fils, 1872.

Barron, L., 'La déportation et les déportés, 1871–1880', *La philosophie positive*, July–August 1880, 41–66.

Bergeret, J., *Le 18 mars: journal hébdomadaire*, London and Brussels, 1871.

Beslay, C., *1830-1848-1870: Mes souvenirs*, Neuchâtel: Imprimerie James Attinger, 1873.

Blanc, L., *Organisation du travail*, 5th edn, Paris: Au bureau de la Société de l'industrie fraternelle, 1847. First published, 1839.

Histoire de la Révolution française, 12 vols., Paris: Langlois et Leclerc, 1847–1862.

L'État et la Commune, Paris: Librairie Internationale, 1866.

Blanqui, L.-A., *L'éternité par les astres* (ed.) L. Block de Behar, Geneva: Éditions Slatkine, 2009. First published, 1872.

L'armée esclave et opprimée: suppression de la conscription enseignement militaire de la jeunesse armée nationale sédentaire, Paris: Au bureau du journal *Ni dieu ni maître*, 1880.

Critique sociale, 2 vols., Paris: Félix Alcan, 1885.

Œuvres complètes, 2 vols. (ed.) A. Münster, Paris: Editions Galilée, 1977.

Borde, F., *Le collectivisme au Congrès de Marseille*, Paris: Delaporte, 1880.

Bottigelli, E., and Willard, C. (eds.), *La naissance du Parti ouvrier français: Correspondance inédite de Paul Lafargue, Jules Guesde, José Mesa, Paul Brousse, Benoît Malon, Gabriel Deville, Victor Jaclard, Léon Camescasse et Friedrich Engels*, Paris: Editions Sociales, 1981.

Brissac, H., *Résumé populaire du socialisme*, Paris: Henri Oriol, 1881.

Travail et prolétariat, Paris: Bureau de la *revue socialiste*, 1886.

Brousse, P., *Le Suffrage universel et le problème de la souveraineté du peuple*, Geneva: Imprimerie Coopérative, 1874.

La crise: sa cause, son remède, Geneva: Éditions du *Révolté*, 1879.

Le marxisme dans l'Internationale, Paris: Imprimerie Nouvelle, 1882.

La propriété collective et les services publics, Paris: Aux bureaux du Prolétaire, 1910. First published, 1883.

Cabet, É., *Le vrai Christianisme suivant Jésus-Christ*, Paris: Au bureau du *Populaire*, 1846.

du Camp, M., *Les convulsions de Paris*, 4 vols., 5th edn, Paris: Hachette, 1881. First published, 1878–1880.

Claretie, J., *Almanach illustré de l'histoire de la Révolution de 1870–71*, Paris: Au bureau du journal *L'Éclipse*, 1872.

Cluseret, G.P., *Mémoires du Général Cluseret*, 3 vols., Paris: Jules Levy, 1887–1888.

Congrès général de l'Association internationale des Travailleurs, *Manifeste adressé à toutes les Associations ouvrières et à tous les Travailleurs, par le Congrès général de l'Association international des Travailleurs tenu à Bruxelles du 7 au 13 Septembre 1874*.

Considerant, V., *Principles of Socialism: Manifesto of Nineteenth-Century Democracy*, (trans.) J. Roelofs, Washington, DC: Maisonneuve Press, 2006. First published in French, 1847.

Constant, B., *De l'esprit de conquête et de l'usurpation, dans leurs rapports avec la civilisation européenne*, 3rd edn, Paris: Le Norment, 1814.

da Costa, G., *La Commune vécue*, 3 vols., Paris: Ancien Maison Quantin, 1903–1905.

Darwin, C., *On the Origin of Species by Means of Natural Selection, or the Preservation of Favoured Races in the Struggle for Life*, London: John Murray, 1859.

Darwin, C.R., *De l'origine des espèces, ou des lois du progrès chez les êtres organisés* (trans.) C.-A. Royer, Paris: Guillaumin & Masson, 1862. First published in English, 1859.

De l'origine des espèces au moyen de la sélection naturelle, ou, la lutte pour l'existence dans la nature (trans.) J.-J. Moulinié, Paris: Reinwald, 1873. First published in English, 1859.

D'Esboeufs, V., *La république telle que nous la voulons: programme révolutionnaire, politique, économique et social*, Geneva: Imprimerie J. Benoit et Compagnie, 1874.

Deville, G. (ed.), *Le Capital de Karl Marx*, Paris: Henry Oriol, 1883.

Deville, G., *L'Évolution du capital*, Paris: Henry Oriol, 1884.

Diderot, D., *Supplément au voyage de Bougainville* (ed.) P. Jimack, London: Grant & Cutler, 1988. First published, 1772.

Digeon, E., *Droits et devoirs de l'anarchie rationnelle*, Paris: Fayard, 1882.

Dumartheray, F., *Aux travailleurs manuels de France: l'artisants de l'action politique*, Geneva: publisher unknown, 1876.

Dunoyer, C., *L'Industrie et la morale considérées dans leurs rapports avec la liberté*, Paris: A. Sautelet, 1825.

Dupont, F., Engels, F., Frankel, L., Le Moussu, C., Marx, K., and Serraillier, A., *L'Alliance de la démocratie socialiste et l'Association internationale des travailleurs: rapport et documents publiés par ordre du congrès internationale de La Haye*, London: A. Darson, 1873.

Engels, F., *Anti-Dühring: Herr Eugen Dühring's Revolution in Science*, (trans.) E. Burns, Moscow: Progress Publishers, 1947. First published in German, 1877.

'Socialism: utopian and scientific', (trans.) E. Aveling, in Engels, F., Lenin, V.I., and Marx, K., *The Essential Left: Four Classic Texts on the Principles of Socialism*, London: Unwin Books, 1960, 105–146. First published in French, 1880.

Engels, F., Lafargue, P. and L., *Correspondence*, 3 vols., (trans.) Y. Kapp, Moscow: Foreign Languages Publishing House, 1959.

Flourens, G., *L'histoire de l'homme: cours d'histoire naturelle des corps organisés au Collège de France*, Paris: Imprimerie de E. Martinet, 1863–1864.

de Greef, G., *Eloges d'Élisée Reclus et de Kellès-Krauz*, Gand: Société cooperative Volksdrukkerij, 1906.

Grousset, P., and Jourde, F., *Les condamnés politiques en Nouvelle-Calédonie: récit de deux évadés*, Geneva: Imprimerie Ziegler, 1876.

Guesde, J., *Essai de catéchisme socialiste*, Paris: Marcel Rivière, 1912. First published, 1878.

Collectivisme et Révolution, Paris: Librairie des Publications Populaires, 1879.

La loi des salaires et ses conséquences, Paris: Bibliothèque socialiste, 1879.

Le collectivisme au Collège de France, Paris: Henry Oriol, 1883.

Services publics et socialisme, Bordeaux: Imprimerie E. Forastié, 1883.

Textes choisis (ed.) C. Willard, Paris: Éditions Sociales, 1959.

Guesde, J., and Lafargue, P., *Le Programme du Parti Ouvrier: son histoire, ses considérations, ses articles*, Paris: Henry Oriol, 1883.

Guillaume, J. (ed.), *Le livre rouge de la justice rurale: documents pour servir à l'histoire d'une République sans républicains*, Geneva: Imprimerie V. Blanchard, 1871.

Guillaume, J., *Idées sur l'organisation sociale*, La Chaux-de-Fonds: Imprimerie Courvoisier, 1876.

L'Internationale: documents et souvenirs (1864–1878), Paris: Société nouvelle de librairie et d'édition, 1905–1910.

Guizot, F.P.G., *Histoire de la civilisation en France depuis la chute de l'empire romain jusqu'à la Révolution française*, 4 vols., 2nd edn, Paris: Didier, 1840.

Hugo, V., *La voix de Guernsey*, Guernsey: Imprimerie T.-M. Bichard, 1867.

Hugo, V., *Quatre-Vingt-Treize*, Paris: Imprimerie J. Claye, 1874.

Kropotkin, P., *Paroles d'un révolté*, Paris: Imprimerie de Lagny, 1885.

Laboulaye, É., *Le parti libéral: son programme et son avenir*, 4th edn, Paris: Charpentier, 1864.

Lafargue, P., *Le droit à la paresse: réfutation du "droit au travail" de 1848*, Paris: Henry Oriol, 1883. First published, 1880.

　Cours d'économie sociale: le matérialisme économique de Karl Marx, Paris: Henry Oriol, 1884.

　'Recherches dur les origines de l'idée du bien et du juste', *Revue philosophique* 20, 1885, 253–267.

　'Socialism in France from 1876–1896' (trans.) E. Aveling, *The Fortnightly Review* 62, 1897, 445–458.

de Lamartine, A., *Histoire des Girondins*, 10 vols., Paris: Hachette, 1881. First published, 1847.

Laporte, É., Magnin, F., and Finance, I., *Le positivisme au Congrès ouvrier: discours des citoyens Laporte, Magnin et Finance*, Paris: Imprimerie P. Larousse et Compagnie, 1877.

Lebeau, E., *Périssent dieu et la prêtraille!*, Geneva: Imprimerie coopérative, 1873.

Lefrançais, G., *Étude sur le mouvement communaliste à Paris en 1871*, Neuchâtel: Imprimerie G. Guillaume Fils, 1871.

　République et Révolution: de l'attitude à prendre par le prolétariat en présence des partis politiques, Geneva: Imprimerie Ve Blanchard, 1873.

　L'idée libertaire dans la Commune de 1871, Cahiers de contre-courant 66, April 1958. First published, 1874.

　De la dictature, Geneva: Imprimerie Ziegler, 1875.

　Un Communard aux électeurs français, Geneva: publisher not specified, 1875.

　Où vont les anarchistes?, Paris: Imprimerie F. Harry, date not specified. First published, 1887.

　La Commune et la Révolution, Paris: Imprimerie Paul Dupont, 1896.

　Souvenirs d'un révolutionnaire, 2nd edn, ed. J. Černy, Paris: Société Encyclopédique française et Éditions de la Tête de Feuilles, 1972. First published, 1903.

Lenin, V.I., *The Paris Commune*, London: Martin Lawrence, 1931.

Leroy-Beaulieu, P., *De la colonisation chez les peuples modernes*, Paris: Guillaumin et Compagnie, 1882. First published, 1874.

Lissagaray, P.-O., *Les huit journées de mai derrière les barricades*, Brussels: Bureau du *Petit journal*, 1871.

　Histoire de la Commune de 1871, Paris: E. Dentu, 1896. First published, 1876.

　Histoire de la Commune de 1871, Paris: Maspero, 1967. First published, 1876.

Littré, É., *Conservation, révolution et positivisme*, Paris: Aux bureaux de la *Philosophie positive*, 1879.

Malon, B., *La troisième défaite du prolétariat français*, Neuchâtel: G. Guillaume Fils, 1871.

　Exposé des écoles socialistes françaises, Paris: Imprimerie de Lagny, 1872.

L'Internationale: son histoire et ses principes, Lyons: Extrait de la *République républicaine*, 1872.

La question sociale: histoire critique de l'économie politique, Lugano: J. Favre, 1876.

Spartacus, ou la guerre des esclaves, Verviers: Imprimerie d'Emile Piette, 1876.

Le Nouveau parti, 2 vols., 3rd edn, Paris: Derveaux, 1882.

Constantin Pecqueur: doyen des écrivains socialistes français d'après ses oeuvres publiées et ses manuscrits, Paris: publisher not specified, 1883.

Précis historique, théorique et pratique du socialisme, Paris: Félix Alcan, 1892.

Marouck, V., *Les grandes dates du socialisme: juin 1848*, Paris: Librairie du Progrès, 1880.

Marx, K., 'Zur Judenfrage', in Ruge, A., and Marx, K., *Deutsch-Französische Jahrbücher*, Paris: Au bureau des Annales, 1844.

Misère de la philosophie: réponse à La philosophie de la misère de M. Proudhon, Paris: A. Frank, 1847.

Discours sur la question du libre-échange, Brussels: Aux frais de l'Association démocratique de Bruxelles, 1848.

The Class Struggles in France, 1848–1850, trans. H. Kuhn, New York: New York Labor News Co., 1924. First published in German, 1850.

The Eighteenth Brumaire of Louis Bonaparte, trans. T. Carver, in eds. M. Cowling and J. Martin, *Marx's Eighteenth Brumaire: (Post)modern Interpretations*, London: Pluto Press, 2002, 19–109. First published in German, 1852.

Das Kapital, Band 1, Hamburg: Verlag von Otto Meissner, 1867.

Le Capital, trans. J. Roy, Paris: Maurice Lachâtre, 1872–1875. First published in German, 1867.

Capital, Volume 1, trans. B. Fowkes, London: Penguin, 1990. First published, 1976. First published in German, 1867.

The Civil War in France, London: Martin Lawrence Ltd, 1933. First published, 1871.

Marx, K., and Engels, F., *The Communist Manifesto*, ed. G. Stedman Jones, trans. S. Moore, London: Penguin Books, 2002. First published in German, 1848.

Marx/Engels Collected Works trans. R. Dixon et al., 50 vols., London: Lawrence and Wishart, 1975–2004. Vols.22; 41–46, 1985–1992.

Mémoire présenté par la Fédération jurassienne de l'Association internationale des travailleurs à toutes les fédérations de l'Internationale, Sonvillier: Au siége du Comité fédéral jurassien, 1873.

Mendès, C., *Les 73 journées de la Commune*, 5th edn, Paris: E. Lachaud, 1871.

Messager, H., *239 lettres d'un Communard déporté: Ile d'Oléron – Ile de Ré – Ile des Pins*, ed. J. Maitron, Paris: Le Sycomore, 1979.

Michel, H., *L'Idée de l'État: essai critique sur l'histoire des théories sociales et politiques en France depuis la Révolution*, Paris: Hachette, 1896.

Michel, L., *La Commune*, Paris: P.V. Stock, 1898.

Souvenirs et aventures de ma vie ed. D. Armogathe, Paris: La Découverte/ Maspero, 1983. First published, 1905–1908.

Je vous écris de ma nuit: correspondance générale – 1850–1904, Paris: Les Éditions de Paris, 1999.

Michelet, J., *Le Peuple*, Brussels: Wouters, 1846.

Histoire de la Révolution française, 9 vols., Paris: Chamerot, 1847–1853.

Mignet, F.A., *Histoire de la Révolution française*, Brussels: Aug. Wahlen et Compagnie, 1824.

de Paepe, C., *Les services publics, précédés de deux essais sur le collectivisme*, Brussels: J. Milot, 1895. First published, 1874.

de Paepe, *Entre Marx et Bakounine: Correspondence* ed. B. Dandois, Paris: Maspero, 1974.

Pain, O., *Henri Rochefort (Paris – Nouméa – Genève)*, Paris: Périnet, 1879.

Pelletan, C., *Questions d'histoire: le comité central et la Commune*, Paris: Lagny, 1879.

La semaine de Mai, Paris: M. Dreyfous, 1880.

Pen-ar-vir, *La révolution française de 1877*, Geneva: Imprimerie Ziegler, 1877.

de Pressensé, E., *Les leçons du 18 mars: les faits et les idées*, Paris: Michel Lévy Frères, 1871.

Prévost-Paradol, L.-A., *La France nouvelle*, Paris: Calmann-Lévy, 1868.

'Programme', *Le Travail*, Saint-Ouen: Imprimerie Jules Boyer, 1879.

Proudhon, P.-J., *Qu'est-ce que la propriété? Ou, recherches sur le principe du droit et du gouvernement*, Paris: J.F. Brocard, 1840.

Les confessions d'un révolutionnaire, pour servir à l'histoire de la revolution de février, Brussels: Delevigne et Callewaert, 1849.

General Idea of the Revolution in the Nineteenth Century, trans. J.B. Robinson, Winchester, MA: Pluto Press, 1989. First published in French, 1851.

Du principe fédératif et de la nécessité de reconstituer le parti de la revolution, Paris: Éditions Bossard, 1921. First published, 1863.

De la capacité politique des classes ouvrières, new edn, Paris: Imprimerie Eugène Heutte, 1873. First published, 1865.

Contradictions politiques: théorie du mouvement constitutionnel au XIXe siècle, Paris: Imprimerie L. Toinon, 1870.

Pyat, F., *Lettre au peuple de Lyon*, London: *Courrier révolutionnaire*, 1875.

Quinet, E., *La République: conditions de la régéneration de la France*, Paris: Le Bord de l'Eau, 2009. First published, 1872.

Reclus, Élie, *Les primitifs: étude d'ethnologie comparée*, Paris: G. Chamerot, 1885.

Reclus, É., *La terre: déscription des phénomènes de la vie du globe*, 2 vols., Paris: Hachette. First published, 1868–1869.

La nouvelle géographie: la terre et les hommes, 19 vols., Paris: Hachette, 1876–1894.

Évolution et révolution: conférence faite à Genève, le 5 mars 1880, Geneva: Imprimerie jurassienne, 1880.

Évolution et révolution: conférence faite à Genève, le 5 mars 1880, 2nd edn, Geneva: Imprimerie jurassienne, 1881.

Evolution and Revolution, London: International Publishing Company, 1885. First published in French, 1880.

Évolution et Révolution, 6th edn, Paris: Imprimerie Habert, 1891. First published, 1880.

Ouvrier, prends la machine! Prends la terre, paysan!, Geneva: Imprimerie jurassienne, 1880.

A mon frère le paysan, Geneva: Imprimerie des Eaux-Vives, 1890.

L'Évolution, la Révolution et l'idéal anarchique, Paris: P.V. Stock, 1898.

Correspondance vol.3, Paris: Alfred Costes, 2010.

Reclus, É., and Guyou, G., *L'anarchie et l'Église*, Paris: Au bureau des "Temps nouveaux", 1901.

Regnard, A., *Études de politique scientifique: la révolution sociale, ses origines, son développement et son but*, London: publisher unspecified, 1876.

Renan, E., *Vie de Jésus*, Paris: Michel Lévy Frères, 1863.

Qu'est-ce qu'une nation? Conférence faite en Sorbonne, le 11 mars 1882, Paris: Calmann Levy, 1882.

Rochefort, H., *L'Évadé: roman canaque*, 2nd edn, Paris: Charpentier, 1880.

Les aventures de ma vie, 5 vols., Paris: Paul Dupont, 1896–1897.

Rocher, A., *La vie du Citoyen Jésus-Christ par le Citoyen Satan*, Geneva: Imprimerie V. Blanchard, 1875.

Schwitzguébel, A., *Chacun pour soi, Dieu pour tous*, Geneva: Imprimerie jurassienne, 1880.

Sieyès, E.J., *Qu'est-ce que le Tiers État?* 3rd edn, Paris: publisher unknown, 1789.

Taine, H., *Les origines de la France contemporaine*, 5 vols., Paris: Hachette, 1875–1893.

Testut, O., *L'Internationale et le jacobinisme au ban de l'Europe*, Paris: E. Lachaud, 1872.

Thiers, A., *Histoire de la Révolution française*, 10 vols., 9th edn, Paris: Furne et Cie, 1823–7.

de Tocqueville, A., *Writings on Empire and Slavery*, ed. J. Pitts, Baltimore, MD: Johns Hopkins University Press, 2000.

Toussenel, A., *Les juifs rois de l'époque: histoire de la féodalité financière*, 2 vols., Paris: L'Imprimerie de Crapelet, 1847.

Tridon, G., *Les Hébertistes* 2nd edn, Brussels: Imprimerie de J.H. Briard, 1871. First published, 1864.

Gironde et Girondins: la Gironde en 1869 et en 1793, Paris: Imprimerie Parisienne, 1869.

Du molochisme juif: études critiques et philosophiques, Brussels: Édouard Maheu, 1884. First published 1869.

Oeuvres diverses, Paris: Imprimerie Jean Allemane, 1891.

Vitet, M.L., *Le christianisme et la société*, Paris: Charles Douniol, 1869.

Vuillaume, M., *Mes cahiers rouges au temps de la Commune*, Paris: Cahiers de la quinzaine, 1908–14.

SECONDARY LITERATURE

Newspapers

L'Aurore (Paris), June 1971; November 1971.

Le Figaro (Paris), March 1971.

France Soir (Paris), November 1971.
Historia (Paris), March 1971.
Paris Jour (Paris), May 1971.
Paris Match (Paris), March 1971.

Other Printed

Abi-Mershed, O.W., *Apostles of Modernity: Saint-Simonians and the Civilising Mission in Algeria*, Stanford, CA: Stanford University Press, 2010.
Agamben, G., *The Coming Community*, trans. M. Hardt, Minneapolis: University of Minnesota Press, 1993.
Ageron, C.-R., *L'anticolonialisme en France de 1871 à 1914*, Paris: Presses universitaires de France, 1973.
Agulhon, M., *The Republic in the Village: The People of the Var from the French Revolution to the Second Republic*, trans. J. Lloyd, Cambridge: Cambridge University Press, 1982. First published in French, 1970.
  Marianne into Battle: Republican Imagery and Symbolism in France, 1789–1880, trans. J. Lloyd, Cambridge: Cambridge University Press, 1981. First published in French, 1979.
  Marianne au pouvoir: l'imagerie et la symbolique républicaines de 1880 à 1914, Paris: Flammarion, 1989.
  The French Republic 1879–1992, trans. A. Nevill, Oxford: Blackwell, 1993. First published in French, 1990.
Agulhon, M., Becker, A., and Cohen, É. (eds.), *La République en représentations: autour de l'oeuvre de Maurice Agulhon*, Paris: Publications de la Sorbonne, 2006.
Aldrich, R., *The French Presence in the South Pacific, 1842–1940*, Basingstoke: Macmillan, 1990.
Aldrich, R. (ed.), *France, Oceania and Australia: Past and Present*, Sydney: University of Sydney Press, 1991.
  France and the South Pacific since 1940, Basingstoke: Macmillan, 1993.
  Greater France: A History of French Overseas Expansion, Basingstoke: Macmillan, 1996.
Aldrich, R., and Connell, J. (eds.), *France in World Politics*, London: Routledge, 1989.
  (eds.), *France's Overseas Frontier: Départements et Territoires d'Outre-Mer*, Cambridge: Cambridge University Press, 1992.
Alexander, R., *Re-Writing the French Revolutionary Tradition*, Cambridge: Cambridge University Press, 2003.
Althusser, L., Balibar, É., Establet, R., Macherey, P., and Rancière, J., *Reading Capital: The Complete Edition* trans. B. Brewster and D. Fernbach, London: Verso, 2015. First published in French, 1965.
Anderson, K., 'The "unknown" Marx's *Capital*, volume I: the French edition of 1872–75, 100 years later', *Review of Radical Political Economics* 15, 1983, 71–80.

Anderson, R.D., *Education in France, 1848–1870*, Oxford: Clarendon Press, 1975.

Angenot, M., *Les grands récits militants des XIXe et XXe siècles: religions de l'humanité et sciences de l'histoire*, Paris: L'Harmattan, 2000.

Le marxisme dans les grands récits: essai d'analyse du discours, Paris: L'Harmattan, 2005.

Armitage, D., *Foundations of Modern International Thought*, Cambridge: Cambridge University Press, 2013.

Auspitz, K., *The Radical Bourgeoisie: The Ligue de l'enseignement and the Origins of the Third Republic 1866–1885*, Cambridge: Cambridge University Press, 1982.

Barbier, F., 'The publishing industry and printed output in nineteenth-century France', in K.E. Carpenter, ed., *Books and Society in History: Papers of the Association of College and Research Libraries Rare Books and Manuscripts Preconference*, New York: R.R. Bowker Company, 1983, 199–230.

Baronnet, J., and Chalou, J., *Communards en Nouvelle-Calédonie: Histoire de la déportation*, Paris: Mercure de France, 1987.

Bayly, C.A., *Recovering Liberties: Indian Thought in the Age of Liberalism and Empire*, Cambridge: Cambridge University Press, 2011.

Bayly, C.A., and Biagini, E.F. (eds.), *Giuseppe Mazzini and the Globalisation of Democratic Nationalism*, Oxford: Oxford University Press, 2008.

Beecher, J., *Victor Considerant and the Rise and Fall of French Romantic Socialism*, Berkeley: University of California Press, 2001.

Behrent, M.C., 'The mystical body of society: religion and association in nineteenth-century French political thought', *Journal of the History of Ideas* 69, April 2008, 219–243.

Bellanger, C. (ed.), *Histoire générale de la presse française*, 5 vols., Paris: Presses universitaires de France, 1969–1976.

Bellet, R., and Régnier, P. (eds.), *Écrire la Commune: témoignages, récits et romans (1871–1931)*, Tusson: Du Lérot, 1994.

Bensimon, F., 'British workers in France, 1815–1848', *Past & Present* 213, 2011, 147–189.

Berenson, E., *Populist Religion and Left-Wing Politics in France, 1830–1852*, Princeton, NJ: Princeton University Press, 1984.

Berenson, E., Duclert, V., and Prochasson, C. (eds.), *The French Republic: History, Values, Debates*, Ithaca, NY: Cornell University Press, 2011.

Bernstein, S., *The Beginnings of Marxian Socialism in France*, New York: Russell & Russell Inc, 1965.

Auguste Blanqui and the Art of Insurrection, London: Lawrence and Wishart, 1971.

Berry, D., and Bantmann, C. (eds.), *New Perspectives on Anarchism, Labour and Syndicalism: The Individual, the National and the Transnational*, Newcastle: Cambridge Scholars Publishing, 2010.

Best, G. (ed.), *The Permanent Revolution: The French Revolution and Its Legacy 1789–1989*, Chicago, IL: University of Chicago Press, 1988.

Blanchard, P., and Lemaire, S., *Culture coloniale: la France conquise par son empire, 1871–1931*, Paris: Éditions Autrement, 2003.

Boime, A., *Art and the French Commune: Imagining Paris after War and Revolution*, Princeton, NJ: Princeton University Press, 1995.

Braka, F., *L'honneur perdu de Gustave Cluseret (1823–1900)*, Paris: Hemisphères, 2018.

Bullard, A., 'Self-representation in the arms of defeat: fatal nostalgia and surviving comrades in French New Caledonia, 1871–1880', *Cultural Anthropology* 12, May 1997, 179–212.

Exile to Paradise: Savagery and Civilization in Paris and the South Pacific, 1790–1900, Stanford, CA: Stanford University Press, 2000.

Caron, J.-C., *Frères de sang: la guerre civile en France au XIXe siècle*, Seyssel: Champ Vallon, 2009.

Paris, l'insurrection capitale, Seyssel: Champ Vallon, 2015.

Carver, T., 'Marx's *Eighteenth Brumaire of Louis Bonaparte*: democracy, dictatorship, and class struggle', in P. Baehr and M. Richter (eds.), *Dictatorship in History and Theory: Bonapartism, Caesarism, and Totalitarianism*, Cambridge: Cambridge University Press, 2004.

César, M., *1871. La Commune révolutionnaire de Narbonne*, Sète: Éditions singulières, 2008.

Chakrabarty, D., *Provincializing Europe: Postcolonial Thought and Historical Difference*, Princeton, NJ: Princeton University Press, 2000.

Clark, C., 'After 1848: the European revolution in government', *Transactions of the Royal Historical Society* 22, 2012, 171–197.

Clark, J.P., and Martin, C. (eds.), *Anarchy, Geography, Modernity: The Radical Social Thought of Élisée Reclus*, Lanham: Lexington Books, 2004.

Conklin, A.L., *A Mission to Civilize: The Republican Idea of Empire in France and West Africa, 1895–1930*, Stanford, CA: Stanford University Press, 1997.

Conklin, A.L., Fishman, S., and Zaretsky, R., *France and Its Empire since 1870*, Oxford: Oxford University Press, 2011.

Cooper, F., and Stoler, A.L. (eds.), *Tensions of Empire: Colonial Cultures in a Bourgeois World*, Berkeley: University of California Press, 1997.

Cordillot, M., *Aux origines du socialisme moderne: La Première Internationale, la Commune de Paris, l'exil*, Paris: Éditions de l'Atelier, 2010.

Cordillot, M., and Latta, C., *Benoît Malon: le mouvement ouvrier, le mouvement republicain à la fin du Seconde Empire*, Lyons: Imprimerie J. André, 2010.

Cornish, W.R., and Clark, G. de N., *Law and Society in England, 1750–1950*, London: Sweet & Maxwell, 1989.

Cowling, M., and Martin, J. (eds.), *Marx's Eighteenth Brumaire: (Post)modern Interpretations*, London: Pluto Press, 2002.

Crapez, M., *La Gauche réactionnaire: mythes de la plèbe et de la race*, Paris: Berg International Editeurs, 1997.

Crouzet, F., 'The historiography of French economic growth in the nineteenth century', *Economic History Review* 61:2, 2003, 215–242.

Curtis, S.A., *Educating the Faithful: Religion, Schooling, and Society in Nineteenth-Century France*, DeKalb: Northern Illinois University Press, 2000.

Darriulat, P., *Les patriotes: la gauche républicaine et la nation 1830–1870*, Paris: Éditions du Seuil, 2001.

Daughton, J.P., *An Empire Divided: Religion, Republicanism, and the Making of French Colonialism, 1880–1914*, Oxford: Oxford University Press, 2006.

Dauphiné, J., *La déportation de Louise Michel: vérité et legends*, Paris: Les Indes Savantes, 2006.

Deluermoz, Q., *Le crépuscule des révolutions 1848–1871*, Paris: Seuil, 2012.

'The IWMA and the Commune: a reassessment', in F. Bensimon, Q. Deluermoz, and J. Moisand, J., *"Arise Ye Wretched of the Earth": The First International in a Global Perspective*, Leiden: Brill, 2018, 107–126.

Commune(s), 1870–1871, une traversée des mondes au XIXe siècle, Paris: Seuil, 2019.

Dening, G., *Readings/Writings*, Melbourne: Melbourne University Press, 1998.

Derfler, L., *Paul Lafargue and the Founding of French Marxism 1842–1882*, Cambridge, MA: Harvard University Press, 1991.

Paul Lafargue and the Flowering of French Socialism, 1882–1911, Cambridge, MA: Harvard University Press, 1998.

Deyon, P., *L'État face au pouvoir local: un autre regard sur l'histoire de France*, Paris: Éditions locales de France, 1996.

Dommanget, M., *Auguste Blanqui au début du IIIe République (1871–1880): dernière prison et ultimes combats*, Paris: Mouton, 1971.

Douglas, B., 'Conflict and alliance in a colonial context: case studies in New Caledonia 1853–1870', *Journal of Pacific History* 15, 1980, 21–51.

'Winning and losing? Reflections on the war of 1878–79 in New Caledonia', *Journal of Pacific History* 26, 1991, 213–233.

Dubois, J., *Le vocabulaire politique et social en France de 1869 à 1872*, Paris: Librairie Larousse, 1962.

Eichner, C.J., '*La citoyenne* in the world: Hubertine Auclert and feminist imperialism', *French Historical Studies* 32:1, 2009, 63–84.

Elwitt, S., *The Making of the Third Republic: Class and Politics in France, 1868–1884*, Baton Rouge: Louisiana State University Press, 1975.

Estebe, J., 'Le centenaire de la Commune par le livre', *Le mouvement social* 86 (January–March 1974), 89–112.

Fougère, L., Machelon, J.-P., and Monnier, F. (eds.), *Les communes et le pouvoir: Histoire politique des communes françaises de 1789 à nos jours*, Paris: Presses Universitaires de France, 2002.

Fournier, É., *La Commune n'est pas morte: les usages politiques du passé de 1871 à nos jours*, Paris: Éditions Libertalia, 2013.

Fox, R., *The Savant and the State: Science and Cultural Politics in Nineteenth-Century France*, Baltimore, MD: Johns Hopkins University Press, 2012.

Fritzsche, P., *Stranded in the Present: Modern Time and the Melancholy of History*, Cambridge, MA: Harvard University Press, 2004.

Furet, F., *Interpreting the French Revolution*, trans. E. Forster, Cambridge: Cambridge University Press, 1981. First published in French, 1978.

La Gauche et la Révolution française au milieu du XIXe siècle: Edgar Quinet et la question du Jacobinisme 1865–1870, Paris: Hachette, 1986.

La Révolution de Turgot à Jules Ferry, Paris: Hachette, 1988.

Furet, F., and Ozouf, M. (eds.), *Le siècle de l'avènement républicain*, Paris: Gallimard, 1993.

Gaboriaux, C., *La République en quête des citoyens: les républicains français face au bonapartisme rural (1848–1880)*, Paris: Presses de la Fondation Nationale des Sciences Politiques, 2010.

Gaçon, G., and Latta, C., *Benoît Malon et La revue socialiste*, Lyons: Imprimerie J. André, 2011.

Gandhi, L., *Affective Communities: Anticolonial Thought, Fin-de-Siècle Radicalism, and the Politics of Friendship*, Durham, NC: Duke University Press, 2006.

Gérard, A., *La Révolution française, mythes et interprétations (1789–1970)*, Paris: Flammarion, 1970.

Gildea, R., *The Past in French History*, New Haven, CT: Yale University Press, 1994.

Children of the Revolution: The French, 1799–1914, London: Allen Lane, 1998.

Girardet, R., *L'Idée coloniale en France de 1871 à 1962*, Paris: Éditions de la Table Ronde, 1972.

Mythes et mythologies politiques, Paris: Éditions du Seuil, 1986.

Girault, J., *Bordeaux et la Commune. 1870–1871*, Périgueux: Fanlac, 2009.

Godineau, L., *La Commune de Paris par ceux qui l'ont vécue*, Paris: Éditions Parigramme, 2010.

Goldberg Moses, C., *French Feminism in the Nineteenth Century*, Albany: State University of New York Press, 1984.

Goto-Jones, C., 'Comparative political thought: beyond the non-Western', in D. Bell (ed.), *Ethics and World Politics*, Oxford: Oxford University Press, 2010.

Gould, R.V., *Insurgent Identities: Class, Community, and Protest in Paris from 1848 to the Commune*, Chicago, IL: University of Chicago Press, 1995.

Goulemot, J.M., 'La rêverie cosmique de Louis Auguste Blanqui', *La Quinzaine littéraire* 1024:16–31, October 2010, p.21.

Gratton, P., *Les luttes des classes dans les campagnes*, Paris: Éditions Anthropos, 1971.

Green, N.L., 'Socialist anti-Semitism, defense of a bourgeois Jew and discovery of the Jewish proletariat: changing attitudes of French socialists before 1914', *International Review of Social History* 30:3, 1985, 374–399.

Greenberg, L.M., *Sisters of Liberty: Marseille, Lyon, Paris and the Reaction to a Centralized State, 1868–1871*, Cambridge, MA: Harvard University Press, 1971.

Grévy, J., *La République des Opportunistes 1870–1885*, Paris: Perrin, 1998.

Gullickson, G.L., *Unruly Women of Paris: Images of the Commune*, Ithaca, NY: Cornell University Press, 1996.

Hanson, S.E., *Post-Imperial Democracies: Ideology and Party Formation in Third Republic France, Weimar Germany, and Post-Soviet Russia*, Cambridge: Cambridge University Press, 2010.

Harris, R., *The Man on Devil's Island: Alfred Dreyfus and the Affair That Divided France*, London: Allen Lane, 2010.

Harvey, D., 'Monument and myth', *Annals of the Association of American Geographers* 69, September 1979, 362–381.

Haynes, C., *Lost Illusions: The Politics of Publishing in Nineteenth-Century France*, Cambridge, MA: Harvard University Press, 2010.

Hazareesingh, S., *Political Traditions in Modern France*, Oxford: Oxford University Press, 1994.

From Subject to Citizen: The Second Empire and the Emergence of Modern French Democracy, Princeton, NJ: Princeton University Press, 1998.

Hazareesingh, S. (ed.), *The Jacobin Legacy in Modern France: Essays in Honour of Vincent Wright*, Oxford: Oxford University Press, 2002.

Intellectual Founders of the Republic: Five Studies in Nineteenth-Century French Republican Political Thought, 2nd edn, Oxford: Oxford University Press, 2005. First published, 2001.

Hobsbawm, E.J., *Primitive Rebels: Studies in Archaic Forms of Social Movement in the 19th and 20th Centuries*, Manchester: Manchester University Press, 1974.

Howorth, J.M., 'The myth of Blanquism under the Third Republic (1871–1890)', *Journal of Modern History* 48, September 1976, 37–68.

Huard, R., *Le suffrage universel en France (1848–1946)*, Paris: Éditions Aubier, 1991.

Hutton, P.H., 'The role of the Blanquist party in left-wing politics in France, 1879–90', *Journal of Modern History* 46, June 1974, 277–295.

'Vico's theory of history and the French revolutionary tradition', *Journal of the History of Ideas* 37, April–June 1976, 241–256.

Hutton, P., *The Cult of the Revolutionary Tradition: The Blanquists in French Politics, 1864–1893*, Berkeley: University of California Press, 1981.

'The role of memory in the historiography of the French Revolution', *History and Theory* 30, February 1991, 56–69.

McInnes, N., 'Les débuts du marxisme théorique en France et en Italie (1880–1897)', *Cahiers de l'Institut de Science Économique Appliquée* 102, June 1960.

James, C.L.R., 'They showed the way to labor emancipation: on Karl Marx and the 75th anniversary of the Paris Commune', *Labor Action* 10, 18 March 1946.

Jennings, J., *Revolution and the Republic: A History of Political Thought in France since the Eighteenth Century*, Oxford: Oxford University Press, 2011.

Johnson, M.P., *The Paradise of Association: Political Culture and Popular Organisations in the Paris Commune of 1871*, Ann Arbor: University of Michigan Press, 1996.

'Memory and the cult of revolution in the 1871 Paris Commune', *Journal of Women's History* 9, 1997, 39–57.

Joughin, J.T., *The Paris Commune in French Politics, 1871–1880*, 2 vols., Baltimore, MD: Johns Hopkins University Press, 1955.

Jousse, E., *Réviser le marxisme? D'Édouard Bernstein à Albert Thomas, 1896–1914*, Paris: L'Harmattan, 2007.

Les hommes révoltés: les origines intellectuelles du réformisme en France (1871–1917), Paris: Fayard, 2017.

Judt, T., *Marxism and the French Left: Studies in Labour and Politics in France, 1830–1981*, Oxford: Clarendon, 1986.

Jun, N.J., and Wahl, S. (eds.), *New Perspectives on Anarchism*, Lanham, MD: Lexington Books, 2010.

Kamenka, E., *Paradigm for Revolution? The Paris Commune 1871–1971*, Canberra: Australian National University Press, 1972.

Katznelson, I., and Stedman Jones, G. (eds.), *Religion and the Political Imagination*, Cambridge: Cambridge University Press, 2010.

Kelly, D., and Cornick, M. (eds.), *A History of the French in London: Liberty, Equality, Opportunity*, London: Institute of Historical Research, 2013.

Kinna, R., *William Morris: The Art of Socialism*, Cardiff: University of Wales Press, 2000.

Koselleck, R., *Futures Past: On the Semantics of Historical Time*, trans. K. Tribe, New York: Columbia University Press, 2004. First published in German, 1979.

Lalouette, J., *La libre pensée en France 1848–1940*, Paris: Éditions Albin Michel, 1997.

La République anticléricale: XIXe–XXe siècles, Paris: Éditions du Seuil, 2002.

Larguier, G., and Quaretti, J. (eds.), *La Commune de 1871: utopie ou modernité?*, Perpignan: Presses universitaires de Perpignan, 2000.

Latta, C. (ed.), *La Commune de 1871: l'événement, les hommes et la mémoire*, Saint-Étienne: Publications de l'Université de Saint-Étienne, 2004.

Lefebvre, H., *La proclamation de la Commune, 26 Mars 1871*, Paris: Gallimard, 1965.

Lefranc, G., *Le mouvement socialiste sous la troisième république*, 2 vols., Paris: Payot, 1977. First published, 1963.

Lehning, J.R., *To Be a Citizen: The Political Culture of the Early French Third Republic*, Ithaca, NY: Cornell University Press, 2001.

Leith, J.A. (ed.), *Images of the Commune: Images de la Commune*, Montreal: McGill-Queen's University Press, 1978.

Lichtheim, G., *Marxism in Modern France*, New York: Columbia University Press, 1966.

The Origins of Socialism, London: Weidenfeld and Nicolson, 1969.

Lidsky, P., *Les écrivains contre la Commune*, Paris: F. Maspero, 1970.

Ligou, D., *Histoire du socialisme en France (1871–1961)*, Paris: Presses Universitaires de France, 1962.

Loubère, L.A., 'The intellectual origins of French Jacobin socialism', *International Review of Socialist History* 4, 1959, 415–431.

Louis, P., *Cent cinquante ans de pensée socialiste*, 2 vols., Paris: Libraire Marcel Rivière, 1938.

Mailhé, G., *Déportations en Nouvelle-Calédonie des communards et des révoltés de la grande Kabylie (1872–1876)*, Paris: L'Harmattan, 1994.

Maitron, J., *Le mouvement anarchiste en France*, 2 vols., Paris: François Maspero, 1975.

Maitron, J., et al. (eds.), *Dictionnaire biographique du mouvement ouvrier français*, 44 vols., Paris: Éditions ouvrières, 1964–1997, vols.4–15, 1967–1977.

Manceron, G., *1885: Le tournant colonial. Jules Ferry contre Georges Clemenceau, et autres affrontements parlementaires sur la conquête coloniale*, Paris: La Découverte, 2007.

Mantena, K., *Alibis of Empire: Henry Maine and the Ends of Liberal Imperialism*, Princeton, NJ: Princeton University Press, 2010.

Marçot, J.-L., *Comment est née l'Algérie française 1830–1850: La belle utopie*, Paris: Éditions de la différence, 2012.

Mason, E.S., *The Paris Commune: An Episode in the History of the Socialist Movement*, New York: The Macmillan Company, 1930.

Matsuda, M.K., *Empire of Love: Histories of France and the Pacific*, Oxford: Oxford University Press, 2005.

Mazauric, C., *L'histoire de la Révolution française et la pensée marxiste*, Paris: Presses Universitaires de France, 2009.

Mehta, U.S., *Liberalism and Empire: A Study in Nineteenth-Century British Liberal Thought*, Chicago, IL: University of Chicago Press, 1999.

Merriman, J., *Massacre: The Life and Death of the Paris Commune of 1871*, New Haven, CT: Yale University Press, 2014.

Metcalf, B., 'Utopian fraud: the Marquis de Rays and La Nouvelle-France', *Utopian Studies* 22, 2011, 104–124.

Milner, J., *Art, War and Revolution in France 1870–1871: Myth, Reportage and Reality*, New Haven, CT: Yale University Press, 2000.

Moggach, D., and Leduc Brown, P. (ed.), *The Social Question and the Democratic Revolution: Marx and the Legacy of 1848*, Ottawa: University of Ottawa Press, 2000.

Moreau, J., *Les socialistes français et le mythe révolutionnaire*, Paris: Hachette, 2003.

Moss, B.H., *The Origins of the French Labor Movement 1830–1914: The Socialism of Skilled Workers*, Berkeley: University of California Press, 1976.

Muthu, S., *Enlightenment against Empire*, Princeton, NJ: Princeton University Press, 2003.

Muthu, S. (ed.), *Empire and Modern Political Thought*, Cambridge: Cambridge University Press, 2012.

Nicolet, C., *L'Idée républicaine en France (1789–1924)*, Paris: Gallimard, 1982.

Nora, P., *Les lieux de mémoire*, 7 vols., Paris: Gallimard, 1984–1992.

Nord, P., *The Republican Moment: Struggles for Democracy in Nineteenth-Century France*, Cambridge, MA: Harvard University Press, 1995.

Noronha-DiVanna, I., *Writing History in the Third Republic*, Newcastle: Cambridge Scholars Publishing, 2010.

Ouennoughi, M., *Algériens et Maghrébins en Nouvelle-Calédonie: Anthropologie historique de la communauté arabo-berbère de 1864 à nos jours*, Algiers: Casbah Editions, 2008.

Ozouf, M., *L'école, l'église et la république 1871–1914*, Paris: Éditions Cana, 1982.

Page Moch, L., *Moving Europeans: Migration in Western Europe since 1650*, Bloomington, IN: Indiana University Press, 1992.

Pérennès, R., *Déportés et forçats de la Commune de Belleville à Nouméa*, Nantes: Ouest Éditions, 1991.

Perovic, S., *The Calendar in Revolutionary France: Perceptions of Time in Literature, Culture, Politics*, Cambridge: Cambridge University Press, 2012.

Pessin, A., *Le mythe du peuple et la société française du XIXe siècle*, Paris: Presses Universitaires de France, 1992.

Pitts, J., *A Turn to Empire: The Rise of Liberal Imperialism in Britain and France*, Princeton, NJ: Princeton University Press, 2005.

'Liberalism and empire in a nineteenth-century Algerian mirror', *Modern Intellectual History* 6, 2009, 287–313.

Plamenatz, J., *The Revolutionary Movement in France 1815–71*, London: Longman, 1965. First published, 1952.

Prélot, M., *L'Évolution politique du socialisme français 1789–1934*, Paris: Éditions Spes, 1939.

Priest, R.D., 'The "great doctrine of transcendent disdain": history, politics and the self in Renan's *Life of Jesus*', *History of European Ideas* 40, 2014, 761–776.

'Reading, writing, and religion in nineteenth-century France: the popular reception of Renan's *Life of Jesus*', *Journal of Modern History* 86, June 2014, 258–294.

The Gospel According to Renan: Reading, Writing, and Religion in Nineteenth-Century France, Oxford: Oxford University Press, 2015.

Przyblyski, J.M., 'Revolution at a standstill: photography and the Paris Commune of 1871', *Yale French Studies* 101, 2001, 54–78.

Rebérioux, M., '*La revue socialiste*', *Cahiers Georges Sorel* 5, 1987, 15–38.

Reynaud Paligot, C., *La République raciale: paradigme racial et idéologie républicaine (1860–1930)*, Paris: Presses universitaires de France, 2006.

Rihs, C., *La Commune de Paris (1871): sa structure et ses doctrines*, Paris: Éditions du Seuil, 1973. First published, 1955.

Roberts, J.M., 'The Paris Commune from the Right', *English Historical Review*, supplement 6, 1973.

Roberts, W.C., *Marx's Inferno: The Political Theory of Capital*, Princeton, NJ: Princeton University Press, 2017.

Rosanvallon, P., *Le moment Guizot*, Paris: Gallimard, 1985.

L'État en France de 1789 à nos jours, Paris: Seuil, 1990.

Le Peuple introuvable: histoire de la répresentation démocratique en France, Paris: Gallimard, 1998.

The Demands of Liberty: Civil Society in France since the Revolution, trans. A. Goldhammer, Cambridge, MA: Harvard University Press, 2007. First published in French, 2004.

Democracy Past and Future, ed. S. Moyn, New York, NY: Columbia University Press, 2006.

The Society of Equals, trans. A. Goldhammer, Cambridge, MA: Harvard University Press, 2013. First published in French, 2011.

Ross, K., *Communal Luxury: The Political Imaginary of the Paris Commune*, London: Verso, 2015. First published in French, 2015.

Rothschild, E., *The Inner Life of Empires: An Eighteenth-Century History*, Princeton, NJ: Princeton University Press, 2011.

Rougerie, J., *Procès des Communards*, Paris: Julliard, 1964.

Paris libre 1871, Paris: Éditions du Seuil, 1971.

1871: jalons pour une histoire de la Commune de 1871, Paris: Presses universitaires de France, 1973.

La Commune 1871, Paris: Presses universitaires de France, 1988.

Paris insurgé: la Commune de 1871, Paris: Gallimard, 1995.

Rubel, M., and Manale, M., *Marx without Myth: A Chronological Study of His Life and Work*, Oxford: Basil Blackwell, 1975.

Rudelle, O., *La République absolue, 1870–1889*, Paris: Publications de la Sorbonne, 1982.

Sessions, J.E., *By Sword and Plow: France and the Conquest of Algeria*, Ithaca, NY: Cornell University Press, 2011.

Shafer, D., *The Paris Commune: French Politics, Culture, and Society at the Crossroads of the Revolutionary Tradition and Revolutionary Socialism*, Basingstoke: Palgrave Macmillan, 2005.

Shineberg, D., '"Noumea no good. Noumea no pay": "New Hebridean" indentured labour in New Caledonia, 1865–1925', *Journal of Pacific History* 26, 1991, 187–205.

Siegel, J., *Marx's Fate: The Shape of a Life*, Princeton, NJ: Princeton University Press, 1978.

Société d'histoire de la révolution de 1848 et des révolutions du XIXe siècle, *Blanqui et les blanquistes*, Paris: Sedes, 1986.

Soltau, R., *French Political Thought in the Nineteenth Century*, London: Ernest Benn Limited, 1931.

Sowerwine, C., *Sisters or Citizens? Women and Socialism in France since 1876*, Cambridge: Cambridge University Press, 1982.

Spitzer, A.B., *The Revolutionary Theories of Louis Auguste Blanqui*, New York: Columbia University Press, 1957.

Stafford, D., *From Anarchism to Reformism: A Study of the Political Activities of Paul Brousse within the First International and the French Socialist Movement 1870–1890*, London: Cox & Wyman, 1971.

Starr, J.B., *Continuing the Revolution: The Political Thought of Mao*, Princeton, NJ: Princeton University Press, 2015. First published, 1979.

Starr, P., *Commemorating Trauma: The Paris Commune and Its Cultural Aftermath*, New York: Fordham University Press, 2006.

Stedman Jones, G., *Languages of Class: Studies in English Working Class History 1832–1982*, Cambridge: Cambridge University Press, 1983.

Karl Marx: Greatness and Illusion, London: Allen Lane, 2016.

Stedman Jones, G., and Claeys, G. (eds.), *The Cambridge History of Nineteenth-Century Political Thought*, Cambridge: Cambridge University Press, 2011.

Sternhell, Z., *La droite révolutionnaire 1885–1914: les origines françaises du fascisme*, Paris: Éditions du Seuil, 1978.

Stoler, A.L., *Along the Archival Grain: Epistemic Anxieties and Colonial Common Sense*, Princeton, NJ: Princeton University Press, 2009.

Stone, J.F., *Sons of the Revolution: Radical Democrats in France 1862–1914*, Baton Rouge, LA: Louisiana State University Press, 1996.

Stuart, R., *Marxism at Work: Ideology, Class and French Socialism during the Third Republic*, Cambridge: Cambridge University Press, 1992.

Tartakowsky, D., *Nous irons chanter sur vos tombes: le Père-Lachaise, XIXe-XXe siècle*, Paris: Aubier, 1999.

Taylor, K., *The Political Ideas of the Utopian Socialists*, London: Frank Cass, 1982.

Thomas, P., *Karl Marx and the Anarchists*, London: Routledge, 1980.

Thomson, D., *Democracy in France since 1870, London: Cassell, 1989.* First published, 1946.

Tillier, B., *La Commune de Paris, révolution sans images? Politique et représentations dans la France républicaine (1871–1914)*, Seyssel: Champ Vallon, 2004.

Todd, D., 'A French imperial meridian, 1814–1870', *Past & Present* 210, 2011, 155–186.

Free Trade and Its Enemies in France, 1814–1851, Cambridge: Cambridge University Press, 2015.

'Transnational projects of empire in France, c.1815–c.1870', *Modern Intellectual History* 12, 2015, 265–293.

Tombs, R.P., *France 1814–1914*, London: Routledge, 1996.

'How bloody was *la semaine sanglante* of 1871? A revision', *The Historical Journal* 55, September 2012, 679–704.

Paris, bivouac des révolutions: la Commune de 1871, trans. J. Chatroussat, Paris: Éditions Libertalia, 2014. First published in English, 1999.

Toth, S.A., 'Colonisation or incarceration? The changing role of the French penal colony in *fin-de-siècle* New Caledonia', *Journal of Pacific History* 34, 1999, 59–74.

Beyond Papillon: The French Overseas Penal Colonies, 1854–1952, Lincoln: University of Nebraska Press, 2006.

Tsuzuki, C., *The Life of Eleanor Marx, 1855–1898: A Socialist Tragedy*, Oxford: Clarendon Press, 1967.

Various, *Le mouvement social: La Commune de 1871, actes du colloque universitaire pour la commémoration du centenaire, Paris les 21–22–23 mai 1971* 79, April–June 1972.

Varley, K., *Under the Shadow of Defeat: The War of 1870–1871 in French Memory*, Basingstoke: Palgrave Macmillan, 2008.

Vincent, K.S., *Pierre-Joseph Proudhon and the Rise of French Republican Socialism*, Oxford: Oxford University Press, 1984.

Between Marxism and Anarchism: Benoît Malon and French Reformist Socialism, Berkeley: University of California Press, 1992.

Weber, E., *Peasants into Frenchmen: The Modernisation of Rural France 1870–1914*, London: Chatto & Windus, 1977.

White, J.D., 'Despotism and anarchy: the sociological thought of L.I. Mechnikov', *The Slavonic and East European Review* 54, July 1976, 395–411.

Willard, C., *Socialisme et communisme français*, Paris: Armand Colin, 1978. First published, 1967.

Le socialisme de la renaissance à nos jours, Paris: Presses Universitaires de France, 1971.

Jules Guesde, l'apôtre et la loi, Paris: Éditions ouvrières, 1991.

Willard, C. (ed.), *La France ouvrière: Histoire de la classe ouvrière et du mouvement ouvrier français* vol. 1, Paris: Éditions sociales, 1993.

Wilson, C.E., *Paris and the Commune 1871–1878: The Politics of Forgetting*, Manchester: Manchester University Press, 2007.

Wright, J., and Jones, H.S. (eds.), *Pluralism and the Idea of the Republic in France*, Basingstoke: Palgrave Macmillan, 2012.

Wu, Y., *The Cultural Revolution at the Margins: Chinese Socialism in Crisis*, Cambridge, MA: Harvard University Press, 2014.

Zeldin, T., *France 1848–1945: Politics and Anger*, Oxford: Oxford University Press, 1979.

Unpublished

Dodds, D., 'Funerals, Trials, and the Problem of Violence in Nineteenth-Century France: Blanqui and Raspail', unpublished PhD thesis, University of Cambridge, 2010.

Dowdall, A., 'Narrating *la Semaine Sanglante*, 1871–1880', unpublished MPhil dissertation, University of Cambridge, 2010.

Godineau, L., 'Retour d'exil: les anciens Communards au début de la Troisième République', unpublished PhD thesis, Université de Paris I Panthéon-Sorbonne, 2000.

Jones, T.C., 'French republican exiles in Britain, 1848–1870', unpublished PhD thesis, University of Cambridge, 2010.

Jousse, E., 'La construction intellectuelle du socialisme réformiste en France, de la Commune à la Grande Guerre', unpublished PhD thesis, Sciences-Po, 2013.

Martinez, P.K., 'Paris Communard refugees in Britain, 1871–1880', unpublished PhD thesis, University of Sussex, 1981.

Websites

'L'Assemblée réhabilite les communards victimes de la répression', *Le Monde*, www.lemonde.fr/societe/article/2016/11/30/l-assemblee-rehabilite-les-communards-victimes-de-la-repression_5040565_3224.html [last accessed 3 April 2018].

Commune de Paris 1871, www.communedeparis1871.fr/fr [last accessed 25 May 2015].

'Ne laissons pas la Commune de Paris aux hipsters!', www.poisson-rouge.info/2015/06/02/ne-laissons-pas-la-commune-de-paris-aux-hipsters/ [last accessed 7 September 2015].

Visual

Kozintsez, G. and Trauberg, L. (dirs.), Новый Вавилон (The New Babylon), 1929.

Watkins, P. (dir.), *La Commune (Paris, 1871)*, 2000.

Index

Abdelkader, 245, 248
Action, revolutionary, 65, 92, 104, 243, 260, 267
  traditional, 10, 15–16, 18, 72, 82, 104,
    112–113, 139, 144, 199
  violent, 73, 134, 200
Adam, Edmond, 233, 275
Adam, Juliette, 233, 275
Africa, 12, 242, 247, 256
  North, 209
  West, 210
Agamben, Giorgio, 227
Ageron, Charles-Robert, 211
Agulhon, Maurice, 170
Albigensians. See Cathars
Algeria, 60, 210, 216, 240, 245, 251–252,
    254–256, 262
Allemane, Jean, 213, 218, 224, 230, 262, 271
Alsace Lorraine, 39, 172, 196, 222
Althusser, Louis, 154
Amnesty, 226
  campaign, 31, 216, 229, 233
  general, 3, 14, 35, 51, 54, 56, 59–61, 76, 122,
    140, 175, 194, 213–214, 216, 226, 228,
    242, 258
  Kabyle, 262
Anarchism, 11, 188, 201, 249. See also Anarchy
  nihilist, 200
Anarchist, 16, 77, 82, 133, 149, 175, 180, 182,
    188, 201, 206, 209, 213, 249
Anarchy
  theory of, 69
Anderson, Kevin, 154, 173
Andrieu, Jules, 28, 39, 42, 75, 94, 96
Angenot, Marc, 157, 181
Anticlericalism, 117–120, 124
  Free Thought Movement, 117–118
Anticolonialism, 211–212, 217, 257, 267–268
  proto-, 255
Anti-Semitism, 195, 271
Arnould, Arthur, 9, 26, 35, 41–44, 46–47, 53, 55,
    69, 73, 75, 84, 89–90, 98, 128, 250, 275

Asia, 12, 216, 242
  East, 223
  South, 209–210
  Southeast, 253
Assemblée Nationale, 2, 4, 21, 39–40, 92, 238
Auclert, Hubertine, 249
Australia, 214–215, 220–221, 223, 261

Babeuf, Gracchus, 10, 90
Bakunin, Mikhail, 10, 15, 149, 175–176, 180,
    273
Ballière, Achille, 97, 213, 221, 223, 231, 261
Baronnet, Jean, 217
Barricades, 2, 49, 130, 228
Barron, Louis, 117, 226, 229–231, 236
Bastille, 99, 101
Bebel, August, 154, 198–199
Beesley, Edward Spencer, 28, 32
Belgium, 3, 53, 240
Bellanger, Claude, 14, 244
Belleville, 1, 228
Berenson, Edward, 115, 151
Bergeret, Jules, 53, 69, 114, 127
Bernstein, Edouard, 14, 150, 202
Bernstein, Samuel, 31, 83
Beslay, Charles, 36, 84, 95
Blanc, Louis, 62, 98, 102, 180, 184, 232
  Organisation du travail, 159, 182
Blanqui, Louis Auguste, 7, 16, 106–111, 197
  as actor, 10, 40, 90, 138, 191, 193, 225
  as author, 85, 110, 114, 129, 180, 193, 270,
    274, 276
    L'éternité par les astres, 107, 129, 158
  as inspiration, 10, 29, 57
Blanquists, 9, 12, 50, 53, 64, 66, 69, 71–75, 87,
    91, 114, 118, 127, 137, 176, 180,
    191–193, 197, 202, 204–206
Boime, Albert, 6
Bonaparte, House of, 41
Bonaparte, Louis-Napoléon. See Napoleon III
Bonapartism, 6, 92, 176, 210, 247

Bonapartist. *See* Bonapartism
Boulanger, Ernest, 8, 12, 204, 271
Boulangism, 213
Bourbon, House of, 236
Bourgeoisie, 104, 109, 255
Brissac, Henri, 55
Britain. *See* United Kingdom
Brousse, Paul, 7, 117, 151, 180, 189–190, 201, 203–204
Brussels, 59, 168
Bullard, Alice, 217, 229, 231, 234
Buonarroti, Filippo, 90

Cabet, Étienne, 115, 235
Capitalism, 22, 170, 191, 255
  development of, 159, 162, 173–174, 181
  industrial, 159–160, 202
Cathars, 98–99
Catholic Church, 100, 115–118, 120, 124–125, 275
  separation of Church and State, 44–45, 117
Catholicism, 99, 118, 123, 125–126
  revival, 125
  social, 115
Catholics, 98, 116, 118, 123
Chalou, Jean, 217
Chambord, Henri, Comte de, 41
Chambre des Députés, 222, 233, 245
Change
  intellectual, 8, 12, 67, 85, 110, 145, 203
  leadership, 12, 86
  natural, 130, 135
  political, 59, 84, 86, 92, 110, 112, 121, 130, 134, 203, 272
  religious, 126
  revolutionary, 77, 81, 84, 107, 131, 135, 139, 235
  social, 10, 82, 86, 95–96, 100, 112–113, 121, 125, 130, 132, 139–140, 145, 159, 170–171, 184, 188, 193, 243, 257, 259, 272
  translational, 158, 162–163, 165–166, 173–174
China, 3, 210, 240, 245, 251–254, 256, 259
  industrialisation, 259
Citizens, 30, 57, 109, 185, 228, 234, 236, 247
  militia, 107
Citizenship, 98
Civilisation, 31, 40, 109, 253, 272
  French, 210, 242
  non-Western, 247, 252–253, 256
  Western, 253, 258, 263
Clark, Christopher, 116, 125
Class, 96, 173, 253, 255
  consciousness, 170

difference, 170
  working class, 30, 39, 46, 62, 134, 186, 227, 244
Clemenceau, Georges, 10, 62, 85, 94, 132, 145, 164, 186, 222, 245, 267, 275
Clericalism, 116–117
Cluseret, Gustave Paul, 53, 69, 91, 95, 271
Code, penal, 225
Colonialism, 209, 212, 217–219, 221, 223–224, 238–239, 241, 245, 263, 268
  agents of, 218, 223
  colonial lobby, 221, 224, 246–248, 257–259, 267
  colonial subjects, 219, 229, 242, 256, 263, 267
  critics of, 237
  settler, 237
Colony, penal, 2, 65, 211, 214–215, 220, 224, 226, 261
  administration, 223, 230–231, 236
Comité central républicain des vingt arrondissements, 39–40
Commemoration, 25, 51, 56, 59–60, 66, 72, 74, 230, 272
  banquets, 40, 64, 86, 107, 261
  funerals, 56–57, 215
  later, 22
Committee of Public Safety, 29, 53, 72
Communes. *See* Organisation:communal
Communism, 3, 22, 67, 119, 181, 198, 250–251
Communist. *See* Communism
Conklin, Alice, 260
Conquest, 242–243, 251
Conseil de la Commune, 28, 33, 40, 44, 49, 54, 215
Conservatives, 29–30, 39, 46, 52, 60, 99, 102, 236, 255
  later, 22
Conspiracy, 10, 28, 66, 74, 86, 90, 106
Constant, Benjamin, 256
Constitution, 96, *See also* Republic:as constitution; Third Republic: constitution
  constitutional guarantees, 94
Cordillot, Michel, 7, 212
Crimes, 251
  communard, 2, 215, 226
  official, 228, 238
  political, 215
Criminals
  common, 226–227, 229
  revolutionaries cast as, 25, 31
Cruise O'Brien, Conor, 83

Culture, 232
  foreign, 217–218, 248, 255, 263
  non-Western, 251–253
  political, 88, 92, 95, 104

Da Costa, Gaston, 72
Darboy, Georges, 2, 22, 49, 71
Darriulat, Philippe, 75, 83
Darwin, Charles, 131, 137
De Lamartine, Alphonse, 231
De MacMahon, Patrice, 60, 63
De Musset, Alfred, 231
De Paepe, César, 188–189
De Saint-Simon, Henri, 115
Declaration of the Rights of Man and the
  Citizen, 90, 104, 198
Democracy, 29–30, 40, 62, 144, 219, 232,
  251–252, 264
Democ-socs. *See* Socialists:democratic
Dening, Greg, 263, 265
Deportation, 2, 15, 77, 139, 240–241, 261–262,
  267, 273
Deportees, 3, 214–219, 221–241, 248, 250, 257,
  261–264, 266–268, 273
  as actors, 217, 220, 223–224, 230, 235–237
  as authors, 213, 216–219, 221, 224–226, 229,
    231–232, 236–238
  as interlocutors, 213, 224, 231, 237, 239
  life, 6, 11, 213, 216
Deputies, 4, 21, 39, 60, 140, 186, 209, 213, 221,
  248
Derfler, Leslie, 152
Dervillers, Prudent, 34, 62
Deville, Gabriel, 104, 118, 140, 155, 167, 178,
  180–181, 183–185, 187, 203
  Le Capital de Karl Marx, 154, 165–167, 181,
    197
Diderot, Denis, 231, 256
Domela Nieuwenhuis, Ferdinand, 32
Dowdall, Alex, 52
Dreyfus, Alfred, 226, 271
  Dreyfus affair, 8, 195, 271
Du Camp, Maxime, 26, 30, 32–33, 37, 46–47,
  51, 53
Dumartheray, François, 81–83, 104
Dunoyer, Charles, 159

Education, 44, 139, 218, 221
  reform, 126, 132
  religious, 117, 124
  secular, 117–118, 275
Elections, 29, 188, 199, 204, 216
  legislative, 12, 39, 140, 197, 213, 271
  municipal, 2, 28, 40
  presidential, 12, 130, 169

Empire, 15, 209–212, 217–218, 221, 223–224,
  238–243, 247, 250–251, 256–259,
  262–263, 266–268, 273
  British. *See* United Kingdom:empire
  as category of analysis, 243, 268
  First. *See* First Empire
  Ottoman, 241
  Second. *See* Second Empire
Engels, Friedrich, 14, 57, 61, 86, 97, 150–151,
  154–155, 164, 167, 196, 198, 201–202,
  204, 270
  Anti-Dühring, 136, 156, 181
England. *See* United Kingdom
Enracinement, republican, 6, 93, 100, 105
Equality, 18, 66, 92, 96, 116, 129, 276–277
  economic, 10
  political, 96
  racial, 256
  social, 46, 187, 193
  universal, 11, 259, 273
Europe, 2, 10, 13, 17, 33, 86, 90, 110, 117, 130,
  171, 175, 185, 194–195, 197, 209, 213,
  216, 221, 233, 237–239, 241–243, 249,
  252, 258, 266–268, 270, 273
  culture, 251, 262
  Eastern, 242
  imperialism, 218, 242, 247, 249, 252, 257,
    263, 266–267
  politics, 15, 18, 32, 86, 101, 154, 186,
    194–195, 200, 205, 222, 238, 241, 263,
    277
  press, 175
  revolution, 3, 82, 84, 115
  society, 30, 84, 86, 149, 264
  Western, 163, 251
Évadés, 215–216, 220, 233, 261, 275
Evolution, 113, 130–142, 144–145, 232, 272
Exile, 3, 6, 12, 15, 25, 33, 37, 41, 58–59, 61, 65,
  70, 76–77, 102, 108, 133, 139, 164, 176,
  194–195, 233, 237, 269–270, 276

Faction, 8, 17, 29, 64, 67–71, 149, 176, 206,
  270, 272
  majority, 29, 53, 72–73
  minority, 29, 35, 53, 71–75
Factory, 159–162, 171, 183
  Factory Acts, 159–160
  inspectorate, 159, 171
  owners, 160–161, 198
Favre, Jules, 227
Federalism, 53, 73, 90, 191
Federalists, 29, 91, 127, 235, 249
Fédération des travailleurs socialistes français. *See*
  Possibilists
Ferré, Théophile, 28, 71–72

Ferry, Jules, 52, 62, 67, 94, 221–222, 245–246, 248, 267
First Empire, 86
First International. *See* International Workingmen's Association
First Republic, 86, 99–100
Flaubert, Gustave, 101
Flourens, Gustave, 42, 130, 137, 209
Fourier, Charles, 115, 234
Fournier, Éric, 9, 24
Fourth Estate, 88–89
Framework, imperial, 243, 268
  intellectual, 11
  legal, 40, 232
  national, 259
  organisational, 195
  revolutionary, 142
  social, 183–184
France, army, 1, 21, 25, 30, 38, 49, 52, 64, 76, 100
  citizens, 41, 101–102, 107, 124, 126, 130, 182, 214, 217, 220, 223, 232, 237, 246–247
  colonialism, 219, 223, 251
  countryside, 73, 113, 121, 169–170, 277
  culture, 124, 212, 231–232
  economy, 170–173, 186, 195, 220–221, 248, 258–259
  history, 85, 94–102, 107–110, 114, 143, 145, 199, 229, 265, 272
  industrialisation, 162, 170–173, 187
  peasantry, 73, 169–170, 172, 184
  politics, 7–8, 11, 15, 17–18, 24–25, 28, 58, 66, 68, 83, 111, 115, 132, 139–141, 144, 186–187, 200, 205, 211, 223–224, 228, 231–232, 236, 238, 243, 246, 272–274
  provinces, 113–129, 143, 170
    provincial communes, 70
  revolution, 2, 29, 31, 82, 95, 115, 142–143, 160, 229, 269, 272
    1789, 3, 31, 82, 86, 90–91, 95–96, 102–103, 110, 276
    1792, 103, 107
    1793, 82, 90, 99, 101, 107
    1830, 31, 44, 82, 86–87, 95, 106
    1848, 30–31, 38, 44, 62, 82, 86–87, 89, 95, 106, 112, 115, 117–119, 121, 128, 130–131, 144, 168, 182
  socialism, 87, 123, 149, 151–157, 166, 173, 176–177, 179–180, 182, 184, 187, 189–191, 193–195, 197–205, 234, 248, 252, 270–271, 273
  society, 8, 26, 47, 83–85, 95–96, 100, 130, 134, 177, 198, 222, 227, 234

Fraternity, 18, 81, 245, 266
  universal, 259
Furet, François, 6, 93, 104, 143

Gaboriaux, Chloé, 170, 172
Gambetta, Léon, 39, 57, 62, 67, 93–94, 96, 103, 116, 231, 233
Gandhi, Leela, 267
Geneva, 3, 70, 133, 144, 175, 240, 249–250
Geographer, 35, 113, 133, 137, 144, 209, 249
Geography, 11, 127, 133, 173
Germany, 39, 97, 168, 172–173, 194–196, 198–199, 210, 222, 226, 242, 245
  anti-Germanism, 196, 199
  army, 2, 38–39, 41, 49, 109, 192, 196
  economy, 171, 184, 186
  expatriates, 150
  industrialisation, 171
  language, 153, 155, 157–158, 162, 164, 166–169
  politics, 198
  socialists, 154, 194, 197–199
Ghosh, Peter, 205
Gildea, Robert, 82
Girardet, Raoul, 211
Girondism, 107
Godineau, Laure, 8, 24
Government of National Defence, 31, 38, 41–42, 76
Grévy, Jules, 93
Grousset, Paschal, 220, 229, 232, 261
Guesde, Jules, 116, 126, 151, 155, 165, 180, 183–184, 188, 198, 237, 273
Guesdists, 9, 13, 17, 21, 71, 118, 127, 137, 140, 150–151, 156, 179–187, 189, 192–193, 197–198, 201–202, 204–206, 244, 273
Guillaume, James, 15, 149, 175–176
Guillotine, 91, 101
Guizot, François, 98
Guyot, Yves, 121

Harris, Ruth, 120
Harrison, Frederic, 28, 32
Haussonville report, 222–223, 234
Hazareesingh, Sudhir, 94
Hugo, Victor, 10, 39, 85, 87, 102, 104, 109, 216, 231, 233, 262, 275
Huguenots, 98. *See also* Protestants
Humbert, Alphonse, 121
Hutton, Patrick, 66, 74, 87, 142

India, 193, 210, 223, 241, 259
Indochina, 245

Industrialisation, 159–160, 163, 174, 182–187, 194
  British. *See* United Kingdom:industrialisation
  Chinese. *See* China:industrialisation
  French. *See* France:industrialisation
  German. *See* Germany:industrialisation
Inequality, 160, 222
  social, 134
Injustice, 40–41, 218
Insurrection, 10, 27, 50, 105, 110, 135, 215
International Workingmen's Association, 7, 13, 31, 37, 149, 153–154, 156–157, 174–178, 180, 189, 192, 195, 212, 227, 240, 273
  Hague Congress, 149, 176
  politics, 176–177
  split, 176, 188, 190
Internationalist. *See* Socialists:international

James, C.L.R., 4
Japan, 250, 264
Jaurès, Jean, 150, 155
Jews. *See* Judaism
Johnson, Martin, 22, 24
Joughin, Jean, 24, 58, 60, 233
Jourde, Francis, 220, 230, 232, 261
Journalist, 9, 30, 33, 35, 41, 54–56, 71, 88, 118, 123, 130, 132, 158, 165, 191, 209, 213, 215, 244, 248, 251, 253, 261
Jousse, Emmanuel, 7, 34, 179, 198, 212
Judaism, 195, 197, 199
July Monarchy, 130, 195, 259
Jura Federation, 13, 175, 180, 249
Justice, 2, 44, 66, 129

Kabylia, 252, 260
  democracy, 251–252, 264
  deportees, 218, 262
  rebellion, 10, 217
  society, 267
Kanaks, 216, 218, 223, 225, 262
  culture, 262
  rebellion, 217–218
Kautsky, Karl, 203
Koselleck, Reinhart, 142
Kropotkin, Peter, 33, 82

Labour, 182, 186, 228, 254
  artisanal, 185–186
  child, 159, 161
  communal. *See* Labour:artisanal
  factory. *See* Labour:industrial
  imported, 216, 223
  industrial, 11, 159–162, 171–172, 183–184, 187

Lachâtre, Maurice, 158, 164, 167, 178
Lafargue, Laura, 21, 181
  as interlocutor, 97, 154–155, 167, 202
Lafargue, Paul, 7, 21, 132, 151, 154–155, 165, 181, 184, 197, 203–204, 244, 271, 273
  as author, 180–181, 183, 185, 187, 203
  Le droit à la paresse, 115, 180, 183
  as interlocutor, 57, 123, 155, 191, 196, 198, 201
  as translator, 156
Law, *Loi Dufaure*, 177, 199
  Loi Falloux, 117–118, 124
  natural, 129, 234, 254–255, 257
  republican, 6, 12, 85, 92–93, 96, 195, 204
  Lois Ferry, 118
Lecler, Adhémar, 132, 136
Lefebvre, Henri, 4, 27, 73
Lefrançais, Gustave, 9, 21, 26, 35, 39, 44–46, 53, 55, 58, 62, 71, 75, 84, 89, 101, 250
Lehning, James, 212
Leith, James, 24
Lenin, Vladimir, 3, 5, 22, 268
Leroy-Beaulieu, Pierre, 210, 214, 220–221, 246, 248
Liberals, 94, 98, 115, 117, 159, 210, 237, 256, 259, 266
  later, 22, 26
Liberty, 92, 96, 225
  impediments to, 159, 184, 219
  municipal, 73
  republican, 88
  traditional symbols of, 88, 108
  work and, 159, 183, 185
Lichtheim, George, 150, 152, 203
Liebknecht, Wilhelm, 154, 198–199
Ligou, Daniel, 151
Lissagaray, Prosper-Olivier, 53, 243–249
  as actor, 192, 276
  as author, 51, 57, 273
  Histoire de la Commune de 1871, 26, 35–36, 53, 243
  as editor, 35, 53, 165, 196, 273
London, 33, 35, 40, 59, 64, 175–177, 239–240, 276
Longuet, Charles, 9, 33, 132

Machinery, 159–160, 171, 184–185
Madagascar, 209, 246
Mailhé, Germaine, 217
Maitron, Jean, 23
Malon, Benoît
  as actor, 21, 35, 39, 151, 204, 271
  as author, 26, 40, 42, 55, 57–58, 63, 69–70, 88–89, 119, 121, 177, 180, 189–190, 198, 240

as editor, 15, 21, 126
as interlocutor, 123
Mantena, Karuna, 252
Mao, Zedong, 3, 5, 22
Marçot, Jean-Louis, 234, 252
Marseilles, 70–71
Martyrdom, 57
Martyrs, 58
  revolutionary, 56, 60, 65, 72
Marx, Eleanor, 35, 59, 244
Marx, Karl, 15, 32, 77, 270
  as actor, 10, 26, 31, 37, 244, 274
  as author, 3, 5, 11, 17, 23, 32–33, 37, 46, 53,
    209, 225, 270–274, 276
  Das Kapital, 155, 158–164, 166–170, 174,
    181–182, 187, 273
  Le Capital, 153, 156, 158–168, 173, 187,
    191
  Misère de la philosophie, 156, 191, 202
  The Civil War in France, 23, 26, 31–32,
    67–68, 154, 156, 169, 181, 203
  as inspiration, 17, 22, 33, 273
  as interlocutor, 32, 244
Marxism, 7, 11, 15, 17, 68, 77, 150–154, 156,
  164, 177, 179, 182, 193–194, 200–205,
  209, 274
  orthodox, 17, 180, 202–203, 205, 270, 273
Marxists, 26, 44, 67, 149–152, 154, 188, 201, 272
  French. *See* Guesdists
Matsuda, Matt, 211, 223
Mazzini, Giuseppe, 138
Mechnikov, Lev, 249–251, 256
Mehta, Uday, 266
Merriman, John, 5, 50
Messager, Henri, 213, 226, 235
Metropole, 222–223, 236, 246, 259
  colony–metropole paradigm, 259
Meunier, Lucien-Victor, 123, 244
Mexico, 210, 240, 250
Michel, Louise, 117, 129, 213, 215, 218, 220,
  228, 231, 262, 275
Michelet, Jules, 98
Midi, 70, 122, 126
Militarism, 219–220, 224, 236, 267
Modernity, 252, 254, 257–258, 264
Monarchism, 6, 210, 232, 236
Monarchists, 60, 92, 118
Monarchy, 41, 236
  July. *See* July Monarchy
Montagnards, 90, 107, 109
Montagne, the. *See* Montagnards
Montmartre, 1, 27, 49, 215
Moral Order, 76
  government, 13, 93, 216, 228, 236
  politicians, 52, 63, 103, 140, 214, 272

Moreau, Jacques, 87
Morris, William, 56, 186
Moss, Bernard, 151, 212
Movement, international, 16, 76, 81, 90–91, 97,
  104, 106, 114, 119–120, 122, 127–128,
  136–139, 141, 149–150, 179, 193–195,
  200, 206, 209, 212, 231–232, 269–270,
  272, 274–277
  Italian, 138
  revolutionary, 1, 9, 11, 14–18, 36–37, 50, 54,
    60–61, 64, 67–68, 70–71, 74
  unified, 18, 81, 272
Mur des Fédérés, 21–22, 56

Napoleon I, 116, 210
Napoleon III, 10, 30, 38, 42, 56, 63, 130, 169,
  210
  1851 *coup d'état*, 38, 109, 130, 169
Naquet, Alfred, 216, 233
Nation, 97–98, 110, 233, 238, 254, 257–258,
  263
National Guard, 2, 27–28, 30, 53, 89, 108
Nationalism, 12, 67, 242, 271
  patriotic, 97
Nationalists, 16, 77, 242, 271
Nature, 84, 112, 130, 137, 143, 145, 200, 234
  force of, 137, 139, 141, 272
  history, 130
  of man, 98
New Caledonia, 2, 6, 10–11, 17, 54, 65, 117,
  212–217, 219–220, 222–223, 226–233,
  235–241, 261–262, 264, 266, 270, 273,
  275
  Ducos peninsula, 215, 230
  Île des Pins, 215, 230
  Île Nou, 215, 224, 230
New York, 261
Newspapers, 13–15, 35, 51, 122–123, 126–127,
  263, 266
  La Bataille, 15, 51, 53, 60, 192, 197, 241–251,
    254, 256–260, 264, 266, 268, 273
  Bulletin de la Fédération jurassienne, 45, 216,
    239–240, 249
  Le Citoyen, 15, 129, 180, 244, 256
  Le Citoyen & La Bataille, 123, 165, 244
  L'Égalité, 15, 26, 34, 38, 51, 74, 108, 137–138,
    157, 180–181, 183, 186, 196–198, 200,
    244
  L'Émancipation, 15, 126
  La Fédération, 12, 15, 51, 69, 84, 91
  L'Intransigeant, 14, 51, 54–55, 57, 60, 84,
    118, 121, 137, 180, 191–192, 219, 256,
    262
  New York Herald, 93, 261
  La Patrie en danger, 107, 109–110

Newspapers (cont.)
  La Patrie en Danger, 84
  Le Prolétaire, 15, 26, 34–35, 41, 54, 58, 60,
     74, 90, 104, 123, 136, 140, 180, 188,
     190, 197, 206, 240, 244
  Qui Vive!, 15, 26, 34, 51, 95–96
  Revue socialiste, 21, 40, 58, 88, 119, 241, 257
  Le Travailleur, 15, 36, 38, 89, 133, 241–243,
     249–261, 263–268
Nicolet, Claude, 6

Oceania, 13, 216, 223, 242
Order, established, 25, 214, 234, 259
  forces of, 98, 100
  party of, 103
  social, 231
Orders, religious, 124
Organisation, communal, 163, 184, 191, 193,
     202, 209, 235
Orléans, House of, 41, 236
Ozouf, Mona, 6, 93

Pacific, South, 2, 17, 214, 229, 234, 238, 241,
     261
Pain, Olivier, 12, 261–262, 270
Pamphleteer, 9, 276
Paris, burning of, 2, 29, 49, 51, 53
Parti Ouvrier Français, 13, 62, 154, 188, 190,
     206
Patriotism, 96–97, 109, 260
  La patrie, 40, 97, 109
Peasantry, property of, 169
Pelletan, Camille
  as actor, 10, 30, 52, 62, 216, 233
  as author, 26, 32, 44, 46–47, 52
Père-Lachaise cemetery, 2, 21, 60
Perin, Georges, 233
Perovic, Sanja, 26
Pétroleuse, 29, 227
Pitts, Jennifer, 256, 259, 266
Plekhanov, Georgi, 133
POF. *See* Parti Ouvrier Français
Police, 176
  informant, 13, 70
  Préfecture de police, 13, 59, 240, 269, 276
  report, 13, 51, 59, 235, 269, 271, 276
Politics, 18, 23, 128, 131, 140–141, 260–261
  international, 11, 22
  moderate, 7
  of everyday life, 129, 141, 272
  of friendship, 267
  party, 13, 67, 110, 123, 138, 154, 177, 182,
     188–189, 194, 201, 205, 221, 274
  revolutionary, 21, 46, 75, 106, 132, 272,
     274–275

Positivists, 131, 164
Possibilists, 9, 13, 71, 127, 136, 152, 180–181,
     186, 188–193, 197, 201, 204–206, 240,
     244
Priest, Robert, 125
Prison, 40, 49, 106, 138, 213, 220, 226, 230,
     270
  Warden, 215
Prisoners, 2, 155, 214, 225–226
  Political, 225, 232, 262
Proletariat, 40, 61, 170, 254, 260
Protectionism, 172, 187, 243, 249, 254,
     256–258
Protestants, 99. *See also* Huguenots
Proudhon, Pierre Joseph, 69, 197
  as author, 180, 182, 184
  as inspiration, 151, 191, 273
Proudhonism, 152
Prussia. *See* Germany
Przyblyski, J.M., 6
Pyat, Félix, 55, 158

Radical Party, 22
Radicalism, 9–10, 90, 177, 198, 234, 267
  student, 10, 132, 145
Radicals, 86, 125, 182, 188, 192, 199, 216, 226,
     233–234, 236, 248, 261, 270, 274
Railways, 122, 135, 137, 248, 260
Reactionary, 29, 31, 47, 129, 170
Reclus, Élisée
  as actor, 113, 133–136, 168
  as author, 9, 119, 141, 144, 209, 235,
     249–251, 253, 255, 260, 264, 272–273
  Évolution et Révolution, 133–136
  as editor, 133
  as inspiration, 11, 133
Regnard, Albert, 257, 260
Religion, 84, 112–129, 139, 143, 170, 232, 247,
     272
  popular, 56
  substitute for, 112, 124
  world, 240
Renan, Ernest, 125, 252
Republic, 185
  ancient, 108
  as constitution, 40–41, 52, 60, 74, 83, 89,
     92–94, 96, 99–100, 103, 134, 145, 199,
     214, 219, 221, 236–238, 247, 275
  as government, 25, 60, 77, 92–94, 96,
     100–101, 103–104, 143–145, 211, 214,
     218, 227–229, 232, 235, 237–238, 266,
     274–275
  as idea, 96, 98–99, 101, 105, 108, 110, 143,
     233, 235–238, 268
  as society, 96

First. *See* First Republic
Roman, 96
Second. *See* Second Republic
Third. *See* Third Republic
Republicanism, 67, 70, 76, 104, 108, 211, 232,
    249, 252, 266
    moderate, 8, 62, 270, 275
    opportunist, 76–77
Republicans, 7, 30, 35, 38, 46–47, 52, 60,
    62–63, 67, 77, 82, 85, 89, 93–94, 98,
    100, 105, 121, 130, 135, 144–145, 210,
    216, 218, 229, 233, 237–238, 244,
    260–262, 272, 274–276
    moderate, 10, 30, 52, 63, 67, 85, 94, 96, 109,
        111, 113, 145, 225, 232–233
    opportunist, 3, 6, 12, 16, 85, 93–94, 96,
        100–103, 105, 109, 118, 133, 139–140,
        142, 145, 195, 213–214, 216, 221, 228,
        236, 270–271, 273, 275
    radical, 10, 30, 42, 47, 52, 63, 67, 85, 94, 100,
        103, 109, 111, 134, 145, 186–187, 209,
        216, 222, 234, 270, 275
    republican community, 12, 99, 111, 145, 275
    revolutionary, 30, 85, 93–94, 106, 111, 145,
        211, 232
Restoration, 103
    Bonapartist, 92
    Monarchical, 52, 60, 92, 140
Restoration, the, 106, 210
Rigault, Raoul, 28, 71
Rights
    democratic, 101, 105, 246–247
    national, 257
    right to be lazy, 185–186
    right to work, 11, 182, 185
    universal, 95, 160
    workers', 187, 257–258
Rihs, Charles, 9, 24
Robespierre, Maximilien, 29, 53, 89, 256
Rochefort, Henri, 54, 94, 118, 191, 211, 213,
    215–216, 218, 233, 261–262, 271
    as author, 54, 93, 127, 228
    as editor, 14–15, 219
    as *évadé*, 215–216, 233, 275
Ross, Kristin, 33, 60
Roubaix, 171–172, 186, 194, 198
Rougerie, Jacques, 4–5, 23–24
Roy, Joseph, 158, 166–167
Royalists. *See* Monarchists
Russia, 133, 210, 241–242, 245, 249–250
    revolution, 2, 22

Sacrifice, 5, 47, 55, 138–139, 144, 232, 237, 250
Saint Bartholomew's Day Massacre, 98
Saint-Simonianism, 106, 234

Saint-Simonians. *See* Saint-Simonianism
San Francisco, 253, 261
Schoelcher, Victor, 62
Science, 129–142, 144–145, 234
Second Empire, 10, 30, 38, 41, 86, 94, 100,
    116–117, 126, 132, 134, 195, 246, 274
    fall, 38, 59, 102
Second International, 8, 12, 271
Second Republic, 101, 109, 112, 116, 130, 168,
    210
    constitution, 210
    fall, 111, 130, 169
Secret societies. *See* Conspiracy
Section française de l'Internationale ouvrière, 22,
    213
Semaine Sanglante, 2, 5, 8, 24, 31, 33–34, 49,
    51–55, 58, 60–64, 71, 98, 105, 225,
    269
Senegal, 221, 223, 261
Separation of Church and State. *See* Catholic
    Church:separation of Church and State
Sessions, Jennifer, 243
Shineberg, Dorothy, 223
Siegel, Jerrold, 168
Sieyès, Emmanuel Joseph, 88, 99
Socialism, 4, 12, 32, 66, 128, 134, 144, 150,
    152, 165, 182–183, 186, 188, 190, 193,
    202–203, 206, 212, 246, 251, 255, 265,
    267–269
    Christian, 115
    federalist, 25, 53, 71, 91
    French. *See* France:socialism
    German. *See* Germany:socialists
    international, 12, 15, 17, 37, 60, 67, 75, 149,
        154, 194–195, 200, 253, 270, 274
    Marxian, 8, 15, 67, 270
    public service, 7, 204
    reformist, 7–8, 271
    revolutionary, 17, 212, 243
Socialists, 16, 21, 29, 32, 39, 45, 47, 77, 87, 98,
    102, 107, 109, 114, 119, 139–140,
    151–152, 155, 157–158, 165, 172, 177,
    180, 184, 187, 190, 193–195, 197–200,
    204, 240, 248, 264, 268, 271, 273–274
    Christian, 116, 120
    democratic, 116, 120, 125
    deputies, 4, 21, 140
    federalist, 9, 91
    international, 29, 49, 61, 82, 155, 186, 194,
        205
    proto-, 90
    public service, 188
    revolutionary, 35, 149, 151, 179–180, 200,
        204, 243–244, 266, 273
    utopian, 115, 195

Solidarity, 50, 81, 121, 194, 231, 253–254, 257,
        259, 262, 266–267, 273, 276
    international, 266
    regional, 254
    revolutionary, 50, 217, 262
    transnational, 264, 268
    universal, 257, 259
    universal proletarian, 253, 255
    of the vanquished, 262
Sorel, Georges, 151, 155–156
Stafford, David, 72, 151, 176
Starr, Peter, 27
State, 6, 40, 170, 238, 241, 264
    bourgeois State, 160, 169, 183
    French State, 17, 52, 75, 96, 116, 213, 236,
        266, 273
    republican State, 77, 92, 100–101, 103, 111,
        142, 144, 182, 225, 227, 229, 237, 275
Stedman Jones, Gareth, 163, 168
Sternhell, Zeev, 7, 271
Stoler, Ann Laura, 218, 267
Struggle, class, 153, 168, 198
    for equality, 116
    power, 149
    revolutionary, 33, 66, 268
Stuart, Robert, 128, 152, 212
Suffrage, female, 249
    universal, 275
Switzerland, 3, 69, 133, 149, 175–176, 240,
        250

Taine, Hippolyte, 29, 41, 46, 51, 99
Talmeyr, Maurice, 191
Technology, 122, 159, 171, 260, 266
Terror, the, 30, 100
Thiers, Adolphe, 22, 31, 47, 68, 72, 94, 98, 106,
        134, 225
Third Republic, 11, 63, 67, 75, 84, 98, 100, 103,
        105, 108, 110–111, 113, 142–144, 170,
        209–210, 214, 219, 225, 229, 232,
        234–238, 242, 246, 248, 259, 263, 275
    constitution, 92, 236
    early, 7, 14–16, 47, 59, 81–82, 85–86, 92,
        102, 105, 118, 120, 124, 132, 150, 152,
        172, 197, 204–205, 211, 213, 227, 243,
        266, 268, 272
    foundation, 1, 38, 100, 112, 133
    politicians, 50
Todd, David, 103, 248
Tolain, Henri, 62
Tombs, Robert, 2, 5, 8, 24, 51, 77, 91, 94, 105
Tonkin affair, 12, 245
Toolkit, revolutionary, 83, 85–86, 100, 112
Toth, Stephen, 211
Trade union, 10, 261

Tradition, 18, 23, 26, 83–85, 89, 109, 116, 151,
        256–257, 266–267, 270, 276
    enlightened, 99–100
    federalist, 71
    radical, 10, 198
    revolutionary, 1, 18, 22, 66, 82–83, 85,
        88–90, 95, 99–101, 104, 107–108, 110,
        112, 142–143, 145, 156, 276
Transnationalism, 249, 257, 260–262, 264–266,
        268
Transportation, 226
Transportees, 226
Tridon, Gustave, 39
Trinquet, Alexis, 225, 228
Tuileries Palace, 51, 53

United Kingdom, 3, 38, 69, 159, 167, 175, 244,
        253, 269
    colonialism, 221, 224, 247
    culture, 259
    economy, 163, 184, 186
    empire, 247
    industrialisation, 171
    socialists, 56
United States, 3, 10, 108, 214, 240
Urbain, Raoul, 38, 261

Vaillant, Édouard, 54, 56, 65, 122, 129
Vallès, Jules, 14–15, 57, 192
Values
    French, 229
    liberal, 90, 94, 103
    republican, 63, 93–94, 219, 232, 237, 247,
        266
Varlin, Eugène, 49
Versailles, 2, 34, 37, 40–42, 63, 65
Vincent, Steven, 151, 212
Violence, 10, 25, 30, 49–50, 52–55, 58, 61–62,
        65, 77
    act of, 2, 215
    experience of, 57, 64–65, 75
    official, 52, 63
    revolutionary, 52, 90–91, 103–104, 112, 144
    symbolic, 72
Virtue, 109, 185, 237
Vuillaume, Maxime, 72

War, 97
    Cold War, 4–5, 22
    Franco-Prussian War, 1, 27, 39, 97, 109, 172,
        196, 198
    Revolutionary Wars, 86, 107–108
    Wars of Religion, 98
Watkins, Peter, 23
Weber, Eugen, 83

Willard, Claude, 151
Wilson, Colette, 6
Workers, 28, 45, 88–89, 107, 109, 116, 123,
    134, 139, 153, 159–167, 169–170,
    183–188, 190, 199, 246, 250, 253–255,
    257–258
  association, 123, 151
  Chinese, 253
  enfranchisement, 138, 162

  European, 171, 253, 258–260, 266, 273
  French, 166, 171–172, 244, 249, 258, 268
  library, 165
  movement, 187, 201–202
  newspaper, 165
  property, 169, 173
  universal, 194, 253–254, 257, 260, 266

Zasulich, Vera, 15, 133, 163

IDEAS IN CONTEXT

Edited by

David Armitage, Richard Bourke, Jennifer Pitts, and John Robertson

1. RICHARD RORTY, J. B. SCHNEEWIND, and QUENTIN SKINNER (eds.)
   Philosophy in History
   Essays in the Historiography of Philosophy
   PB 9780521273305

2. J. G. A. POCOCK
   Virtue, Commerce and History
   Essays on Political Thought and History, Chiefly in the Eighteenth Century
   PB 9780521276603

3. M. M. GOLDSMITH
   Private Vices, Public Benefits
   Bernard Mandeville's Social and Political Thought
   HB 9780521300360

4. ANTHONY PAGDEN (ed.)
   The Languages of Political Theory in Early Modern Europe
   PB 9780521386661

5. DAVID SUMMERS
   The Judgment of Sense
   Renaissance Naturalism and the Rise of Aesthetics
   PB 9780521386319

6. LAURENCE DICKEY
   Hegel: Religion, Economics and the Politics of Spirit, 1770–1807
   PB 9780521389129

7. MARGO TODD
   Christian Humanism and the Puritan Social Order
   PB 9780521892285

8. LYNN SUMIDA JOY
   Gassendi the Atomist
   Advocate of History in an Age of Science
   PB 9780521522397

9. EDMUND LEITES (ed.)
   Conscience and Casuistry in Early Modern Europe
   PB 9780521520201

10. WOLF LEPENIES
    Between Literature and Science: The Rise of Sociology
    PB 9780521338103

11. TERENCE BALL, JAMES FARR, and RUSSELL L. HANSON (eds.)
    Political Innovation and Conceptual Change
    PB 9780521359788

12. GERD GIGERENZER et al.
    The Empire of Chance
    How Probability Changed Science and Everyday Life
    PB 9780521398381

13. PETER NOVICK
    That Noble Dream
    The "Objectivity Question" and the American Historical Profession
    HB 9780521343282
    PB 9780521357456

14. DAVID LIEBERMAN
    The Province of Legislation Determined
    Legal Theory in Eighteenth-century Britain
    PB 9780521528542

15. DANIEL PICK
    Faces of Degeneration
    A European Disorder, c.1848–c.1918
    PB 9780521457538

16. KEITH BAKER
    Inventing the French Revolution
    Essays on French Political Culture in the Eighteenth Century
    PB 9780521385787

17. IAN HACKING
    The Taming of Chance
    HB 9780521380140
    PB 9780521388849

18. GISELA BOCK, QUENTIN SKINNER, and MAURIZIO VIROLI (eds.)
    Machiavelli and Republicanism
    PB 9780521435895

19. DOROTHY ROSS
    The Origins of American Social Science
    PB 9780521428361

20. KLAUS CHRISTIAN KOHNKE
The Rise of Neo-Kantianism
German Academic Philosophy between Idealism and Positivism
HB 9780521373364

21. IAN MACLEAN
Interpretation and Meaning in the Renaissance
The Case of Law
HB 9780521415460
PB 9780521020275

22. MAURIZIO VIROLI
From Politics to Reason of State
The Acquisition and Transformation of the Language of Politics 1250–1600
HB 9780521414937
PB 9780521673433

23. MARTIN VAN GELDEREN
The Political Thought of the Dutch Revolt 1555–1590
HB 9780521392044
PB 9780521891639

24. NICHOLAS PHILLIPSON and QUENTIN SKINNER (eds.)
Political Discourse in Early Modern Britain
HB 9780521392426

25. JAMES TULLY
An Approach to Political Philosophy: Locke in Contexts
HB 9780521430609
PB 9780521436380

26. RICHARD TUCK
Philosophy and Government 1572–1651
PB 9780521438858

27. RICHARD YEO
Defining Science
William Whewell, Natural Knowledge and Public Debate in Early Victorian Britain
HB 9780521431828
PB 9780521541169

28. MARTIN WARNKE
The Court Artist
On the Ancestry of the Modern Artist
HB 9780521363754

29. PETER N. MILLER
   Defining the Common Good
   Empire, Religion and Philosophy in Eighteenth-Century Britain
   HB 9780521442596
   PB 9780521617123

30. CHRISTOPHER J. BERRY
   The Idea of Luxury
   A Conceptual and Historical Investigation
   PB 9780521466912

31. E. J. HUNDERT
   The Enlightenment's 'Fable'
   Bernard Mandeville and the Discovery of Society
   HB 9780521460828
   PB 9780521619424

32. JULIA STAPLETON
   Englishness and the Study of Politics
   The Social and Political Thought of Ernest Barker
   HB 9780521461252
   PB 9780521024440

33. KEITH TRIBE
   Strategies of Economic Order
   German Economic Discourse, 1750–1950
   HB 9780521462914
   PB 9780521619431

34. SACHIKO KUSUKAWA
   The Transformation of Natural Philosophy
   The Case of Philip Melanchthon
   HB 9780521473477
   PB 9780521030465

35. DAVID ARMITAGE, ARMAND HIMY, and QUENTIN SKINNER (eds.)
   Milton and Republicanism
   HB 978521551786
   PB 9780521646482

36. MARKKU PELTONEN
   Classical Humanism and Republicanism in English Political Thought
   1570–1640
   HB 9780521496957
   PB 9780521617161

37. PHILIP IRONSIDE
   The Social and Political Thought of Bertrand Russell

The Development of an Aristocratic Liberalism
HB 9780521473835
PB 9780521024761

38. NANCY CARTWRIGHT, JORDI CAT, LOLA FLECK, and THOMAS E. UEBEL
Otto Neurath: Philosophy between Science and Politics
HB 9780521451741

39. DONALD WINCH
Riches and Poverty
An Intellectual History of Political Economy in Britain, 1750–1834
PB 9780521559201

40. JENNIFER PLATT
A History of Sociological Research Methods in America
HB 9780521441735
PB 9780521646499

41. KNUD HAAKONSSEN (ed.)
Enlightenment and Religion
Rational Dissent in Eighteenth-Century Britain
HB 9780521560603
PB 9780521029872

42. G. E. R. LLOYD
Adversaries and Authorities
Investigations into Ancient Greek and Chinese Science
HB 9780521553315
PB 9780521556958

43. ROLF LINDNER
The Reportage of Urban Culture
Robert Park and the Chicago School
HB 9780521440523
PB 9780521026536

44. ANNABEL BRETT
Liberty, Right and Nature
Individual Rights in Later Scholastic Thought
HB 9780521562393
PB 9780521543408

45. STEWART J. BROWN (ed.)
William Robertson and the Expansion of Empire
HB 780521570831

46. HELENA ROSENBLATT
Rousseau and Geneva

From the First Discourse to the Social Contract, 1749–1762
HB 9780521570046
PB 9780521033954

47. DAVID RUNCIMAN
Pluralism and the Personality of the State
HB 9780521551915
PB 9780521022637

48. ANNABEL PATTERSON
Early Modern Liberalism
HB 9780521592604
PB 9780521026314

49. DAVID WEINSTEIN
Equal Freedom and Utility
Herbert Spencer's Liberal Utilitarianism
HB 9780521622646
PB 9780521026864

50. YUN LEE TOO and NIALL LIVINGSTONE (eds.)
Pedagogy and Power
Rhetorics of Classical Learning
HB 9780521594356
PB 9780521038010

51. REVIEL NETZ
The Shaping of Deduction in Greek Mathematics
A Study in Cognitive History
HB 9780521622790
PB b 9780521541206

52. MARY S. MORGAN AND MARGARET MORRISON (eds.)
Models as Mediators
Perspectives in Natural and Social Science
HB 9780521650977
PB 9780521655712

53. JOEL MICHELL
Measurement in Psychology
A Critical History of a Methodological Concept
HB 9780521621205
PB 9780521021517

54. RICHARD A. PRIMUS
The American Language of Rights

HB 9780521652506
PB 9780521616218

55. ROBERT ALUN JONES
The development of Durkheim's Social Realism
HB 9780521650458
PB 9780521022101

56. ANNE MCLAREN
Political Culture in the Reign of Elizabeth I
Queen and Commonwealth 1558–1585
HB 9780521651448
PB 9780521024839

57. JAMES HANKINS (ed.)
Renaissance Civic Humanism
Reappraisals and Reflections
HB 9780521780902
PB 9780521548076

58. T.J. HOCHSTRASSER
Natural Law Theories in the Early Enlightenment
HB 9780521661935
PB 9780521027878

59. DAVID ARMITAGE
The Ideological Origins of the British Empire
HB 9780521590815
PB 9780521789783

60. IAN HUNTER
Rival Enlightenments
Civil and Metaphysical Philosophy in Early Modern Germany
HB 9780521792653
PB 9780521025492

61. DARIO CASTIGLIONE AND IAIN HAMPSHER-MONK (eds.)
The History of Political Thought in National Context
HB 9780521782340

62. IAN MACLEAN
Logic, Signs and Nature in the Renaissance
The Case of Learned Medicine
HB 9780521806480

63. PETER MACK
Elizabethan Rhetoric
Theory and Practice

HB 9780521812924
PB 9780521020992

64. GEOFFREY LLOYD
The Ambitions of Curiosity
Understanding the World in Ancient Greece and China
HB 9780521815420
PB 9780521894616

65. MARKKU PELTONEN
The Duel in Early Modern England
Civility, Politeness and Honour
HB 9780521820622
PB 9780521025201

66. ADAM SUTCLIFFE
Judaism and Enlightenment
HB 9780521820158
PB 9780521672320

67. ANDREW FITZMAURICE
Humanism and America
An Intellectual History of English Colonisation, 1500–1625
HB 9780521822251

68. PIERRE FORCE
Self-Interest before Adam Smith
A Genealogy of Economic Science
HB 9780521830607
PB 9780521036191

69. ERIC NELSON
The Greek Tradition in Republican Thought
HB 9780521835459
PB 9780521024280

70. HARRO HOPFL
Jesuit Political Thought
The Society of Jesus and the state, c.1540–1640
HB 9780521837798

71. MIKAEL HORNQVIST
Machiavelli and Empire
HB 9780521839457

72. DAVID COLCLOUGH
Freedom of Speech in Early Stuart England
HB 9780521847483

73. JOHN ROBERTSON
   The Case for the Enlightenment
   Scotland and Naples 1680–1760
   HB 9780521847872
   PB 9780521035729

74. DANIEL CAREY
   Locke, Shaftesbury, and Hutcheson
   Contesting Diversity in the Enlightenment and Beyond
   HB 9780521845021

75. ALAN CROMARTIE
   The Constitutionalist Revolution
   An Essay on the History of England, 1450–1642
   HB 9780521782692

76. HANNAH DAWSON
   Locke, Language and Early-Modern Philosophy
   HB 9780521852715

77. CONAL CONDREN, STEPHEN GAUKROGER AND IAN HUNTER (eds.)
   The Philosopher in Early Modern Europe
   The Nature of a Contested Identity
   HB 9780521866460

78. ANGUS GOWLAND
   The Worlds of Renaissance Melancholy
   Robert Burton in Context
   HB 9780521867689

79. PETER STACEY
   Roman Monarchy and the Renaissance Prince
   HB 9780521869898

80. RHODRI LEWIS
   Language, Mind and Nature
   Artificial Languages in England from Bacon to Locke
   HB 9780521874750

81. DAVID LEOPOLD
   The Young Karl Marx
   German Philosophy, Modern Politics, and Human Flourishing
   HB 9780521874779

82. JON PARKIN
   Taming the Leviathan
   The Reception of the Political and Religious Ideas of Thomas Hobbes in England 1640–1700
   HB 9780521877350

83. D. WEINSTEIN
Utilitarianism and the New Liberalism
HB 9780521875288

84. LUCY DELAP
The Feminist Avant-Garde
Transatlantic Encounters of the Early Twentieth Century
HB 9780521876513

85. BORIS WISEMAN
Lévi-Strauss, Anthropology and Aesthetics
HB 9780521875295

86. DUNCAN BELL (ed.)
Victorian Visions of Global Order
Empire and International Relations in Nineteenth-Century Political Thought
HB 9780521882927

87. IAN HUNTER
The Secularisation of the Confessional State
The Political Thought of Christian Thomasius
HB 9780521880558

88. CHRISTIAN J. EMDEN
Friedrich Nietzsche and the Politics of History
HB 9780521880565

89. ANNELIEN DE DIJN
French Political thought from Montesquieu to Tocqueville
Liberty in a Levelled Society?
HB 9780521877886

90. PETER GARNSEY
Thinking About Propety
From Antiquity to the Age of Revolution
HB 9780521876773
PB 9780521700238

91. PENELOPE DEUTSCHER
The Philosophy of Simone de Beauvoir
Ambiguity, Conversion, Resistance
HB 9780521885201

92. HELENA ROSENBLATT
Liberal Values
Benjamin Constant and the Politics of Religion
HB 9780521898256

93. JAMES TULLY
Public Philosophy in a New Key
Volume 1: Democracy and Civic Freedom
HB 9780521449618
PB 9780521728799

94. JAMES TULLY
Public Philosophy in a New Key
Volume 2: Imperialism and Civic Freedom
HB 9780521449663
PB 9780521728805

95. DONALD WINCH
Wealth and Life
Essays on the Intellectual History of Political Economy in Britain, 1848–1914
HB 9780521887533
PB 9780521715393

96. FONNA FORMAN-BARZILAI
Adam Smith and the Circles of Sympathy
Cosmopolitanism and Moral Theory
HB 9780521761123

97. GREGORY CLAEYS
Imperial Sceptics
British Critics of Empire 1850–1920
HB 9780521199544

98. EDWARD BARING
The Young Derrida and French Philosophy, 1945–1968
HB 9781107009677

99. CAROL PAL
Republic of Women
Rethinking the Republic of Letters in the Seventeenth Century
HB 9781107018211

100. C. A. BAYLY
Recovering Liberties
Indian Thought in the Age of Liberalism and Empire
HB 9781107013834
PB 9781107601475

101. FELICITY GREEN
Montaigne and the Life of Freedom
HB 9781107024397

102. JOSHUA DERMAN
Max Weber in Politics and Social Thought
From Charisma to Canonizaion
HB 9781107025882

103. RAINER FORST (translated by CIARAN CRONIN)
Toleration in Conflict
Past and Present
HB 9780521885775

104. SOPHIE READ
Eucharist and the Poetic Imagination in Early Modern England
HB 9781107032736

105. MARTIN RUEHL
The Italian Renaissance in the German Historical Imagination
1860–1930
HB 9781107036994

106. GEORGIOS VAROUXAKIS
Liberty Abroad
J. S. Mill on International Relations
HB 9781107039148

107. ANDREW FITZMAURICE
Sovereignty, Property and Empire, 1500–2000
HB 9781107076495

108. BENJAMIN STRAUMANN
Roman Law in the State of Nature
The Classical Foundations of Hugo Grotius' Natural Law
HB 9781107092907

109. LIISI KEEDUS
The Crisis of German Historicism
The Early Political Thought of Hannah Arendt and Leo Strauss
HB 9781107093034

110. EMMANUELLE DE CHAMPS
Enlightenment and Utility
Bentham in French, Bentham in France
HB 9781107098671

111. ANNA PLASSART
The Scottish Enlightenment and the French Revolution
HB 9781107091764

112. DAVID TODD
Free Trade and its Enemies in France, 1814–1851
HB 9781107036932

113. DMITRI LEVITIN
Ancient Wisdom in the Age of the New Science
HB 9781107105881

114. PATRICK BAKER
Italian Renaissance Humanism in the Mirror
HB 9781107111868

115. COLIN KIDD
The World of Mr Casaubon
Britain's Wars of Mythography, 1700–1870
HB 9781107027718

116. PETER SCHRÖDER
Trust in Early Modern International Political Thought, 1598–1713
HB 9781107175464

117. SIMON GROTE
The Emergence of Modern Aesthetic Theory
Religion and Morality in Enlightenment Germany and Scotland
HB 9781107110922

118. NIALL O'FLAHERTY
Utilitarianism in the Age of Enlightenment
The Moral and Political Thought of William Paley
HB 9781108474474

119. GREGORY CONTI
Parliament the Mirror of the Nation
Representation, Deliberation, and Democracy in Victorian Britain
HB 9781108428736

120. MARK MCCLISH
The History of the Arthaśāstra
Sovereignty and Sacred Law in Ancient India
HB 9781108476904

121. WILLIAM SELINGER
Parliamentarism
From Burke to Weber
HB 9781108475747

122. JULIA NICHOLLS
Revolutionary Thought After the Paris Commune, 1871–1885
HB 9781108499262